Noble's Wedding Venues Guide
Third Edition

Copyright
The Noble Publishing Company
Pavillon (Publishing) Limited
The Old Corn Store
Hawkhurst
Kent TN18 5EU
Tel: 01580 752404

First edition 1996
Second edition 1997
This edition 1998

All rights reserved.
No part of this publication may be copied, reproduced,
stored in a retrieval system or transmitted in any form
or by any means electronic, mechanic, photocopy, recording
or otherwise, without the prior permission of the publishers.

Editor: Janet Simpson

The publishers have made every effort to ensure that the information
contained in this book is correct at the time of going to press.
They cannot, however, accept any responsibility for any
errors or inaccuracies contained herein.

ISBN: 0 9528 144 12

Concept and design by Pavillon (Publishing) Ltd
Front cover concept by Ken Bentley
Illustration by Camilla Dowse
Printed in the UK by Chandlers

FOREWORD

Getting married can be both the most enjoyable, and the most stressful, of times. However, the recent change in the law, which opened up new opportunities for couples to marry outside the conventional church or registry office locations, took away one source of stress for many couples. Now, for the first time, we are all able to choose a venue to exactly fit our interests, style and budget; and, if we so desire, stay in the same building for our reception.

There is only one problem. How do we find out about these elusive licensed premises. This is the problem we set out to solve at Noble's in 1995, when we began research for the very first edition of Noble's Wedding Venues Guide. At the time only 800 venues were licensed, and coverage across England and Wales was patchy. Three years on and, with the publication of our third edition, we find that the number of licensed venues has doubled, and that interest in "alternative' weddings has blossomed.

Noble's original aims and objectives have hardly altered. We still aim to be as comprehensive as humanly possible. We still present extensive information on both ceremony and reception facilities in a easy-to-use format. Sadly, we still do not have complete entries on every venue, but this is not for lack of effort on our researchers' part. Some venues, it seems, still do not appreciate the value of a free entry in the UK's only dedicated and comprehensive wedding venues guide. It is their loss.

However the good news is that the choice of venues is now better than ever. Castles, theatres, football clubs, exclusive hotels, ancient monuments, ships, private homes, caves, zoos, racecourses, etc. These are all available, and often at very reasonable rates. So whether you fancy exclusive use of a top hotel, or an informal gathering with a pie and a pint, Noble's can point the way.

My advice, therefore, is to think carefully about the kind of wedding you really crave, and then open these pages. Cast your geographical net wider than you might for a conventional wedding, and I am certain that you will find the exact venue that can turn your dreams into reality. After all, the premises on these pages have arranged everything from a Caribbean barbecue wedding with a steel band by the pool, to a Gothic-theme wedding where the bride and groom both wore black.

Happy hunting and have a great, great day.

Janet Simpson, Editor.

Finding the correct county

Entries in Noble's Wedding Venues Guide are listed alphabetically by county, and alphabetically within each county. We have taken current physical county boundaries to define where a venue is located, although some may have a different county in their postal address, or may still be using old county names. Much to many people's surprise, Middlesex no longer exists, for example, and many places that were once in Surrey, Essex or Kent are now in fact in Greater London. Similarly, places that were once in Cheshire or Lancashire now form part of Greater Manchester. To add to the confusion, several new counties were introduced in April 1996, while others disappeared off the map. For entries formerly in North Humberside, for instance, you should now look up the East Riding of Yorkshire or Kingston upon Hull. Avon has been divided into Bath and North East Somerset, North Somerset and South Gloucestershire. Wales has also changed considerably, with several old county names returning.

A few facts on civil wedding ceremonies

All venues in England and Wales that can hold a civil wedding ceremony on their premises only hold a licence for the room or rooms deemed acceptable by the local registrar. You cannot marry anywhere else on the premises. By law, these licensed premises must have a roof and be a permanent structure. You can, therefore, get married on a permanently moored boat, but not on one that cruises up and down a river. Similarly, you can get married in a football club boardroom, but not on the pitch (although you can usually have your photos taken there). The nearest you will get to an al fresco civil ceremony is one held in a conservatory or orangery, or a permanent garden gazebo - but not many of these are licensed.

It is the registrar local to the venue who will perform your wedding ceremony, and he/she must be booked by you, along with the venue. You must also notify the local registrar where you live that you intend to marry and where.

Tips for your search

Assuming that you want exclusive use of your chosen venue, it is wise to get early confirmation that this is possible. Some of the larger venues may host several weddings in a day. While this may not pose a problem, it can be embarrassing and upsetting is certain facilities, such as the garden or toilets, are shared.

If you are limited to wines offered by the venue, insist on a tasting session, so that you know you will get what you want, at a price you can afford.

If you or your guests want to stay nearby, ask the venue if it operates preferential rate agreements with local hotels or guest houses.

Finally, in order to make it easier for your guests to find the venue, ask if location maps can be provided for you to send out with the wedding invitations.

CONTENTS

Foreword 3
How to use 5
Key to Symbols 8

ENGLAND
Bath & North East Somerset 9
Bedfordshire 10
Berkshire 11
Bristol 16
Buckinghamshire 17
Cambridgeshire 20
Cheshire 24
Cornwall 35
Cumbria 39
Derbyshire 45
Devon 50
Dorset 55
Durham 58
East Riding of Yorkshire 60
East Sussex 61
Essex 65
Gloucestershire 70
Hampshire 74
Hartlepool 81
Hereford & Worcester 81
Hertfordshire 86
Isle of Wight 91
Kent 91
Kingston upon Hull 99
Lancashire 99
Leicestershire 107
Lincolnshire 111
London 113
Manchester 129
Merseyside 134
Norfolk 137
Northamptonshire 139
North East Lincolnshire 140
North Lincolnshire 140
Northumberland 141
North Yorkshire 143
Nottinghamshire 149
Oxfordshire 151
Shropshire 154
Somerset 156
South Gloucestershire 158
South Yorkshire 159
Staffordshire 160
Suffolk 164
Surrey 168
Tyne & Wear 173
Warwickshire 175
West Midlands 179
West Sussex 183
West Yorkshire 187
Wiltshire 194
York 197

WALES
Bridgend 198
Caerphilly 198
Cardiff 199
Carmarthenshire 200
Ceredigion 200
Conwy 200
Denbighshire 201
Flintshire 201
Gwynedd 202
Isle of Anglesey 202
Monmouthshire 203
Neath Port Talbot 203
Newport 204
Powys 205
Rhondda Cynon Taff 206
Swansea 207
Torfaen 207
Vale of Glamorgan 207
Wrexham 207

Stop Press 208

Index 209

CEREMONY FACILITIES

 Building of historic interest

 Seated capacity

 Total capacity seated and standing

 Wheelchair access

 Area suitable for indoor photography

 Area suitable for outdoor photography

Price guide: This is the starting price for hiring the venue for the ceremony. This price does not include the registrar's fees, which are usually around £150.

Catering: This is the starting price for catering (food only) per head at the venue. Where possible we quote prices for both buffets and sit down meals.

RECEPTION FACILITIES

 Capacity - waited service

 Capacity - buffet

 Marquee available (with capacity if known)

 In-house catering

 Contract catering or Self-catering

 Contract catering approved list only

 Liquor licence

 Late night liquor licence

 Area for displaying gifts

 Changing room available

 Flowers can be provided

 Cake can be provided

 Cake knife and stand can be provided

 Toastmaster can be arranged

 Photographer can be arranged

 Dancing/disco can be arranged

 Piped music available

 Live music can be arranged

 Entertainment or stage can be arranged

 Accommodation on site (with number of rooms)

KEY TO SYMBOLS

Ashton Court Mansion
Ashton Court Estate
Long Ashton, Bristol
North Somerset BS41 9JN
T: 0117 9633438 F: 0117 9530650
Contact: Christopher Wood
Operations Manager

Ceremony

This is a Grade I listed 16th Century mansion house set in 900 acres of parkland, which helicopters and hot air balloons may use. The Music Room and panelled lounges are licensed for ceremonies which can take place here on any day of the year, but must be followed by reception at the house.
Price guide: £460

Reception

Testimony to the organisational skills of this venue, the first wedding held here was organised by fax with an Australian couple who arrived in the UK one week prior to the big day. All types of ethnic cuisine can be provided.
Catering: Buffets from £5.95pp + vat. Sit down from £18pp + vat.

Assembly Rooms
& Museum of Costume
Bennett Street, Bath, BA1 2QH
T: 01225 477782/86
F: 01225 477476
email: ruth-warren@bathnes.gov.uk
Contact: Ruth Warren, Sales Officer

Ceremony

This building (now National Trust) was built in 1771 to house Georgian Assemblies. Its suite of rooms, Ballroom, Octagon and Tea Room, was restored in 1991. They are linked in sequence, as well as to the central vestibule. Furnishings include paintings by Gainsborough and Hoare and 18th Century crystal chandeliers. Private tours can be arranged. Up to three ceremonies are allowed per day, every day except Sunday and Christmas Day.

Price guide: Packages from £160

Reception

An hourly rate is charged for rooms for receptions. Catering options range from canapes to Georgian themed menus.
Catering: from £10pp

Bath Spa Hotel
Sydney Road, Bath BA2 6JF
T: 01225 444424 F: 01225 444006
Contact: Myfanwy Rogers
Banqueting Sales Co-ordinator

Ceremony

This is a Grade I listed Georgian mansion set in 7 acres of formal gardens featuring a temple and a grotto. The property is owned and run by Forte. Five rooms are licensed for ceremonies and are available for weddings on any day of the week. Only one ceremony is allowed here per day, and must be followed by reception at the venue.
Price guide: from £400

Reception

Wedding reception packages are available, as well as a host of services, including nursery and baby-sitting.
Catering: from £32pp

Combe Grove Manor Hotel
Brassknocker Hill
Monkton Combe,
Bath BA2 7HS
T: 01225 834644 F: 01225 834961
Contact: Banqueting Co-ordinator

Ceremony

This elegant manor house, set in 82 acres of gardens and woodland, was built in 1698 and is now a hotel and country club. Two rooms are licensed for wedding ceremonies; the largest housing 100 (in the more recently built Garden Lodge), while the smallest, The Drawing Room, takes 50 and is located within the manor house itself. There is limited wheelchair access.
Price guide: from £250

Reception

The hotel can arrange everything from horses and carriage to fireworks and hot air balloons. Both helicopters and hot air balloons can land on site. For those who can't resist the water, the canal is a mere half a mile away.
Leisure facilities on site include tennis, swimming and golf. Couples booking their reception at Combe Grove can book the Fourposter Suite at a special price of £100 B&B for their wedding night.. The hotel also offers a honeymoon package, and special bridal beauty treatments.
Catering: Buffets from £5pp Sit down from £25pp

Guildhall
High Street, Bath BA1 5AW
T: 01225 477782 or 477786
F: 01225 477476
email: ruth-warren@bathnes.gov.uk
Contact: Ruth Warren, Sales Officer

Ceremony

This National Trust, listed building (completed 1778), houses a famous banqueting room featuring 18th Century chandeliers and neo-classical decoration; including plasterwork and gilding. This, and the adjoining Aix-en-Provence Room, are found on the first floor. Both rooms are reached via the Adam-style Grand Staircase.
Price guide: Packages from £120

Reception

BATH & NORTH SOMERSET

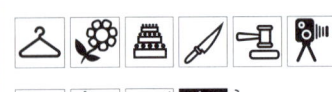

An hourly rate is charged for the rooms for receptions. The caterer of your choice may be used at this venue. Accommodation is not available on the premises, but preferential rates have been agreed with local establishments.

**Leigh Court
Abbots Leigh
North Somerset BS8 3RA**
T: 01275 373393   F: 01275 374681
Contact: General Manager

Ceremony

An early 19th Century, Greek revival style Grade II listed mansion set in 25 acres of parkland, Leigh Court is two miles from the M5 and 3 miles from the centre of Bristol.
Price guide: £350

Reception

While overnight accommodation is not available on the premises, special rates have been negotiated with local hotels. Leigh Court has nine rooms for hire; a cellar, which can take up to 50, five rooms on the ground floor, and a further three rooms on the first floor.
Catering: from £24pp

**Pump Room & Roman Baths
Stall Street, Bath, BA1 1LZ**
T: 01225 477782 or 477786
F: 01225 477476
email: ruth-warren@bathnes.gov.uk
Contact: Ruth Warren, Sales Officer

Ceremony

The 2000 year old torch-lit Roman Baths, and world-famous Georgian Pump Room (completed in 1795), is now owned by the National Trust. The complex includes the Concert Room, Drawing Room, Smoking Room, Terrace and Roman Baths. As few as 20 and as many as 400 can be accommodated for the wedding ceremony. Three ceremonies per day is the maximum number allowed, and on any day except Christmas Day. Special features can include guided tours of the Roman Baths, lit by flares.
Price guide: Package, including photographs of Bride and Groom, from £120.

Reception

An hourly rate is charged for the rooms. The only rooms available during the day are the Smoking Room and Drawing Room (for up to 40). Catering specialities by the appointed contract caterers include themed dinners; Georgian, Roman, etc. Overnight accommodation is not available on the premises, but the Pump Room has preferential rates with local establishments.
Catering: from £10pp

**Theatre Royal
Sawclose, Bath BA1 1ET**
T: 01225 448815   F: 01225 444080
Contact: Ann Meddings, Operations Manager

Ceremony

For the theatrically minded, ceremonies can even take place on the stage at the Theatre Royal, to a capacity audience of 950! Four other rooms in the 1805 suite are also licensed. These rooms are designed by a leading theatre designer and each has its own entrance, kitchen and bar. Wheelchair access is limited to the auditorium. An unlimited number of weddings can take place here on any day of the year except Christmas Day.
Price guide: from £200

Reception

While no accommodation is available on the premises, the theatre has preferential rate agreements with local hotels and guest houses.
Catering: from £16pp

ALSO LICENSED
Priston Mill   01225 460234
Royal Crescent Hotel   01225 739955
Winter Gardens   01934 417117

very helpful.

**Barns Hotel, Cardington Road
Bedford, Beds MK44 3SA**
T: 01234 270044   F: 01234 273102
Contact: Rachelle Ranson, Conference Manager or Matthew Bryam Operations Manager

Ceremony

This riverside hotel comprises a 13th Century tithe barn and a 16th Century manor house. Couples may arrive and depart by boat. Numerous rooms are licensed for ceremonies (limited wheelchair access), allowing for group sizes from 10 to 120. Ceremonies can take place on Saturdays and Sundays.
Price guide: from £195

Reception

Catering: Buffets from £10.50pp. Sit down from £16.50pp

**Beadlow Manor
Golf & Country Club
Nr Shefford, Beds SG17 5PH**
T: 01525 860800   F: 01525 861345
Contact: Simon Johnson, Sales & Marketing Manager

Ceremony

The Club is set in 300 acres of rural Bedfordshire and features two 18-hole golf courses and lakes. The original building dates from the mid-19th

Century, but there have been modern additions over the years.
Two suites are available for ceremonies, the olde worlde style Bedfordshire Suite with a sitting capacity of up to 85, and the larger Manhattan Suite.
Wheelchair access is more difficult to the older parts of the building. Ceremonies cannot be held without a reception.
Price guide: £85

Reception

Italian food is a speciality. The wedding package includes a complimentary suite for the couple in their wedding night, and use of the Club's own cake stand and knife. In addition to the rooms on the premises, the Club has other accommodation nearby. In the past, the Club has hosted Medieval and Gothic style weddings (all in black), has organised fireworks and allowed helicopters to land in the grounds. Guests staying overnight have full complimentary use of the health centre which includes sauna and Jacuzzi.
Price guide: Buffet from £7.35pp Sit down from £19.70pp

Flitwick Manor
Flitwick, Beds MK45 1AE
T: 01525 712242 F: 01525 718753
Contact: General Manager

Ceremony

Flitwick Manor is set in its own grounds with a croquet lawn and tennis court. The listed building offers two rooms for wedding ceremonies, accommodating 24 and 40 people. In 1996 only one ceremony was allowed per day, on any day except Christmas Day and Good Friday.
As we go to press, the hotel is undergoing a change of ownership, so prices and facilities may yet change.
Price guide: £100

Reception

Flitwick boasts a celebrity chef, and can be available exclusively for your wedding for 24 hours. Otherwise, weddings will usually finish by 6pm.
Catering: £35 to £50pp

Moore Place Hotel
The Square, Aspley Guise
Milton Keynes MK17 8DW
T: 01908 282000 F: 01908 281888
Contact: Brian Haddleton, Food & Beverage Manager

Ceremony

This Georgian mansion, originally built as a family home, is set in the village of Aspley Guise. Two rooms are licensed for ceremonies: the Greenhouse Restaurant (80 max) and the Buckingham Suite (15 max). The restaurant is set in a courtyard overlooking a water cascade and ornamental pond. Ceremonies can take place here any day of the week between 8am and 6pm, but must be accompanied by reception at the hotel.
Price guide: from £70

Reception

Food and drink packages pre-booked for Friday, Sunday or a Bank Holiday will be entitled to a 10% discount. Special accommodation rates are also offered for wedding guests.
Catering: £18.95pp

Woburn Abbey
Woburn, Beds MK43 0TP
T: 01525 290666 F: 01525 290271
Contact: Nigel Robinson
Catering Manager

Ceremony

Woburn Abbey is a stately home set in 1 3,000 acre deer park. Guests must be seated at the ceremony, which can take place in one of two rooms, but there is ample capacity for most wedding parties. The smaller of the two marriage rooms (the Lantern Room) has the capacity for up to 70. Ceremonies must be followed by reception at the Abbey.
Price Guide: £500 + vat

Reception

There is no accommodation on the premises, but preferential rates are available locally.
Catering: from £27.50pp

ALSO LICENSED
Shuttleworth Centre 01767 626200
Swiss Gardens 01767 627666
Woodlands Manor Hotel 01234 363281

Aurora Garden Hotel
14 Bolton Avenue, Windsor
T: 01753 868686 F: 01753 831394
Contact: Josephine Currie, Managing Partner, or Duty Manager

Ceremony

This country house hotel and restaurant is situated in a residential park of the town and set in its own acre of gardens. Up to three ceremonies per day are permitted in the Lavender Suite.
Price Guide: £250

Reception

The in-house catering team can provide vegetarian or ethnic dishes if required.
Catering: from £16.95pp

The Bear at Hungerford
Charnham Street
Hungerford, Berks
T: 01488 82512 F: 01488 684357
Contact: Joanne Clayton, Sales Manager

BERKSHIRE

Ceremony

This English Heritage property allows ceremonies on any day, with a maximum of two ceremonies per day.
Price guide: from £200

Reception

A honeymoon suite is offered free of charge to the wedding couple as part of the package.
Catering: Buffet from £6.95pp. Sit down from £22pp (inc drinks)

**Berystede Hotel, Bagshot Road
Sunninghill, Ascot, Berks**
T: 01344 23311 F: 01344 873061
Contact: Debbie Guy, Sales Manager

Ceremony

Only one ceremony is permitted per day at this hotel which is set in nine acres of landscaped gardens. There is one ceremony room, which has limited wheelchair access.
Price guide: £175

Reception

Despite the acreage around the hotel, there is unfortunately no suitable site for helicopters or balloons. However, the hotel is able to arrange all the facilities you are likely to require from music and entertainment to toastmaster and transport.
Catering: Buffets from £24.50pp. Sit down package from £48pp.

**Boulters Lock Hotel
Maidenhead, Berks SL6 8PE**
T: 01628 21291 F: 01628 26048
Contact: Jean Dunstone, Sales

Ceremony

The hotel (built in 1726 as a miller's house) is set on Boulters Island and has panoramic views of the River Thames. The hotel features in Jerome K Jerome's novel 'Three Men in a Boat'. Ceremonies are allowed on any day of the week, but confetti is not permitted.
Price guide: £250

Reception

The hotel has its own pontoon, so bride and groom could arrive or leave their wedding by boat. Accommodation is available at the hotel, and the hotel also has preferential arrangements with other local establishments.
Catering: from £25pp

**Bull Inn, High Street
Bisham, Berks**
T: 01628 484734 F: 01628 898424
Contact: Andres Lopez, Owner

Ceremony

Up to two ceremonies a day can take place in the ceremony room at the Bull, a traditional public house and restaurant.
Price guide: £200

Reception

The Bull is happy to cater for children separately to the main wedding party.
Catering: Buffets from £12pp. Sit down from £17.50pp.

**Calcot Hotel
98 Bath Road
Calcot, Reading
Berks**
T: 01189 416423 F: 01189 451223
Contact: Claire Piercey
Banqueting Co-ordinator

Ceremony

Up to two ceremonies are permitted on any day except Christmas Day and Boxing Day.
Price guide: £600

Reception

Catering: £18pp

**Cantley House Hotel
Milton Road, Wokingham
Berkshire RG40 5QG**
T: 01189 789912 F: 01189 774294
Contact: Julie Carey, General Manager or Charlotte Gallacher, Banqueting Manager

Ceremony

This Victorian country house, set in 59 acres, was formerly the home of the Marquis of Ormonde. Up to two ceremonies are permitted on any day of the week.
Price guide: £250

Reception

Catering: from £38pp (including drinks).

**Cliveden
Taplow, Maidenhead
Berkshire SL6 0JF**
T: 01628 68561 F: 01628 661837
Contact: Kate Hewlett, Sales

Ceremony

Once the home of Lady Astor, Cliveden was built in 1851 and is set in 375 acres

of landscaped grounds high above the Thames. Ceremonies, only one per day, can only take place here if the reception is also at Cliveden.
Price guide: £7,000 (see below)

Reception

Cliveden's wedding package for 56 guests includes use of various suites, accommodation on the eve and night of the wedding for bride and groom, and flowers. This package price does not include food and drink (one star Michelin). While entertainment and dancing are allowed, they must not interfere with the normal running of the hotel, or inconvenience other guests, which precludes loud bands or discos. This, of course, does not apply if you take over the whole hotel (190 guests with accommodation for up to 37 couples), plus a band and dinner, for £45,000.
Price guide: POA

**The Copper Inn
Church Road, Pangbourne**
T: 01189 842244 F: 01189 845542
Contact: Jenny Ellis, Conferences and Events

Ceremony

This early 19th Century coaching inn is set in gardens within the village of Pangbourne. Only one ceremony can take place per day in the inn's Chiltern Suite.
Price guide: £100

Reception

The Inn offers Mediterranean style food. While there is no room on the premises for evening dances, the Inn can arrange for the hire and licensing of the adjacent Pangbourne Hall and can, of course, provide the catering.
Catering: £25pp

**Courtyard by Marriott Reading
Bath Road
Padworth, Reading
Berkshire RG7 5HT**
T: 01189 714411 F: 01189 714442
Contact: Tim Cadman
General Manager

Ceremony

Part of the Whitbread Hotel Company, The Courtyard is a modern AA/RAC three-star hotel with a very traditional ambience. The hotel is available for wedding ceremonies on any day of the week except Sundays, with only one ceremony permitted per day.
Price guide: £600

Reception

Catering: from £19.50pp

**Donnington Valley Hotel
Old Oxford Road
Donnington, Newbury**
T: 01635 551199 F: 01635 551123
Contact: Barbara, PA to MD, or Jo

Ceremony

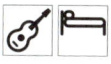

This 58 bedroomed hotel and golf course, situated on the outskirts of Newbury, allows only one ceremony per day, but on any day of the week.
Price guide: £250

Reception

Catering: from £34.50pp

**Easthampstead Park
Conference Centre
Wokingham RG40 3DF**
T: 01189 780686 F: 01189 793870
Contact: Doug Wass, Manager

Ceremony

This is a Victorian country house (Grade II listed), set in 60 acres of parkland. Wedding ceremonies are allowed on all days except Bank Holidays. One ceremony per day.
Price guide: £200

Reception

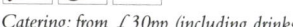

Catering: from £30pp (including drinks)

**Foley Lodge Hotel, Stockcross
Newbury RG20 8JU**
T: 01635 528770 F: 01635 528398
Contact: Kathy Kernutt, Banqueting

Ceremony

This Victorian hunting lodge offers up to two ceremonies per day in its Wellingtonia Room.
Price guide: £600

Reception

Unusual weddings that have apparently taken place at Foley Lodge include Druid, Gypsy and Italian celebrations - so the hotel is clearly adaptable!
Catering: from £21.95pp

**Hanover International Hotel
Pingewood, Reading RG30 3UN**
T: 01189 500885 F: 01189 391996
Contact: Elaine Mickley
Business Development Manager

BERKSHIRE

BERKSHIRE

Ceremony

The hotel is set by its own 33 acre lake (well-known for water-skiing). The Windsor Room is licensed and is available any day of the week, with two ceremonies permitted per day. Ceremonies held here do not have to be followed by reception at the venue.
Price guide: £400

Reception

As well as menu packages, the hotel offers drinks packages and can also tailor-make a menu for you. The wedding package includes complimentary room for the bride and groom on the wedding night, or at any other Hanover International hotel within six months, complementary six month membership of the leisure club for bride and groom, and free fun packs for children.
Catering: Buffets from £15pp. Sit down from £20pp.

Harte & Garter Hotel
High Street, Windsor
T: 01753 863426 F: 01753 831394
Contact: Richard Varney, GM

Ceremony

The hotel is directly opposite the main entrance to Windsor Castle. The newly refurbished hotel boasts a regally decorated Victorian ballroom.
Two rooms are licensed and are available any day of the week with one ceremony per day. Ceremonies must be followed by reception at the hotel.
Price guide: £200

Reception

Catering: Buffet from £17.50pp. Sit down from £22pp.

The Hideout
Easthampstead Park
Wokingham RG40 3BT
T: 01344 778686 or 750044
Contact: Mr or Mrs Bailey, Owners

Ceremony

This public house and Thai restaurant offers two wedding rooms, which have limited wheelchair access. The building is set in 80 acres of secluded grounds with 'no risk of disturbing the neighbours'.
Price: POA

Reception

Naturally, Thai food is the catering speciality here. The restaurant obviously likes a good party and has a full unconditional entertainment licence until 2am. There is room on site for helicopters or hot air balloons.
Catering: Buffets from £7pp. sit down from £15pp

Hollington House Hotel
Woolton Hill
Newbury RG20 9XA
T: 01635 255100 F: 01635 255075
Contact: Miss Christy Williams

Ceremony

This Edwardian country residence, set in 14 acres of woodland gardens, allows only one ceremony per day, but on any day during the year. Confetti is not permitted.
Price guide: from £150

Reception

Catering at the house is traditional English with French influences. While several services are offered by the venue itself, others, namely the cake, photography, a disco, live music and stage can all all be arranged on your behalf.
Catering: from £35pp

Jarvis Elcot Park Hotel
Elcot, Newbury RG20 8NJ
T: 01488 658100 F: 01488 658288
Contact: Peter Browning/Juliana Pardo Wedding Co-ordinators

Ceremony

Part of the Jarvis Hotels group, this is a country house hotel with extensive lawns overlooking the Kennett Valley. The Old Restaurant and Balmoral Suite are both licensed for weddings, which can take place here any day of the year. Ceremonies here do not have to followed by reception at the hotel. Confetti is not permitted.
Price guide: from £250 (with reception). Concessions can be negotiated for Friday or Sunday weddings.

Reception

The hotel claims excellent food and friendly service. Helicopters and hot air balloons can land on site by arrangement.
Catering: from £22.50pp

The Manor House
Church Road
Aldermaston RG7 4HP
T: 01189 819333 F: 01189 819025
Contact: Margaret Redding, Function Organiser

Ceremony

This Grade II Victorian mansion, set in 137 acres, allows only one ceremony on any day except Bank Holidays. Leisure facilities at the hotel include tennis, putting, croquet and snooker. Disabled access to the ceremony room is via a

ramp on the outside of the building. The Manor House is now fully booked for 1998, and only has Saturdays available for the first three months of 1999.
Price guide: £165

Reception

Catering: from £33pp

Mill House Hotel & Restaurant
Old Basingstoke Road
Swallowfield
Reading RG7 1PY
T: 01189 883124   F: 01189 885550
Contact: Kim Pybuf, Partner

Ceremony

Built in 1823, the Mill House originally formed part of Stratfield Saye estate, home to the 1st Duke of Wellington. Its wedding packages include an MC, four-poster bridal suite for the couple, floral arrangements, silver cake stand and knife, red carpet on arrival and colour coordinated linen.
Price guide: £185

Reception

A selection of drinks packages and menus are designed to help the couple plan their perfect day.
Catering: from £20pp

Monkey Island Hotel
Bray on Thames SL6 2EE
T: 01628 23400   F: 01628 784732
Contact: Sue Cook, Conference & Banqueting

Ceremony

Set on an island in the Thames, this Grade I listed building is a Regency style hunting lodge, once the residency of the Duke of Marlborough. It can be reached via a footbridge, boat or helicopter. The hotel how has three rooms licensed for ceremonies.
Price guide: £500

Reception

There are various rooms to choose from, including one over the river. While a marquee is available, this is not recommended for full catering. Limousine, executive coach, boat hire and care hire are all available. The package includes overnight room and champagne.
Catering: £75pp (package)

New Mill Restaurant
New Mill Road, Eversley,
Berks RG27 0RA
T: 01189 732105   F: 01189 328780
Contact: Anthony Finn, GM

Ceremony

This Grade II listed restored watermill can be hired on any day of the year up to a maximum of three ceremonies in a day.
Price guide: from £200

Reception

New Mill is known for its award-winning British cooking. A list of local accommodation can be provided.
Price guide: from £200

Oakley Court Hotel
Windsor Road, Water Oakley
Windsor SL4 5UR
T: 01753 609988   F: 01628 637011
Contact: Conference & Banqueting

Ceremony

This four-star hotel is set in 35 acres of landscaped gardens sweeping down to the River Thames.
Price guide: £1,000 (£500 in package)

Reception

The hotel offers a comprehensive wedding package from £75 per person, which includes drinks (including champagne on arrival and for toasts), flowers, evening disco or harpist playing throughout the meal, toastmaster, and overnight accommodation for bride and groom. Special accommodation rates are also available for guests. For the reception, children under 5 are free, and children between the ages of 5 and 12 are charged at half price.
Catering: from £75pp (package)

The Old Mill
Station Road, Aldermaston
Berks RG7 4LD
T: 01189 712365   F: 01189 712371
Contact: Robin or Diane Arlott Owners

Ceremony

This Grade II listed building is set in 20 acres alongside the river Kennet. Ceremonies can take place on any day of the week in the Stable Room.
Price Guide: £50-£200

Reception

The restaurant, which recently hosted a reception for a Blind Date couple, offers home cooked food. While accommodation is available on site, a list of local establishments is available.

BERKSHIRE

There is room for helicopters or hot air balloons to land on site, and couples may arrive or depart by boat.
Catering: Buffets from £8pp. Sit down from £13pp.

**Royal Berkshire Hotel
London Road, Sunninghill
Ascot SL5 0PP**
T: 01344 23322 F: 01344 27100
Contact: Conference Office

Ceremony

This old manor house, dating from 1705, was originally built for the Churchill family. It is now a Hilton International hotel under the Country Style brand. The hotel is set in 15 acres of landscaped garden, with a sunken garden as a special feature. Two ceremony rooms are available on any day of the year.
Price guide: from £500

Reception

The hotel offers wedding packages starting at £60pp: This includes drinks, overnight accommodation for the bride and groom and preferential overnight rates for guests.
Catering: from £60pp

**Taplow House Hotel
Berry Hill
Taplow, Maidenhead
Berks SL6 0DA**
T: 01628 670056 F: 01628 773625
Contact: Rachel Shepherd
Banqueting Coordinator

Ceremony

Taplow House stands in six acres of grounds featuring protected trees. The hotel offers a choice of two rooms for ceremonies, which can take place on any day except Christmas Day. Confetti is permitted outside only.
Price guide: £250

Reception

Special children's menus are offered at the Taplow House. As well as offering accommodation, the hotel has preferential rate agreements with several other local establishments.
Catering: from £25pp

ALSO LICENSED
*Ascot Racecourse 01344 203871
Bel & Dragon 01628 521263
CIM 01628 427500
Civil Service College 01344 634250
Holiday Inn Maidenhead 01628 623444
Inn on the Green 01628 482638
Knights Out 01189 595510
Reading Town Hall 01189 399820
Sir Christopher Wren's House 01753 861754
Sonning Golf Club 01189 693332
Waterside Inn 01628 771966
Wokingham Town Hall 01189 783185*

**The Beeches
Broomhill Road, Brislington
Bristol BS5 4RG**
T: 0117 972 8778 F: 0117 971 1968
Contact: Sharon Barr, Marketing Manager

Ceremony

This Victorian mansion, set in 22 acres, is now a conference and training centre. The Freeland and Lanesbrough rooms are licensed for ceremonies which can take place here on any day except Christmas Day, with only one permitted per day. Ceremonies not followed by reception here can only take place on weekdays.
Price guide: £195

Reception

Unusual weddings to have taken place here have included a triple wedding when three sisters all got hitched at the same time. The venue is also a second division football club, Bristol Rovers, so supporters often get married here, and can be photographed with the players.
Catering; Buffets from £5.90pp. Sit down from £15pp.

**Cadbury House Country Club
Frost Hill, Congresbury
Bristol BS19 5AD**
T: 01934 834343 F: 01934 834390
Contact: Christine Pepler
Deputy Manager

Ceremony

This is an 18th Century house set in 14 acres of private parkland. It is currently a restaurant and leisure club (with pool golf, etc), but an 80 bedroom hotel is planned. Up to three ceremonies a day are allowed. Confetti is not permitted.
Price guide: £75

Reception

Catering for children under 14 will be quoted at a reduced rate, although the club with not normally provide separate catering for children.
Catering: from £16pp

**Forte Crest Bristol
Filton Road, Hambrook
City of Bristol BS16 1QX**
T & F: 0117 956 4242
Contact: Chris Swire
Banqueting Manager

Ceremony

The hotel is set in its own extensive landscaped grounds featuring two ornamental ponds. It has two rooms with a license to hold weddings, the smaller of which can accommodate up to 25 guests. Up to two ceremonies are permitted per day on any day of the week.
Price guide: from £100

Reception

The wedding package features an all-inclusive price which includes drinks on arrival, with the meal and also for toasts, plus flowers and complimentary overnight accommodation for bride and groom.
Catering: from £29.50pp

**Goldney Hall
University of Bristol,
Lower Clifton Hill Road
Bristol BS8 1BH**
T: 0117 926 5698 F: 0117 929 3414
Contact: Ann Longney, Hall Secretary

Ceremony

This university hall of residence has its own listed 18th Century formal gardens set in seven acres, featuring a folly and a grotto. Ceremonies can take place in the Mahogany Parlour on any day except Christmas Day. Ceremonies on Saturday or Sunday must be followed by a reception at the hall. Confetti is not permitted.
Price guide: from £175

Reception

There are 30 self-contained flats within the hall, but these are only available during vacation time; July to September.
Catering: POA

**Parkside Hotel, 470 Bath Road,
Brislington, Bristol BS4 3HQ**
T & F: 0117 971 1461
Contact: Moira Gould, Banqueting

Ceremony

Ceremonies can take place in the Tudor Room or the Clifton Room, which have limited wheelchair access.

Only one ceremony is permitted per day. Ceremonies not followed by reception at the venue are only permitted on Saturdays between October and April, although they can, of course, take place during the week at any time of year.
Price guide: £350

Reception

Catering: from £25pp

**SS Great Britain, Gt Western Dock
Gas Ferry Road, BS1 6TY**
T: 0117 922 5737 F: 0117 930 4358
Contact: Carol Wilkins, Purser

Ceremony

The historic SS Great Britain was built in Bristol in 1843 as a liner and cargo vessel. It is now undergoing restoration, with the first class dining saloon restored in 1992 to its original 1843 condition. Up to four ceremonies are permitted, on all days except Bank Holidays. Confetti on the quayside only.
Price guide: £295

Reception

Accommodation is not available on board, but preferential rates have been agreed with local establishments.
Catering: from £20pp

**Swallow Royal Hotel
College Green, Bristol BS1 5TA**
T: 0117 925 5100 F: 0117 925 9951
Contact: Lynne Taylor,
Wedding Co-ordinator

Ceremony

The Swallow Royal is a listed Victorian building (1863), occupying a central position next to the cathedral. Only one ceremony is permitted per day. Three rooms are available for ceremonies with capacities ranging from 40 to 200. Days not available include Christmas Day, Good Friday and Easter Sunday. Confetti is not allowed.
Price guide: from £175.

Reception

Catering from £23pp.

ALSO LICENSED
*Avon Gorge Hotel 0117 9738955
Council House 0117 922 2366
Mansion House 0117 926 5698*

**Bassetsbury Manor
Bassetsbury Lane
High Wycombe, HP11 1BB**
T: 01494 421889 F: 01494 421808
Contact: Alan Stafford, Hall Manager,
or Russell Page on 01494 421883

Ceremony

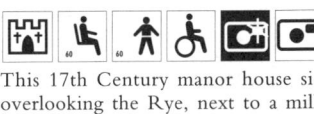

This 17th Century manor house sits overlooking the Rye, next to a millstream. Three rooms are available for ceremonies; two of which can be made into one. Ceremonies can take place here from Thursday to Sunday, but not on Christmas Day or New Year's Day.
Price guide: £50 (Mon-Sat) £75 (Sun)

Reception

While the Manor has appointed contract caterers, couples can use their own caterers if preferred. From April to October, when the croquet lawns are in use, only a small marquee can be erected. The Manor recently hosted a Medieval themed wedding, with authentic music, food and costume.
Catering: from £8pp

BUCKINGHAMSHIRE

Burnham Beeches Hotel
Grove Road
Burnham, Bucks SL1 8DP
T: 01628 429955 F: 01628 603994
Contact: Laura Gee,
Events Co-ordinator

Ceremony

This Georgian manor is set in over ten acres of grounds on the edge of Burnham Beeches. Two rooms are available for ceremonies, the smaller and oldest of which can accommodate up to 40 guests. Up to three ceremonies per day are permitted at the hotel, on any day of the week.
Price guide: £200

Reception

One of the main reception suites opens on to lawns, making it ideal for summer receptions. The hotel has arranged fireworks for weddings and couples have arrived and left by helicopter.
Catering: £45pp (package inc drinks)

Compleat Angler Hotel
Marlow Bridge,
Marlow,
Bucks SL7 1RG
T: 01628 484444 F: 01628 486388
Contact: Ms Micky Dunsbier

Ceremony

This country house hotel sits on the banks of the river Thames within walking distance of the centre of Marlow, a short drive to Heathrow, and 30 miles from the centre of London. Two rooms are licensed for ceremonies; the smallest of which has a sitting capacity for 60.
Price guide: from £200 (with reception). £500 for ceremony only.

Reception

Catering: from £65pp (inc drinks)

Court Garden House
Pound Lane, Marlow,
Bucks SL7 2AE
T: 01628 898080 F: 01628 473277
Contact: Gillian Hayes, Functions & Bookings Officer

Ceremony

This conference and function centre is near the river in the centre of town. Three rooms are licensed for ceremonies with capacities from 15 to 100.
Price guide: from £150

Reception

Children can be catered for separately at the reception. While there is no accommodation on the premises, a list of local establishments can be provided. Helicopters and hot air balloons can land on site, by arrangement, and couples can arrive/depart this venue by boat.
Catering: from £34pp

Dorton House
Dorton, Aylesbury,
Bucks HP18 9NG
T: 01844 238237 F: 01844 238505
Contact: Christine Shaw, Commercial Director

Ceremony

Dorton House is a prep school in a Jacobean mansion set in its own 70 acre estate. The Saloon is licensed for wedding ceremonies which may take place here at the weekends only during term time, but on any day of the week at other times. Ceremonies may take place here without the reception.

Confetti is not permitted.
Price guide: £500

Reception

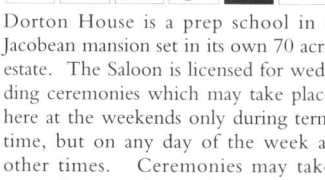

While no accommodation is available on the premises, a list of local establishments can be provided.
Catering: Buffets from £6.95pp Sit down from £25pp.

Forte Posthouse
Aston Clinton Road, Aylesbury
Bucks HP22 5AA
T: 01296 393388 F: 01296 334387
Contact: Leigh Knowles, Conference & Banqueting

Ceremony

This modern hotel, which features a courtyard (decked in flowers in the summer), has two suites available for wedding ceremonies; the smaller takes up to 40 guests. Ceremonies must be followed by reception here.
Price guide: £250

Reception

Catering: Buffets from £6.95pp. Sit down from £16.50pp

The Grovefield Hotel
Taplow Common, Burnham
Bucks SL1 8LP
T: 01628 603131 F: 01628 668078
Contact: Jacqui Bagnall, GM or Tracey Lynch, Conference Manager

Ceremony

A turn of the century Edwardian house set in eight acres, Grovefield Hotel can

accommodate wedding ceremonies on any day of the week.
Price guide: £250

Reception

The hotel offers several wedding and catering packages. Special touches includes ice carving, petits fours with the bride's and groom's names on, and bread rolls in the couple's initials.
Catering: £42.50 (package including accommodation)

**Hatton Court Hotel
Bullington End, Hanslope
Bucks MK19 7BQ**
T: 01908 510044 F: 01908 510945
Contact: Catherine Banfield, Conference and Events Sales Manager

Ceremony

This country house is set in six acres of private gardens. It is described as 'typical mid-Victorian architecture with gothic mullioned windows and main porchway'. The interior features include an oriental lounge and a conservatory. The marriage room is only available on Fridays and Saturdays.
Price guide: POA

Reception

The sit down meal packages may start at £29.50, but rises to £67.50 per head. The latter includes delicacies such as 'Charentais melon filled with ragout of lobster tail and king scallops with a truffle and hazelnut vinaigrette' - and that's just for starters! Local entertainment is provided by Towcester Racecourse (7 miles), and Silverstone (10 miles).
Catering: Buffets from £7.50pp. Sit down from £29.50pp

**Missenden Abbey
Management Centre
Great Missenden,
Bucks, HP16 0BD**
T: 01494 866811 F: 01494 866737
Contact: Sue Newman, Marketing Executive

Ceremony

This restored 12th Century abbey is a management centre from Monday to Friday, but is available for weddings at the weekends (usually including Fridays). Ceremonies are limited to one per day. Two marriage rooms are available.
Price guide: £300

Reception

As well as the Abbey Library, where the stained glass windows are an attractive feature, Missenden offers a choice of three adjoining dining rooms, available singly or together. The ceremony price guide is reduced to £125 if the reception is also held at the Abbey. Hire of the Abbey for a reception is £850.
Catering: £25pp

Pinewood Studios, Pinewood Rd, Iver, Bucks SL0 0NH
T: 01753 656953 F: 01753 653616
Contact: Vivienne Harrison

Ceremony

The Ballroom, The Green Room and The Gatsby Room are all part of Pinewood Studios and are licensed for weddings. Wheelchair access is limited.
Price guide: POA

Reception

Catering: Buffets from £20pp. Sit down from £32pp.

Stoke Park, Park Road, Stoke Poges, Bucks SL2 4PG
T: 01753 717171 F: 01753 717181
Contact: Joanne Scott, Sales Manager

Ceremony

This is a Grade I Palladian mansion set in 300 acres of golf course. Three rooms are licensed.
Price guide: from £350

Reception

Catering: from £25pp

Stowe Landscape Gardens, Stowe, Buckingham, MK18 5EH
T: 01280 822850 F: 01280 822437
Contact: Paula Hutton

Ceremony

This National Trust Property features four temples within a highly acclaimed landscaped garden. Each of the temples may be hired for your wedding, with the Temple of Venus, by name at least, perhaps being the most appropriate for marriage ceremonies. Weddings may take place here on any day of the year.
Price guide: from £600

Reception

There are no indoor reception facilities in the temples themselves. Catering capacity is limited by marquee size. Helicopters and hot air balloons may land in the gardens if required.
Catering: POA

**Stowe School, Stowe
Buckingham,
Bucks MK18 5EH**
T: 01280 813650 F: 01280 822769
Contact: Ms Chris Shaw, Commercial Director

BUCKINGHAMSHIRE

19

BUCKINGHAMSHIRE - CAMBRIDGESHIRE

Ceremony

Stowe School is an attractive period building set in extensive grounds. It offers couples a choice of three rooms for their ceremony: The Music Room (100); The Marble Hall (200); and The Blue Room (40).
Price guide: £350 - £850

Reception

Catering: Buffets from £12.50pp. Sit down from £28pp

**Tythrop Park, Kingsey
Aylesbury, Bucks HP17 8LT**
T: 01865 351203 F: 01865 351613
Contact: JR Parke, Events Manager

Ceremony

This Carolean house is set in 60 acres of mature grounds. Ceremonies are held in the galleried hall where there is a minimum capacity for 20 guests.
Price guide: £500

Reception

Catering: Buffets from £21pp. Sit down from £27.50pp

**Villiers Hall, 3 Castle Street
Buckingham, Bucks Mk18 1BS**
T: 01280 822444 F: 01280 822113
Contact: Jean Rush, House Manager

Ceremony

This Grade II listed old town hall features a refurbished ballroom.

Price guide: £300

Reception

The Villiers Hotel will tailor menus to each couple's requirements and also offers complimentary sampling of selected dishes. The wedding package includes preferential overnight rates for all guests, and a complimentary first anniversary dinner for bride and groom.
Catering: £15-£25pp

**Waddesdon Manor (The Dairy),
Queen Street, Waddesdon,
Aylesbury, Bucks HP18 0JW**
T: 01296 651236 F: 01296 651142
Contact: Mrs Soames

Ceremony

Set in a private area of the grounds of Waddesdon Manor (National Trust), this converted model dairy features a central courtyard with a water garden. Two rooms have licences: the Wintergarden and the West Hall. Ceremonies can take place on any day at the management's discretion. Confetti is not permitted.
Price guide: £4000

Reception

Catering: from £45pp

**Wycombe Swan, St Mary Street,
High Wycombe, HP11 2XE**
T: 01494 514444 F: 01494 538080
Contact: Roger Keele, Asst GM

Ceremony

The main licensed area in this theatre is the Oak Room (130 seated), but the Swan Theatre is also licensed (1076). Confetti is not permitted.
Price guide: £250 + vat

Reception

The in-house contract caterer at The Swan is Top Hat (contact Frank Cortner 01494 537777). A list of local accommodation is available on request.
Catering: Buffets from £4.50pp. Sit down from £16pp.

**Bell Inn, High Street
Stilton, Cambs PE7 3RA**
T: 01733 241066 F: 01733 245173
Contact: Mrs Kate Robinson, Manager

Ceremony

This listed 15th Century coaching inn is the birthplace of Stilton cheese. The Inn's Marlborough Suite is licensed for weddings which can take place here on Fridays and Sundays only. Ceremonies must be followed by a reception at the Inn.
Price guide: £100

Reception

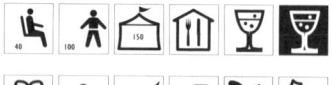

The Inn is Egon Ronay recommended.
Catering: Buffets from £8pp. Sit down from £15pp.

**Brook House Motel
Brook Street, Soham, Cambs**
T & F: 01353 720324
Contact: Mrs WM Day

Ceremony

Ceremonies can take place here on any day of the week except Bank Holidays.
Price Guide: £100 (free with reception)

Reception

Catering: £5 - £15pp

Chilford Halls
Linton, Cambs CB1 6LE
T: 01223 892641 F: 01223 894056
Contact: Rosemary Neilson

Ceremony

Chilford Halls is a small estate of 50 acres owned by the Alper family. The estate boasts the largest vineyard in Cambridgeshire, and has a 12 acre field for any outdoor activity. Three separate areas are available for ceremonies in the main building (which dates from the mid-18th Century); the smallest of which seats up to 65 (30 would be the minimum number of guests for a ceremony). Ceremonies can take place on any day of the year except Christmas Day, Boxing Day, New Year's Eve or New Year's Day.
Price guide: £250

Reception

One of the most unusual features of the venue is that Chilford Halls can provide its own estate bottled wine for your reception. A variety of standard menus is available to simplify food selection. Special services include ribbon displays and balloon nets.
Catering: £8.75pp to £35pp

The Dolphin Hotel
Bridge Foot
London Road
St Ives,
Cambs
PE17 1EP
Tel: 01480 466966 Fax: 01480 495597
Contact: Stephanie Hubbard, GM

Ceremony

The Dolphin is in the town centre and has river frontage and a large garden with patio area. Couples can arrive and depart by boat. The Meadow Suite is licensed and one ceremony can take place here per day on any day of the year. Confetti is not permitted.
Price guide: £200

Reception

Catering: from £16pp

The Grange
Old North Road, Kneesworth
Nr Royston, Cambs SG8 5DS
Tel: 01763 248674 Fax: 01763 246641
Contact: Patsy Toulson or Jack Thompson

Ceremony

The Grange is a private Georgian farm house with Victorian conservatory and a barn. Weddings followed by reception here have exclusive use of the house. Ceremonies can take place here on any day of the year except between Christmas and New Year.
Price guide: £47

Reception

The 'up and coming' chef at The Grange apparently does particularly good Indian and Italian cuisine, as well as a 'rather good' Beef Wellington.
Catering: from £38pp

Greshams, Owen Webb House,
1 Gresham Road,
Cambridge CB1 2ER
T: 01223 354012 F: 01223 312749
Contact: Mrs Rosemary Kershaw, Secretary/Administrator

Ceremony

Greshams is a club based in a listed building in the centre of Cambridge. Greshams stands in its own grounds overlooking Parker's Piece and Fenners Cricket Ground. The conservatory opens out onto a private walled garden with lawns.
The Conference Room and Oak Room have licences for wedding ceremonies which can take place here on any day except Bank Holidays. Ceremonies here do not have to be followed by a reception at the venue.
Price guide: £50 to secure venue

Reception

While there is no accommodation on the premises, there is plenty of accommodation nearby.
Catering: Buffets from £4.50pp. Sit down from £12.50pp

The Haycock Hotel, Wansford,
Peterborough, Cambs PE8 6JA
T: 01780 782223 F: 01780 783508
Contact: Andrew Underwood, GM

Ceremony

The Haycock is a 17th Century coaching inn set in award winning gardens in the village of Wansford. The hotel offers two licensed rooms where ceremonies can take place on any day of the week.
Price guide: £100 - £200

Reception

Three rooms are available where traditional cuisine is offered alongside modern and international dishes.
Catering: From £21.95pp

CAMBRIDGESHIRE

**Hinchingbrooke House
Brampton Road, Huntingdon
Cambs PE18 6BN**
T: 01480 452119 F: 01480 432054
Contact: Mrs Pauline Steel,
Lettings Officer

Ceremony

This English Heritage property is the ancestral home of the Cromwells. Wedding ceremonies can currently only take place here on a Saturday. Confetti is not permitted. Ceremonies must be followed by a reception at the house. In addition to the ceremony fee, there is a fee of £650 for booking the whole of the ground floor of the house, which becomes yours for the day.
Price guide: from £80

Reception

The Old Dining Room, with access to the York Stone Terrace, is one of the many rooms within Hinchingbrooke House available for receptions. The Hinchingbrooke Performing Arts Centre is also situated within the grounds of the house.
Catering: Buffets from £2.95pp Sit down from £15pp

**Newnham College
Sidgwick Avenue
Cambridge
Cambs CB3 9DF**
T: 01223 335801 F: 01223 357736
Contact: Mrs Heather Wynn

Ceremony

Founded in 1871, Newnham College is one of the only all-women colleges at Cambridge. Built from Victorian red brick in the Queen Anne revival style, it has three rooms for ceremonies, with capacities up to 100. During the University term, ceremonies can only take place on a Saturday. Other days when weddings are not possible include Christmas Day and New Year's Day. Up to two ceremonies are allowed per day. Confetti is not permitted.
Price guide: £150

Reception

The college offers an array of international wines to choose from.
Catering: £18 - £27pp

Officers Mess Conference Centre, Imperial War Museum Duxford, Cambs CB2 4QR
T: 01223 833686 F: 01223 836959
Contact: Mary Myers, Sales and Conference Manager

Ceremony

This is part of the Imperial War Museum Complex and is operated by Ring & Brymer, a division of Gardner Merchant Leisure. Four rooms are licensed with capacities ranging from 40 to 200. Ceremonies must be followed by a reception at the venue.
Price guide: £200

Reception

A 1940s' themed wedding recently took place here, the ideal venue to arrive and/or depart by plane, helicopter or hot air balloon. Wedding photos can be taken alongside the vintage planes. Ring & Brymer boasts an award winning chef at this venue. Fireworks can also be arranged on your behalf.
Catering: Buffets from £13.50pp. Sit down from £20.50pp

**Old Bridge Hotel
1 High Street, Huntingdon
Cambs PE18 6TQ**
T: 01480 52681 F: 01480 411017
Contact: Samantha Webb,
Sales & Reservations Manager

Ceremony

This Georgian, ivy covered, building sits on the banks of the River Ouse. Up to two ceremonies are permitted per day.
Price guide: £75

Reception

Catering: from £17.95

**Oliver's Lodge Hotel
Needingworth Road
St Ives, Cambs PE17 4JP**
Tel: 01480 463252 Fax: 01480 461150
Contact: Christopher Langley,
Managing Director

Ceremony

This Victorian hotel (with recent extensions) has four rooms licensed for civil ceremonies.
Price guide: £100

Reception

Catering specialities at Oliver's include individual Beef Wellingtons, Chicken and Asparagus En Croute, and whole sirloin or fillet of beef carved in front of your guests. A room can be made available for the bride and groom during their wedding day at no extra charge.
Catering: £7 - £21pp

**The Pink Geranium
Station Road, Melbourn
Cambs SG8 6DX**
T: 01763 260215 F: 01763 262110
Contact: Charles Ockenden, Manager or Sally Saunders, Proprietor

Ceremony

This 15th Century thatched, pink, cottage has a conservatory and enclosed south facing garden. The conservatory and Garden Room hold the wedding licence. These rooms have limited wheelchair access. Ceremonies must be followed by a reception at the Pink Geranium.
Price guide: FOC

Reception

Catering: Buffets from £20pp. Sit down from £25pp

Robinson College
Cambridge CB3 9AN
T & F: 01223 339140
Contact: Roger Greeves, College Chaplin

Ceremony
Ceremony and wedding facilities at the College are only available to members of the College.

Royal Cambridge Hotel
Trumpington Street,
Cambridge CB2 1PY
T: 01223 351631 F: 01223 352972
email: royalcambridge@msihotels.co.uk
Contact: Rebeca Rendell, Wedding Co-ordinator

Ceremony

The Royal Cambridge is a Georgian building located in the heart of Cambridge. Five rooms are licensed for weddings, with two ceremonies permitted per day on any day of the year. Ceremonies here must be followed by a reception at the venue.
Price guide: FOC

Reception

As well as a bespoke service, the hotel offers a wedding package for a minimum of 60 guests, which include overnight accommodation for bride and groom, and resident disco for your evening function. Packages start at £28.25pp.
Catering: Buffets from £12.95pp. Sit down from £14.75pp

Sheene Mill Hotel
Station Road,
Melbourn, Cambs SG8 6DY
T: 01763 261393 F: 01763 261376
Contact: Sally Saunders, Proprietor

Ceremony

This listed 17th Century water mill is set on the River Mel in three acres of gardens. Three rooms are licensed for ceremonies, including the conservatory. Ceremonies here must be followed by reception at the venue.
Price guide: FOC

Reception

The Mill boasts celebrity chef Steven Saunders, who has appeared on Ready Steady Cook. Helicopters and hot air balloons may land on site.
Catering: Buffets from £10pp. Sit down from £20pp

Slepe Hall Hotel, Ramsey Road
St Ives, Cambs PE17 4RB
T: 01480 463122 F: 01480 300706
Contact: Mr T O'Connell, Partner

Ceremony

This Grade II listed building was formerly a girls' school. Three ceremony rooms are available on any day of the week. There is no charge for the ceremony room if the reception is also here.
Price guide: from £50

Reception

Catering: Buffets from £6.75pp Sit down from £12.50pp

Swallow Hotel
Lynch Wood
Peterborough
Cambs PE2 6GB
T: 01733 371111 F: 01733 236725
Contact: Mrs Wendy Bannister, Sales Office Manager

Ceremony

This modern hotel is set in 11 acres, including an ornamental lake. It also features its own leisure club. Two licensed rooms available.
Price guide: £80

Reception

Catering: Buffet from £9pp Sit down from £20pp

Wadenhoe House, Management Training Centre, Wadenhoe, Peterborough, Cambs PE8 5SS
T: 01832 720777 F: 01832 720410
Contact: Carron McMillan, Client Manager

Ceremony

This Grade II listed building is a Jacobean manor house, with three licensed rooms which are available on Saturdays and Sundays only. Ceremonies here must be followed by reception at the venue. Couples may arrive and depart by boat or air.
Price guide: £300

Reception

CAMBRIDGESHIRE

CAMBRIDGESHIRE - CHESHIRE

Wadenhoe offers a wedding package at £55 per person. This includes exclusive use of the house and grounds until 7pm, drinks, three course meal or buffet, flowers, cake stand and knife, and changing room for bride and groom. There is a discount for children under 10 years old. Evening reception facilities and entertainment are also offered.
Catering: £55pp (package)

ALSO LICENSED
Abington Hall 01223 891162
The Castle 01480 860505
The George Coaching Inn 01480 810307
Heydon Grange 01763 208988
Homerton College 01223 507151
The Moller Centre 01223 465500
Quy Mill Hotel 01223 293383
Royal British Legion, Ely 01353 778330
The Sibson Inn 01780 782327
Swynford Paddocks 01638 570234

Alderley Edge Hotel
Macclesfield Road
Alderley Edge
Cheshire SK9 7BJ
T: 01625 583033 F: 01625 586343
Contact: Denise Buck, Conference Manager

Ceremony

Originally a mill owner's private residence (1850), this country house hotel is set in its own grounds with views over the surrounding countryside. Ceremonies can take place on any day of the week (except Christmas Day and New Year's Eve), in one of three rooms, and are restricted to one per day.
Price guide: £100

Reception

The hotel holds two AA rosettes for its food and has its own bakery. Wedding packages start from £35pp and include complimentary four-poster honeymoon suite, use of a changing room all day, and special rates for wedding guests. The reception suite is self-contained with its own bar and cloakrooms.
Catering: Buffets from £8.95pp
Sit down from £17.50

Arley Hall
Arley, Nr Northwich, Cheshire
Tel: 01565 777353 Fax: 01565 777465
Contact: Mr Eric Ransome, Estate Manager

Ceremony

Arley Hall is the ancestral home and estate (over 2000 acres) of Viscount Ashbrook. It is a mock Jacobean house, built in the 1840s, and features a Grade II listed hall, distinctive ceilings and wood panelling, and famous gardens. Ceremonies are limited to one per day, on any day except Christmas. Confetti is not permitted.
Price guide: P.O.A.

Reception

The Hall's caterer will 'provide whatever your require', although children cannot be catered for separately. While accommodation is not available on the premises, a list of local accommodation, with which the Hall has preferential rates, can be provided. Suppliers of services not offered by the Hall itself can be recommended.
Catering: P.O.A.

Astbury Water Park
Newcastle Road,
Congleton
Cheshire, CW12 4HL
T: 01260 299771 F: 01260 298960
Contact: Restaurant Manager

Ceremony

This outdoor pursuits centre has its own restaurant overlooking the 43 acre lake. Weddings can take place here on any day except Sundays and Bank Holidays.
Price guide: P.O.A.

Reception

The Park can arrange cars, horses and carriages, and balloons.
Catering: £4.95 - £18.95pp + VAT

The Belfry Hotel
Stanley Road,
Handforth,
Cheshire SK9 3LD
T: 0161 437 0511 F: 0161 499 0597
Contact: Juanita Brown, Conference & Banqueting

Ceremony

This modern, family-run hotel, set in private gardens, is situated near the airport and is available for ceremonies every day except Sundays and Bank Holidays.
Price guide: POA

Reception

Overnight accommodation for the bride and groom is offered as part of the wedding package. A special rate of £30pp Room Only is available for wedding guests wishing to stay overnight, available Friday to Sunday inclusive.
Catering: from £18pp

Brereton Hall
Sandbach
Cheshire CW11 9RZ
T: 01477 535516 F: 01477 533093
Contact: Ian Bell, Operations Manager

Ceremony

This Grade I listed private house, completed in 1585, is claimed to be the first brick built mansion in Cheshire. The house recently came under new ownership, and the ground floor is now

reserved solely for functions. Only one wedding is permitted per day.
Price guide: £300

Reception

Brereton Hall now has its own in-house catering team. By the end of 1998, a bridal suite should also be available for overnight accommodation.
Catering: £20 - £40pp

The Bridge Hotel
Prestbury, Macclesfield
Cheshire SK10 4DQ
T: 01625 829326 F: 01625 827557
Contact: Mrs Elaine Grange, Director

Ceremony

Once a row of timbered cottages (dating from 1626), The Bridge Hotel stands by the River Bollin in the village of Prestbury. The hotel has two marriage rooms, both of which have patios and views over the gardens. Ceremonies are restricted to one per day on any day except Sunday.
Price guide: £750

Reception

The hotel offers a broad selection of dishes from which couples can compile their own menus. Children cannot be catered for separately. The wedding package includes an overnight stay for the newly weds.
Catering: from £9.55pp (three course)

The Bull's Head Hotel
Mill Street, Congleton
Cheshire CW12 1AB
T: 01260 273388 F: 01260 298049
Contact: Mr Foster, Restaurant Manager

Ceremony

This renowned coaching house dates from 1641. Only one ceremony is permitted here per day, on any day of the year. The Bull's Head will allow couples to get married on the premises without also holding their reception at the venue.
Price guide: £75

Reception

The Bull's Head has a licence for drinks with supper only. The site is suitable for a marquee with a capacity of up to 120 guests. Children can be catered for separately, if required.
Catering: from £18.50pp

Carden Park Hotel
Carden, Chester CHB 9DQ
T: 01829 731000 F: 01829 731032
Contact: Sarah Pritchard, Deputy General Manager or Jane McNay, Conference Manager

Ceremony

This golf spa and resort is set in 750 acres. The Shooting Lodge and Suite and the Carden Suite are licensed for ceremonies which can take place on any day of the year. Ceremonies must be followed by reception at the hotel.
Price guide: £250

Reception

Weddings held on a Sunday or Bank Holiday will be entitled to a discount of up to 20%. Prices quoted are guaranteed to September 1999. Food on offer will appeal to to foodies; 'Bruschetta of Asparagus, Cream Cheese and Parma Ham with Black Olive Dressing' is named as one of many appealing starters, for example. There is a sensible wine list with house wines starting at £11.95.
Catering: Buffets from £9.95pp.
Sit Down from £25pp.

The Chester Grosvenor
Eastgate, Chester, Cheshire
T: 01244 324024 F: 01244 313068
Contact: Alison Plenderleith

Ceremony

This well-known 130 year old city centre hotel has four marriage rooms available for ceremonies on any day of the year.
Price guide: from £125

Reception

In addition to the above services, the hotel can also provide a red carpet, silver for the tables, personalised menus, and special accommodation rates for guests.
Catering: from £25pp

Chester Town Hall
Northgate Street, Chester
Cheshire
T: 01244 324324 F: 01244 341965
Contact: Linda Clements, Marketing

Ceremony

The Town Hall allows up to three ceremonies per day on any day except Sundays and Bank Holidays. Confetti is not permitted.
Price guide: £200 -£250

Reception

You can bring in your own caterer for the wedding reception, therefore we cannot offer any price guide.

CHESHIRE

25

CHESHIRE

The Chestergate Banqueting Suite
40 Chestergate, Stockport
Cheshire SK1 1NT
T: 0161 480 3048 F: 0161 476 0734
Contact: Sarah Clayton, Banqueting Manager

Ceremony

The Banqueting Suite, located in the centre of town, is part of United Norwest Co-Operatives Ltd. Ceremonies can take place in any of the function rooms.
Price guide: FOC with reception

Reception

This venue says it is able to arrange for discounts off gifts, cars and flowers.
Catering: Buffets from £5.99pp. Sit down from £10.95pp

The Chimney House Hotel
Congleton Road, Sandbach
Cheshire CW11 0ST
T: 01270 764141 F: 01270 768916
Contact: Jill Galley, Banqueting

Ceremony

The Chimney House, which belongs to the Country Club Hotel Group, is a tudor style half timbered building set in eight acres of woodland. Up to two ceremonies per day can take place in the Patio Restaurant on any day of the year. Helicopters and hot air balloons can use the grounds.
Price guide: £100

Reception

Catering: Buffets from £7pp Sit down from £16pp

Cottons Hotel
Manchester Road,
Knutsford
Cheshire WA16 0SU
T: 01565 650333 F: 01565 755351
Contact: Sandy Taylor, Banqueting Manager

Ceremony

This purpose-built modern hotel has a French New Orleans theme, and is part of the Shire Inns group. Up to three ceremonies can take place here each day on any day of the week. It is not possible to hold ceremonies here without also booking the reception at the hotel.
Price guide: F.O.C.

Reception

In keeping with the theme of the hotel, the restaurant offers cajun and creole dishes. The hotel also has its own leisure centre offering an indoor swimming pool, whirlpool, sauna, solarium and gym.
Catering: from £17pp

Crabwall Manor
Parkgate Road, Mollington
Chester, Cheshire CH1 6NE
T: 01244 851666 F: 01244 851400
Contact: Keith Raxter, Deputy Manager

Ceremony

This Grade II listed building (dating from 1077) became a hotel in 1987, and is now a member of the Small Luxury Hotels of the World. The hotel is set in 11 acres of wooded parkland, with landscaped gardens. A maximum of two weddings can be held here at any one time, in any of the three marriage rooms.
Price guide: £200

Reception

Head Chef at the Manor is Michael Truelove (formerly of the two Michelin starred Box Tree Restaurant in Ilkley). The Manor itself has now gained three AA Rosettes for its food. The Manor's approach is very flexible and, while there are some services it cannot offer itself, it has contacts with many nationally acclaimed professionals. As part of the wedding package, wedding guests are offered special overnight rates. The hotel has its own helipad.
Catering: from £23pp

Craxton Wood Hotel
Parkgate Road
Puddington, Cheshire
T: 0151 339 4717 F: 0151 339 1740
Contact: Mrs Petranca

Ceremony

Craxton Wood allows only one ceremony per day on any day except Sundays and Bank Holidays. The ceremony must be followed by reception at the hotel.
Price guide: FOC

Reception

Catering: from £21.85pp

Crewe Hall, Weston Road,
Crewe, Cheshire CW1 6UZ
T: 01270 253333 F: 01270 253322
Contact: Kieran Parker,
Wedding Co-ordinator

Ceremony

This 17th Century mansion was owned by The Queen until February 1998. It is a Jacobean building with 11 rooms licensed for civil wedding ceremonies which may take place here with as few as four guests. While wheelchair access

is limited the Hall offers 'helpful staff'. Weddings may take place here any day except Sunday.
Price guide: £200 - £500

Reception

Food here is described as 'The best of traditional English with influences from across the world. While accommodation is not yet available on the premises as we go to press, around 20 bedrooms are planned for the end of 1998, with a further 100 planned for the middle of 1999. Helicopters and hot air balloons may land on site.
Catering: from £35pp

Crewe Municipal Buildings
Earle Street, Crewe, CW1 2BJ
T: 01270 537569 F: 01270 537605
Contact: David Owen

Ceremony

The Civic Suite comprises two rooms which can be used for weddings. Up to four weddings per day are permitted here, on any day except Bank Holidays. Confetti is not allowed.
Price guide: from £120

Reception

Couples may choose their own caterers, therefore we are unable to give a price guide. Catering for the reception could be provided by the venue if requested, however. A piano is available.

The Crown Hotel
High Street, Nantwich CW5 5AS
Tel: 01270 625283 Fax: 01270 628047
Contact: Phillip J Martin, General Manager

Ceremony

This Grade I listed building, built in 1583, is situated in the town centre. The Minstrels' Gallery and Royal Cavalier Room hold licences for ceremonies on any day of the year except Christmas Day. Ceremonies must be followed by reception at the hotel.
Price guide: £50

Reception

Catering: POA

De Vere Lord Daresbury Hotel
Chester Road, Daresbury
Warrington, Cheshire
T: 01925 267331 F: 01925 601666
Contact: Miss Mary Clark

Ceremony

This four star hotel and leisure club, near the home village of Lewis Carroll, gives priority to ceremonies with receptions booked at the hotel. If this is the case, there is no room hire charge for the ceremony.
Price guide: FOC (with reception)

Reception

The hotel offers a 20% reduction on the food costs if the wedding is held on a Sunday. Also included in the wedding package is a complimentary bridal suite, typed menus, and candelabra. The hotel also has a resident pianist.
Catering: Buffets from £8.50pp Sit down from £16pp

Ellesmere Port Civic Hall
Civic Way,
Ellesmere Port
Cheshire L65 0BE
T: 0151 356 6780 F: 0151 355 0508
Contact: Miles Veitch, Manager

Ceremony

This impressive civic building, in the centre of town, has two licensed rooms; the Main Hall (480) and the Function Room (120). Both are available on all days except Christmas and New Year holidays.
Price guide: £40

Reception

A list of local accommodation can be provided by the venue.
Catering: Buffets from £5pp. Sit down from £12pp.

Everglades Park Hotel
Derby Road, Widnes
Cheshire WA8 0UJ
T: 0151 495 2040 F: 0151 424 6536
Contact: Bill Heslop, General Manager

Ceremony

This purpose-built modern hotel, which has gardens to the rear and a swimming pool, allows up to three ceremonies per day on any day of the year. Receptions must be booked with the ceremony.
Price guide: from £50

Reception

Catering: £15pp (three courses)

Finney Green Cottage
134 Manchester Road
Wilmslow, Cheshire SK9 2JW
T: 01625 533343 F: 01625 548579
Contact: Kay or Pat Johnson

Ceremony

This historic listed guest house dates from the

16th Century. Weddings may take place in the dining room, which will take 30 people standing, although the room has been approved for up to 50.
Price guide: £100

Reception
Reception facilities cannot be provided at the cottage. The three bedrooms are priced from £40 per night.

Fir Grove Hotel
Knutsford Old Road, Warrington Cheshire WA4 2LD
T: 01925 267471 F: 01925 601092
Contact: Liz Hesketh, Banqueting

Ceremony

This hotel, restaurant and public house offers two ceremony rooms; the Grappenhall Suite (up to 200) and the Appleton (up to 110). Up to three ceremonies are permitted per day, on any day except Christmas Day. Confetti is not permitted.
Price guide: £100

Reception

Catering: from £12pp

Forte Posthouse Runcorn
**Wood Lane
Beechwood, Runcorn
Cheshire WA7 3HA**
T: 01928 714000 F: 01928 712681
Contact: Barbara Gerring

Ceremony

There are no restrictions on the number of weddings that can be held per day at the Posthouse. Ceremonies can also be held on any day of the year.
Price guide: POA

Reception

Catering: from £17pp

The Four Seasons Hotel
Hale Road, Hale Barns, Cheshire WA15 8XW
T: 0161 904 0301 F: 0161 980 1787
Contact: Joanne Moore, Debra Kay, Conference Co-ordinators

Ceremony

The hotel, only minutes from Manchester Airport, boasts 'fabulous courtyard gardens'. All of the hotel's suites are licensed for ceremonies which can take place here on any day, although the hotel gets busy with parties at Christmas time. Ceremonies must be followed by a reception.
Price guide: FOC with reception

Reception

The hotel has hosted many Jewish weddings and is happy for Kosher caterers to use their kitchens.
Catering: Buffets from £7.95pp. Sit down from £19pp.

Hartford Hall
**81 School Lane
Hartford, Northwich
Cheshire CW8 1PW**
T: 01606 75711 F: 01606 782285
Contact: Margaret Livingstone-Evans, Manager

Ceremony

This former nunnery and manor house, which dates from the 16th Century, still retains many period features, and is set in its own grounds. Ceremonies can take place in the Nun's Room (home of the resident ghost) on any day except Sundays and Christmas Day. Only one ceremony can take place per day.
Price guide: from £75 (£20 with reception)

Reception

In addition to more formal receptions, the venue offers informal midweek champagne specials (from £9.95pp) which are held in the garden, weather permitting.
The Hall can provide a complimentary room for the bride and groom. Should their own accommodation be booked up, other establishments will be recommended.
Catering: Buffets from £15pp Sit down from £20pp

The Hunting Lodge
**Adlington Hall
Adlington, Macclesfield
Cheshire SK10 4LF**
T: 01625 827595 F: 01625 820797
Contact: Julie Williams/Helen Broadhead

Ceremony

The Hunting Lodge is a converted Georgian mews in the grounds of Adlington Hall. The Lodge is a banqueting suite, and holds a wedding licence for the entire suite which can be sectioned off as required. The Lodge is hired out on an exclusive use basis. Helicopters and balloons can take off from the grounds with special permission from the Hall.
Price guide: from £100

Reception

Catering: Buffets from £8.60pp Sit down from £17.85pp

Jarvis Abbots Well Hotel
**Whitchurch Road
Christleton, Chester CH3 6PQ**
T: 01244 332121 F: 01244 335287
Contact: Karen Freeman, Sales

Ceremony

The Abbots Well allows for up to three ceremonies per day on any day of the year, including Bank Holidays. Confetti is not permitted. The price of the ceremony varies between £100 and £250 depending on the size of the wedding party.
Price guide: from £100

Reception

Flowers are usually included in the wedding package at the hotel, which can also supply fun packs for children, menu cards and one month's free use of the health club. The hotel also offers to send out your wedding invitations at their expense.
Catering: Buffets from £7.50. Sit down from £16.50

**Lion & Swan Hotel
Swan Bank, Congleton
Cheshire CW12 1JR**
T: 01260 273115 F: 01260 299270
Contact: Mr Simms/Julie Bratt

Ceremony

This three star hotel and restaurant was formerly a 15th Century coaching inn, and is based in the town centre. Weddings can take place in one of two ceremony rooms on any day of the year.
Price guide: £25

Reception

If you book a full day at the hotel, the bride and groom will be offered the bridal suite, free of charge, for their wedding night. Wedding guests are also offered a discount.
Catering: Buffets £6.25pp . Sit down £11.50pp

**Mere Golf & Country Club
Chester Road, Mere, Knutsford,
Cheshire WA16 6LJ**
T: 01565 830155 F: 01565 830713
Contact: Yvette Roule, Conference & Banqueting Co-ordinator

Ceremony

Mere is a private golf and country club. Several rooms are licensed for weddings which can take place here any day of the year except Christmas Day.
Price guide: POA

Reception

Helicopters may use the club grounds.
Catering: from £25pp

**Mollington Banastre Hotel
Parkgate Road, Chester**
T: 01244 851471 F: 01244 851165
Contact: Banqueting Manager

Ceremony

This country house dating from 1857 is set in over eight acres, which includes formal gardens, croquet lawns and tennis.
Price guide: from £150

Reception

Specialities of the house include a pig roast barbecue. The hotel has also arranged fireworks for wedding parties.
Catering: from £19.50pp

**Mottram Hall Hotel
Wilmslow Road
Mottram St Andrew SK10 4QT**
T: 01625 828135 F: 01625 828950
Contact: Helen Russell

Ceremony

This Georgian hotel permits up to three ceremonies per day, on any day of the year except Sunday. Confetti is not permitted.
Price guide: £150

Reception

Catering: from £21.00pp

**Neston Civic Hall
Hinderton Road, Neston
South Wirral, Cheshire**
T: 0151 336 3991 F: 0151 353 0064
Contact: Anne Tudor, Information Officer

Ceremony

This Victorian building is close to the town centre, and has a large grassed area to the rear. It has recently been refurbished and modernised and now offers two ceremony rooms. Ceremonies can take place here any day but Christmas Day or Good Friday.
Price guide: POA

Reception

While there is catering available on site, you may also bring in your own caterers to this venue. The venue can recommend florists, photographers and entertainment.
Price guide: POA

**Nunsmere Hall Hotel
Tarporley Road, Oakmere
Northwich, Cheshire CW8 2ES**
T: 01606 889100 F: 01616 889055
Contact: Malcolm McHardy, Director

Ceremony

CHESHIRE

CHESHIRE

This historic hall is surrounded on three sides by a 60 acre lake. Helicopters and balloons can also land on site. Only one ceremony is permitted here per day, and this may take place in one of three licensed rooms on any day of the week. The room hire fee includes flowers and harpist.
Price guide: £500

Reception

Catering: Sit down from £26.50

The Oakland Hotel
Millington Lane
Gorstage, Weaverham
Northwich CW8 4SU
T: 01606 853249   F: 01606 852419
Contact: Chris Kay

Ceremony

Up to two ceremonies per day can take place in the Restaurant.
Price guide: £25

Reception

Catering: Buffets from £4.50pp Sit down from £15.50pp

Old Hall Hotel
High Street, Sandbach
Cheshire CW11 1AL
T: 01270 761221   F: 01270 762551
Contact: CPJ Reysenn, director

Ceremony

This Grade I listed building features an original Elizabethan facade. The Tudor room is licensed for ceremonies which can take place here on any day.
Price guide: £100

Reception

Catering: Buffets from £9.25pp Sit down from £25pp.

Paddington House Hotel
514 Manchester Road,
Paddington, WA1 3TZ
T: 01925 816767   F: 01925 816651
Contact: Pat McKay, Conference & Banqueting Co-ordinator

Ceremony

Price guide: POA

Reception

Catering: POA

Park Royal International Hotel
Stretton Road, Stretton
Warrington
Cheshire
WA4 4NS
T: 01925 730706   F: 01925 730740
Contact: Mrs Mfanwy Quine, Sales & Marketing Manager

Ceremony

The modern Park Royal allows up to four ceremonies per day on any day of the year.
Price guide: POA

Reception

As part of the wedding package, the hotel offers complimentary overnight accommodation, champagne and flowers for bride and groom on their wedding night. An extension adding about 30 more bedrooms to the hotel should be completed this year.
Catering: POA

The Parkgate Hotel
Boathouse Lane
Parkgate Cheshire L64 6RD
T: 0151 336 5001 F: 0151 336 5084
Contact: Mrs J Campbell, Proprietor

Ceremony

The hotel is located on the Dee estuary, 10 miles from Chester. It has several function rooms ranging in capacity from 35 guests to 250.
Price guide: £100

Reception

In addition to accommodation on the premises, the hotel can recommend other local establishments with which it has preferential rates.
Catering: from £6pp

Peckforton Castle
Stone House Lane, Peckforton
Cheshire CW6 9TN
T: 01829 260930   F: 01829 261230
Contact: Mrs E Graybill, Director

Ceremony

Peckforton claims to be the only intact Medieval style castle in Britain - it was actually built during the Victorian era and is now Grade I listed and was used for the filming of Robin Hood. Three rooms are available for ceremonies; the Library (for 60), the Octagonal Stone Dining Room (for 120) and The Great Hall (for 200). Ceremonies can take place here any day except Sundays, between 11am and 4pm. Blessings can also take place here in the castle's own chapel.
Price guide: from £100

Reception

The castle is able to offer a medieval banquet, in keeping with the building, complete with open fire, and ceremonial sword for cutting the cake. Children (2-12 years) are catered for at a discount rate. The Castle can also arrange a barn dance or a concert harpist, as well as a professional disco. It can even organise a horse and carriage if required. A peal of wedding bells can also be arranged.
Catering: from £17.50

**Pinewood Thistle Hotel
180 Wilmslow Road, Handforth
Wilmslow, SK9 3LG**
T: 01625 529211 F: 01625 536812
Contact: Kirsten Pennie, Conference & Banqueting Co-ordinator

Ceremony

Situated a few minutes from Manchester Airport, this modern hotel has five rooms licensed for ceremonies, with a minimum capacity for 60 guests from April to September. Ceremonies must be followed by reception here.
Price guide: FOC

Reception

Catering: Buffets from £7pp. Sit down from £19.50pp

**Portal Golf & Country Club
Arderne Hall
Cobblers Cross Lane,
Tarporley
Cheshire CW6 0DJ**
T: 01829 733933 F: 01829 733928
email: portalgolf@aol.com
Contact: Ann Fleet, Sales Department, or Tony Alexander, General Manager

Ceremony

This golf and country club is set in 300 acres, The Castle Suite is licensed and ceremonies can take place here on any day of the year. Ceremonies here must be followed by reception at the club.
Price guide: FOC

Reception

Helicopters and hot air balloons may land on site at the club.
Catering: Buffets from £16pp. Sit down from £24.50pp

**Portal Premier
Forest Road, Tarporley
Cheshire CW6 9AZ**
T: 01829 733884 F: 01829 733666
Contact: Julie Kite, Function Manager

Ceremony

Just to confuse you, there are two golf courses at the Portal Club; the Championship course and the Premier course, each with club houses attached. The Premier course was the first to gain a wedding licence and is licensed for two rooms which are available any day except Bank Holidays. Ceremonies here do not have to be followed by reception on site.
Price guide: POA

Reception

Catering: POA

**The Queen Hotel
City Road, Chester CH1 3AH**
T: 01244 350100 F: 01244 318483
Contact: Stephen Lee, GM

Ceremony

This Victorian building, built in 1860, is Grade II listed and located just outside the city centre. Only one ceremony is permitted per day, on any day of the year.
Price guide: £125

Reception

Catering: from £22pp

**The Racecourse
Chester, Cheshire CH1 2LY**
T: 01244 323170 F: 01244 344971
Contact: Ray Walls, Racecourse Manager

Ceremony

Chester is the oldest racecourse in the country and can permit ceremonies on any day but is dependent on the racing calendar. Ceremonies can take place in the Long Room, and the Board Rom on the County Stand and the Leverhulme Suite.
Price guide: POA

Reception

While there is no accommodation at the racecourse, a list of local establishments with which the course has preferential rate agreements is available on request.
Catering: from £15pp

**Rake Hall Hotel
Rake Lane, Little Stanney
Chester CH2 4HS**
T: 0151 355 9433 F: 0151 355 0526
Contact: Ken Hughes, GM

CHESHIRE

31

CHESHIRE

Ceremony

The Rake Suite and the Garden Suite both hold licences. Ceremonies may take place here on any day of the year. Helicopters and hot air balloons may use the grounds of the Hall.
Price guide: FOC

Reception

Catering: Buffets from £5.95pp Sit down from £10.95pp

Rookery Hall Hotel
Worleston, Nantwich CW5 6DQ
T: 01270 610016 F: 01270 626027
Contact: Belinda Ryan, Sales Manager

Ceremony

Ceremonies can take place here any day except Sunday, but must be followed by a reception at the hotel. Only one ceremony is permitted per day.
Price guide: P.O.A.

Reception

Catering: from £32.50pp

Rowton Hall Hotel
Whitchurch Road, Rowton
T: 01244 335262 F: 01244 335464
Contact: Mrs D Begbie, Hotel Director

Ceremony

This country manor house, built in 1779, stands in eight acres of award winning gardens. Four rooms are licensed taking from 10 to 200 guests on any day except Sunday and Bank Holidays. Helicopters and hot air balloons can make use of the grounds.
Price guide: £100

Reception

Catering: Buffets from £13.35pp Sit down from £19.70pp

Sandhole Farm
Hulme Walfield, Congleton
Cheshire, CW12 2JH
T: 01260 224419 F: 01260 224766
Contact: Veronica Worth, Proprietor

Ceremony

This is a privately owned farmhouse, with a former stable block converted into 15 en-suite bedrooms. Weddings can take place here on any day except Sundays.
Price guide: £100

Reception

You can bring in your own caterer to Sandhole Farm, so we are unable to provide a price guide. A drinking licence can be applied for as required.
Catering: P.O.A.

Stanneylands Hotel
Stanneylands Road
Wilmslow, Cheshire SK9 4EY
T: 01625 525225 F: 01625 537282
Contact: Ms Tracy Lavin, Conference & Banqueting Manager

Ceremony

The Stanneylands Hotel claims extensive and unusual gardens. It will permit one ceremony per day on any day except Christmas Day, Boxing Day, New Year's Eve and New Year's Day.
Price guide: £100

Reception

The cuisine at the hotel holds two AA Rosettes.
Catering: from £17.75pp

Statham Lodge Hotel
Warrington Road
Statham, Lymm WA13 9BP
T: 01925 752204 F: 01925 757406
Contact: Reception

Ceremony

This Georgian manor house is set in its own landscaped grounds featuring an 8-hole pitch and putt course.
Four rooms are licensed for ceremonies, two of which are on the ground floor and have good wheelchair access. Ceremonies can take place on any day except Christmas Day, Boxing Day, New Year's Eve and New Year's Day.
Price guide: from £75

Reception

In the past the hotel has hosted medieval banquets, Caribbean weddings and Indian weddings. A discount is offered to wedding guests who wish to stay overnight at the hotel.
Catering: Buffets from £5.50pp Sit down from £17pp

Sutton Hall,
Bullocks Lane, Sutton,
Macclesfield SK11 0HE
T: 01260 253211 F: 01260 252538
Contact: R Bradshaw, Proprietor

Ceremony

Sutton Hall is a listed, 16th Century, part timber framed building by the canal. The Dining Room and Library are licensed for ceremonies, which must be followed by reception at the venue.
Price guide: POA

Reception

Catering: from £25pp

**Tabley House
Knutsford
Cheshire WA16 0HB**
T: 01565 750151 F: 01565 653230
Contact: Peter Startup, Administrator, or Brenda Fold, Assistant

Ceremony

This Grade I listed Palladian mansion belongs to The Victoria University of Manchester. It has two rooms licensed for ceremonies; The Gallery (100) and The Portico (50). The house is technically available on any day of the year, but it is recommended to avoid 2-4.30pm Thursday to Sunday, as the house is then open to the public. Real rose petals are preferred to paper confetti, and are traditional at Tabley.
Price guide: £75 + £1pp over 10 people

Reception

Tabley allows couples to arrange wedding receptions at the house in their own style, with their own suppliers: but is happy to offer plenty of ideas.
Price guide: P.O.A.

**Tatton Park
Knutsford
Cheshire WA16 6QN**
T: 01565 632914 F: 01565 650179
Contact: Karen Hay, Events & Function Manager

Ceremony

Tatton Park, owned by the National Trust, claims to be the most visited historic attraction in the north of England. It offers four marriage rooms, ranging in capacity from 40 to 400. These include Lord Egerton's Apartment (for 43) which features a covered balcony that overlooks the Italian garden, deer park and lakes. Confetti is not permitted.
Price guide: from £300

Reception

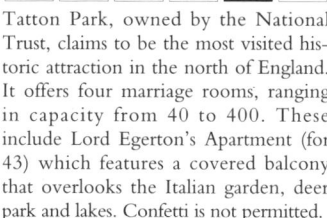

In addition to the above services Tatton Park can provide a PA system, and stage lighting.
Catering: from £15pp

**Walton Hall
Walton Lea Road, Higher Walton
Warrington, Cheshire**
T: 01925 263797 F: 01925 861868
Contact: Nick Iddon, Hall Manager

Ceremony

Wedding ceremonies at this listed building are permitted on any day except Sundays and Bank Holidays. Up to four ceremonies per day.
Price guide: £150

Reception

Catering: from £15pp

**Warmington Grange
School Lane, Warmington
Sandbach, Cheshire CW11 3QN**
T: 01270 526276/257/412
F: 01270 526413
Contact: Christopher Wright, Owner

Ceremony

Lord Crewe's former shooting and hunting lodge, set in landscaped gardens with 'water features', is 200 years old and Grade II listed. Ceremonies can take place in Lancelot's Garden Suite or in the Drawing Room. Wheelchair access is limited.
Price guide: £100

Reception

While no accommodation is available on the premises, the Grange has preferential rate agreements with local establishments. There is plenty of room in the gardens for helicopters and balloons to land on site.
Catering: Buffets from £3.50pp Sit down from £12.50pp

**The White Lion Inn
Main Road, Weston
Crewe, Cheshire CW2 5NA**
T: 01270 500303 F: 01270 500303
Contact: Mrs AJ Davies, Proprietor

Ceremony

Originally a Tudor farmhouse, the Inn has now been extended to offer a hotel, restaurant and bars; the heavily beamed lounge bar is in the original part of the building. Outside there are gardens and a bowling green. The ceremony room is in the more modern conference room, and weddings can take place here on any day except Bank Holidays. Preference is given to those holding their reception at the inn.
Price guide: £95

Reception:

Catering: from £17pp

**Wildboar Hotel & Restaurant
Whitchurch Road, Nr Beeston
Tarporley, Cheshire CW6 9NW**
T: 01829 260309 F: 01829 261081
Contact: Jane Slaney/Sue Duxbury

CHESHIRE

33

CHESHIRE

Ceremony

This black and white 17th Century hunting lodge is a typical building of the area. Ceremonies can take place in The Gallery and the Penthouse Suite.
Price guide: £150

Reception

This venue holds an AA Rosette for its cuisine. A four-poster honeymoon suite is available for bride and groom, and is offered free if the reception is also booked here. Discounted accommodation is also offered for wedding guests. If a marquee is required, a fountain can be set up as an unusual centrepiece. There is room on site for helicopters and balloons.
Catering: Buffet from £9.85pp.
Sit down from £16pp

Willington Hall Hotel
Willington
Tarporley, Cheshire CW6 0NV
T: 01829 752321 F: 01829 752596
Contact: Mr R Pigot, Owner

Ceremony

This neo-Elizabethan manor house was actually built in 1825, and was converted to a hotel by the owning family nearly 20 years ago. The house is set in its own park with a lake.
Two rooms have licenses for ceremonies. These are available on any day except Sundays and Bank Holidays.
Price guide: POA

Reception

Wedding parties have exclusive use of the house, although sadly evening parties are not possible. It is possible for helicopters and hot air balloons to land on site.
Catering: £18pp

Wilmslow Moat House Hotel
Altrincham Road
Wilmslow, Cheshire SK9 4LR
T: 01625 889988 F: 01625 539357
Contact: Conference Office

Ceremony

This modern hotel is three miles from the airport. It is currently designed in a Swiss chalet style, but a £1.5m refurbishment will soon add a conservatory (extending the restaurant): plus improve facilities for the disabled. The hotel has a garden to the side which runs alongside the River Bollin. The reception must also be at the hotel.
Price guide: F.O.C. (with reception)

Reception

The hotel is very popular for Indian weddings, for which the hotel welcomes specialist caterers to its kitchens. The hotel offers several reception packages, including drinking packages starting at £6.75pp.
Catering: Buffet from £6.20pp.
Sit down from £15.50pp

Wincham Hall Hotel
Hall Lane, Wincham
Cheshire CW9 6DG
T: 01606 43453 F: 01606 40128
Contact: Sarah, Hotel Manager
or Jackie Myers, Marketing Manager

Ceremony

This period country residence (part is listed) is set in five acres of landscaped grounds with a walled garden and lily pond. The hotel has a licence for three rooms ranging in capacity from 15 to 100. The smaller room on the first floor has no wheelchair access. Ceremonies can take place here on any day except Sundays and Christmas Day, and are restricted to one per day. It is not possible to hold wedding ceremonies here without also booking reception facilities. Confetti is allowed at the Wincham Hall Hotel. The hotel says it can offer a number of unusual services to weddings parties.
Price guide: from £50

Reception

The hotel offers a comprehensive mid-week reception package which includes the 'eight essential services' (everything but the stress!) such as hire of two suits, video and vintage car, for 40 wedding guests at £2290. Guest numbers over the 40 are charged at £17.50 per head. A complimentary bridal suite is offered to the couple if there are over 50 wedding guests. The grounds are suitable for use by hot air balloons and helicopters.
Catering: Buffet from £7.95pp Sit down from £15.50pp

Winnington Hall
Winnington Lane
Northwich,
Cheshire CW8 4DU
T: 01606 784177 F: 01606 741873
Contact: Shirley Jones, Manager

Ceremony

This listed building is both a restaurant and conference centre. It can host up to two ceremonies per day, every day of the year except Sundays, Christmas Day and Boxing Day. If required, ceremonies can be held without booking the venue's reception facilities. Confetti is not allowed.
Price guide: £100

Reception

The Winnington Hall claims to specialise in first rate food, and can provide balloons for wedding parties.
Price guide: £20pp

34

ALSO LICENSED
The Big Lock, Middlewich 01606 833489
Chester Moat House 01244 899988
Grosvenor Pulford,01244 570560
Holly Lodge Hotel 01477 537033
Hoole Hall, Chester 01244 350011
Hooton Golf & Squash Centre, Little Inglewood, Ledsham 0151 339 5105
Jarvis Crewe 01270 588615
The Lymm Hotel, 01925 752233
Manchester Airport Moat House 01625 889988
The Manor House,01270 884000
Old Orleans 01244 311518
The Patten Arms, 01925 636602
The Plough at Eaton 01625 529211
Quality Friendly 01606 733064
Reaseheath Hall 01270 625131
Saxon Cross 01270 763281
Sleepers Hotel 01270 585555
The Woodhey Hotel, 0151 339 5121

Alverton Manor
Tregolls Road
Truro, Cornwall TR1 1XQ
T: 01872 76633 F: 01872 222989
Contact: Barbara Wren, Admin Manager

Ceremony

The Manor is a Grade II listed former convent set in six acres. It has two marriage rooms; the Old Chapel/Great Hall and the Library. There is no room hire charge if the reception is in the same room. Ceremonies are not allowed without a reception.
Price guide: £150 (for Saturday)

Reception

A complimentary bridal suite is provided for the couple on their wedding night.
Catering: from £12.95pp

Atlantic Hotel
Dane Road, Newquay, Cornwall
T: 01637 872244 F: 01637 874108
Contact: Mrs Stones, Manager

Ceremony

The hotel is available to hold ceremonies seven days a week.
Price guide: £150

Reception

The hotel has 90 bedrooms but also operates preferential rate agreements with local hotels and guest houses. In addition to the services indicated, the hotel offers a red carpet, and champagne breakfast.
Price guide: £9.50pp

Barrowfield Hotel
Hilgrove Road
Newquay, Cornwall TR7 2QY
T: 01637 878878 F: 01637 879490
Contact: Mrs Fran Bradshaw

Ceremony

Price guide: £50

Reception

Catering: from £10.00pp

Budock Vean Hotel
Mawnan Smith, Falmouth TR11 4QJ
T: 01326 250288 F: 01326 250892
Contact: Judy Carter, Assistant Manager

Ceremony

This golf and country house hotel is set in 65 acres of gardens and woodlands with its own foreshore to the Helford River. Couples can arrive and depart by boat, dependant upon the tide. Helicopters and hot air balloons can also land on site. Only one ceremony is allowed per day, and three ceremony rooms are offered.
Price guide: from £100

Reception

Free accommodation is offered to the couple on their wedding nights, and guests are offered discount rates.
Catering: Sit down from £12pp

The Bullers Arms Hotel
Marhamchurch EX23 0HB
T: 01288 361277 F: 01288 361541
Contact: Tony Perry, GM

Ceremony

Price guide: Min £400 on reception

Reception

Catering: Sit down from £10.50pp

Carlyon Bay Hotel
St Austell, Cornwall PL25 3RD
T: 01726 812304 F: 01726 814938
Contact: Mr P J Brennan, Manager

Ceremony

Dramatically located on craggy cliffs above the Bay, this venue enjoys spectacular sea views. In addition, the hotel is set in 250 acres of grounds, including championship golf course and pool.
Price guide: from £100

CORNWALL

Reception

The hotel features 73 en-suite bedrooms.
Catering: from £14pp

The Castle
Bude, Cornwall EX23 8LG
T: 01288 353576 F: 01288 353576
Contact: Peter Judson, Town Clerk

Ceremony

The Castle, which houses the local town council, was built in the early 19th Century by Sir Goldsworthy Gurney, and is set on the sands of the Atlantic coast. Ceremonies are held in the The Council Chamber Monday to Saturday excluding all Bank Holidays.
Price guide: £100

Reception
No reception facilities are provided.

The China Fleet Country Club
Saltash, Cornwall PL12 6LJ
T: 01752 848668 F: 01752 848456
email: sales@china-fleet.co.uk
Contact: Functions &
Event Co-ordinator

Ceremony

This leisure club, with pool, golf, etc, is a mixture of old and new, set in rolling cornish countryside, with views of the River Tamar and only 10 minutes from the centre of Plymouth. Two rooms are licensed.
Price guide: £100 (depending on package)

Reception

Couples can arrive here by boat or air.
Catering: Buffets from £6.95pp Sit down from £15pp.

The Dower House
Fentonluna Lane, Padstow,
Cornwall PL28 8BA
T & F: 01841 532317
Contact: Paul/Patricia Brocklebank, Proprietors

Ceremony

This Grade II listed building is now a small hotel on the edge of Padstow town. The terrace overlooks the Camel estuary and the distant hills of Bodmin moor. Three rooms are licensed for ceremonies; the lounge, bar and dining room.
Price guide: £200

Reception

The hotel has hosted a medieval wedding here, and also specialises in barbecues and curries. You can choose your own caterer.
Catering: Buffets from £12pp. Sit down from £15pp

Falmouth Beach Resort Hotel
Gyllyngvase Beach, Seafront,
Falmouth, Cornwall TR11 4NA
T: 01326 318084 F: 01326 319147
email: falbeach@aol.com

Ceremony

This is an AA 3-star hotel with seafront location. Two rooms are currently licensed and a third will be added by the end of 1998. Ceremonies here must be followed by a reception at the hotel.
Price guide: £50 with reception

Reception

Couples can arrive and depart from this venue by boat, and helicopters can land on the beach. The menus are traditional with house wines starting at £7.60 a bottle.
Catering: Buffets from £8.25pp. Sit down from £10.75pp.

Green Lawns Hotel
Western Terrace
Falmouth, Cornwall TR11 4QJ
T: 01326 312734 F: 01326 211427
Contact: Mrs Symons, Manageress

Ceremony

Price guide: F.O.C (with reception)

Reception

Catering: from £7.50pp

Hannafore Point Hotel
West Looe, Cornwall PL13 2DG
T: 01503 263273 F: 01503 263272
Contact: Brian Payne, GM

Ceremony

The hotel overlooks Looe Bay and offers ceremonies seven days a week excluding Christmas Day and Boxing Day.
Price guide: from £150

Reception

Catering: from £10pp

Headland Hotel, Newquay
Cornwall TR7 1EW
T: 01637 872211 F: 01637 872212
Contact: Mrs Carolyn Armstrong, Proprietor & Director

Ceremony

This Grade II listed building is set on a Cornish headland surrounded by sea, just yards from Newquay's Fistral Beach. Ceremonies are free of charge with receptions. A fee of £10 per person is made for ceremonies only.
Price guide: F.O.C. or POA

Reception

Although the hotel offers catering facilities for as many as 600, they are equally happy to cater for intimate groups. The hotel prides itself on the provision of fresh local produce, with seafood being a speciality. A complimentary overnight stay at the hotel is offered to couples with reduced rates for friends and relatives. In addition to the services indicated, the hotel has its own hot air balloon giving couples the opportunity to fly away from their wedding in true style.
Catering: POA

Hotel California,
Pentire Crescent
Newquay, Cornwall TR7 1PU
T: 01637 879292   F: 01637 875611
Contact : Manager

Ceremony

The hotel has four rooms licensed to hold ceremonies; the largest with a standing capacity of 500. Ceremonies are available seven days a week excluding Christmas Day, Boxing Day and New Year's Eve. Ceremonies are free of charge if held in conjunction with receptions.
Price guide: from £40

Reception

Catering: £12.50pp

Land's End Hotel
Land's End, Sennen
Penzance, Cornwall TR19 7AA
T: 01736 871844   F: 01736 971599
Contact: Mr Richard Smith, Hotel Manager

Ceremony

Set on a cliff-top overlooking Land's End Point, the hotel has two marriage rooms, The Atlantic Restaurant (overlooking the sea) and the Ocean Conservatory. Up to three ceremonies per day: on any day of the year.
Price guide: from £75

Reception

Catering: from £12.75pp

Penmere Manor Hotel
Mongleath Road, Falmouth
Cornwall TR11 4PN
T: 01326 211411   F: 01326 317588
Contact: Debbie Collins, Conference & Function Coordinator

Ceremony

This Georgian manor house has five acres of secluded wooded gardens and a view of Falmouth Bay. Three rooms are licensed for ceremonies.
Price guide: £50 - £150

Reception

The Head Chef here has two Rosettes for cuisine and service. The restaurant has a menu dedicated to lobster, while the cellar has a choice of over 100 wines. The hotel has a leisure club with indoor and outdoor swimming pools.
Catering: Buffets from £6.95pp. Sit down from £10.50pp

Polhawn Fort
Military Road, Rame
Torpoint, Cornwall PL10 1LL
T: 01752 822864   F: 01752 822341
Contact: John Wicksteed, Proprietor

Ceremony

This Grade II listed Napoleonic coastal fort, situated on the Rame Peninsular, is available for private and exclusive use only, and is generally hired for a full weekend period. Because the Fort is hired on an exclusive basis ceremonies may be held any day of the week with no restrictions on Bank Holidays. Prices for the hire of the Fort (from £1,595 to around £3,500) include the cost of the ceremony, and use of all facilities (including tennis court).

Reception

Catering is on a contract basis and, although the Fort has a list of recommended caterers available, couples may provide their own, subject to facility fees. The Fort features two grand master bedrooms, four double bedrooms and two single bedrooms, sleeping up to 20 guests in total, however a list of further local accommodation is available. All the services indicated are available by arrangement. The Fort is complete with all modern conveniences.
Catering: P.O.A.

The Queens Hotel
The Promenade, Penzance
Cornwall TR18 4HG
T: 01736 62371   F: 01736 50033
Contact: Vyvyan Jenkin, GM

Ceremony

CORNWALL

37

CORNWALL

All function rooms at this Victorian seaside hotel overlook the sea. Three rooms are used for wedding ceremonies.
Price guide: from £100

Reception

Couples holding ceremony and reception at the hotel are offered a complimentary room for the night while their guests are offered a discount on accommodation. Unusual weddings here have included a medieval banquet including roast pig.
Catering: Buffets from £5.20pp Sit down from £10.20pp

Rose-in-Vale Country House Hotel, Mithian, St Agnes Cornwall TR5 0QD
T: 01872 552202 F: 01872 552700
Contact: Mrs V M Arthur, Proprietor

Ceremony

This Grade II listed country house dates back to the 1760s and is set in 11 acres of woods, pasture and gardens. Ceremonies are available seven days a week with a maximum of two permitted per day.
Price guide: from £75

Reception

The hotel has its own marquee sited in the grounds. This features a bar and a dancefloor. In addition, a classical pianist is available to take advantage of the hotel's own baby grand piano. On application, a room will be made available for the bride and groom to change in. Amongst other plaudits, the hotel boasts an RAC Merit Award and has been graded as an AA three star hotel.
Catering: from £12pp

Royal Duchy Hotel Cliff Road, Falmouth Cornwall TR11 4NX
T: 01326 313042 F: 01326 319420
Contact: Mr Darryl Reburn, Hotel Manager

Ceremony

Ceremonies are available Monday to Saturday excluding Good Friday and Christmas Day. Ceremonies without receptions are permitted. Prices vary with the time of year.
Price guide: F.O.C. (with reception)

Reception

Catering is in-house and the hotel holds an AA Rosette for its cuisine. A wide selection of sample menus is available.
Catering: from £16pp

St Mellion Hotel, Golf & Country Club Near Saltash, Cornwall PL12 6SD
T: 01579 351351 F:01579 350116
email: stay@st-mellion.co.uk
Contact: Mark Lovell, Conference & Banqueting Manager

Ceremony

The Club is set in a 450 acre estate. Three rooms are licensed for ceremonies for a minimum of 10 guests. Confetti is not permitted.
Price guide: £400

Reception

The hotel provides a comprehensive pack of information to help you plan the details of your wedding, giving local as well as national contacts. Helicopters and hot air balloons may use the grounds.
Catering: from £22.50pp

Trevigue Crackington Haven, Bude Cornwall EX23 0LQ
T: 01840 230418 F: 01840 230418
Contact: Gayle Crocker, Wedding Co-ordinator

Ceremony

This National Trust owned farmhouse is built around a cobbled courtyard and offers ceremonies seven days a week with only one permitted per day.
Price guide: POA

Reception

Catering is in-house and, although the farmhouse holds a liquor licence, this does not extend to a late night licence. Trevigue prides itself on the use of top quality produce enhanced by the subtle use of sauces, herbs and seasonings. The venue has hosted live music in the past, such as classical string quartets. In addition to the three bedrooms situated in the farmhouse, a further two rooms are located in the Mediterranean-style annex a few hundred yards from the main building.
Catering: from £12pp

ALSO LICENSED

Bella Vista Hotel 01637 872244
Carbis Bay Hotel 01736 795311
Coombe Barton Inn 01840 230345
Falcon Hotel 01288 352005
Mullion Cove Hotel 01326 240328
The Porthminster Hotel 01736 795221
Sconner House Inn 01503 230297
St Michaels Hotel 01326 312707
The Valley Club 01503 263281

Abbey House Hotel
Abbey Road, Barrow in Furness
Cumbria LA13 0PA
T: 01229 838282 F: 01229 820403
Contact: Heather Holding,
Sales Manager

Ceremony

This Lutyens building was built in 1914 and is set in 14 acres in front of Furness Abbey. Five rooms are licensed and are available any day of the week. Helicopters and hot air balloons can use the grounds.
Price guide: from £75

Reception

Catering: Buffets from £5.50 Sit down from £12pp

Armathwaithe Hall Hotel
Bassenthwaithe Lake
Keswick, Cumbria, CA12 4RE
T: 017687 76551 F: 017687 76220
Contact: Joan Tomkinson,
Sales Manager

Ceremony

This 17th Century former stately home is now a family owned and run hotel, set in 400 acres of lakeside grounds. Special features include wood panelled public rooms and log fires. Three rooms are available for ceremonies, which can only be conducted here if the reception is also held on the premises.
Price guide: from £75

Reception

In addition to the services above, both wedding cars, and horses and carriages, can be arranged by the hotel.
Catering: from £18.95pp

Broad Oaks,
Bridge Lane
Troutbeck,
Nr Windermere
Cumbria LA23 1LA
T: 01539 445560 F: 01539 488766
Contact: T Pavolyn, Owner

Ceremony

Weddings at this country house can only be arranged if accommodation is also taken.
Price guide: from £150

Reception

Catering: from £19pp

Broughton Craggs Hotel
Great Broughton
Cockermouth
Cumbria CA13 0XW
T: 01900 824400 F: 01900 825350
Contact: Sandra Taylor

Ceremony

This hotel and restaurant is willing to conduct up to two ceremonies per day, seven days a week, even if the reception is not held at the venue. Two rooms (The Craggs Lounge and The Main Dining Room) are licensed and confetti is allowed.
Price guide: F.O.C. (with reception)

Reception

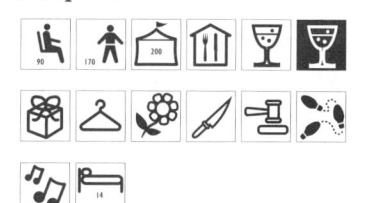

Price guide: P.O.A.

The Burnside Hotel
Kendal Road
Bowness on Windermere
Cumbria LA23 3EP
T: 015394 42211 F: 01394 43824
Contact: Mrs Brenda Watson

Ceremony

Set in its own gardens overlooking Lake Windermere, The Burnside has four rooms that are licensed for weddings. Ceremonies can be held daily throughout the year.
Price guide: £100

Reception

Again, the hotel offers several rooms, according to requirements. A wide range of services is offered, including reduced accommodation rates for guests.
Catering: from £16pp

Castle Inn Hotel
Bassenthwaithe
Nr Keswick
Cumbria CA12 4RG
T: 017687 76401 F: 017687 76604
Contact: Liz Arnell, Sales Manager

Ceremony

The Castle Inn enjoys views of Bassenthwaite Lake and the highest mountains in England. Five rooms hold wedding licences, ranging in capacity from 2 to 175.
Price guide: from £50

Reception

Catering: Buffets from. £6.95pp Sit down from £15pp

CUMBRIA

39

CUMBRIA

The Coot on the Tarn Restaurant
Great Urswick, Ulverston,
Cumbria LA12 0SP
T: 01229 586264 F: 01229 588425
Contact: Mrs Sharon Sutcliffe, Wedding Coordinator

Ceremony

The restaurant is set in landscaped gardens which lead down to a lake. The Function Room and Upstairs Lounge are licensed for ceremonies which can take place here any day of the week.
Price guide: from £50

Reception

The restaurant offers several traditional set menu options, and can also prepare oriental stir fry dishes.
Catering: Buffets from £4.50 Sit down from £15.95pp

Cragwood Country House Hotel
Ecclerigg,
Windermere
Cumbria LA23 1LQ
T: 015394 88177 F: 015394 42145
Contact: Phil Hornby, Manager

Ceremony

Cragwood is a traditional country house hotel, set in 20 acres of gardens and woodland, and is the sister venue to Merewood. The ceremony room here can seat up to 50 people, and is available daily throughout the year.
Price guide: £100

Reception

Catering: from £22pp

Crown Hotel
Wetheral
Carlisle, Cumbria CA4 8ES
T: 01228 561888 F: 01228 561637
Contact: Lynn Parratt, Banq Manager

Ceremony

Ceremonies are offered daily throughout the year. Three rooms are available, seating from 15 up to 150 people. Room hire includes a floral arrangement.
Price guide: from £75

Reception

Extra services include red carpet on arrival, and reduced accommodation rates for guests.
Catering: from £13.95pp

Dalston Hall Hotel,
Dalston, Nr Carlisle,
Cumbria CA5 7JX
T: 01228 710271 F: 01228 711273
Contact: Trevor Tiffin, General Manager

Ceremony

This 15th Century mansion house set in extensive gardens was built in William the Conquerer's time. Two rooms are licensed for ceremonies; The Baronial Hall and Sir John Dalston's Study. These are available on any day of the week. Ceremonies here do not have to be followed by reception at the hotel other than on Fridays and Saturdays.
Price guide: from £65

Reception

Catering: Buffets from £10.95pp. Sit down from £26.95pp

Eccle Riggs Manor Hotel
Foxfield Road
Broughton in Furness
Cumbria LA20 6BN
T: 01229 716398 F: 01229 716958
Contact: Ms Vanessa Hayes, GM

Ceremony

A maximum of two ceremonies can be held daily except Christmas Day.
Price guide: from £85

Reception

Catering: from £5pp

Ennerdales Country House Hotel
Cleator
Cumbria CA23 3DT
T: 01946 813907 F: 01946 815260
Contact: James Lamb, GM

Ceremony

This Grade II listed building is set in landscaped gardens with fountain. The Fountain Room and Muncaster Rooms are licensed for ceremonies, which here must be followed by reception. Helicopters and hot air balloons may use the grounds.
Price guide: £100

Reception

Catering: Buffets from £8pp Sit down from £13pp

Glenridding Hotel, Glenridding
Ullswater CA11 0PB
T: 017684 82228 F: 017684 82555
Contact: Paula Scott, Marketing

Ceremony

Three rooms are licensed at this hotel and are available on any day of the year.
Price guide: £100

Reception

Catering: from £17.50pp

Greenhill Hotel
Red Dial, Wigton, CA7 8LS
T: 016973 43304 F: 016973 45168
Contact: Marianne Phillips

Ceremony

The Library, Conservatory, Dining Room and Function Suite are all licensed, and capable of accommodating parties from 20 to 250.
Price guide: from £50

Reception

Catering: Buffets from £7pp. Sit down from £15pp

Gretna Chase Hotel
Sark Bridge
Gretna, Cumbria DG1 5JB
T: 01461 337517 F: 01461 337766
Contact: Margaret or Patricia, Banqueting Manageresses

Ceremony

Two ceremony rooms are licensed at the Gretna Chase. Weddings can be held Sunday to Thursday. Confetti is not permitted.
Price guide: from £85

Reception

Although this hotel has a Dumfriesshire postcode, it is actually on the English side of the border. Built in 1856 for runaway couples, the hotel offers the romance of getting married in Gretna, while remaining under English law. It is set in award-winning gardens.
Catering: £12.50 - £19.50pp

Greystoke Castle, Greystoke
Penrith, Cumbria CA11 0TG
T: 017684 83722 F: 017684 83072
email: douglas.weymouth@lineone.net
Contact: Douglas Weymouth, Events Manager

Ceremony

This listed building is a private house and garden with its own lake. Features include a panelled great hall and views to the Pennines.
Price guide: from £300

Reception

Catering: Buffets from £14pp Sit down from £22pp

Holbeck Ghyll Country House Hotel, Holbeck Lane
Windermere, Cumbria LA23 1LU
T: 015394 32375 F: 015394 34743
Contact: David or Patricia Nicholson, Proprietors

Ceremony

This up-market 19th Century hunting lodge features views over Lake Windermere. Three of its rooms are licensed for wedding ceremonies,

The Lounge, The Lonsdale Room and the Terrace Restaurant, allowing for a minimum of two and maximum of 40 guests. Lawns, lakes and the Langdale mountains offer an appealing backdrop to photographs. There is no suitable site for helicopters to land.
Price guide: £50

Reception

This venue has two AA Rosettes for its cuisine.
Catering: Buffets from £20pp. Sit down from £25pp

Keswick Country House Hotel
Station Rd, Keswick CA12 4NQ
T: 017687 72020 F: 017687 71300
Contact: Stephanie Muir, Banqueting Co-ordinator

Ceremony

This Victorian building set in four acres of award winning gardens, is now a 4-star hotel and part of the Principal Hotels group. It is only a short walk from the centre of Keswick. Three rooms are licensed here including the Conservatory.
Price guide: £100

Reception

Catering: Buffets from £6.50pp. Sit down from £15pp.

Lakeside Hotel
Newby Bridge
Cumbria
LA12 8AT
T: 015395 31207 F: 015395 31699
Contact: Jonathon Robb or Kate Willock

CUMBRIA

41

CUMBRIA

Ceremony

This traditional lakeland coaching inn is set on the south shore of Lake Windermere, with its own jetties and boats. Three separate areas of the hotel have been granted a licence, but only one ceremony is permitted per day.
Price guide: from £195

Reception

The hotel has an AA Rosette and an RAC award for its food and restaurant. The price below is based on the hotel's wedding packages, which include drinks. The hotel can arrange hour long 'cocktail' cruises on the lake for up to 200 people: appropriate between day and evening receptions. Hot air balloons can also take off from behind the hotel.
Catering: from £29.50pp

The Langdale Chase Hotel
Windermere
Cumbria CA23 1LW
T: 015394 32201 F: 015394 32604
Contact: Mr Thomas Noblett, GM

Ceremony

This lakeside hotel features large gardens and views across the lake to the mountains. Five rooms are licensed. Couples can arrive or depart by boat here or make a grand entrance or exit by helicopter or balloon.
Price guide: £50

Reception

Catering: Buffets from £9pp. Sit down from £14pp

Leeming House Hotel
Watermillock, Ullswater
Nr Penrith, Cumbria CA11 0JJ
T: 017684 86622 F: 017684 86443
Contact: General Manager

Ceremony

This Forte hotel is set in 27 acres on the shores of Ullswater. There are three marriage rooms which are offered any day except Christmas Day and New Year's Day. There is no room hire charge if the reception is also at the hotel. For ceremonies only, price depends on time of year and day.
Price guide: F.O.C. (with reception) or P.O.A.

Reception

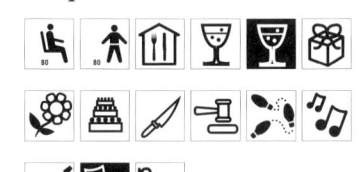

This busy hotel (two AA Rosettes) is not really able to cater for evening functions unless the whole hotel is taken on an exclusive use basis. However, between March and October, a steam boat (for up to 200) operates on the lake. This can be hired for dinner/dances, etc. The hotel also has a helipad and space for hot air balloons. Cake makers and photographers can both be recommended.
Catering: from £27.50pp (3-course meal)

Linthwaite House Hotel
Crook Road
Windermere
Cumbria LA23 3JA
T: 015394 88600 F: 015394 88601
Contact: Tina Slingo or Anne Marie Lennon

Ceremony

This hotel is set in 14 acres of grounds with views of Lake Windermere. The three licensed rooms range in capacity from 24 to 64 and are available any day except Sunday, and the Christmas and New Year Bank Holidays. Ceremonies must be followed by a reception here. Couples may arrive or depart by boat and may leave by hot air balloon.

Price guide: from £150

Reception

The hotel prides itself on its use of local produce in its modern British cuisine. Exclusive use of the entire hotel is possible - in fact recently a couple flew their entire family over from Hong Kong for their wedding here.
Catering: Buffet from £19pp
Sit down from £26pp

Low Wood Hotel
Windermere, Cumbria LA23 1LP
T: 015394 33338 F: 015394 34072
Contact: Teresa Whiteside, Sales Manager

Ceremony

The Low Wood is situated on the shores of Lake Windermere with views across the lake to the Langdale Pikes. Numerous rooms are licensed for weddings which can take place here any day of the year except Christmas Day. Ceremonies must be followed by reception at the hotel.
Price guide: £200

Reception

Helicopters and hot air balloons may use the hotel grounds, and couples can arrive and/or depart from their wedding by boat.
Catering: from £13.95pp

Merewood Country House Hotel
Ecclerigg
Windermere
Cumbria LA23 1LH
T: 015394 46484 F: 015394 42128
Contact: Christopher Dalzell, Manager

42

Ceremony

Merewood is the sister hotel of Cragwood. Weddings are possible for parties of up to 70 people, throughout the year, with one allowed per day. An administration cost of £50 is charged.
Price guide: £50

Reception

Catering: from £20pp

Michael's Nook
Country House Hotel
Grasmere, Cumbria LA22 9RP
T: 015394 35496 F: 015394 35645
Contact: Janette, Executive Assistant

Ceremony

This hotel has three licensed rooms: the Dining Room, the Drawing Room and the Oak Room. One ceremony per day can be held seven days per week but Saturday availability is limited in season. Restricted wheelchair access.
Price guide: from £75

Reception

Wedding cake, photography and live music can all be provided on arrangement. Children cannot be catered for separately. Michael's Nook does not operate preferential rate agreements with any local hotels.
Catering: £27.50 - £38pp

Mirage at Milton Hall
Brampton
Cumbria CA8 1JA
T: 016977 41774 F: 016977 2800
Contact: June Aston, Administrator

Ceremony

Mirage is the recently refurbished function suite at Milton Hall and is in a country setting with extensive views. Only one ceremony per day can be held at Mirage, but this must be followed by a reception at the venue.
Price guide: No charge

Reception

Helicopters and balloons can land and take off in the grounds of Mirage. The venue can provide a list of local establishments with accommodation.
Catering: Buffets from £6pp
Sit down from £15pp

Muncaster Castle, Ravenglass,
Cumbria CA18 1RQ
T: 01229 717614 F: 01229 717010
Contact: Anne Hudson, Commercial Director

Ceremony

This Grade I listed building has extensive gardens and an owl centre on site. Several rooms are licensed including the Library, Great Hall and State Dining Room, and are available on any day of the year.
Price guide: from £500

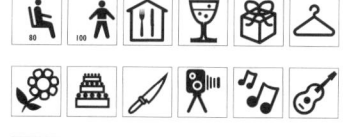

Reception

Catering: Buffets from £6pp. Sit down from £15pp

Naworth Castle
Brampton, Cumbria CA8 2HF
T: 016977 3229 F: 016977 3679
Contact: Colleen Hall, Events Manager

Ceremony

Wedding ceremonies at Naworth Castle (which dates from 1335) are held in the Old Library, (100 seated - 150 standing).
Price guide: £300 plus vat

Reception

Wedding breakfasts are held in the Great Hall (200 seated), with additional rooms available on request. All weddings exclusive use only. The smallest wedding held here so far was for two people!
Horse riding, clay pigeon shooting and fishing are also all available here.
Catering: from £18pp, plus vat

North Lakes Hotel
Ullswater Road, Penrith
Cumbria CA11 8QT
T: 01768 868111 F: 01768 868291
Contact: Hilary Carruthers, Banqueting Manager

Ceremony

The North Lakes has four rooms available for weddings, for groups of 2 to 200 people. Ceremonies are possible daily, all year round, except for Easter Sunday and Christmas Day. Confetti is not allowed.
Price guide: from £50

Reception

The hotel can arrange a wide range of additional services.
Catering: from £19.95pp

Old England Hotel
Church Street, Bowness
on Windermere LA23 3DF
T: 015394 42444 F: 015394 43432
Contact: Valerie Lockley, Banqueting

CUMBRIA

43

CUMBRIA

Ceremony

Four rooms hold a licence (Belle Isle, Lake, Garden & Bury), with one or two ceremonies per day available 365 days of the year. The hotel has its own jetties and gardens.
Price guide: £80 - £150

Reception

Catering: £18pp

Samling at Dovenest
Ambleside Road
Windermere
Cumbria LA23 1LR
T: 015394 31922 F: 015394 30400
Contact: Brigette Beser,
Sales Manager

Ceremony

Samling is apparently the Cumbrian word for 'gathering', for those of you wondering. Those gathering here would enjoy an 18th Century building, now a sophisticated private hotel available for exclusive use. The house is set in 67 acres of landscaped gardens with a pond. Ceremonies here must be followed by reception. The Samling offers an inclusive package for 20 which includes 24 hour use of the house and grounds, with dinner, bed and breakfast and lunch, plus drinks, all for £350 per couple, or £250 per person. The Samling is a three minute walk from Lake Windermere. Helicopters and hot air balloons may use the grounds.
Price guide: £250pp (for inclusive 24 hr package)

Reception

The overnight accommodation is in 10 suites (ie with sitting room each). The chef, who uses local produce where possible, is a former chef for David Bowie.
Catering: This is an all-in package - see above.

Skiddaw Hotel
Main Street, Keswick, CA12 5BN
T: 017687 72071 F: 017687 74850
Contact: Maria, Sales Manager

Ceremony

This town centre hotel offers four ceremony rooms accommodating a minimum of four guests. Confetti is not permitted.
Price guide: from £45

Reception

Catering: Buffets from £15pp Sit down from £13pp

Stakis Keswick Lodore
Swiss Hotel, Borrowdale
Keswick, Cumbria CA12 5UX
T: 017687 77285 F: 017687 77343
Contact: Valerie Ayre, Deputy Manager

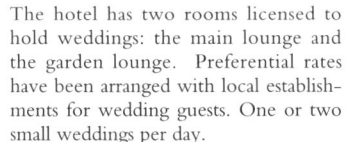

Ceremony

The hotel has two rooms licensed to hold weddings: the main lounge and the garden lounge. Preferential rates have been arranged with local establishments for wedding guests. One or two small weddings per day.
Price guide: from £125

Reception

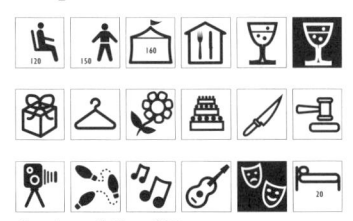

Catering: £15 - £25pp

Swan Hotel, Newby Bridge
Cumbria LA12 8NB
T: 015395 31681 F: 015395 31917
Contact: Wendy Eden

Ceremony

The Swan is situated at the southern tip of Lake Windermere. Ceremonies are restricted to one per day, but the hotel is not available over the Easter holiday weekends, Spring Bank Holiday or the late Summer Bank Holiday.
Price guide: £125

Reception

Local specialities include venison, Morecambe Bay Shrimps and Cumberland Farmhouse Cheese.
Catering: £25pp

Tufton Arms Hotel
Market Square
Appleby in Westmoreland
Cumbria CA16 6XA
T: 017683 51593 F:017683 52761
Contact: Teresa Burton

Ceremony

This 16th Century old coaching inn, with Victorian additions, is located in the centre of Appleby. Four rooms are licensed, two on the ground floor and with good wheelchair access.
Price guide: £90 (FOC if reception costs over £500)

Reception

The Tufton Arms holds an AA Rosette for its cuisine and is AA, RAC, Egon Ronay and Johanssen recommended.
Catering: from £12.50pp

**Tullie House
Museum & Art Gallery
Castle Street, Carlisle CA3 8TP**
T: 01228 34781 F: 01228 810249
Contact: Barbara Lamont, Bookings

Ceremony

This award-winning Museum offers ceremonies in the Victorian Function Room: the original lecture theatre. The Grade I listed building provides an excellent backdrop for photography, both indoors and in the gardens. Room hire is charged at £130 if the reception is held at Tullie House, and at £230 otherwise.
Price guide: from £130

Reception

The Garden restaurant offers classical menus.
Catering: from £13.50pp

**Ullswater Hotel
Glenridding, Penrith, CA11 0JJ**
T: 017684 82444 Fax: 017684 82303
Contact: David Mohum

Ceremony

The Ullswater Hotel is set in 40 acres of private grounds on the shores of Lake Ullswater with three landing jetties, a helipad and separate children's play area. The hotel is also situated 200 yards from the Ullswater Steamer, which is available for private hire for trips on the lake.
Price guide: P.O.A.

Reception

Catering: £13.50 - £25pp

**Victoria Park Hotel, Victoria Rd,
Barrow in Furness, LA14 5JS**
T: 01229 821159 F: 01229 870303
Contact: Mr I Alexander, Owner

Ceremony

Two rooms are licensed at the hotel and are available every day. Ceremonies must be followed by a reception.
Price guide: FOC

Reception

Catering: Buffets from £5pp. Sit down from £11pp.

**Wordsworth Hotel
Grasmere
Cumbria LA22 9SW**
T: 015394 35592 F: 0153 94765
Contact: Robin Lees, General Manager

Ceremony

The Wordsworth offers a maximum of two ceremonies per day, excluding Christmas and New Year. Up to 120 people can be accommodated in the ceremony room.
Price guide: from £100

Reception

The reception facilities are suitable for up to 110 people for waited service, or for 120 for a buffet. A marquee could be used, for up to 150. The hotel has its own overnight accommodation, or can arrange preferential rates with local establishments.
Catering: from £11.50pp

STOP PRESS
Appleby Castle 01768 351402
Beech Hill Hotel 01539 442137
Bower House Inn
Castle Green
The Chase Hotel
Grove Court Hotel
Irton Hall
Ladstock Country House, 017687 78210
Lisdoonie Hotel
Lovelady Shield
Netherwood Hotel, 015395 32552
Scafell Hotel
Washington Central Hotel, 01900 65772

**Breadsall Priory Hotel
Moor Road
Morely, Nr Derby
Derbyshire DE7 6DL**
T: 01332 832235 F: 01332 833509
Contact: The Manager

Ceremony

This listed building used to belong to the Darwin family. Set in 400 acres of mature parkland, it offers ceremonies seven days a week with no restrictions on the time of year.
Price guide: £200

Reception

Parking is available for up to 300 cars.
Catering: £19.95 - £35pp

**Brookfield Hall on Long Hill
Long Hill, Buxton
Derbyshire, SK17 6SU**
T: 01298 24151 F: 01298 24151
Contact: Roger Handley, Owner

Ceremony

This Victorian manor house is set in 10 acres of grounds and has been restored to its original state. Two rooms are licensed; the reception hall and the drawing room, with capacities varying from 10 to 60. Ceremonies are available without receptions but are more expensive.

DERBYSHIRE

Price guide: £58.75 - £117.50

Reception

The Hall offers a complimentary overnight suite for the couple, while reduced accommodation rates in the hotel's seven remaining bedrooms can be arranged for wedding guests. Children can be catered for separately, if required.
Catering: from £18.50pp

Dales & Peaks Hotel
Old Road, Darley Dale
Matlock DE4 2ER
T: 01629 733775
Contact: Mr Banks, Owner

Ceremony

The hotel is housed in a Victorian building with a 3/4 acre walled garden. The Red House Stables, adjacent to the hotel, house a vintage car and carriage museum, the exhibits of which were recently used in the film of Jane Eyre. These vehicles can also be used for weddings. Two rooms in the hotel are licensed for ceremonies. Ceremonies on a Saturday must be followed by reception at the hotel.
Price guide: £50

Reception

Evening functions are not possible at the hotel.
Catering: from £16.95 (inc drinks)

Darwin Forest Country Park
Darley Moor
Darley Two Dales
Matlock DE4 5LN
T: 01629 732428 F: 01629 735015
Contact: Quentin Gregory

Ceremony

This £5million holiday complex is set in 50 acres and has over 80 self-catering log cabins. For this reason, ceremonies here should be booked alongside catering and accommodation. Helicopters and hot air balloons can use the site.
Price guide: from £100

Reception

Catering: POA

Donington Manor Hotel
Castle Donington
Derby DE74 2PP
T: 01332 810253 F: 01332 850330
Contact: CN Grist, Director

Ceremony

The Rawdon Room in this 18th Century coaching inn is licensed for ceremonies, and is available any day of the year except over the Christmas period.
Price guide: POA

Reception

Catering: POA

The Donington Thistle Hotel
East Midlands Airport
Castle Donington
Derby DE74 2SW
T: 01332 850700 F: 01332 850823
Contact: Lisa Maycock, Tracey Miles, Conference & Banqueting Coordinators

Ceremony

This is a modern hotel, with a more traditional interior featuring antiques and tapestries, etc. The Southwell Suite is licensed for ceremonies and is available any day of the year except Christmas Day and New Year's Day.
Price guide: from £200

Reception

This hotel clearly aims to please and is happy to help wherever needed. They will even let you create your own menu. Helicopters and aeroplanes can use this site.
Catering: Buffets from £10pp. Sit down from £18.75pp

East Lodge Country House Hotel
Rowsley, Matlock DE4 2EF
T: 01629 734474 F: 01629 733949
Contact: Mrs Mills, Proprietor

Ceremony

The hotel was once the East Lodge to Haddon Hall and is set in 10 acres of grounds. It is set on the outskirts of the Derbyshire Peak District and has two rooms licensed to hold ceremonies with capacities of 20 and 70. One ceremony per day is permitted, and only if held in conjunction with reception.
Price guide: £150

Reception

Catering: from £18.95pp

Elvaston Castle
Borrowash Road
Elvaston
Derby
DE72 3EP
T: 01332 571343 F: 01332 758751
Contact: Lesley Law, Assistant Area Manager

Ceremony

This listed building is set in an historic garden and parkland estate, and now operates as a museum, with camping and a riding centre in the grounds. It is run by Derbyshire County Council. The Gothic Hall is licensed for ceremonies which can take place here on any day except Sundays and Bank Holidays. Ceremonies can take place here without reception, but confetti is not permitted.
Price guide: £125

Reception

Catering is provided by Mrs Kemps cafe on site, who can be contacted directly on 01159 231494. Flowers are usually provided at the Castle. Helicopters and hot air balloons may land on site with the relevant approval. The Castle is a 'no smoking' zone and confetti is not permitted on site.
Catering: POA

Forte Posthouse Derby
Pastures Hill, Littleover
Derby DE23 7BA
T: 01332 518668 F: 01332 518668
Contact: Debbie Hale, Meeting and Conference Manager

Ceremony

The main part of this building, which is set in 4 acres of gardens, dates from the 19th Century. The bedrooms are said to be modern, however. Three rooms are licensed for ceremonies which can take place at any time except over the Christmas and New Year holidays. Ceremonies here must be followed by a reception at the hotel.
Price guide: £150 - £325

Reception

Catering: Buffets from £10.95pp.
Sit down from £15.50pp

Hassop Hall
Hassop, Nr Bakewell
Derbyshire
T: 01629 640488 F: 01629 640577
Contact: Mr Chapman, Owner

Ceremony

Ceremonies are available from Monday to Saturday, but must be followed by a reception here. Confetti is not permitted.
Price guide: POA

Reception

A late night drinking licence is held for the restaurant and residential guests only. The hotel offers its own pianist for receptions.
Price guide: POA

Heanor & Loscoe Town Hall
Market Place, Heanor
Derbyshire DE75 7AA
T: 01773 533050
Contact: DR Bostock, Town Clerk

Ceremony

This town centre, Grade II listed, building (recently rescued from dereliction) provides three ceremony rooms with capacities ranging from 15 to 210. Weddings can take place here on any day of the year.
Price guide: £25

Reception

Outside caterers or self catering is permitted at the Town Hall, and drinks licences can be obtained if required.

Kedleston Hall, Derby DE22 5JH
T: 01332 842191 F: 01332 841972
Contact: Property Manager

Ceremony

This National Trust Property offers three ceremony rooms with capacities ranging from 30 to 100. Ceremonies can take place on Thursdays and Fridays only from April to October. At other times, only by arrangement with the Property Manager.
Price guide: from £200

Reception

Catering: from £21pp

Lion Hotel & Restaurant
Belper, Derbyshire DE56 1AX
T: 01773 824033 F: 01773 828393
Contact: Ian Miller

Ceremony

This olde worlde hotel, dating from the 18th Century, is sited in the centre of Belper. Three rooms are licensed.
Price guide: £100

Reception

The wedding package at the hotel includes complimentary overnight accommodation for bride and groom, complimentary floral arrangements, menu cards, toastmaster, discounts for children and accommodation discounts for guests. Drinks packages start at £5.95pp.
Catering: from £11.95

Locko Park,
Sponden
Derby DE21 7BW
T: 01332 662785 F: 01332 281942
Contact: Miss GL Phillipson, Assistant Agent

Ceremony

This listed private house is set in formal gardens and surrounded by parkland. The Picture Gallery, Dining Room and Billiard Room are all licensed for cere-

DERBYSHIRE

DERBYSHIRE

monies and are available on Wednesdays, Fridays and Saturdays from 1st April to 30th October inclusive.
Price guide: from £275

Reception

All catering is managed in-house, and is arranged on an individual basis, hence no price guides. While discos and modern music are not permitted, classical music is welcomed.

Mackworth Hotel
Ashbourne Road
Derby
DE22 4LY
T: 01332 824324 F: 01332 824692
Contact: Banqueting Manager

Ceremony

This listed building also features a permanent marquee and offers ceremonies on all days except Sunday.
Price guide: £150

Reception

Catering: from £15.95pp

Makeney Hall
Makeney, Milford
Derbyshire DE56 0RS
T: 01332 842999 F: 01332 842777
Contact: Janet Gould, Operations Manager

Ceremony

A Victorian country house hotel, Makeney Hall is set in six acres of gardens on the edge of the Derwent Valley. Helicopters can land on site. Five rooms are licensed for ceremonies and are available on any day, now including Sundays and Bank holidays. Receptions must also be booked at this venue.
Price guide: £100

Reception

Catering: Buffets from £7.50pp. Sit down from £23pp

The Maynard Arms Hotel
Main Road, Grindleford
Derbyshire S32 2HE
T: 01433 630221 F: 01433 630445
Contact: Jonathan and Joanne Tindall, General Managers

Ceremony

Built in 1898, this is a traditional coaching inn with views over its landscaped gardens an the Hope Valley. Three rooms are licensed for ceremonies.
Price guide: £50 - £150

Reception

Catering: Buffets from £8.25pp. Sit down from £18pp

Mickleover Court Hotel
Mickleover, Derby DE3 5XX
T: 01332 521641 F: 01332 523644
email: hotel.reservations@virgin.co.uk
Web site: www.virgin.com
Contact: Conference & Banqueting

Ceremony

This modern Virgin-managed hotel was originally designed with the disabled in mind and features customised bedrooms. Ceremony capacities range from 40 to 300. Figures quoted here are for 1997, however, as the management was not helpful in updating this entry. We trust they will be more helpful to potential customers.
Price guide: from £80

Reception

The hotel prides itself on its catering specialities including Italian and traditional cooking. The hotel can provide red carpet, wedding car and table plans.
Catering from £8.95pp

Midland Hotel
Midland Road, Derby DE1 2SQ
T: 01332 345894 F: 01332 293522
Contact: Jane Cryer, Deputy GM

Ceremony

This traditional style building dates back to the middle of the 19th Century and features a tree lined garden. Ceremonies are available without receptions at a cost of £500, and are not available on Sundays or Bank Holidays.
Price guide: £150 (with reception)

Reception

Wedding guests are offered reduced overnight accommodation rates.
Catering: from £21.15 (including drinks)

Morley Hayes
Main Road, Morley
Derby DE7 6DG
T: 01332 780480 F: 01332 781094
Contact: Functions Manager

Ceremony

The Morley Hayes is a family owned and run 18 hole golf course, function

suite, bar and restaurant. Three rooms are licensed for weddings. Helicopters and hot air balloons can use the grounds.
Price guide: £350

Reception

Catering: Buffets from £7.45pp Sit down from £17pp

New Bath Hotel
New Bath Road
Matlock Bath
Derbyshire DE4 3PX
T: 01629 583275 F: 01629 580268
Contact: Celina Tann

Ceremony

The hotel offers ceremonies Monday to Saturday.
Price guide: £75

Reception

Catering: £18.95pp

Oaklands Manor
Long Hill,
Buxton
Derbyshire
SK17 6ST
T: 01298 72565 F: 01298 73053
Contact: Keith Highet, Manager

Ceremony

This banqueting and business centre is set in a Victorian manor house overlooking the Wye Valley. Two rooms are available for ceremonies.
Price guide: £50

Reception

Catering: Buffets from £7.75pp Sit down from £13.75pp

Riber Hall,
Matlock, Derbyshire DE4 5TU
T: 01629 582795 F: 01629 580475
email: info@riber-hall.co.uk
Contact: Pat Robinson, Under Manager

Ceremony

Riber is one of Derbyshire's old country houses, dating from the 15th Century. Features include a walled garden and orchard and it has been nominated by the AA as one of the most romantic hotels in Britain. Three rooms are licensed for ceremonies which must be followed by a reception on the premises.
Price guide: £100

Reception

Catering: from £20pp

Ringwood Hall Hotel
Brimington
Chesterfield
Derbyshire S43 1DQ
T: 01246 280077 F: 01246 472241
Contact: Joanne Cutt,
Group Co-ordinator

Ceremony

Set in 28 acres of gardens, Ringwood Hall offers three rooms for ceremonies. Up to six ceremonies are permitted per day on any day of the year.
Price guide: POA

Reception

Helicopters and hot air balloons can use the Hall grounds, which have also been host to firework displays.
Catering: Buffets from £6.95
Sit down from £15.95

Risley Hall Hotel
Derby Road
Risley
Derbyshire DE72 3SS
T: 0115 939 9000 F: 0115 939 7766
Contact: Sales & Marketing Manager

Ceremony

This 16th Century Grade II listed building is set in five acres of gardens. The Baronial Hall, where ceremonies take place, was once the Prince of Wales' hunting lodge.
Price guide: £150

Reception

Flower arrangements are included in the standard wedding package.
Catering: from £23.50pp

Royal Regency Banqueting Suites
Wharncliffe Road
Ilkeston, Derby DE7 5HF
T: 0115 932 7777 F: 0115 932 4386
Contact: Helen Beard

Ceremony

This venue is a member of the Ilkeston Co-op Group. One room, the Queen Elizabeth II room, is licensed to hold ceremonies on any day of the week.
Price guide: from £100

Reception

DERBYSHIRE

49

DERBYSHIRE - DEVON

Five rooms are available for receptions with varying capacities of 50 to 350. Although there is no accommodation on site, a list of local establishments with preferential rate agreements is provided on request.
Catering: from £12pp

**St Elphins School
Darley Dale
Matlock, Derbyshire DE4 2HA**
T: 01629 733263 F: 01629 733956
email: admin@st-elphins.co.uk
Contact: Mrs E Ainscough, Bursar

Ceremony

St Elphins is an independent school for girls. It is set in attractive grounds and has its own chapel. Six rooms are licensed with capacities ranging from 20 to 400. Ceremonies are difficult to arrange in term time as this is a residential school, but all enquiries are welcome.
Price guide: £35

Reception

The school's in-house catering team offers all types of catering, including ethnic dishes.
Catering: Buffets from £6pp. Sit down from £10.50pp

**Swallow Hotel, J28 M1
Carter Lane East
South Normanton
Derbyshire DE55 2EH**
T: 01773 812000 F: 01773 813413
Contact: Julie Naughton or Justine Wilson, Conference Coordinators.

Ceremony

Ceremonies here must be followed by a reception on the premises.
Price guide: £16

Reception

Catering: Buffets from £6.10pp. Sit down from £16.25pp

**Yew Lodge Hotel
Packington Hill
Kegworth
Derby DE74 2DF**
T: 01509 672518 F: 01509 674730
Contact: Carol Patrick/Katrina Andries Conference & Banqueting.

Ceremony

This hotel, restaurant and conference centre offers two ceremony rooms which are available any day of the year. The hotel features gardens and a lounge with an open fire.
Price guide: £350

Reception

The hotel can arrange most wedding requirements, including fireworks, and has even hosted a double wedding for twins.
Catering: Buffet from £7.50pp Sit down from £12.50pp

ALSO LICENSED
Crown Inn   01773 832310
Derbyshire County Office 01629 580000
East Lodge 01629 734474
Fischers at Baslow Hall 01246 583259
The Homestead 01332 544300
Indian Community Centre 01332 342792
International Hotel 01332 369321
Jarvis Newton Park 01283 703568
The Lund Pavilion 01332 383211
Old Vicarage Restaurant 0114 247 5814
Pride Park Stadium 01332 202202

Sandpiper Hotel 01246 450550
Sitwell Arms Hotel 01246 435226
Springwood House 01332 840757
Three Fishes Hotel 01246 250096
Trent College 0115 946 2848

**Barton Hall, Kingskerswell Road
Torquay, Devon TQ2 8JY**
T: 01803 328748 F: 01803 315605
Contact: Laura Mildiner, Customer Services Manager

Ceremony

Barton Hall is a leisure village with outdoor pool, tennis courts, etc. Four rooms are licensed for ceremonies and are available on any day of the year except Bank Holidays. Ceremonies here must be followed by a reception on the premises.
Price guide: POA

Reception

Catering: Buffets from £5.25pp Sit down from £11.75pp

**Bishops Court Hotel,
Lower Warberry Rd,
Torquay**
T: 01803 294649 F: 01803 291175
Contact: Mrs L Irving, Functions

Ceremony

Three rooms are licensed, with a minimum capacity for 20.
Price guide: £200 - £300

Reception

Catering: Buffets from £5.95pp Sit down from £12.75pp

DEVON

**Bitton House, Bitton Park Road
Teignmouth, Devon TQ14 9DF**
T: 01626 775030
Contact: Mr Lambert, Town Clerk

Ceremony

Bitton House is set in its own grounds and has a gun deck with cannons and balustrading, suitable for wedding photographs (it takes about 30 people).
Price guide: from £45

Reception

Couples may bring their own caterers to this venue, although several can be recommended by Bitton House.
Catering: from £3.50 (buffet) £7.50 (waited)

**Boringdon Hall Hotel
Colebrook
Devon PL7 4DP**
T: 01752 344455 F: 01752 346578
Contact: Melanie White/Elaine Whitehead

Ceremony

This Grade I listed mansion sits in its own grounds on the edge of Dartmoor. Interior features include a Great Hall with minstrel's gallery.
Price guide: £175

Reception

Boringdon Hall's wedding package includes a 50% discount for all children under 11. Infants are catered for free. Other facilities at the hotel include indoor pool, sauna, tennis and a nine-hole pitch and putt golf course.
Catering: £17.50pp

**Buckland-Tout-Saints Hotel
Goveton, Kingsbridge
Devon TQ7 2DS**
T: 01548 853055 F: 01548 856261
Contact: Julie Hudson

Ceremony

This Queen Anne mansion is set in extensive grounds featuring a terrace, where a jazz band can play by arrangement. Three rooms are licensed for ceremonies. Helicopters and hot air balloons can use the grounds.
Price guide: from £50

Reception

Discos and dances can take place in the marquee, as the house is not suitable. Past weddings have featured a jazz band playing on the terrace.
*Catering: Buffets from £15pp
Sit down from £25pp*

**Burgh Island Hotel
Burgh Island, Bigbury on Sea
Devon TQ7 4BG**
T: 01548 810514 F: 01548 810243
Contact: Tony Porter, Proprietor

Ceremony

Burgh Island Hotel is an Art Deco building, built in 1929, set on its own 26 acre tidal island. It can be reached across the sands when the tide is out (6 hours a day), or via the hotel's own sea tractor when the tide is in. The hotel also has its own smugglers' pub on the island (built 1336), as well as a helipad. The nature of the hotel means that it is most suitable for smaller wedding groups, or larger groups if it is taken on an exclusive use basis. (An exclusive-use 2-day package for 36 people, including meals is £7822). One of its claims to fame is that Edward and Mrs Simpson apparently retreated to the hotel to escape the press. It is not possible to hold ceremonies here without also holding the reception at the hotel. Confetti is not permitted. A changing room can be provided for bride and groom on the wedding day, subject to availability.
Price guide: from £150 + vat

Reception

Fish and seafood are a speciality of the hotel which has its own lobster fisherman in season (May to September). The hotel can recommend cake makers. Dances and other live entertainment can only be permitted if the hotel is taken on an exclusive use basis. Overnight accommodation is offered in suites, with their own lounges.
Catering: from £32pp (sit down including canapes and coffee with petits fours)

**Deer Park Hotel
Weston, Honiton
Devon EX14 0PG**
T: 01404 41266 F: 01404 46598
Contact: Janet Gwynn, Hospitality

Ceremony

This Georgian mansion (built 1720) is set in 35 acres of parkland. Ceremonies can take place on any day except Christmas Day and New Year's Eve, but must be followed by reception at the hotel. Helicopters and hot air balloons can use the grounds.
Price guide: £150 + vat

Reception

Catering: from £16pp + vat

**The Devon Hotel
Matford, Exeter EX2 8XU**
T: 01392 59268 F: 01392 413142
Contact: Mr Parkhouse

Ceremony

51

DEVON

The Devon Hotel is 10 minutes from the centre of Exeter, and has three rooms licensed for ceremonies. Ceremonies must be followed by reception at the hotel.
Price guide: £200

Reception

Catering: Buffets from £5.50pp. Sit down from £13pp

The Duke of Cornwall
Millbay Road, Plymouth
Devon PL1 3LG
T: 01752 266256 F: 01752 600062
Contact: Melanie Williams, Conf. Manager

Ceremony

This Grade II listed building was apparently once described by Sir John Betjeman as the finest example of Victorian architecture in Plymouth. It is now a Best Western hotel, with three AA and RAC stars. Inside it retains many original features including a sweeping staircase.
Price guide: £200

Reception

The hotel holds two AA rosettes for fine food.
Catering: from £6.95pp

Durrant House Hotel
Heywood Road, Northam
Devon EX39 3QB
T: 01237 472361 F: 01237 421709
Contact: Maria Borg, Owner

Ceremony

This old Georgian mansion set in three acres, has its own swimming pool, sauna and solarium, and is developing a leisure complex. Ceremonies can take place in one of three rooms; the Venetian Banqueting Suite, the Regency Room and the Garden Room. Ceremonies can take place here on any day except Bank Holidays.
Price guide: £50

Reception

The venue can arrange horse and carriage for you. Helicopters would have to land nearby, however, as there are overhead cables close to the site.
Catering: from £11.50 (buffet) - £14pp (waited)

East Devon Council Offices
The Knowle, Sidmouth
Devon EX10 8HL
T: 01395 516551 F: 01395 577853
Contact: Diana Vernon, Admin Officer or Jeff Bailey, Technical Services Manager

Ceremony

Three rooms have been granted a licence for civil wedding ceremonies at Knowle; The Council Chamber (max 170), the Committee Room (max 85) and the Members' Area (max 160). The building is set in 16 acres of parkland overlooking Lyme Bay. Ceremonies can only take place here on Saturday.
Price guide: from £63.50

Reception

Couples can provide their own caterer for receptions at this venue, therefore a price guide cannot be given.

Eggesford Barton, Eggesford
Chulmleigh, Devon EX18 7QU
T: 01769 580255 F: 01769 580256
email: heyeseggesfordb@compuserve.com
Contact: PN Heyes, Owner

Ceremony

This is a listed period building, set in 100 acres, with a riverside setting. Three rooms are licensed; The Milk Parlour, The Great Barn and The Studio. They are available on any day except Sundays.
Price guide: £250 - £800

Reception

Catering: Buffets from £13pp. Sit down from £20pp

Escot House & Gardens
Escot, Ottery St Mary EX11 1LU
T: 01404 822188 F: 01404 822903
Contact: Mrs Lucy Kennaway, Owner

Ceremony

Escot is a Georgian manor house set in parkland and gardens with lake views. Five rooms are licensed for ceremonies for a minimum of 20 guests. Helicopters and hot air balloons may use the grounds, and boating is possible on the lake.
Price guide: £150

Reception

A speciality of the kitchens is wild boar farmed on the estate. Past weddings have included bride and groom arriving on horseback, and a humanist wedding ceremony.
Catering: Buffets from £5pp
Sit down from £10pp

Haldon Belvedere (Lawrence Castle), Higher Ashton, Exeter
T & F: 01392 833668
Contact: Ian Turner, Manager

Ceremony

This secluded, listed building has panoramic views over Devon. The building is owned by The Devon Historic Buildings Trust, and includes an apartment which is also let. Two rooms are licensed for ceremonies, each with its own character.
Price guide: from £200

Reception

Couples may choose their own caterer for this venue, or this can be arranged for you. Many services can be recommended, including a piper. Both helicopters and hot air balloons may land on site.
Catering: P.O.A.

Huntsham Court
Huntsham, Tiverton EX16 7NA
T: 01398 361365 F: 01398 361456
Contact: Andrea Bolwig, Owner

Ceremony

Ceremonies at this Grade II listed Victorian gothic country house can take place on any day of the year, with only one permitted per day.
Price guide: £250

Reception

The Court provides British and continental style cuisine.
Catering: P.O.A.

Imperial Hotel
Park Hill Road, Torquay
Devon TQ1 2D
T: 01803 294301 F: 01803 298293
Contact: Food & Beverage Manager

Ceremony

This well-known resort hotel can hold ceremonies on any day except Sunday.
Price guide: £200

Reception

In addition to the above services, the hotel can also print menus and place cards for you.
Catering: P.O.A.

Langstone Cliff Hotel
Dawlish Warren
Dawlish, Devon EX7 0NA
T: 01626 865155 F: 01626 867166
Contact: Geoffrey or Mark Rogers, Partners

Ceremony

Langstone Cliff is a Grade II listed building set in its own grounds of 19 acres, on Devon's south coast. It has an outdoor pool and a hard tennis court.
Price guide: £200

Reception

Transport, balloons and a cabaret can all be organised by the hotel, which can also offer barbecues, supper dances and children's parties and teas.
Catering: from £9pp

Lewtrenchard Manor
Lewdown
Okehampton
Devon EX20 4PN
T: 01566 783256 F: 01566 783332
Contact: Mrs S Murray, Owner

Ceremony

The Manor was built in about 1600 and was once the home of the composer of 'Onward Christian Soldiers'. Internally, the house features ornate ceilings and oak panelling, carvings and open fireplaces. It is now the home of the Murray family. Four rooms are licensed for ceremonies. The grounds can be used by hot air balloons and helicopters.
Price guide: £200

Reception

Catering: from £22.50pp

Moorlands Link Hotel
Yelverton
Devon PL20 6DA
T: 01822 852245 F: 01822 855004
Contact: Irene, Functions Co-ordinator

Ceremony

Up to two ceremonies per day can take place at Moorlands Link, but ceremonies must be followed by a reception at the hotel. Weddings can take place any day except during the festive season. Confetti is not permitted. Wheelchair access to the Ballroom is limited.
Price guide: from £150

Reception

Overnight accommodation can be offered at a special rate to your wedding guests.
Catering: P.O.A.

Northcote Manor
Burrington
Nr Exmoor
Devon EX37 9LZ
T: 01769 560501 F: 01769 560770
Contact: Norbert Spichtinger, Owner

DEVON

DEVON

Ceremony

The Manor is a Grade II listed building and the former estate of the Earls of Bedford and Portsmouth. It is set in 20 acres of lawns, landscaped gardens and woodland, and features a tennis court and golf practise area. There are also horses available for riding. One ceremony can take place here on any day of the year.

The Manor offers a wedding package which includes marriage ceremony in the Oak Room (not registrar's fees), use of the Northcote Room for reception, overnight stay in the honeymoon suite, use of a vintage Rolls Royce and a free night in a double room on the couple's first anniversary, all for £395.
Price guide: P.O.A.

Reception

"Sophisticated Continental" cuisine.
Catering: £20pp - £40pp

Old Forde House, Brunel Road
Newton Abbot, Devon TQ12 4XX
T: 01626 61101
Contact: Mrs A Livingston, Administrator

Ceremony

This is a Grade I listed manor house, with gardens, dating from 1600. It is currently owned by Teignbridge District Council, and has four rooms licensed for civil ceremonies, including the Victorian Kitchen. These are available on the first Saturday of the month only, and not during the administrator's annual leave, or during Bank Holidays. Up to two ceremonies are permitted on any one day. Smoking is not permitted on the premises, and confetti must be of the biodegradable variety. Wheelchair access to the Main Hall only.
Price guide: £150

Reception

There are no reception facilities at Old Forde.

Park Hotel
Taw Vale, Barnstaple, Devon
T: 01271 72166 F: 01271 23157
Contact: Michael Woodford, Manager

Ceremony

The Park Hotel is five minutes from the town centre in a park and riverside location. Two rooms are licensed for ceremonies.
Price guide: £200

Reception

Catering: Buffets from £4.95 Sit down from £12.50pp

Powderham Castle
Kenton, Exeter
Devon EX6 8JQ
T: 01626 890243 F: 01626 890729
Contact: Tim Faulkner, General Manager

Ceremony

Powderham Castle dates from Medieval times and has been the historic family home of the Earl of Devon for over 600 years. It is set within an extensive landscaped deer park alongside the River Exe. The castle was also used as the location for the film "The Remains of the Day", staring Anthony Hopkins and Emma Thompson. The castle is usually only available for ceremonies on Saturday, but ceremonies can be held on other days by arrangement. Confetti is not allowed.
Price guide: £500

Reception

Catering at the castle is through a contract caterer which can be of your choice, hence it is not possible to give a price guide. A list of local accommodation with which the castle has preferential rate agreements is available on request.

The Royal Hotel
Barnstaple Street
Bideford
Devon EX39 4AZ
T: 01237 472005 F: 01237 478957
Contact: Mr Nigel Maun

Ceremony

The Royal was originally built by a merchant in the 18th Century and is sited by the River Torridge. Couples can arrive and depart by boat. Three rooms are licensed for ceremonies.
Price guide: from £45 + vat

Reception

Traditional English carvery is one of the specialities of the house. Complimentary overnight accommodation is offered to bride and groom if the reception is booked here.
Catering: Packages including drink from £15.90pp

Tavistock Town Hall
Tavistock
Devon PL19 0AU
T: 01822 617232
Contact: Mr Cridland, Town Hall Supervisor

Ceremony

Two ceremony rooms are available in this 1860's building in the main square in the centre of Tavistock. These are available on any day except Bank Holidays.
Price guide: £65 (local residents) £85 (to those living outside the area)

Reception

Couples may appoint their own caterers for receptions at the Town Hall. The bar is licensed until 2am on all days except Saturday when it is licensed until midnight.

Tiverton Castle
Tiverton
Devon EX16 6RP
T: 01884 253200 F: 01884 254200
Contact: Mr & Mrs AK Gordon, Owners

Ceremony

This Grade I listed medieval castle is easily accessed from the M5 and Tiverton Parkway station. Four rooms are licensed for ceremonies, which can take place on any day except Sunday. Access is also limited when the castle is open to the public. Wheelchair access is limited.
Price guide: 1-30 people £250 (2hrs)
30-70 people £300 (2hrs)

Reception

The accommodation on offer is self-catering (with 4-keys rating). Prices for hiring the castle for reception start at £300 for the hire of castle for three hours after the reception (1-30 people), and rises to £500 for three hours, reception only for 70 people and over. Catering is extra by arrangement with the Castle's contract caterers.
Catering: POA

Tiverton Hotel, Blundells Road
Tiverton EX16 4DB
T: 01884 256120 F: 01884 258101
Contact: Brigitte Kuipers, Events Manager

Ceremony

This town centre hotel has three licensed rooms.
Price guide: from £70

Reception

The hotel says it offers a wide variety of vegetarian dishes. It will also give discounts for children dining at the reception.
Catering: From £12.50pp

ALSO LICENSED
Bickleigh Castle   01884 855363
Buckerell Lodge Hotel   01392 52451
Crossmead Centre   01392 273703
Elfordleigh Hotel   01752 336428
Gypsy Hill Hotel   01392 465252
The Horn of Plenty 01822 832528
Kingston House 01803 762235
Kitley, Plymouth   01752 881555
Manor House Hotel   01647 440355
Market Hall, Holsworthy   01237 476711
Medland Manor   01647 24042
Overmead Hotel 01803 295666
Saunton Sands Hotel 01271 890212
Whitechapel Manor   01769 573377
Yarner, Bovey Tracey 01364 661354

Bridge House Hotel
2 Ringwood Road
Longham,
Nr Ferndown
Dorset
BH22 9AN
T: 01202 578828 F: 01202 572620
Contact: Simon Ball, Manager

Ceremony

The hotel is set on the banks of the River Stour, and has an island garden. Three suites are licensed and are available on any day except Christmas Day.
Price guide: from £70

Reception

Themed weddings held here have included both a 1960's and a Teddy Boy's wedding!
Catering: Buffets from £3.95pp. Sit down from £10.95pp

Carlton Hotel
East Overcliff, Bournemouth
Dorset BH1 3DN
T: 01202 552011 F: 01202 299573
Contact: General Manager

Ceremony

This hotel was in the process of being sold as we went to press, so couples would be advised to call the hotel for an update on prices. Below is the 1996 entry.
The Carlton Hotel sits overlooking Bournemouth Bay with views to the Needles on the Isle of Wight, Studland Point and the Purbecks. One ceremony is permitted here per day on any day of the year. It is not possible to book a ceremony here without also booking reception facilities, however.
Price guide: £150

Reception

In addition to the services above, the hotel can provide linen to your colour choice and candelabra. The wedding package also includes complimentary overnight accommodation for bride and groom. Helicopters can land by arrangement.
Catering: from £23.50pp

Coppleridge Inn
Motcombe, Shaftesbury SP7 9HW
T: 01747 851980 F: 01747 851858
Contact: David Dawson, Manager

Ceremony

The Inn is a converted 17th Century farm set in 15 acres of meadow and woodland. The Inn's function room is an oak timbered former barn. Ceremonies can take place here on any day of the year.
Price guide: £100

Reception

DEVON - DORSET

55

DORSET

The Inn offers dishes using its own free range chickens.
Catering: £5pp - £20pp

Dorchester Municipal Buildings
High East Street
Dorchester, Dorset
T: 01305 265840 F: 01305 266085
Contact: Miss Lousie Harding, Administrator

Ceremony

The Municipal Buildings are Grade II listed and date from the mid 19th Century. The Buildings comprise a suite of rooms ranging in capacity from 40 to 120. Up to two ceremonies a day can take place here on any day except Sunday, Christmas Day and Boxing Day. Confetti is not permitted.
Price guide: £50

Reception

Couples may choose their own caterers for this venue: kitchens will be made available.
Catering: P.O.A.

The Guildhall
Bridge Street, Lyme Regis
Dorset DT7 3QA
Tel: 01297 445175 Fax: 01297 443773
Contact: Mrs C Bright

Ceremony

The Guildhall claims 'spectacular' coastal views, which take in both the Cobb and the Golden Cap. This ancient building's history dates back to the Stuart period. Ceremonies take place in the main Council Chamber, which was formerly the local court-house, with its curved ceiling and coat of arms. Ceremonies can take place any day except Sunday and Bank Holidays.
Price guide: £75

Reception
The nearest venue for receptions is the Marine Theatre. Contact the Manager Mr Peter Hammond for details (01297 442394)

Hotel Rembrandt
12-16 Dorchester Road
Weymouth
Dorset DT4 7JU
T: 01305 764000 F: 01305 764022
Contact: Rebecca Buckland, Hotel Administrator

Ceremony

The Rembrandt offers two marriage rooms, the Garden Room (max 100) and the Aylesbury Room (max 70). These are available on any day except Christmas Day, New Year's Eve and New Year's Day. There is now an area suitable for outdoor photography.
Price guide: £150

Reception

In addition to the range of services listed above, the hotel can provide a choice of coloured linen, special archway ribbons for use in the reception decorations, complimentary bridal suite for the couple on the wedding night, 1st anniversary meal and special accommodation rates for wedding guests.
Catering: from £5.95pp (buffet) to £16pp (waited)

Langtry Manor Hotel
Derby Road, East Cliff
Bournemouth, Dorset BH1 3QB
T: 01202 553887 F: 01202 290115
Contact: Tara Howard, GM

Ceremony

This listed building was built by Edward VII for his mistress Lillie Langtry. The marriage room is the Dining Room which features an inglenook fireplace, minstrel's gallery, huge stained glass windows, chandeliers and 16th Century tapestries. Ceremonies can take place here on any day except Christmas Day and Boxing Day. Confetti is not permitted.
Price guide: £200

Reception

For the reception waiters and waitresses will be dressed in mob caps and frilly aprons in true Edwardian style. The reception can take place in the Dining Room or in the Royal Suite in the Langtry Lodge. The latter room is also available for your evening party. The Manor also offers several honeymoon suites with four poster beds or spa baths. Lillie's room, for instance, features a four poster bed and heart shaped corner bath. Edward VII's own personal bedroom is also available.
Catering: £14.95pp - £27pp

The Manor Hotel
West Bexington
Dorchester
Dorset
DT2 9DF
T: 01308 897616 F: 01308 897035
Contact: Richard Childs, Proprietor

Ceremony

Mentioned in the Doomsday Book, The Manor is an ancient stone building set within 500 yards of Chesil Beach. Three rooms have wedding licences, but these have limited wheelchair access.
Price guide: from £100

Reception

Helicopters and hot air balloons can land on site here, but despite its proximity to the sea, couples could not realistically arrive or depart by boat.
Catering: Buffet from £12pp. Sit down from £15pp

DORSET

The Mansion House Hotel
Thames Street
Poole
Dorset BH15 1JN
T: 01202 685666 F: 01202 665709
Contact: Jackie Godden, MD

Ceremony

This Georgian house is set in a town mews just off Poole's busy quay. It is a Grade II listed building with an elegant feature staircase. Ceremonies can take place here on any day of the year.
Price guide: £125

Reception

The hotel offers modern English cuisine. As part of the wedding package, the hotel offers a complimentary bridal suite and special rates.
Catering: P.O.A.

Purbeck House Hotel
91 High Street
Swanage
Dorset BH19 2LZ
T: 01929 422872 F: 01929 421194
email: purbeckhouse@easyco.uk
Contact: Christine Cruse, Proprietor

Ceremony

Purbeck is a Grade II listed building, with gardens. It is in the centre of Swanage and only 300 yards from the sea front. Three rooms are licensed, including the Garden Conservatory.
Price guide: £125

Reception

Catering: Buffets from £9.95pp. Sit down from £12.50pp

Royal Chase Hotel
Shaftesbury, Dorset SP7 8DB
T: 01747 853355 F: 01747 851969
Contact: Leanne Ashmore, Conference & Sales Co-ordinator

Ceremony

The Royal Chase has two rooms licensed for weddings. The venue also has numerous leisure facilities including an indoor swimming pool, Turkish steam room and solarium. Confetti is not permitted on the premises.
Price guide: £150

Reception

The hotel has an AA two rosette credited restaurant. The cellars are said to be suitable for smaller functions, while larger functions here have included a medieval banquet in the restaurant, 'Chasers'.
Catering: Buffets from £4pp Sit down from £12pp

Salterns Hotel
38 Salterns Way
Lilliput, Poole
Dorset BH14 8JR
T: 01202 707321 F: 01202 707488
Contact: Linda Hioco, Marketing & Events Manager

Ceremony

Salterns Hotel enjoys a waterside location and boasts views over Poole Harbour from the two wedding rooms. Wheelchair access is limited.
Price guide: £125

Reception

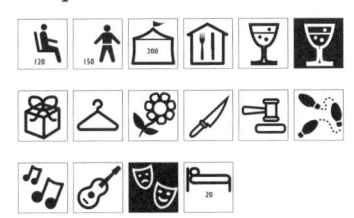

The hotel has an AA two rosette credited restaurant. Helicopters can land on site, and the hotel can arrange arrival or departure by boat if requested.
Catering: Buffets from £7.75pp Sit down from £19.50pp

Sherborne Hotel
Horsecastles Lane
Sherborne
Dorset DT9 6BB
T: 01935 81391 F: 01935 81693
Contact: Mrs Sue Murphy, Conference & Banqueting Coordinator

Ceremony

this is a modern hotel set within four acres of lawned gardens. The Raleigh Room is licensed for ceremonies on any day except Christmas Day and Boxing Day.
Price guide: from £200

Reception

Catering: Buffets from £4.95pp. Sit down from £16pp

Stafford House
West Stafford
Dorchester
Dorset
DT2 8AA
T: 01305 263668 F: 01305 266903
Contact: Mrs Kay Pavitt, Owner

Ceremony

Jane Austen's Emma was recently filmed in the grounds at Stafford House (Emma was proposed to under the oak!). If that's not enough romance or glamour, Hardy apparently also wrote The Waiting Supper about the [...] Grade I listed pr[...] private riverside w[...] and the Drawing [...] for weddings wh[...] on any day of th[...]
Price guide: from £[...]

DORSET - DURHAM

Reception

A choice of contract caterers is offered for those wishing to hold their reception at the house, so prices vary depending on what is required.
Catering: POA

Summer Lodge Hotel
Evershot, Dorset DT2 0JR
T: 01935 83424 F: 01935 83005
Contact: Adam Smith, Assistant Manager

Ceremony

This listed building claims a four acre walled garden. Three rooms are available for ceremonies which can take place here on any day of the year.
Price guide: £200 - £400

Reception

Wedding packages are available here, and full details will be sent on request.
Catering: from £21pp

Swallow Highcliff Hotel
105 St Michael's Road
West Cliff
Bournemouth BH2 5DU
T: 01202 557702 F: 01202 292734
Contact: Barbara Crabb, Conference and Banqueting Sales Manager

Ceremony

This Victorian cliff-top hotel overlooks Bournemouth beach. Two suites are available for ceremonies; the Shaftesbury Suite and the Purbeck Suite. Weddings may take place here on any day of the year.
Price guide: £250

Reception

Additional services to those mentioned above include a red carpet, and champagne for the bride and groom on arrival.
Catering: from £14pp

Wimborne Minster Town Hall
37 West Borough
Wimborne Minster BH21 1LT
T & F: 01202 881655
Contact: Joyce Ulman, Bookings Officer

Ceremony

The Council Chamber is licensed and available for ceremonies on any day of the week except Sundays and Bank Holidays.
Price guide: from £75

Reception

The kitchens here are available for self-catering. There are also several good hotels and restaurants within walking distance.

Winter Gardens Hotel
Tregonwell Road
Bournemouth, Dorset BH2 5NU
T: 01202 555769 F: 01202 551330
Contact: Lorraine Ayrton, Front of House Manager

Ceremony

Only one ceremony per day is permitted at the Winter Gardens Hotel. This can be held on any day of the week, except Sunday. There is no wheelchair access to the hotel. The hotel permits confetti.
Price guide: from £50

Reception

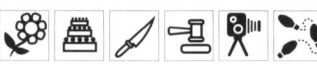

The hotel can offer themed weddings or cater for special dietary requirements.
Catering: from £6pp

Yenton Hotel
5 Gervis Road
East Cliff
Bournemouth
Dorset BH1 3ED
T: 01202 556334 F: 01202 298835
Contact: Mr M C McIntosh, Proprietor

Ceremony

The Yenton is set in an acre of gardens on a tree lined avenue. The Tudor Restaurant and Brodies Restaurant are both licensed for civil ceremonies, which can take place here on any day of the year except Christmas Day.
Price guide: P.O.A.

Reception

The chef at the hotel was head chef at a five star hotel before joining the Yenton. The hotel specialises in barbecues and garden parties and can arrange all kinds of entertainment including discos, bands and cabaret artists.
Catering: £5pp - £25pp

ALSO LICENSED
Avonmouth Hotel 01202 483434

Bishop Auckland Town Hall
Market Place
Bishop Auckland
Co Durham DL 14 7NP
T: 01388 602610 F: 01388 604960
Contact: Gillian Wales, Centre Manager

Ceremony

This Grade II listed civic building is located in the town centre and offers four ceremony rooms. These are available on any day except Bank Holidays.
Price guide: £22

Reception

Catering: Buffets from £1.50pp Sit down from £9.95pp

**The Bowes Museum
Newgate
Barnard Castle
Co Durham DL12 8NP**
T: 01833 690606 F: 01833 637163
Contact: Mrs G Conran, Curator

Ceremony

The Bowes Museum offers the Spanish Gallery and the Music Room for ceremonies on Thursdays, Fridays and Saturdays. It is closed on Christmas Day, Boxing Day and New Year's Day. Confetti is not permitted.
Price guide: from £350

Reception
There are no reception facilities at this venue.

**The George Hotel
Piercebridge, Darlington
Co Durham DL2 3SW**
T: 01325 374576 F: 01325 374577
Contact: Mrs Jennifer Wain, Owner

Ceremony

This old coaching inn, with a landscaped riverside setting, offers ceremonies seven days a week.
Price guide: £45

Reception

The George Hotel prides itself on its family-owned personal touch. As part of its wedding package, the hotel offers free overnight accommodation in the bridal suite for the bride and groom. The hotel also gives a 10% discount off the normal accommodation rates for wedding guests. The reception price guide quoted below includes drinks.
Catering: £22pp

**Headlam Hall Hotel
Nr Gainford, Darlington
Co Durham DL2 3HA**
T: 01325 730238 F: 01325 730790
Contact: David Jackson, Manager

Ceremony

This listed building is set in large formal gardens in a secluded rural location. Two ceremony rooms are available on any day of the week except Saturday, with only one ceremony permitted per day. There is room in the grounds for helicopters and hot air balloons to take off.
Price guide: £150

Reception

Catering: Buffets from £15.50pp Sit down from £17.50pp

**Lord Crewe Arms Hotel
Blanchland
Co Durham DH8 9SP**
T: 01434 675251 F: 01434 675337
Contact: Wendy Hart, Receptionist

Ceremony

This scheduled ancient monument offers ceremonies seven days a week with one permitted per day. Ceremonies are only accepted in conjunction with receptions. Confetti is allowed.
Price guide: POA

Reception

The hotel site is suitable for a marquee with unlimited capacity, while the hotel's restaurant holds an AA rosette.
Catering: from £16.75pp

**The Morritt Arms Hotel
Greta Bridge
Rokeby, Nr Barnard Castle
Co Durham DL12 9SE**
T: 01833 627232 F: 01833 627392
Contact: Barbara-Anne Johnson, Owner.

Ceremony

The Morritt Arms Hotel is a 17th Century listed building built on the site of a Roman settlement which is still visible today. Its Dickens bar features murals by John Gilroy. Ceremonies are available seven days a week with a maximum of two permitted per day. Ceremony prices vary according to number of guests, from £150 for 25 people, £200 for 25-75 people and £250 for 75-150 people.
Price guide: from £150.

Reception

The hotel has 17 individual, en-suite rooms, some featuring four poster or traditional brass beds - a bridal suite is also available. The site is suitable for a marquee to a capacity of 500.
Catering: from £10pp

Pockerley Manor, Beamish Open Air Museum DH9 0RG
T: 01207 231811 F: 01207 290933
Contact: Helen Franklin, Interpretation Assistant

Ceremony

DURHAM

Pockerley Manor is a Georgian farmhouse which reflects the lifestyles of the 1820s. A tram will take guests to Pockerley, while an Armstrong Whitworth limousine carries the bride and groom. The ceremony rooms are the Period Parlour and the Kitchen, but are not available between June and August inclusive, or on Bank Holidays. The terraced gardens are said to be a good backdrop for photographs.
Price guide: from £350 + vat

Reception

A light buffets or drinks reception is available, but full seating is not possible (unless in a marquee). Catering would have to be organised by bride and groom.

Shotton Hall
Peterlee
Co Durham SR8 2PH
T: 0191 5862491 F: 0191 5860370
Contacts: Kay Colborn, Deputy Town Clerk and Billy Davies, Banqueting

Ceremony

Shotton Hall, built in 1760 and set in 17.5 acres of grounds, is available to hold ceremonies seven days a week, excluding Christmas Day, New Year's Day, Good Friday and Boxing Day. A maximum of four ceremonies per day are permitted. The price guide to hold ceremonies varies according to the time of week; £20 for weekdays and £30 at weekends and Bank Holidays. The master staircase provides a good setting for indoor photography.
Price guide: from £20

Reception

Reception facilities include a waited service with a capacity of 180 and buffet service for 280. Although Shotton Hall does not have accommodation facilities, a list of accommodation is available.
Catering: from £3.50pp

Walworth Castle Hotel
Walworth, Darlington DL2 2LY
T: 01325 485470 F: 01325 462257
Contact: Mrs RA Culley

Ceremony

This 12th Century castle is set in 18 acres of gardens and woodland and offers six ceremony rooms.
Price guide: from £50

Reception

Catering: Buffets from £5.50pp Sit down from £14.95pp

STOP PRESS
Hardwicke Hall Manor Hotel
01429 836326
Helme Park Hall Hotel 01388 730970
The Raven Country Hotel 01207 560367

Carlton Towers, Carlton, Goole DN14 9LZ
T: 01405 861662 F: 01405 861917
Contact: Steve Randall, Events Manager

Ceremony

This is a Victorian gothic country house is set amidst 250 acres of parkland. Five state rooms are licensed and are available on any day of the year. Up to three ceremonies are permitted per day.
Price guide: £150 + vat

Reception

A list of local accommodation with which Carlton Towers has rate agreements, is available on request.
Catering: from £30pp

Country Park Inn, Cliff Road
Hessleforeshore
Hessle, HU13 0HB
T: 01482 644336 F: 01482 644336
Contact: Mrs Cross, Conference & Banqueting Co-ordinator

Ceremony

The original part of the building dates back to the 1800s while the Function Suite is a modern addition. The Function Suite is actually set on the banks of the Humber and is only a matter of inches away at high tide. One room is licensed to hold ceremonies at the conference centre, seven days a week, with no restrictions on the number held per day. It is possible to hold ceremonies without reception facilities and confetti is permitted.
Price guide: £200

Reception

Catering prices start from £8.50 a head for a buffet style reception, increasing to £12.50 a head, for a banquet style format. The Conference Centre would like to point out that any catering provisions, including religious or dietary requirements, will be considered. Although no accommodation is available on the premises, the centre operates preferential rate agreements with several local hotels and guest houses.
Catering: from £8.50pp

Grange Park Hotel
Main Street
Willerby, HU10 6EA
T: 01482 656488 F: 01482 655848
Contact: Karen Amann, Conference/Banqueting Co-ordinator

Ceremony

The hotel has two rooms licensed to hold ceremonies, the Mulberry Suite and the Birch Suite. The hotel also features extensive car parking facilities, a helipad and 11 acres of landscaped gardens. Ceremonies must be followed by

a reception on the premises.
Price guide: £150 - £200

Reception

A complimentary overnight stay is available for the bride and groom, although a honeymoon suite is also available at a 50% discount. Special accommodation rates are available for wedding guests and, when full, the hotel has preferential rates with other local establishments. The hotel offers English cooking in a modern style. The adjoining pub and restaurant which specialises in Italian cuisine. Buffets are also available.
Catering: from £16.50pp sit down

Rowley Manor Hotel
Little Weighton, HU20 3XR
T: 01482 848248 F: 01482 849900
Contact: Mario F Ando, Proprietor

Ceremony

This listed Georgian country house is set in 34 acres of lawns, rose gardens and parklands and was once the rectory to St Peter's Church which is also found within the grounds. The rectory is said to have been built in 1621, and in 1928 the house was purchased by a shipping magnate who commissioned the famous pine panelling by Grinling Gibbons which now forms a central feature in the study where ceremonies take place. Ceremonies are available throughout the week, excluding Saturdays.
Price guide: from £100 + vat

Reception

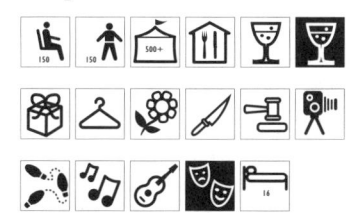

The Manor boasts a selection of menus, including those that allow the guests to carve meats at their own table. The Manor specialises in fresh produce and fresh fish. A typical drinks package starts at £8.75 a head.
Catering: from £19.95pp

Rudstone Walk, South Cave
Nr Beverley HU15 2AH
T: 01430 422230 F: 01430 424552
Contact: Laura Greenwood, General Manager

Ceremony

This conference centre is set in its own 100 acres at the foot of the Yorkshire Wolds. The Main Room is licensed for ceremonies which can take place here on any day except Christmas Day and New Year's Day.
Price guide: £260 (1998) £300 (1999)

Reception

Catering: from £28.50pp

ALSO LICENSED (SEE HULL)
Forte Posthouse (Hull) 01482 645212
Tickton Grange 01964 543666

The Anchor Inn, Anchor Lane
Barcombe, Nr Lewes BN8 5BS
T: 01273 400414 F: 01273 401029
Contacts: Mrs Jaci Bovet-White, Proprietor

Ceremony

This rural 18th Century riverside smuggling inn offers its oriental style Pagoda Room for wedding ceremonies on any day except Bank Holidays.
Price guide: £175 (£100 with reception)

Reception

The Inn tailors each menu to suit. If your reception is for over 20, the honeymoon suite is offered free for bride and groom to use on their wedding night. Couples can arrive here by helicopter or balloon, which the Inn can arrange. In addition, the Inn has 30 of its own flat bottomed six seater hand-propelled boats. The Inn also has its own white Rolls Royce and access to other classic cars.
Catering: Buffets from £7.50pp. Sit down from £12.50pp

Anne of Cleves House
52 Southover High Street
Lewes, East Sussex BN7 1JA
T: 01273 474610 F: 01273 486990
Contacts: Stephen Watts, Senior Custodian

Ceremony

Although it bears her name, this Tudor property was part of Anne of Cleves' estate from which she received rent. It is now a local history museum owned by the Sussex Archaeological Society. Ceremonies can take place in the East Room on Fridays, Saturdays and Sundays.
Price guide: £200

Reception

Outside caterers would have to be appointed for a reception at the house. Tudor weddings have, not surprisingly, proved popular here.

Barnsgate Manor Vineyard
Herons Ghyll
Uckfield TN22 4DB
T: 01825 713366 F: 01825 713543
Contact: Keith Johnson, Proprietor

Ceremony

An old stone flagged barn is the marriage room on this 55 acre estate, which is also home to 60 llamas and alpacas. Ceremonies can take place on any day.
Price guide: £200

Reception

EAST RIDING OF YORKSHIRE - EAST SUSSEX

61

EAST SUSSEX

Receptions can be held at the Manor House Restaurant or the Ashdown Restaurant and Disco Cellar, both of which have patios and views over Ashdown Forest. The vineyard's own wine is, naturally, available for receptions, and includes white and rose wines, as well as an apple wine.
Catering: POA

Beauport Park Hotel
Battle Road, Hastings TN38 8EA
T: 01424 851222 F: 01424 852465
Contact: Stephen Bayes, General Manager

Ceremony

Beauport Park is a Georgian country house (1719) set in 35 acres of woodland and garden, and situated just three miles from Hastings and Battle. Ceremonies can take place here on any day except over the Christmas holiday.
Price guide: £175 (£125 with reception)

Reception

Your reception at Beauport Park can take place in an air-conditioned suite. Both the hotel's restaurant and its cocktail bar overlook the formal Italian and sunken gardens. Children under 12 years old are charged at two-thirds full price, while children under three years old are catered for free. Special weekend rates can be offered to your wedding guests. The hotel can also offer a PA system if required.
Catering: from £16.50pp

Bentley Wildfowl
& Motor Museum
Halland
Lewes
East Sussex BN8 5AF
T & F: 01825 840573/841322
Contact: Barry Sutherland, Manager

Ceremony

The Motor Museum and Wildfowl Collection are set in the grounds of the Bentley Estate, which covers some 100 acres and includes Bentley House, a Tudor farmhouse that has been converted into a Palladian style mansion. The Museum prefers that weddings do not take place on Bank Holiday weekends. While confetti is not permitted, rice is.
Price guide: £150

Reception

While there is in-house catering, you can also appoint a contract caterer from an approved list. A late night drinking licence can be applied for if required. In addition to the services offered above, the Museum can also provide a veteran, vintage or classic car from its collection. A list of local accommodation is available.
Catering: £10 - £50pp

Brickwall House, Northiam
Nr Rye, East Sussex TN31 6NL
T: 01797 252001 F: 01797 252567
email: post@frewcoll.demon.co.uk
Contact: Peter Mould, Director

Ceremony

This independent school is housed in a listed building, with extensive grounds and gardens. The Grand Drawing Room is licensed for ceremonies which can only take place here on Saturdays and Sundays.
Price guide: £200 - £400

Reception

Helicopters and hot air balloons may use the site on arrangement.
Catering: Buffets from £17.50pp. Sit down from £25pp

Buxted Park Country House Hotel
Buxted Park, Uckfield TN22 4AY
T: 01825 732711 F: 01825 732770
Contact: Lisa Collins, Conference & Banqueting Co-ordinator

Ceremony

This is a Georgian mansion, dating from 1725. The hotel is set in 312 acres of parkland featuring exotic plants and lakes. The Library is the licensed marriage room which is available any day of the year.
Price guide: £150

Reception

Receptions can take place in the hotel's restaurant (for 45) or in its newly renovated Orangery (for 50). Larger parties can be catered for in the Ballroom and Coat of Arms Lounge.
Catering: £47.50pp

Cinque Ports Hotel
Bohemia Road, Hastings TN34 1ET
T: 01424 439222 F: 01424 437277
Contact: Colin Wilson, General Manager

Ceremony

Cinque Ports allows wedding ceremonies in it Library on any day of the year.
Price guide: £65

Reception

Catering: Buffets from £6.50pp. Sit down from £12.75pp

EAST SUSSEX

De La Warr Pavilion, Marina
Bexhill on Sea, TN40 1DP
T: 01424 212023 F: 01424 787940
Contact: Nick Crane

Ceremony

This 1930's Grade I listed civic building is a popular film set (Poirrot was filmed here), and is situated on the seafront with views across the channel. This Art Deco building has one ceremony room which is available on any day except Christmas Day. Confetti is not permitted.
Price guide: £100

Reception

Two rooms are available for receptions. You may choose your own caterer for this venue.

The Dower House
Bayham Abbey, TN8 8DE
T: 01732 778024
Contact: Abigail Penney, Manager

Ceremony

The Dower House (built c1750) was once the home of Lord Camden (of Camden Town fame) and was built in the grounds of what was once an abbey (founded 1208). The ruins of the abbey remain in the grounds, very near to the house, and can be seen from the ceremony room windows. The house (Georgian Gothic in style) and abbey are now under the management of English Heritage.
There is no electric light in the ceremony room itself, and weddings have been held here in candlelight. Confetti should be flower petals only. Hot air balloons may use the grounds and horses and carriage may drive anywhere in the abbey grounds.
Price guide: £250

Reception

A marquee is set in the grounds for larger parties, and you can choose your own caterer. Receptions in the house carry restrictions of no smoking and no beer. Wedding parties have exclusive use of the grounds in the evening (the abbey is often open to the public).

The Grand Hotel, Kings Road
Brighton BN1 2FW
T: 01273 321188 F: 01272 202694
Contact: Conference Manager

Ceremony

This famous hotel, built in 1865 and a listed building, is situated on Brighton's seafront. The Empress Suite is licensed for wedding ceremonies. This breaks down into four separate rooms, the smallest of which will seat 40. Ceremonies must be followed by a reception at the hotel.
Price guide: from £250

Reception

Catering: Packages including drinks, from £39pp

Herstmonceux Castle
Hailsham, BN27 1RP
T: 01323 834479 F: 01323 834499
Contact: Banqueting Co-ordinator

Ceremony

Herstmonceux is a 15th Century brick moated castle. It has four rooms licensed for weddings, including the Ballroom, which features wood panelling and a painted Palladian ceiling. It overlooks an Elizabethan walled garden and courtyard.
Price guide: £250

Reception

Overnight accommodation is available at Bader Hall on the castle estate.
Catering: £18.55 - £29.95pp

Horsted Place
Little Horsted, Uckfield
T: 01825 750581 F: 01825 750240
Contact: Sally Chapman, Conference & Banqueting Co-ordinator

Ceremony

This Victorian Gothic mansion permits only one ceremony per day, for a minimum of 20 guests. Confetti is only allowed outside.
Price guide: from £200

Reception

Horsted Place can also arrange car hire if required. A bedroom is usually available on site.
Catering: £POA

The Manor Barn
c/o Bexhill Old Town
Preservation Society,
8 High Street, Bexhill TN40 2HA
T: 01424 220231
Contact: Miss Madeley, Secretarial Services Manager

Ceremony

This was once the ballroom of the late Earl De La Warr and is set amongst the ruins of the Earl's old manor house in a parkland setting. The ceremony licence is held for the hall only
Price guide: £54

Reception

The Manor Barn may be hired for the reception. It is licensed for music and dancing and there is a bar. Couples may bring in caterers of their choice to use the 'spacious well-equipped kitchen'.

Netherfield Place
Battle
East Sussex
TN33 9PP
T: 01424 774455 F: 01424 774024
Contact: Michael Collier, Proprietor, or Nicky Keeling, Assistant Manager

EAST SUSSEX

Ceremony

This country house hotel set in 30 acres has a licence for its Bayeux Room, which has limited wheelchair access and is available on all days except Bank Holidays.
Price guide: POA

Reception

Helicopters and hot air balloons may use the grounds.
Catering: Buffets from £7.50pp. Sit down from £18pp

**Newick Park, Newick
East Sussex BN8 4SB**
T: 01825 723633 F: 01825 723969
Contact: Virginia Childs, GM

Ceremony

This Grade II listed Georgian building features Victorian gardens with views of the lake to the South Downs. The Library is the ceremony room and is available all year.
Price guide: from £100 (with reception)

Reception

Newick boasts an award-winning chef.
Catering: from £20pp

**The Old Ship Hotel, Kings Road
Brighton BN1 1NR**
T: 01273 329001 F: 01273 820718
Contact: Alison Tanner

Ceremony

The Old Ship is housed in a Regency building (Grade I listed) and claims to be Brighton's oldest hotel. It is situated on Brighton's seafront, opening up interesting opportunities for outdoor photography. Ceremonies can take place here on any day of the year, but must be followed by a reception at the hotel.
Price guide: POA

Reception

Receptions can take place in the Paganini Ballroom, or the Regency Suite, or both rooms can be used together. Four smaller rooms are also available for receptions of between 20 and 75 guests.
Catering: from £20pp

**The Palace Pier
Madiera Drive
Brighton BN2 1TW**
T: 01273 609361 F: 01273 684289
Contact: RG Stevens, Deputy GM

Ceremony

This famous pier features Victoria's Bar and Palm Court Restaurant which are available for ceremonies from Monday to Friday, but not during Bank Holidays. Ceremonies must be followed by a reception here.
Price guide: POA

Reception

Catering: from £6pp

**The Powdermills Hotel
Powdermills Lane
Battle TN33 0SP**
T: 01424 775511 F: 01424 774540
Contact: Nick Walker, Manager

Ceremony

The Powdermills Hotel is housed in a listed building (built 1720), that was originally a famous gunpowder mill. The hotel is set in 150 acres. Confetti is not permitted.
Price guide: £175

Reception

The Powdermills Hotel claims a famous chef, and has won many awards for its cuisine.
Catering: £20pp - £25pp

**Queens Hotel, 1-5 Kings Road
Brighton BN1 1NS**
T: 01273 321222 F: 01273 203059
Contact: Sally Dossetter, Conference & Event Coordinator, or Nichola Humphrey

Ceremony

Ceremonies can take place on any day of the year at this seafront hotel. Wheelchair access is limited. Outdoor photography can take place in the gardens near to the hotel.
Price guide: £175

Reception

Catering: £16.50pp

**Royal Pavilion
Brighton BN1 1EE**
T: 01273 292815 F: 01273 292871
Contact: Sam Shaw,
Wedding Co-ordinator

Ceremony

The Royal Pavilion is the extraordinary seaside palace of King George IV. The ceremony takes place in the Red

Drawing Room which retains much of the original 1820's oriental decorative scheme. Ceremonies take place on Fridays and Saturdays except Boxing Day and Christmas Day. Rose petals and rice are the only forms of confetti permitted.
Price guide: from £325

Reception

Catering for receptions must be arranged by the couple. A list of local accommodation is available.
Catering: POA

Uckfield Civic Centre
Bell Farm Lane
Uckfield TN22 1AE
T: 01825 761659 F: 01825 765757
Contact: Catering Manager

Ceremony

This conference centre and restaurant offers specially good facilities for the disabled, including ramps and lifts. Ceremonies may be held here on any day of the week except Sunday.
Price guide: £200

Reception

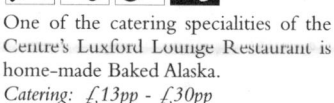

One of the catering specialities of the Centre's Luxford Lounge Restaurant is home-made Baked Alaska.
Catering: £13pp - £30pp

ALSO LICENSED
Boship Farm Hotel 01323 844826
Cavendish Hotel 01323 410222
Charleston Manor 01323 871617
Chatsworth Hotel 01323 411016
Deans Place Hotel 01323 870248
Glynde Place 01273 858224
Holmbush House 01435 813078
Leeford Place Hotel 01424 772863
White Friars Hotel 01323 832255
Winston Manor Hotel 01892 652772

Chigwell Manor Hall
144 Manor Road
Chigwell, Essex IG7 5PX
T: 0181 500 2432 F: 0181 500 9926
Contact: Francis Rogers, Director

Ceremony

The banqueting hall have one room licensed to hold ceremonies, with a minimum capacity of 30.
Price guide: POA

Reception

A list of accommodation offering preferential rates is available.
Catering: from £15pp

Colchester Town Hall
High Street
Colchester CO1 1FR
T: 01206 282200 F: 01206 282228
Contact: Richard Buckle, Town Serjeant

Ceremony

This listed Victorian building has three rooms licensed to hold ceremonies; the Council Chamber (80), the Grand Jury Room (100) and the Moot Hall (400). Ceremonies are held on Saturdays and Sundays.
Price guide: from £100

Reception

The Town Hall offers various ceremony and reception packages including a ceremony wedding breakfast and an evening reception deal. Catering is entirely on a contract basis to be supplied by the individual. The civic gardens, approximately five minutes walk away, are recommended for photography. Piped music is available in the Moot Hall only.
Catering: POA

Cumberland Banqueting Suite
Pembury Road
Westcliff-on-Sea SS0 8DX
T: 01702 346656 F: 01702 344662
Contact: Mr M Nelkin, MD

Ceremony

The banqueting suit has two rooms licensed to hold ceremonies; the Ballroom and the Princess Suite. Ceremonies are free of charge if held in conjunction with a reception on the premises.

Reception

Catering: from £15pp

Essex Golf & Country Club
Earls Colne, Colchester CO6 2NS
T: 01787 224466 F: 01787 224410
Contact: Kate Alden, Functions Manager

Ceremony

The function rooms of this club overlook the 18 hole golf course. Two rooms are licensed for ceremonies and are available all year except for Christmas Day. Ceremonies must be followed by reception here.
Price guide: POA

Reception

Catering: from £13.50pp

Fennes, Fennes Road
Bocking, Braintree CM7 5PL
T: 01376 324555 F: 01376 551209
Contact: Edward James Tabor, Proprietor

EAST SUSSEX – ESS

65

ESSEX

Ceremony

Fennes, a private house, is a Grade II listed building set in a mature, partly moated, garden and parkland. It is available to hold ceremonies seven days a week. The ceremony, which takes place in the Drawing Room, (or the attached pavilion), overlooking the water fountain, is free of charge if held in conjunction with the reception.
Price guide: from £200

Reception

Reception catering facilities may take place in the Dining Room. However, for parties of over 30, receptions transfer to the house's solid floor, centrally heated pavilion which can be adapted to suit. Catering may be provided in-house. Preferential rates with numerous local hotels and guest houses can be arranged, and Fennes can provide transport. The venue fee for the reception starts at £500.
Catering: from £22 + vat. Drinks packages start at £7.50 + vat.

Forte Posthouse
Cranes Farm Road
Basildon SS14 3DG
T: 01268 533955 F: 01268 530119
Contact: Sarah Lane

Ceremony

This modern hotel is situated beside a lake in its own landscaped gardens. Ceremonies are available seven days a week.
Price guide: from £90

Reception

In addition to the services indicated here, the hotel offers free car parking and, for weddings of 20 adult guests and over, the bride and groom are offered complimentary wedding night accommodation, full English breakfast, champagne and flowers - a first anniversary celebration is also provided.
Catering: from £7.95pp

The Friary
East Essex Adult Community College, Carmelite Way,
Maldon CM9 5FJ
T: 01621 853337 F: 01621 850286
Contact: Mike Cork, Site Manager

Ceremony

This adult community college is housed in a listed building, with gardens, in a central location. The Lounge and Hall are licensed where ceremonies can take place at the weekends during term time, and any day of the week outside term.
Price guide: from £200

Reception

Preferential rates are available for local accommodation.
Catering: from £4pp

Friern Manor Country House Hotel
Lower Dunton Road
Dunton, Brentwood CM3 3SL
T: 01268 543222 F: 01268 419739
Contact: Mark Ansell, General Manager

Ceremony

This Grade II listed Georgian manor has three licensed areas with varying capacities from 15 to 150. Ceremonies are available seven days a week excluding Boxing Day.
Price guide: £150

Reception

The manor has five bedrooms but also operates preferential rate agreements with other local hotels and guest houses. The venue boasts three baby grand pianos. Ethnic cuisine is also available.
Catering: from £19.50pp

The Heybridge Hotel, Roman Rd
Ingatestone CM4 9AB
T: 01277 355355 F: 01277 353288
Contact: Cypriella Kyprianau or Beverley Ashcroft

Ceremony

This Tudor building dates back to 1494. The hotel now specialises in conferences and banqueting, and offers three ceremony rooms for a minimum of four guests. Ceremonies must be followed by a reception at the hotel.
Price guide: POA

Reception

Catering: from £18pp

The Lawn, Hall Road
Rochford SS4 1PJ
T: 01702 203701 F: 01702 204752
Contact: Mrs Keddie, Owner

Ceremony

This Grade II listed Georgian mansion is set in three acres of grounds featuring rose gardens. The Blue Drawing Room is licensed to hold ceremonies which are permitted seven days a week and are free of charge if held in conjunction with receptions.
Price guide: £390

Reception

A list of four approved caterers is available. The marquee can be linked directly to the house. The two large 'Brides' bedrooms, although not available for overnight accommodation, provide changing facilities for the bride and groom or family. The house has a preferential rate agreement with a good local hotel. The hotel has good car parking facilities.
Catering: Buffets from £13pp. Sit down from £15pp

Layer Marney Tower
Nr Colchester CO5 9US
T & F: 01206 330784
Contact: Sheila Charrington, Owner

Ceremony

This Tudor gatehouse dates back to 1520. It has three licensed rooms with capacities from 10 to 200. There is wheelchair access to two of the rooms. Ceremonies are available seven days a week with restrictions on Christmas Day and New Year. One ceremony only on Saturday afternoons.
Price guide: £200

Reception

A list of local accommodation is available.
Catering: POA

Leez Priory
Hartford End
Chelmsford CM3 1JP
T: 01245 362555 F: 01245 361079
Contact: Angela Nicholson

Ceremony

This Grade I listed Tudor country house also features an ancient monument and has six rooms licensed to hold ceremonies. The rooms have varying capacities from 40 to 130, only some of which have wheelchair access. Ceremonies are available seven days a week, with only one permitted per day on an 'exclusive use guaranteed' basis. The Priory does not allow ceremonies to be performed here unless the reception follows.
Price guide: from £200

Reception

The Priory has three double bedrooms, all en-suite, and features a lakeside lodge which sleeps four. A list of local accommodation is also available.
Leez Priory is a sister venue to Clearwell Castle, Gloucestershire.
Catering: from £29.50pp sit down. Buffets from £10.50.

Maison Talbooth, Stratford Road
Dedham, Colchester CO7 6HN
T: 01206 322367 F: 01206 322752
Contact: Marian Barwell, Manager

Ceremony

Maison Talbooth is a Victorian country house set in the heart of Constable country. The hotel lounge is available for ceremonies any day of the week except Christmas Day. Ceremonies must be followed by a reception.
Price guide: £175

Reception

Receptions take place at The Talbooth Restaurant. Couples can arrive and depart by boat, and helicopters and hot air balloons can also use the grounds.
Catering: Buffets from £35pp. Sit down from £48pp

The New Oysterfleet, Knightswick Rd, Canvey Island SS8 7UX
T: 01268 510111 F: 01268 511420
Contact: Julio Moscoso, GM

Ceremony

This conference centre enjoys a town centre location, overlooking a lake. Ceremonies may take place in the Lakeside Room on any day of the year. Confetti is not permitted.
Price guide: POA

Reception

Catering: POA

Newland Hall, Roxwell
Chelmsford CM1 4LH
T: 01245 231010 F: 01245 231463
email: info@newland.co.uk
Contact: Tracy Hunt, Events Manager

Ceremony

This is an outdoor events and conference centre, housed in a Grade II listed Tudor manor house set in over 100 acres of grassland, woodland and lakes. The Henry VIII Room is licensed for ceremonies which can take place here any day of the year. Confetti is not permitted.
Price guide: £250

Reception

Helicopters and hot air balloons may use the grounds.
Catering: Buffets from £7.50pp. Sit down from £20pp.

Orsett Hall Hotel
Prince Charles Avenue
Orsett
Grays RM16 3HS
T: 01375 891402 F: 01375 891135
Contact: Stephen Haynes, Managing Director

67

ESSEX

Ceremony

This 17th listed building is set in 12 acres of grounds and has ceremonies available seven days a week, excluding Saturdays during the months May to September.
Price guide: £175

Reception

Three rooms are available to hold receptions with varying capacities of 30 to 150. The provision of a toastmaster is included in the price of the reception.
Catering: from £20pp

Packfords Hotel
16 Snakes Lane West
Woodford Green IG8 0BS
T: 0181 504 2642 F: 0181 505 5778
Contact: Simon Packford, Owner

Ceremony

The hotel offers ceremonies six days a week, with Sundays being unavailable.
Price guide: £100

Reception

Catering: from £18pp

Parsonage Farm Guest House
Parsonage Farm
Abridge Road
Theydon Bois CM16 7NN
T: 01992 814242 F: 01992 814242
Contact: Mr Steve Dale or Mrs Marion Dale, Events Managers

Ceremony

This listed farmhouse is set in its own gardens, and features oak timber throughout. Ceremonies are available seven days a week.
Price guide: £150

Reception

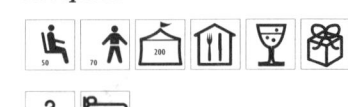

The guest house prides itself on its Provence style a la carte French menus, but regrets that children cannot be catered for separately.
Catering: from £25pp

Pontlands Park Hotel
West Hanningfield Road
Great Baddow
Chelmsford CM2 8HR
T: 01245 476444 F: 01245 478393
Contact: Mr Anthony Bell, General Manager

Ceremony

Pontlands Park is a Victorian mansion, originally built in 1879 and set in its own grounds. Ceremonies are available seven days a week.
Price guide: £200

Reception

Catering: £30pp

Prince Regent Hotel
Manor Road
Woodford Bridge IG8 8AE
T: 0181 505 9966 F: 0181 506 0807
Contact: John Parket, Banqueting Manager

Ceremony

This Grade II lsted building is available to hold ceremonies seven days a week, with a maximum of three per day. Confetti is allowed. The price varies from £75 to £250.
Price guide: from £75

Reception

Catering facilities are provided in-house, although contract caterers are permitted on days other than Saturdays. Chauffeured cars are offered in addition to the services indicated.
Catering: £25pp

The Roebuck
North End
Buckhurst Hill IG9 5QY
T: 0181 505 4636 F: 0181 504 7826
Contact: Banqueting Co-ordinator

Ceremony

The hotel was originally an 18th Century coaching inn and has three rooms licensed, with capacities varying from 25 to 150. However, there is wheelchair access to only two of the rooms. Ceremonies are available seven days a week.
Price guide: Package £125+

Reception

Indoor photography is recommended on the hotel's feature staircase, whilst the green in front of the hotel is recommended for outside photographs.
Catering: £20pp

Rose & Crown Hotel
East Gates, Colchester CO1 2TZ
T: 01206 866677 F: 01206 866616
Contact: Diana Warren, Front of House Manager

Ceremony

This 15th Century Tudor inn is now a listed building, and has recently under-

gone refurbishment. Three ceremony rooms are offered, suitable for 4 to 100 guests.
Price guide: POA

Reception

Catering: Buffets from £7.95pp. Sit down from £23.50pp

**South Lodge Hotel
196 New London Road
Chelmsford
Essex CM2 0AR**
T: 01245 264564 F: 01245 492827
Contact: Wedding Co-ordinator

Ceremony

This original Georgian house has a ceremony capacity of 40 and offers ceremonies seven days a week with no restrictions on the number permitted a day. Confetti is allowed.
Price guide: £100

Reception

Catering facilities are in-house and to a maximum of 100. The hotel has 42 bedrooms but also operates preferential rate agreements with local hotels and guest houses.
Catering: from £12pp.

**Stifford Moat House
(now Lakeside Moat House)
High Road, North Stifford
Grays, Essex RM16 5UE**
T: 0170-8 719988 F: 01375 390426
Contact: Mrs Pat Hackett, Banqueting Coordinator

Ceremony

This Georgian country house is set in 6.5 acres of garden in the village of North Stifford. The Terrace and Orchard rooms are licensed for ceremonies which can take place here on any day of the year.
Price guide: POA

Reception

Catering: POA

**Three Rivers Golf & Country Club
Stow Road, Cold Norton
Nr Purleigh, Essex CM3 6RR**
T: 01621 828631 F: 01621 828060
Contact: Andrew Rimmington, Banqueting Manager

Ceremony

The ceremony room, the Lake Suite, is available any day of the week, with only one ceremony permitted per day. Helicopters and hot air balloons can land on site.
Price guide: from £250

Reception

Catering: Buffets from £8pp Sit down from £14pp

**Tower Hotel, Main Road
Dovercourt, Harwich CO12 3PJ**
T & F: 01255 504952
Contact: Mrs Lynn Sherwood, GM

Ceremony

This listed period building overlooks the river. It offers one ceremony room, The River Room which is available on any day of the week. Confetti is permitted outside only.
Price guide: £100

Reception

The hotel offers a choice of two honeymoon suites.
Catering: Buffets from £8pp Sit down from £12pp

**The Westcliff Hotel
Westcliff Parade
Westcliff-on-Sea SS0 7QW**
T: 01702 345247 F: 01702 431814
Contact: Mrs Sarah Davidson, Conference and Banqueting Manager

Ceremony

The hotel has one room licensed to hold ceremonies with a maximum capacity of 100. Ceremonies are available seven days a week with no restriction on the number held per day. Confetti is allowed.
Price guide: £250

Reception

The catering price guide ranges from under £10 to a maximum of £22. The hotel has 55 bedrooms in total with reduced rates offered to wedding guests, and a wide range of bridal suites available. In addition to the services indicated here, the hotel can also recommend car hire facilities.
Catering: from £7.75pp.

**Whitehall Hotel
Church End
Broxted, Essex CM6 2BZ**
T: 01279 850603 F: 01279 850385
Contact: Jonathon Beck, Assistant Manager

Ceremony

ESSEX

69

ESSEX - GLOUCESTERSHIRE

The family owned Whitehall Hotel is an Elizabethan manor house set in a walled garden. The hotel is conveniently situated for Stansted Airport. Three rooms are licensed, The Butlers Suite, the Audley Suite and the Restaurant, and these are available on Fridays, Saturdays and Sundays. Confetti is not permitted.
Price guide: £350

Reception

The hotel offers several wedding and party packages which include drinks, with discounts offered for Friday or Sunday weddings.
Catering: from £20pp

Wivenhoe House Hotel
Wivenhoe Park
Colchester
Essex CO4 3SQ
T: 01206 863666 F: 01206 868532
Contact: Jenny Hall, Sales Manager

Ceremony

Wivenhoe is a Georgian mansion house, which now operates as a hotel and conference centre. Ceremonies can take place in any of three rooms on Fridays, Saturdays or Sundays, or on any other day by arrangement.
Price guide: £97 - £153

Reception

While the hotel can provide contacts for many extra services, it prefers not to 'recommend these'.
Catering: Buffets from £9.40pp. Sit down from £17.40pp

ALSO LICENSED
Churchgate Manor Hotel 01279 420246
The Coach House 01371 850228
Crondon Park Golf Club 01277 841115
Down Hall Country House Hotel 01279 731441
Kingsford Park Hotel 01206 734301

Marygreen Manor Hotel, 01277 225252
Thurrock Masonic Hall 01375 375695
Warren Golf Club, Maldon 01245 223258

Bear of Rodborough Hotel
Rodborough, Stroud GL5 5DE
T: 01453 878522 F: 01453 872523
Contact: Mr Hutton, General Manager

Ceremony

This 17th Century building is surrounded by 500 acres of National Trust land. The Garden Room is available for wedding ceremonies every day except Christmas Day.
Price guide: from £50

Reception

The restaurant serves traditional English cuisine. If the hotel is full, other local establishments can be recommended for your guests.
Catering: from £14pp

Bell's Hotel
Lord's Hill
Coleford, Glos GL16 8BD
T: 01594 832583 F: 01594 832584
Contact: Charlotte Clifford-Weston, GM

Ceremony

This hotel and golf club offers one ceremony per day, seven days a week: but only in conjunction with receptions. There is no room charge for the ceremony. Confetti is not permitted.
Price guide: FOC (with reception)

Reception

The Bell's Hotel is attached to the Forest of Dean Golf Club, which is open to non-members.
Catering: from £12pp

Calcot Manor Hotel
Calcot, Glos GL8 8YJ
T: 01666 890391 F: 01666 890394
Contact: Paul Sadler, Manager

Ceremony

Calcot Manor is one of the oldest tithe barns in the country, and is available for ceremonies Monday to Saturday.
Price guide: £150

Reception

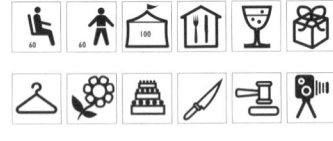

Only one large event is possible per day.
Catering: from £17pp

Charingworth Manor
Charingworth
Chipping Camden
Glos GL55 6NS
T: 01386 593555 F: 01386 593353
Contact: Pamela Jackson, Sales Manager

Ceremony

This historic country house is set on a private estate in the rolling Cotswold countryside. The Conservatory and The Long Room hold wedding licences and are available any day of the year.
Price guide: £500

Reception

Catering: Buffets from £30pp Sit down from £35pp

Cheltenham Racecourse
Prestbury
Cheltenham
Glos GL50 4SH
T: 01242 570150 Fax: 01242 579356
Contact Sheila Day, Manager

GLOUCESTERSHIRE

Ceremony

The ceremony room is available daily throughout the year, although it would be wise to avoid Gold Cup Day. Two ceremonies are possible per day.
Price guide: £50 (with reception)

Reception

As one might expect from a venue used to dealing with large crowds, Cheltenham Racecourse emphasises the flexibility of its catering services. It is excellently equipped to deal with groups from as small as 10 up to larger parties of up to 350. Please note that the venue's in-house team is also available for outside catering assignments.
Catering: from £18pp

Clearwell Castle
Church Road
Clearwell, Coleford GL16 8LG
T: 01594 832320   F: 01594 835523
Contact: Angela Nicholson, General Manager

Ceremony

This Grade II listed stately home offers ceremonies Friday to Sunday.
Price guide: Inclusive package

Reception

Catering: Buffet from £10.50pp. Sit down from £29.50pp

The Close Hotel
Tetbury, Glos GL8 8AQ
T: 01666 502272   F: 01666 504401
Contact: Sophia McLeod or Jonathon Dawson

Ceremony

Part of the Virgin Collection, The Close Hotel, a small country house hotel, offers up to two ceremonies daily, excluding Bank Holidays.
Price guide: £199

Reception

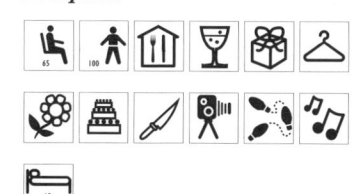

The hotel can be hired on an exclusive use basis, from £2,500.
Catering: Buffets from £8.95pp

The Fleet Inn and Restaurant
Twyning
Tewkesbury, Glos GL20 6DG
T: 01684 274310
Contact: Roy Probin, Catering Manager

Ceremony

The Fleet enjoys a riverside setting, where couples can arrive and depart by boat. The Avon Conservatory is the licensed wedding room and is available on any day of the year. Ceremonies must be followed by a reception at the Inn.
Price guide: FOC (with reception)

Reception

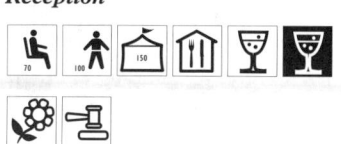

Catering: Buffets from £4.25pp Sit down from £14.95pp

Forte Posthouse Gloucester
Crest Way, Barnwood GL4 7RX
T: 01452 613511   F: 01452 371036
Contact: Karen Godden or Abby Meredith, Conference Co-ordinators

Ceremony

This three-star hotel is set in its own grounds, and offers two suites for ceremonies on Fridays, Saturdays and Sundays. Ceremonies here must be followed by reception on the premises.
Price guide: £95

Reception

The hotel can provide helium-filled balloons to decorate the venue.
Catering: Buffets from £14.50pp. Sit down from £18.50pp

The Fossebridge Inn
Fossebridge, Cheltenham
Glos GL54 3JS
T: 01285 720721   F: 01285 720793
Contact: Tim or Caroline Bevan

Ceremony

This is a Grade II listed Tudor building housing a pub and set in gardens with a lake. The Board Room and River Restaurant are licensed for ceremonies which can take place here on any day of the year.
Price guide: £60

Reception

The pub holds an AA Rosette for its food. Helicopters and hot air balloons may use this site.
Catering: from £12.95pp

Frogmill Inn
Shipton Oliffe
Cheltenham, Glos GL54 4HT
T: 01242 852237   F: 01242 820237
Contact: John Griffith, Proprietor

Ceremony

Frogmill Inn dates from the Domesday

GLOUCESTERSHIRE

Book and is set in five acres.
Price guide: £50

Reception

Two dining areas, one for up to 60, one for up to 200. Can cater for special diets.
Catering: from £15pp

Grapevine Hotel
**Sheep Street,
Stow-on-the-Wold GL54 1AU**
T: 01451 830344 F: 01451 832378
Web site: http://www.vines.co.uk/
Contact: Peter Dann, GM

Ceremony

This 17th Century hotel offers a maximum of two ceremonies per day, seven days a week, in its Georgian Room or Restaurant.

Reception

A conservatory restaurant, canopied by a grapevine, seats 80 for waited service. The two AA rosetted restaurant offers modern English cuisine with Continental influences.
Catering: from £15pp

Greenway
**Shurdington
Cheltenham
Glos GL51 5UG**
T: 01242 862352 F: 01242 862780
Contact: David A White, Proprietor

Ceremony

Greenway is a 16th Century manor house set in ten acres. Ceremony facilities are available daily except Sundays, subject to a maximum of one event per day, in conjunction with reception bookings. No confetti.
Price guide: from £135

Reception

The restaurant holds three rosettes. The hotel offers various packages that can be tailored to your individual needs. A typical example, including wines/champagne, costs £55pp. The management is happy to arrange additional services, such as car hire and hairdressing.
Catering: from £27.50pp

Hare & Hounds Hotel
**Westonbirt, Tetbury
Glos GL8 8QL**
T: 01666 880233 F: 01666 880241
Contact: Jeremy Price or Martin Price, Proprietors

Ceremony

The hotel offers ceremonies every day of the year, subject to a maximum of two daily. The Cotswold stone building is set in its own large gardens.
Price guide: from £150

Reception

Catering: from £18pp

Hatherly Manor Hotel
**Down Hatherly Lane
Down Hatherly, Glos GL2 9QA**
T: 01452 730217 F: 01452 731032
Contact: Maria Heap, Conference and Banqueting Manager

Ceremony

This 17th Century manor house, set in 37 acres, is available for ceremonies in one of five licensed suites.
Price guide: £150

Reception

The Manor House has an AA Rosette for its food.
Catering: from £18.95pp

Hatton Court Hotel
**Upton Hill
Upton St Leonards
Glos GL4 8DE**
T: 01452 612412 F: 01452 612945
Contact: Jacqui Peachey, Conference & Banqueting Manager

Ceremony

Hatton Court is a 17th Century Cotswold manor house, set in seven acres of gardens and 30 acres of pasture. Its position at 600 ft above sea level provides excellent views over the Severn Valley. One ceremony is possible per day, excluding the Christmas and New Year holiday period.
Price guide: £95

Reception

Catering from £24.95pp

Jarvis Bowden Hall Hotel
**Bondend Lane
Upton St Leonards GL4 8ED**
T: 01452 614121 F: 01452 611885
Contact: Rachel Swaffield, Wedding Consultant

Ceremony

72

This is a Grade II listed Regency building with private grounds and lawns leading to a lake. Numerous rooms are licensed for ceremonies, including The Lakeside Suite. Ceremonies here must be followed by a reception.
Price guide: £150

Reception

A recent wedding here included a casino evening for guests.
Catering: Buffets from £15pp Sit down from £22pp

Lords of the Manor
Upper Slaughter
Cheltenham Glos GL54 2JD
T: 01451 820243 F: 01451 820696
Contact: Richard Young, General Manager

Ceremony

This former rectory dates from the 17th Century, and is set in eight acres of grounds including a trout lake and parkland. It offers facilities for one ceremony daily from Monday to Saturday throughout the year.
Price guide: from £200

Reception

The award-winning restaurant offers reception facilities for a maximum of 120, but up to 400 could be accommodated in a marquee. Accolades include a Michelin star and three AA rosettes.
Catering: from £26pp

Manor House Hotel
High Street
Moreton-in-Marsh GL56 0LJ
T: 01608 650501 F: 01608 651481
Contact: Miss Meriel Neighbour, GM

Ceremony

This listed building dates back to 1545. It has links with the Creswyke family and has its own resident ghost, and a priest hole. The Four Shires Suite is licensed and will take from 50 to 108 guests.
Price guide: £150

Reception

The AA Rosetted restaurant can prepare vegan and vegetarian dishes on request.
Catering: Buffets from £16.50pp Sit down from £20pp

Painswick Hotel
Painswick, Stroud GL6 6UF
T: 01452 812160 F: 01452 814059
Contact: Julia Robb, Manager

Ceremony

This Grade II listed Palladian style stone building was formerly a rectory. It is set in its own gardens featuring a croquet lawn. Ceremonies are possible from Monday to Friday, with only one per day. Confetti is not permitted. Ceremonies can only be held with a reception.
Price guide: £60

Reception

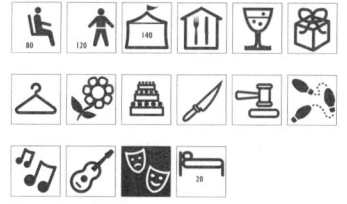

Catering: £18pp

Painswick House
Painswick
Glos GL6 6TH
T: 01452 813646 F: 01452 813204
Contact: Lady Dickinson, Proprietor

Ceremony

Painswick House is a privately owned Georgian stately home, and permits one ceremony per day throughout the year.
Price guide: POA

Reception

In-house catering is available, although alternative arrangements can be made for larger parties.
Catering: POA

Pittville Pump Room
Pittville Park
Cheltenham
Glos GL52 3JE
T: 01242 523852 F: 01242 526563
Contact: Mr Chris Aldred, Manager

Ceremony

This neo-classical Grade I listed building is managed by Cheltenham Borough Council and houses the Cheltenham Spa waters. Ceremonies can be held daily, excluding Christmas Day, subject to a maximum of four per day. There are several rooms available.
Price guide: £150 per ceremony

Reception

The Pump Room offers flexible menus, allowing guests to choose between courses on the day. A list of local accommodation options is available.
Catering: from £15pp

Prestbury House
Hotel & Restaurant
The Burgage, Prestbury
Cheltenham Glos GL52 3DN
T: 01242 529533 F: 01242 227076
Contact: Jacqueline Whitbourn, Proprietor

GLOUCESTERSHIRE

GLOUCESTERSHIRE - HAMPSHIRE

Ceremony

This 300 year old country manor house is Grade II listed and set in four acres of grounds. The Georgian and Oak rooms hold the wedding licence and are available any day of the year, with one ceremony only per day.
Price guide: POA

Reception

Catering: POA

Puckrup Hall (now Stakis)
Tewkesbury GL20 6EL
T: 01684 296200 F: 01684 850788
Contact: Conf & Banq Manager

Ceremony

This Regency mansion is set in over 140 acres of parkland, and has its own 18 hole golf course. The hotel's Gloucester Suite has the wedding licence. This room can be divided into four, with a minimum capacity for 20. Ceremonies are restricted to one per day.
Price guide: £150

Reception

Two rooms are available for receptions; the Gloucester Suite and the Ballroom. The hotel has its own helipad and an area for hot air balloons. Drinks packages start at £9.25pp.
Catering: from £25pp

The Queens Hotel, Promenade
Cheltenham, GL50 1NN
T: 01242 514724 F: 01242 262538
Contact: Vicky Hickson, Wedding Co-ordinator

Ceremony

Up to five ceremonies per day are permitted in a choice of three rooms. Confetti is not permitted indoors or out.
Price guide: £150

Reception

Catering: Buffets from £17.50pp. *Sit down from* £20pp.

Stonehouse Court Hotel
Stonehouse, Glos GL10 3RA
T: 01453 825155 F: 01453 824611
Contact: Rebekah Murphy, Business Co-ordinator

Ceremony

This Grade II listed manor house (1601), is built in typical Cotswold stone and is set in six acres of secluded gardens. Three rooms are available for wedding ceremonies and range in capacity from 20 to 80. Only the larger room is suitable for wheelchair access. Helicopters and hot air balloons may use the grounds.
Price guide: £150

Reception

Catering: from £18pp

Stratton House Hotel
Gloucester Road
Cirencester
Glos GL7 2LE
T: 01285 651761
Contact: Claire Mallen

Ceremony

This country house hotel is set in its own grounds, 1/2 mile from Cirencester.
Price guide: POA

Reception

Catering: POA

The Swan Hotel
Bibury, Glos GL7 5NW
T: 01285 740695 F: 01285 740473
Contact: John Stevens, GM

Ceremony

The Swan offers facilities for daily ceremonies throughout the year.
Price guide: from £150

Reception

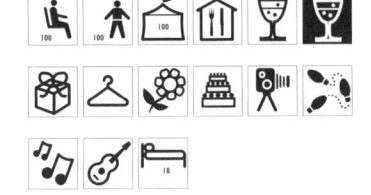

Catering: £15-60pp

ALSO LICENSED
The Beehive 01242 579443
Cheltenham Park Hotel 01242 222021
Great Tythe Barn 01666 502475
Ireley Grounds 01242 603736
The Old Rectory Hotel 01242 673766
Tewkesbury Park Hotel 01684 295405
Wyck Hill House Hotel 01451 831936

Alton House Hotel
Normandy Street
Alton
Hants GU34 1DW
T: 01420 80033 F: 01420 89222
Contact: David Knights, General Manager

Ceremony

Set near the centre of the old market

town of Alton, this Victorian built hotel has over two acres of landscaped gardens and an outdoor pool.
Price guide: £60

Reception

Recommendations can also be given for horse and carriages, cars, video and balloons.
Catering £21.50

**Ashburn Hotel
Station Road
Fordingbridge
Hants SP6 1JP**
T: 01425 652060 F: 01425 652150
Contact: Terri Robson, Director

Ceremony

The hotel is set in landscaped gardens. Its Garden Room is licensed for ceremonies and is available on Wednesdays and Saturdays.
Price guide: £100

Reception

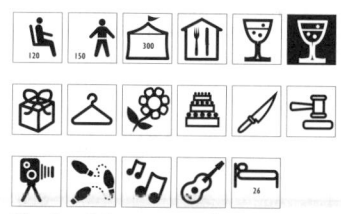

The hotel has an award winning chef and can offer a vegetarian menu, a medieval banquet or an Elizabethan feast.
Catering: Buffets from £7pp. Sit down from £12pp

**Bartley Lodge Hotel
Cadnam, Hants SO40 2NR**
T: 01703 812248 F: 01703 812075
Contact: Rachel Smith, Manager
(T: 01703 283717)

Ceremony

This Grade II listed hunting lodge (1759) is set in eight acres of parkland and walled gardens. Interior features include a minstrel's gallery and a grand oak panelled room. Two rooms are available for ceremonies. Only one ceremony is permitted per day.
Price guide: from £200

Reception

A late night drinking licence will be applied for on request. Special catering features include barbecues and spit roasts. A complimentary bridal suite on the wedding night is part of the wedding package. In the past, couples have had firework displays in the grounds, and one couple even parachuted in for their wedding! The Lodge is part of Care Hotels plc which has four other country houses in the area, offering special rates for guests.
Catering: from £18pp

**Botleigh Grange Hotel
Hedge End
Southampton, Hants SO30 2GA**
T: 01489 787700 F: 01489 788535
Contact: Conference co-ordinator

Ceremony

This 17th Century country house is set in parkland with lakes and a sweeping drive. Ceremonies can take place here any day of the week, with a space of 90 minutes left between weddings. Confetti is only allowed outside.
Price guide: £100

Reception

Catering: £18.95

Botley Park Hotel, Winchester Road, Boorley Green SO32 2UA
T: 01489 780888 F: 01489 789242
Contact: Tonia Mullins, Sales Manager

Ceremony

The hotel is set in 176 acres of parkland golf course. The Knightwood Oak Suite is licensed for ceremonies which can take place on any day of the year.
Price guide: £150

Reception

Place cards, table plans and personalised menus are all services offered at the hotel.
Catering: Buffets from £8.30pp. Sit down from £22.50pp.

**The Burley Manor Hotel
Burley, Ringwood BH24 4BS**
T: 01425 403522 F: 01425 403227
Contact: Andrew Rogers, GM

Ceremony

This RAC/AA 3 star hotel is set in five acres of landscaped grounds with an outdoor pool. One ceremony per day is allowed on any day excluding Sundays and Bank Holidays.
Price guide: £200

Reception

The hotel can help you to arrange balloons, helicopters and horse drawn carriages.
Catering: from £19.75

Celebration Plaza, 3 Terminus Terrace, Southampton SO14 3DT
T: 01703 322260/40 F: 01703 366646
Contact: David Onslow, GM

Ceremony

HAMPSHIRE

75

HAMPSHIRE

This restaurant and nightclub is owned by Matthew Le Tissier and Mike Osman. The ground floor nightclub and restaurant area is licensed for ceremonies which can take place here on any day except Bank Holidays.
Price guide: POA

Reception

Catering: POA

**Chewton Glen Hotel
Christchurch Road
New Milton, Hants BH25 6QS**
T: 01425 275341 F: 01425 272310
Contact: Thierry Lepinoy, Banqueting Manager

Ceremony

A renowned health and country club with five stars AA and RAC rating, Chewton Glen offers wedding ceremonies on any day of the week and allows up to two ceremonies per day. No confetti is allowed.
Price guide: £350

Reception

Chewton Glen's catering has earned it one Michelin star. Discos and live music are available upon discussion with the hotel.
Catering: £30pp

**Chilworth Manor, Chilworth
Southampton SO16 7PT**
T: 01703 767333 F: 01703 701743
Contact: Susan Walker, Sales & Marketing Executive

Ceremony

This Edwardian manor house, set in 36 acres of parkland, now operates as a conference centre. The GK Chesterton room is licensed for ceremonies which can take place on Saturdays and Sundays. Ceremonies here must be followed by a reception at the venue.
Price guide: £250

Reception

Helicopters and hot air balloons may use the grounds. The manor offers a complete wedding package which include red carpet, MC, inclusive room hire and extension to liquor licence, and overnight accommodation for bride and groom. House wines start at £10.50.
Catering: from £25pp

**The Crown Hotel, High Street
Lyndhurst SO43 7NF**
T: 01703 282922 F: 01703 282751
Contact: Kirsty Attridge, Conference & Sales Manager

Ceremony

The Crown features stone mullioned windows, panelled rooms and period decor, and claims to have the character and style of the classic English country house. The Palmer Room is licensed for ceremonies which can take place at any time except the Christmas period. Ceremonies must be followed by a reception at The Crown.
Price guide: £325 (including registrar and room)

Reception

Catering: Buffet from £8.95 Seated from £17.50

**Elmers Court Country Club
South Baddesley Road
Lymington, Hants SO41 5BZ**
T: 01590 676011 F: 01590 679780
Contact: Banqueting Manager

Ceremony

This Tudor manor is set in 25 acres with lawns sweeping down to the Solent. One room, the Waterford Room, is licensed for ceremonies on any day except Christmas Day. There is room in the grounds for helicopters and hot air balloons.
Price guide: £200

Reception

A new development of Country Club Suites are now available for overnight stays here, with special rates available for wedding guests. However, the venue is able to offer a complimentary suite to the newly weds as part of the wedding package. Elmers Court can provide seasonal menus, and while there is currently no late night drinking licence, this can be applied for. Special entertainments can be arranged.
Catering: £22.50pp

**Essebourne Manor Hotel
Hurstbourne Tarrant
Andover, Hants SP11 0ER**
T: 01264 736444 F: 01264 736725
Contact: I Hamilton, Proprietor

Ceremony

This country house hotel holds a wedding licence for its Dining Room. This is available seven days a week, with one ceremony permitted per day.
Price guide: £200

Reception

Helicopters and hot air balloons may use the grounds.
Catering: POA

76

The Falcon Hotel
68 Farnborough Road
Farnborough, Hants GU14 6TH
T: 01252 545378   F: 01252 522539
Contact: Mandy Childs, GM

Ceremony

This town centre hotel has one room licensed for ceremonies, which is available any day except Christmas Day. The ceremony room hire fee is reduced to £35 if you also hold your reception at the venue. A small patio is the only area available for outdoor photography.
Price guide: £75

Reception

While there is no late night drinking licence for non-residents, this can be applied for if required. The reception package (and price guide below) includes a drink on arrival as well as the room hire.
Catering: £20.65pp

The Forest Park Hotel
Rhinefield Road
Brockenhurst
Hants SO42 7ZG
T: 01590 622844   F: 01590 623948
Contact: Sales Manager

Ceremony

Originally built as a vicarage, this venue became an hotel in 1902. The hotel, set in four acres, boasts a tennis court, outdoor heated pool, and log cabin sauna. Weddings can take place in the Morant Room on any day of the week, with only one ceremony permitted per day.
Price guide: £125

Reception

Catering: from £20pp

Forte Posthouse
Herbert Walker Avenue
Southampton SO15 1HJ
T: 01703 330777   F: 01703 332510
Contact: Michelle Murphy, Conference & Banqueting Manager

Ceremony

The Posthouse is situated in the centre of Southampton, next to The Mayflower Park. The Hampshire Suite is licensed and available on any days except the 11th -20th of September.
Price guide: £200

Reception

The hotel can recommend a variety of dress designers with different styles. A 1970s' style wedding recently took place here.
Catering: Buffets from £8.75pp   Sit down from £16.50pp

The Fountain Court Hotel
Frost Lasne, Hythe
Southampton, Hants SO45 3NE
T: 01703 846310   F: 01703 847295
Contact: Mrs V Harris, Proprietress

Ceremony

Built in 1856, the hotel boasts intricate decor, a garden fountain and an undergarden chamber. The Garden Room holds the wedding licence and is available any day except Christmas Day and Good Friday. There is no ceremony room hire fee if your reception is also held at the hotel.
Price guide: FOC (with reception)

Reception

The hotel offers a wide vegetarian menu, as well as a children's menu, with cuisine ranging from Cajun to oriental, French and American. Helicopters and hot air balloons can use the site.
Catering: Buffets from £5pp   Sit down from £12.50pp

The Grange Hotel
London Road
Alton, Hants GU34 4EG
T: 01420 86565   F: 01420 541346
Contact: Sandra Ford,
Function and Conference Co-ordinator

Ceremony

This 3-star, 4-crown, privately owned hotel is set in two acres of gardens. Two rooms are licensed for ceremonies seating a minimum of 20 guests. Ceremonies are not usually available on a Saturday here, depending on the size of the wedding.
Price guide: £100

Reception

Catering: Buffets from £7.95pp. Sit down from £23.50 (inc drinks)

Highclere Castle
Highclere, Hants RG15 9RN
T: 01635 253210   F: 01635 810193
Contact: Lindsey Giles, Event Co-ordinator

Ceremony

Highclere Castle is a listed building and is claimed to be the finest Victorian home still in existence. Ceremonies can take place in the Library Room or the Salon. The venue encourages late afternoon civil ceremonies and receptions during the Castle's open season from May to September. Confetti is not permitted.
Price guide: £1000 + vat

Reception

HAMPSHIRE

HAMPSHIRE

Catering: POA

HMS Warrior
HM Naval Base
Portsmouth, Hants PO1 2QX
T: 01705 291379   F: 01705 821283
Contact: Mrs Sorel Mitchell, Special Events Manager

Ceremony

This restored 1860's warship lies within Portsmouth's Historic Dockyard. Ceremonies take place in the Captain's Cabin. Availability on application. Confetti and smoking are not permitted, and ladies are requested not to wear high heels.. Photography is allowed on the upper deck, the main gun deck and in the Captain's Cabin.
Price guide: £500

Reception

Receptions may be held on board after the ship is closed to the public following a late afternoon ceremony. These are held in the Wardroom (20), on the Half Deck (up to 50) or on the Gun Deck for larger numbers. There is a choice of two contract caterers who will obtain the relevant drinks licence and can provide cake stand and knife if required. Advice on local accommodation is available together with a wide choice of photographers and musicians.
Catering £10-£25

Lainston House Hotel
Sparsholt
Winchester, Hants SO21 2LT
T: 01962 863588   F: 01962 776248
Contact: Patsy Enright, Sales & Marketing Manager

Ceremony

This William and Mary, 17th Century, country house hotel is set in 63 acres of parkland featuring a lime tree avenue. One ceremony is permitted per day on any day except Christmas and New Year but only with a reception.
Price guide: from £200

Reception

Lainston House offers several rooms for receptions including the Dawley Barn (a 17th Century half-timbered barn). For larger numbers a marquee can be set up on the lawn adjacent to the dining room. Wedding menus include Gourmet and Gastronomique options for a maximum of 16 people. Reception room hire of £775 includes a toastmaster.
Catering: from £28pp

Lismoyne Hotel
Church Road
Fleet, Hants GU11 8NA
T: 01252 628555   F: 01252 811761
Contact: Marcus Can Hagen, GM

Ceremony

This 4-crown, AA 3-star, hotel can offer ceremonies on any day.
Price guide: £375

Reception

Car hire can also be arranged by the venue.
Catering: £19pp

Lyndhurst Park Hotel
High Street
Lyndhurst
Hants
SO43 7NL
T: 01703 283923   F: 01703 283019
Contact: Sue Cotton, Banqueting Manager

Ceremony

Located on the edge of the New Forest, Lyndhurst Park is set in its own gardens of five acres. The hotel has one room licensed for wedding ceremonies, which can take place on any day of the week. The hotel allows up to four ceremonies per day.
Price guide: from £160

Reception

Marquee only for daylight hours.
Catering: £22pp

Old Thorns Hotel & Golf Course
Griggsgreen, Liphook GU30 7PE
T: 01428 724555   F: 01428 724555
Contact: GM Jones, General Manager

Ceremony

Only one ceremony per day is permitted in the function suite at the hotel.
Price guide: POA

Reception

Catering: POA

Mottisfont Abbey
Mottisfont, Romsey SO51 0LP
T: 01794 340757   F: 01794 341492
Contact: Julie Evans, Visitor Services Manager

Ceremony

This National Trust property is set on a tributary to the River Test. Its grounds feature lawns and gardens, (including a

collection of old-fashioned roses), while inside the house is a room painted by Whistler. The Morning Room, which has views over the south lawns, holds the Ceremony licence, while the adjacent Old Dining Room is often used for the reception. Ceremonies can take place here from Wednesday to Saturday inclusive. Confetti is not permitted.
Price guide: POA

Reception

Catering at the Abbey includes fresh local produce such as trout from the River Test and Mottisfont Rose Petal Ice Cream.
Catering: POA

**New Place Management Centre
High Street, Shirrell Heath
Southampton, Hants SO32 2JH**
T: 01329 833543 F: 01329 833259
Contact: Sue Conduct

Ceremony

This Grade I listed building was designed by Sir Edwin Lutyens and is set in 30 acres of landscaped gardens and woodland. It also has a swimming pool.
Price guide: £150

Reception

Cuisine by Laurent Beaunier, ex-Boulestin. Venue hire for the reception will be £1500 in 1999.
Catering: from £25pp

**Newtown House Hotel
Manor Road, Hayling Island
Hants PO11 0QR**
T: 01705 466131 F: 01705 461366
Contact: Lynda Witkowski, Hotel Manageress

Ceremony

The restaurant at this hotel holds the wedding licence. Ceremonies can take place here at any day in the year.
Price guide: £150

Reception

Catering: Buffets from £19pp. Sit down from £24pp

**Portsmouth Football Club
Fratton Park
57 Frogmore Road
Portsmouth, Hants PO3 8RA**
T: 01705 731204 F: 01705 734124
Contact: Commercial Manager

Ceremony

The club's Board Room is the marriage room. Ceremonies can take place on any day when there is not an afternoon home match.
Price guide: £200

Reception

Catering: POA

**Portsmouth Marriott
North Harbour
Portsmouth, Hants PO6 4SH**
T: 01705 383151 F: 01705 388701
Contact: Tiffany Rowe, Meetings Manager

Ceremony

The Mary Rose Suite can take a minimum of 70 guests with only one ceremony allowed per day, on any day

except the Christmas period. Ceremonies at the hotel must be followed by reception here. Confetti is only permitted outside.
Price guide: Currently no charge.

Reception

The hotel offers a comprehensive wedding package which includes cake, flowers and disco. Late night drinking licence for residents.
Catering: from £34.50pp

**The Potters Heron Hotel
Ampfield
Nr Romsey, Hants SO51 9ZF**
T: 01703 266611 F: 01703 251359
Contact: Helen Crawford, Conference & Banqueting Sales Co-ordinator

Ceremony

This thatched building, surrounded by woodland, offers its Ampfield Suite for wedding ceremonies. Up to four ceremonies per day may take place on any day of the year.
Price guide: £100

Reception

Catering: from £18pp

**Rhinefield House Hotel
Rhinefield Road
Brockenhurst, Hants SO42 7QB**
T: 01590 622922 F: 01590 622800
Contact: Lisa Schofield, or Stephanie Waine, Conference & Banqueting co-ordinators

Ceremony

HAMPSHIRE

79

HAMPSHIRE

The hotel, part of Virgin Hotels, is set in the New Forest. Ceremonies can take place in the Orangery conservatory or the regal style Kings Room. The hotels award-winning gardens have been restored to the original 1890's design, with maze and formal parterres.
Price guide: £250

Reception

Rhinefield features a model of Westminster Hall, as well as an authentic recreation of part of the Alhambra Palace in Granada (these are not marriage rooms). It has three AA and RAC stars as well as an AA Rosette. Accommodation discounts are available.
Catering: £26 - £32pp

**The Royal Armouries
Fort Nelson,
Down End Road
Fareham,
Hants PO17 6AN**
T: 01329 233734 F: 01329 822092
E-mail: tpridmore@armouries.org.uk
Contact: Tony Pridmore

Ceremony

Fort Nelson is a scheduled ancient monument and is the Royal Armouries Museum of artillery. Smoking is only allowed in designated areas and confetti is not permitted. Two rooms are licensed for ceremonies: the Officers Mess Ante Room (50) and The Point of the Redan(100). Wheelchair access is limited. Ceremonies may take place here any day, at the discretion of The Keeper.
Price guide: from £300

Reception

A reception may be held at the fort following a late afternoon ceremony.
Catering: Buffets from £7.50pp Sit down from £16.50pp

**St Leonards Hotel
Ringwood Road
St Leonards BH24 2NP**
T: 01425 471220 F: 01425 480274
Contact: Alison or Mark Price, General Managers

Ceremony

The hotel, set in four acres of land, offers three ceremony suites, with a minimum capacity for just two. Ceremonies can take place here on an day except Sundays.
Price guide: £85

Reception

The hotel says it can cater for all special dietary needs. Wedding guests are offered a 15% discount on room rates.
Catering: Buffets from £5.95pp. Sit down from £13.95pp

**The Solent Hotel
Rookery Avenue, Whiteley
Fareham, Hants PO15 7AJ**
T: 01489 880000 F: 01489 880007
Contact: Nikki Carpenter, Banqueting

Ceremony

This purpose-built hotel features log fires, polished stone floors and cherry-wood panelling. Two rooms are licensed; the Hambledon Suite and the Carisbrick Suite (the smaller seating up to 100). Up to two ceremonies are permitted per day, but the ceremony must be followed by reception at the hotel.
Price guide: No charge

Reception

There is no room hire charge for the reception at the Solent. Options include a red carpet, menu cards, and a four poster bridal suite with champagne. Reduced rate accommodation is available for wedding party guests.
Catering: £23.50-£32.50

**Southdowns Hotel & Restaurant
Trotton, Rogate
Petersfield, Hants GU31 5JN**
T: 01730 821521 F: 01730 821790
Contact: Mr Vedovato

Ceremony

This country hotel has a licence to hold ceremonies in the Lounge or the Harting Suite, offering a minimum capacity of 10 people. Only one ceremony is permitted per day. Only biodegradable confetti is allowed.
Price guide: £250

Reception

The hotel can help to organise cars and more unusual modes of transport such as carriages and helicopters. A 10% discount is offered to guests who stay for two or three nights.
Catering: from £15pp

**Tyrells Ford Hotel
Avon, Nr Christchurch
Hants BH23 7BH**
T: 01425 672646 F: 01425 672262
Contact: Collette Birkbeck, GM

Ceremony

This 18th Century family owned manor house is set in ten acres of grounds on the edge of the New Forest. The Lounge (with minstrel's gallery) is licensed for ceremonies and is available all days of the year. Ceremonies here must be followed by reception at the venue. Confetti is not permitted. Helicopters may use the grounds.
Price guide: £125

Reception

Catering: from £16.85pp

The Wessex Centre
Sparsholt College
Winchester, Hants SO21 2NF
T: 01962 776647   F: 01962 776636
Contact: Anne McDonald, Catering & Conference Manager

Ceremony

The Wessex Centre is part of Sparsholt Agricultural College which is set in over 400 acres. One room is licensed, The Jane Austen Suite, to which wheelchair access is limited. The Suite is available on any day of the year except over the Christmas and New Year period. Ceremonies must be followed by a reception at the centre.
Price guide: £50

Reception

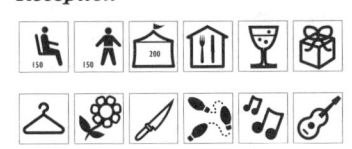

Helicopters and hot air balloons may use the grounds.
Catering: Buffets from £12.50. Sit down from £14pp

The Westover Hall
Park Lane
Milford on Sea
Hants SO41 0PT
T: 01590 643044   F: 01590 644490
Contact: Stewart Mechem/Nicola Musetti, Proprietors

Ceremony

This Grade II listed Victorian mansion overlooks the Solent and the Isle of Wight. The building features a minstrel's gallery and stained glass. The Nuffield Suite, which has limited wheelchair access, is licensed, and ceremonies can take place here on any day of the year. Confetti is not permitted.
Price guide: £250

Reception

Cuisine at the Hall has a strong Italian influence. The Hall may take the prize for the most romantic wedding, as one couple apparently had dinner on the beach before paddling in the sea.
Catering: from £17.50pp

Winchester Guildhall
The Broadway
Winchester, Hants SO23 9LJ
T: 01962 840820   F: 01962 878458
Contact: Kelly Vaughan

Ceremony

This listed Victorian building has two marriage rooms; the Mayor's Parlour (seats 20) and the Conference Chamber (seats 150). The latter has limited wheelchair access.
Price guide: £50

Reception

There is one elected contract caterer to the Guildhall. Recommendations can be given for discos and live music.
Catering: POA

ALSO LICENSED
'68', Fareham   01329 221338
The Beaulieu Hotel   01703 293344
Busketts Lawn Hotel   01703 292272
Careys Manor Hotel   01590 623551
The Game Larder   01264 610414
Montague Arms Hotel   01590 612324
Parkhill Country House Hotel   01703 282944
Romans Country House Hotel   01734 700421
Stanwell House Hotel   01590 677123
Tylney Hall   01256 764881

The Marine Hotel
5-7 The Front
Seaton Carew, Hartlepool
T: 01429 266244   F: 01429 864144
Contact: Wedding Co-ordinator

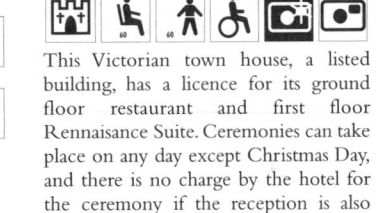

Ceremony

This Victorian town house, a listed building, has a licence for its ground floor restaurant and first floor Rennaisance Suite. Ceremonies can take place on any day except Christmas Day, and there is no charge by the hotel for the ceremony if the reception is also held in house.
Price guide: F.O.C. (with reception) - £200

Reception

The hotel offers a traditional four course menu, although other menus can be arranged through the manager. The hotel will offer reduced price accommodation for wedding guests.
Catering: £8.25 - £16.75pp

The Abbey Hotel, Abbey Road,
Great Malvern WR14 3ET
T: 01684 892332
Contact: Sharon Haw, Sales Coordinator

Ceremony

Set in the centre of Malvern, The Abbey adjoins the old Bendictine Priory and boasts beautiful views over hills and the Severn Valley. Six rooms are licensed including the Priory View Restaurant.
Price guide: POA

Reception

Catering: Buffets from £13.75pp. Sit down from £16pp

HAMPSHIRE - HARTLEPOOL - HEREFORD & WORCESTER

81

HEREFORD & WORCESTER

Allt Yr Ynys
Country House Hotel
Walterstone HR2 0DU
T: 01873 890307 F: 01873 890539
Contact: Howard Williams, Proprietor

Ceremony

Allt Yr Ynys is a Grade II listed building located in the Brecon Beacons National Park. It has a riverside location, and features a knot garden. Three rooms are licensed including the Jacobean Drawing Room, and are available every day of the year. Confetti is not permitted.
Price guide: £25 - £100

Reception

The hotel boasts an AA two rosette restaurant. Helicopters and hot air balloons may use the grounds.
Catering: Buffets from £15pp Sit down from £17pp

Avoncroft Museum of Historic Buildings
Stoke Heath, Bromsgrove
Worcs B60 4JR
T: 01527 831363/831886
F: 01527 876934
Contact: Judy Lines, Manager

Ceremony

The Museum of Historic Buildings, Guesten Hall, has a medieval roof set within a modern, specially designed building. On site is a Victorian 'tin' church which can be used for blessings. The New Guesten Hall holds a ceremony licence and weddings can take place here on any day except Bank Holidays. Confetti is not permitted.
Price guide: £300

Reception

Helicopters and hot air balloons may use the grounds.
Catering: Buffets from £5pp Sit down from £15pp

Aylestone Court Hotel
Hereford
T: 01432 341891 F: 01432 267691
Contact: Mrs Holloway, Owner

Ceremony

This Georgian hotel is set in one acre of gardens. Ceremonies are held in The Orangery on any day of the year.
Price guide: P.O.A.

Reception

Price guide: P.O.A.

Berrington Hall
Leominster, Hereford HR6 0DW
T: 01568 615721 F: 01568 613263
Contact: Mrs Y Osborne, Manager

Ceremony

This National Trust owned, Grade I listed building was designed by Henry Holland and is set above the River Lugg with views to the Black Mountains and Brecon Beacons. Capability Brown created the lake in the grounds which features an artificial island. Three rooms hold ceremony licences, but these have limited wheelchair access. They are, however, available all year. Only biodegradable confetti is permitted, and photography cannot be allowed inside the house.
Price guide: from £300

Reception

Reception facilities are offered from November 1st to March 15th. Dancing and music is permitted in a marquee.
Price guide: POA

Burford House, Burford
Nr Tenbury Wells WR15 8HQ
T: 01584 810777 F: 01584 810673
Contact: Andrew Kinniburgh, Site Assistant Manager

Ceremony

The House's panelled entrance hall leads to the Burford House Gardens, which features four acres of lawns and is home to the National Clematis Collection. Ceremonies are available Monday to Saturday excluding Bank Holidays. The price guide to hold the ceremony includes the use of the grounds for photography.
Price guide: £150

Reception

Reception facilities are not available in the House itself, although a marquee is available with a capacity of 500. Catering is on a contract basis but does not have to be from an approved list.
Catering: P.O.A.

Dormy House Hotel
Willersley Hill
Broadway,
Worcs WR12 7LF
T: 01386 852711 F: 01386 858636
Contact: Nicola Sinclair, Sales Manager

Ceremony

This hotel, a converted 17th Century Cotswold farmhouse, has three marriage rooms, each with limited wheelchair access. These are available on any day except Christmas Day and Boxing Day.
Price guide: £150

Reception

The hotel has two AA Rosettes and is RAC recommended. Ethnic, Kosher and vegetarian food can be prepared.
Catering: from £19.50pp

HEREFORD & WORCESTER

Eastnor Castle
Eastnor, Ledbury
Herefordshire HR8 1RL
T: 01531 633160 F: 01531 631776
Contact: Simon Foster, Administrator

Ceremony

This privately owned 'fairytale' castle is set in the Malvern Hills and surrounded by a deer park and a lake. The Castle's Gothic Drawing Room holds the ceremony licence, and this room has limited wheelchair access. Weddings can take place here on any day except Sundays and Bank Holidays, and weekdays during July and August.
Price guide: £250

Reception

Helicopters and hot air balloons can use the Castle grounds.
Catering: POA

Elms Hotel
Abberley
Nr Worcester WR6 6AT
T: 01299 896666 F: 01299 896804
Contact: Mrs Paula Aczel

Ceremony

The hotel's "Gallery Room" is licensed to hold ceremonies which are not available on Sundays and Bank Holidays and has a minimum capacity of 10. Although there is wheelchair access to the hotel, there is no disabled WC. It is not possible to hold ceremonies without reception facilities also.
Price guide: £250

Reception

The hotel's restaurant has been awarded two AA rosettes. In addition to the services indicated, which include free use of an antique cake stand and knife, the hotel is happy to organise any further services for the couple. For instance, menu cards, place names and even bud vases can be provided at no extra cost.
Catering: POA

Fownes Hotel
City Walls Road
Worcester WR1 2AP
T: 01905 613151 F: 01905 23742
Contact: Wendy Hyde, Events Manager

Ceremony

Fownes Hotel is located in the city centre next to the canal. Four rooms are licensed and are available on any day of the year.
Price guide: £70 - £80

Reception

The hotel offer numerous packages, with optional extras, such as the toastmaster (from £125), place cards (£1 per 10) and disco (from £175). Packages include overnight accommodation for bride and groom, drinks and printing of menus, and start at £25pp. There is also the 'fine dining' option, with menu items individually priced.
Catering: from £25pp - £35pp

Grafton Manor
Bromsgrove
Worcs B61 7HA
T: 01527 579007 F: 01527 575221
Contact: Stephen Morris, Managing Partner

Ceremony

The Manor dates from 1567, but was substantially rebuilt in the early 18th Century. Two rooms (with limited wheelchair access) are available for ceremonies on any day of the year. Ceremonies must be followed by reception at the Manor. The Manor boasts its own chapel which is available for blessings after the civil ceremony.
Price guide: £125

Reception

Grafton caters for weddings on an exclusive use basis.
Catering: from £33.75

Granary Hotel & Restaurant
Shenstone, Nr Kidderminster
Worcs DY10 4BS
T: 01562 777535 F: 01562 777722
Contact: Sue Taylor, Wedding Co-ordinator

Ceremony

Up to three ceremonies per day are allowed at the hotel. Ceremonies can only be held here if the reception is also at the hotel.
Price guide: from £125

Reception

A traditional carvery can be offered by the hotel, as well as table plans if required.
Catering: from £14.50pp

Hanbury Hall
School Road
Hanbury, Droitwich
Worcs WR9 7EA
T: 01527 821214 F: 01527 821251
Contact: Grace Elford, Property Manager

Ceremony

HEREFORD & WORCESTER

This National Trust property offers its Drawing Room, Hall and Library for wedding ceremonies. These are available at any time from November to March but from April to October the Hall (with sweeping staircase and log fire) is available mornings only from Sunday to Wednesday. Exclusive use is provided of all ground floor rooms and the 20 acre garden. There are restrictions for indoor photography.

Price guide: from £400. £800 for ceremony and reception

Reception

Helicopters and hot air balloons may use the grounds. Catering can be provided by National Trust Enterprises, or couples may choose their own caterers at this venue.
Catering: POA

Hereford Town Hall
St Owen Street HR12 2PJ
T: 01432 362521
Contact: J Arnold, Communications Assistant

Ceremony

This listed building has approval for four rooms, including the Assembly Hall and the Council Chamber. All rooms have limited wheelchair access. Confetti is not permitted.
Price guide: from £20

Reception

Couples would need to arrange for their own caterers at the Town Hall.

Hopton Court, Cleobury Mortimer, Kidderminster DY14 0EF
T: 01299 270734 F: 01299 271132
Contact: C Woodward, Owner

Ceremony

Hopton Court is an English Heritage, Grade II listed building, with a refurbished conservatory. The house dates from 1776 and is set in 1800 acres. Four rooms are licensed for ceremonies including the Conservatory, and these are available any day except Sundays.
Price guide: £50

Reception

All international cuisine can be provided, claims the venue.
Catering: Buffets from £7.50pp Sit down from £18.75pp

The Hundred House Hotel
Great Witley, WR6 6HS
T: 01299 896888 F: 01299 896588
Contact: Brian Offord, Manager

Ceremony

The hotel offers three licensed rooms. Ceremonies here must be followed by reception at the hotel.
Price guide: £100

Reception

Catering: Buffets from £10pp. Sit down from £17pp

Jarvis Heath Hotel
Habberley Road, Bewdley
Nr Kidderminster DY12 1LJ
T: 01299 400900 F: 01299 400921
Contact: Louise Allen, Events Coordinator

Ceremony

The Jarvis Heath Offers for rooms on any day of the year.
Price guide: POA

Reception

Jarvis has put together a Themes and Dreams brochure to inspire your event - they can even provide disposable cameras for every guest. Themes that are already packaged include a Venetian Masquerade Ball, a Night At the Oscars and a Magical Theme. A recent event involved recreating the inside of a circus tent for a party of 300.
Catering: Buffets from £6.45pp

Lygon Arms
Broadway
Worcester WR12 7DU
T: 01386 852255 F: 01386 858611
Contact: Simon Hancox

Ceremony

This 16th Century coaching inn, set in the heart of the village, is situated at the foot of the Cotswolds and features antique furniture and log fires. Only one ceremony is allowed per day.
Price guide: from £300

Reception

A cake maker and photographer can be recommended by the hotel.
Catering: from £20.75pp

New Priory Hotel
Stretton Sugwas
Hereford HR4 7AR
T: 01432 760264 F: 01432 761809
Contact: KJ Benjamin, Owner

Ceremony

This old vicarage, now an hotel and restaurant, is set in over 3 acres of grounds. The Breakfast Bridal Room is available for ceremonies on any day of the year.

Price guide: £50

Reception

The New Priory can offer vegetarian menus. Helicopters and hot air balloons can use the site.
Catering: Buffets from £5pp Sit down from £8.50pp

**Pengethley Manor Hotel,
Pengethley Park
Ross on Wye HR9 6LL**
T: 01989 730211 F: 01989 730238
Contact: Paul Forster, General Manager

Ceremony

This listed Georgian country house is set in 15 acres of gardens. Five rooms are licensed for ceremonies, and are available on any day of the year.
Price guide: £75

Reception

The hotel boasts chef Ferdinand Van Der Knaap. An unusual event hosted here recently was on the theme of a Victorian Tea Party. In addition to the accommodation offered on the premises, the hotel has preferential rate agreements with other local establishments.
Catering: From £20pp

**Penrhos Court
Kington HR5 3LH**
T: 01544 230720 F: 01544 230754
Contact: Daphne Lambert, Owner

Ceremony

Dating back to 1280 there are three periods to the main house, including the great medieval Cruck Hall and an Elizabethan wing with oak beams. Only one ceremony per day is permitted.
Price guide: £120

Reception

Penrhos prides itself on its organic produce which is grown in the Court's own garden. The Court has 19 bedrooms, two of which have four poster beds.
Price guide: from £20pp

**Redditch Town Hall
Alcester Street
Ringway, Redditch B98 8AH**
T: 01527 64252 F: 01527 65216
Contact: Mrs Heather Hayes, Room Bookings

Ceremony

Located in the town centre, Redditch Town Hall offers a Wedding Room and the Council Chamber for wedding ceremonies.. These can take place on any day except Bank Holidays. The Mayor of Redditch was the first person to get married here.
Price guide: £50

Reception

Catering: POA

**Salford Hall Hotel
Abbotts Salford
Evesham
Worcs WR11 5UT**
T: 01386 871300 F: 01386 871301
Contact: Sally Pearce, General Manager

Ceremony

This Tudor manor is a Grade I listed building, restored six years ago. Up to two ceremonies are permitted per day, on any day except Christmas Day. Confetti is not permitted.
Price guide: £100

Reception

The Hotel has two AA Rosettes for its cuisine. It is possible to take over the whole hotel, with a minimum of 30 bedrooms.
Catering: from £25pp

**The Stourport Manor Hotel
Hartlebury Road,
Stourport on Severn DY13 9LT**
T: 01299 289955 F: 01299 878520
Contact: Elena Bueno, Conference & Banqueting Co-ordinator

Ceremony

Set in 23 acres of grounds, the hotel is the former home of Sir Stanley Baldwin. It has five rooms licensed for ceremonies, including the Magellans Restaurant.
Price guide: from £150

Reception

Catering: Buffets from £5.25pp. Sit down from £17.50pp

**Wood Norton Hall
BBC Wood Norton
Evesham WR11 4YB**
T: 01386 420364 F: 01386 420679
Contact: Lucy Biltcliff, Sales Executive

Ceremony

The Wood Norton estate is now owned by the BBC. It was once owned by a French aristocratic family whose presence can still be felt in the decor of the house. The Orleans Room is licensed for ceremonies.
Price guide: POA

HEREFORD & WORCESTER

HEREFORD & WORCESTER - HERTFORDSHIRE

Reception

A variety of rooms are available for the wedding breakfast. The property can be hired on an exclusive use basis. For your entertainment, the Hall boasts a Billiard Room and indoor leisure activities such as squash court, swimming pool, snooker tables and multi gym. Outside there are tennis courts and a croquet lawn.
Catering: POA

The Chase Hotel
Gloucester Road
Ross on Wye HR9 5LH
T: 01989 763161 F: 01989 768330
Contact: Natasha Sturgess-Turton, Sales Manager

Ceremony

The Garden Room, Oak Suit and Restaurant are all licensed for ceremonies and are available any day of the year. Confetti is not permitted.
Price guide: £100

Reception

Catering: From £20pp

ALSO LICENSED
Bank House Hotel 01886 833551
The County Hotel 01432 299955
Earls Croome Court 01684 592372
Munstone House 01432 267122
The Nash 01905 821397
St Andrews House Hotel 01905 779677
Vale Golf & Country Club 01386 462781

The Alban Arena Civic Centre
St Albans
Herts AL1 3LD
T: 01727 861078 F: 01727 865755
Contact: Mr R Cramer or Mr R Daynes

Ceremony

This modern building in the centre of St Albans offers its Main Foyer, Lower Foyer or Auditorium as ceremony venues. These are available on any day of the year. Confetti is not permitted.
Price guide: from £200

Reception

Catering at this venue can be provided by the in-house team, or you can provide your own catering.
Catering: Buffets from £4pp. Sit down from £10pp

Barley Town House, Church End, Barley, Royston SG8
Contact: PW Smith, Chairman of Management Committee on 01763 848561 or I Wilde, Booking Officer on 01763 848276

Ceremony

This is a Grade II listed timber framed building dating from 1520. The Undercroft is licensed for ceremonies and is available on any day of the year. Wheelchair access is to the ground floor only.
Price guide: from £100

Reception

The managers for this property pride themselves on allowing couples a lot of freedom to organise the wedding day as they wish. You can arrange your own caterers, although the local pub can help out in running the bars if required. Weddings previously held here have included a medieval reception, with a pig roasted at the rear of the building.

Briggens House Hotel
Stanstead Road
Stanstead Abbots SG12 8LD
T: 01279 829955 F: 01279 793685
Contact: Georgian Young, Banqueting

Ceremony

Briggens is a Grade II listed, 17th Century, building set in 80 acres of parkland. Three rooms are licensed.
Price guide: from £500

Reception

As part of the wedding package, bride and groom can expect a complimentary changing room and Executive Room, as well as menus and place cards.
Catering: Buffets from £15pp. Sit down from £23.50pp.

Cheshunt Marriott Hotel
Halfhide Lane
Turnford, Broxbourne
Hertfordshire EN10 6NG
T: 01992 451245 F: 01992 440120
Contact: Andrea Moughan

Ceremony

This modern hotel does not have any restrictions on the number of ceremonies held per day and confetti is permitted. The cost of holding the ceremony varies from £300 during weekdays to £250 at weekends.
Price guide: from £250

Reception

Catering: Packages from £38.50pp

Edgwarebury Hotel
Barnet Lane
Elstree
Herts WD6 3RE
T: 0181 953 8227 F: 0181 207 3668
Contact: Zandra Fraser, Conf and Banqueting Manager

HERTFORDSHIRE

Ceremony

The hotel is built in the Tudor manor house style featuring big stone fireplaces and carved oak. It is set in 10 acres of grounds. Three rooms hold licences and these are available on any day of the year. Ceremonies here must be followed by reception at the hotel.
Price guide: from £250

Reception

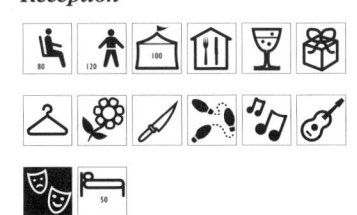

Catering: Buffets from £10.50pp sit down from £26.95pp

Elstree Moat House
Barnet By Pass
Borehamwood WD6 5PU
T: 0181 214 9988   F: 0181 207 3194
Contact: Catherine Heaton

Ceremony

The capacity for the ceremony varies from a minimum of 20 to a maximum of 500. Ceremonies are available seven days a week excluding Saturday, subject to management discretion.
Price guide: POA

Reception

Although catering is in-house, the hotel also offers a choice of contract caterers, but from an approved list only.
Catering: Buffets from £8.50pp Sit down from £24.95pp

Fanhams Hall
Fanhams Hall Road
Ware, Herts SG12 7PZ
T: 01920 460511   F: 01920 469187
Contact: House Manager

Ceremony

Set in 27 acres of gardens, this listed Jacobean style building has a modern pavilion extension which has views over a small landscaped lake. Ceremonies are available throughout the week excluding Sundays, dependent upon conference bookings. The Hall does not accept bookings for ceremonies only.
Price guide: £200

Reception

In addition to the Hall's 85 bedrooms, two honeymoon/VIP suites are available. A late night drinking licence is available until midnight and the Hall is happy to recommend any services you may require.
Catering: £25pp

The Glen Eagle Hotel
1 Luton Road
Harpenden
Hertfordshire AL5 2PX
T: 01582 760271   F: 01582 460819
Contact: David Hunter, GM

Ceremony

This country house style hotel is set in award winning gardens, and holds no restrictions on the availability of ceremonies.
Price guide: POA

Reception

The hotel offers reduced rates for accommodation to those members of the wedding party wishing to stay at the Glen Eagle Hotel on a Friday, Saturday or Sunday night.
Catering: from £21pp

Green End Park Hotel
Dane End
Near Ware, Hertfordshire
T: 01920 438344   F: 01920 438523
Contact: Valerie Hutcheon, Assistant to the Proprietor

Ceremony

This hotel and restaurant is a listed building and has its Louis Room licensed to hold ceremonies. The room has a seating capacity of 70 and the hotel is more than happy to combine a mixture of seated and standing guests to a maximum of 80. Ceremonies are available without receptions while confetti is permitted outside only.
Price guide: £175-250

Reception

Catering is in-house, and a marquee is available for a maximum of 200 guests.
Catering: £28pp

Hanbury Manor Hotel
Ware, Herts SG12 0SD
T: 01920 487722   F: 01920 487692
Contact: Josefine Strygstryg

Ceremony

Only one ceremony is available per day, which must be held in conjunction with a reception.
Price guide: from £300

Reception

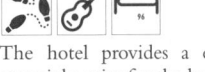

The hotel provides a complimentary overnight suite for the bride and groom including breakfast. In addition to the services indicated, the hotel offers the bridal party a horse and carriage and use

of vintage cars.
Catering: from £30pp

Hatfield Lodge Hotel
Comet Way, Hatfield
Hertfordshire AL10 9NG
T: 01707 272661 F: 01707 256282
Contact: The Conference Department

Ceremony

This modern hotel has three rooms licensed to hold ceremonies with capacities from 35 to 100. Ceremonies must be followed by reception here.
Price guide: from £120

Reception

Flower arrangements are included in the price of the ceremony.
Catering: from £26.95pp

Hilton National Hotel
Elton Way, Watford
Hertfordshire WD2 8HA
T: 01923 235881 F: 01923 220836
Contact: Matthew Wykes

Ceremony

Ceremonies are available in the Registrar's suite for up to 30 and in the New Hertford Suite which can only be reserved in conjunction with a wedding breakfast (minimum of 120 guests).
Price guide: from £100

Reception

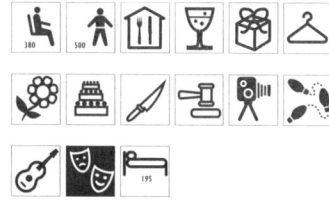

Although the hotel's catering is in-house, a list of outside contract caterers is available. However it is acceptable for the couple to supply their own contract caterer. The hotel boasts kosher and ethnic cuisine expertise.
Catering: from £35pp

Jarvis International
Hemel Hempstead
Hemel Hempstead Road
Redbourn, Herts AL3 7AF
T: 01582 792105 F: 01582 792001
Contact: Merissa Lohan, Conference & Events Sales Manager

Ceremony

The hotel boasts a complete package of services to make the wedding day as simple as possible for the couple. The package includes, amongst other things, free accommodation for the couple on the night of the wedding, special overnight rates for wedding guests, and fun packs to keep children occupied during speeches.
Price guide: £250

Reception

Catering: £20pp

Jarvis Comet Hotel
301 St Albans Road West
Hatfield, Herts AL10 9RH
T: 01707 265411 F: 01707 264019
Contact: General Manager

Ceremony

This Grade II listed art deco building has been renovated to its former glory. Southpoint and the Pioneer Suite are both licensed for wedding ceremonies.
Price guide: £245

Reception

Catering: Buffet from £8pp Sit down from £18pp

Knebworth Park
The Manor Barn
Old Knebworth, Herts SG3 6PY
T: 01438 813825 F: 01438 813003
Contact: Clive Duffey, Events Manager

Ceremony

This 16th Century tithe barn is set in 250 acres of deer park with Knebworth House, Gardens and Barns Banqueting Centre available for the reception and photographs.
Price guide: £300

Reception

Receptions are undertaken in-house by the award-winning Lytton Catering. Accommodation is available at the Novotel hotel set within the park, and a list of other local accommodation is also available.
Catering: £19.75pp

The Manor
St Michael's Village
Fishpool Street
St Albans, Herts AL3 4RY
T: 01727 854444 F: 01727 848909
Contact: Helen Jones

Ceremony

The original Manor House was built around 1512 on medieval foundations and is now a Grade II listed building set in five acres of award winning grounds. Only one ceremony per day is permitted.
Price guide: from £225

Reception

A late night drinking licence is available for residents of the Manor only.
Catering: from £24.50

HERTFORDSHIRE

Offley Place
Kings Walden Road
Great Offley
Hertfordshire SG5 3DS
T: 01462 768787 F: 01462 768724
Contact: Carrie Horwood, Manager

Ceremony

This conference and training venue is a listed building, with parts dating back to the 16th Century, and was once a stately home. Set in its own grounds with orchards and rose gardens, Offley Place has three rooms licensed with capacities from 25 to 80.
Price guide: £100

Reception

For a fee of £500 Offley Place may be hired on an exclusive basis with exclusive use of the grounds and staff. The couple are offered a complimentary overnight suite while staff are quick to point out that although accommodation is provided, and is clean and comfortable, it is not to hotel standards.
Catering: £16-25pp

The Old Palace
Hatfield Park
Hatfield AL9 5NE
Tel: 01707 262055 / 272738
Fax: 01707 260898
Contact: Banqueting Manager

Ceremony

Originally built in the late 15th century, the Old Palace was acquired by King Henry VIII in 1538 and became the childhood home of Queen Elizabeth 1st. The Palace has two room licensed, the Great Hall and the Riding School with capacities varying from 220 to 400. Ceremonies are only available in conjunction with receptions and are not permitted on Sundays, Good Friday and Christmas Day.
Price guide: from £100

Reception

Although the Palace does not have accommodation available on the premises, a list of local accommodation is available. In addition to the services indicated, the Old Palace offers themed receptions; Elizabethan, of course.
Catering: £26.50pp

Pearse House, Parsonage Lane
Bishops Stortford, Herts
T: 01279 757400 F: 01279 506591
Contact: Mrs V McGregor, Deputy Director

Ceremony

Pearse House is a privately owned conference centre with residential facilities, and allows only one ceremony per day. Confetti is permitted outside only.
Price guide: £150-250

Reception

The House prides itself on a 'one stop shop facility' to relieve the couple of any further wedding worries. A children's crèche is available during formalities and preferential rates are offered for guests staying overnight.
Catering: £12.50-33.50pp

The Ponsbourne Park Hotel
Newgate Street Village
Nr Hertford, Herts SG13 8QZ
T: 01707 876191 F: 01707 875190
Contact: Functions Manager

Ceremony

This old country house, set in 170 acres of grounds, was once the hunting lodge of King Henry VIII. The hotel has two rooms licensed, which are available seven days a week although there is limited availability from Monday-Thursday.

Price guide: from £100

Reception

Catering: from £19pp

The Priory
High Street, Ware
Hertfordshire SG12 9AL
T: 01920 460316 F: 01920 484056
Contact: Mrs Janet Buttery, Town Clerk, Ware Town Council

Ceremony

The Priory is a Grade I listed building and scheduled ancient monument, and was originally a friary founded in 1338. Confetti is not permitted.
Price guide: from £160

Reception

Receptions can take place in The Priory Hall or the rebuilt Victorian conservatory. Both rooms overlook and lead onto the river and gardens. Room hire for the reception is from £240. Although accommodation is not available at the Priory, a list of local accommodation is available which offers preferential rates agreements.
Catering: £30pp

Quality Clock Hotel
The Link Road
Welwyn, Hertfordshire AL6 9XA
T: 01438 716911 F: 01438 714065
Contact: Tina, Conf & Banqueting

Ceremony

The hotel features a clock tower outside the main reception and offers only one

89

ceremony per day if held in conjunction with a reception. Ceremonies are generally conducted between 10am-4pm and are available without receptions.
Price guide: POA

Reception

Couples are able to compile their own menu package for maximum flexibility and choice, which may also reduce costs. Children's entertainment such as Punch and Judy shows are available during formalities. A complimentary overnight bridal suite is available as well as preferential rates for guests.
Catering: POA

Shendish Manor
London Road
Apsley, Hemel Hempstead
Herts HP3 0AA
T: 01442 232220 F: 01442 230683
Contact: Tom Concannon, GM

Ceremony

Shendish Manor is a large stately listed building offering leisure facilities such as a golf course and health club, as well as conference facilities. Two rooms are licensed for ceremonies and are available any day of the year. Confetti is not permitted.
Price guide: POA

Reception

Shendish Manor has a New Zealand and Asian chef. Helicopters and hot air balloons may use the grounds.
Catering: from £24.95

Sopwell House Hotel
Cottonmill Lane, St Albans
T: 01727 864477 F: 01727 845636
Contact: Jeremy Hollands, Banqueting

Ceremony

This four star, Georgian country house hotel, was once the country home of Lord Mountbatten and is set in 11 acres of gardens and grounds. Two ceremonies are allowed per day. Confetti is permitted.
Price guide: from £300

Reception

The hotel also operates preferential rate agreements with other local hotels and, in addition to the services indicated, is willing to organise balloons, place cards, menu printing, table plans, car hire, beauty therapy and leisure facilities for the couple.
Catering: from £30pp

Tewin Bury Farm
Nr Welwyn AL6 0JB
T: 01438 717793 F: 01438 840440
Contact: Veronica Winterbourne, Functions Manager

Ceremony

This 17th Century listed barn, situated on the banks of the river Mimram, is available for ceremonies every day excluding Saturday. Ceremonies are available only in conjunction with receptions.
Price guide: £150

Reception

Receptions are offered in either the tithe barn, stable or the farmhouse itself, with capacities varying from 20 to 200. Some of the farm's accommodation consists of two storey suites which are suitable for families and sleep four people.
Catering: £23.70pp

Vintage Court Hotel
Vintage Corner
Puckeridge, Nr Ware SG11 1SA
T: 01920 822722 F: 01920 822877
Contact: Sue Wright, Banqueting Sales

Ceremony

This modern hotel has two rooms licensed and features small but pleasant gardens suitable for photography.
Price guide: £150

Reception

The hotel has 24 bedrooms, all of which are either double or twin bedded.
Catering: from £19.85pp

Jarvis International Hotel
A41 Watford By Pass, Watford
Herts WD2 8HQ
T: 0181 950 6211 F: 0181 950 5804
Contact: Jane Knowles, Wedding Consultant

Ceremony

Six rooms are available for ceremonies, including the Ballroom on the Park. These are available any day of the year and have limited wheelchair access.
Price guide: £150 - £400

Reception

Many services can be recommended, including suppliers of vehicles, horse and carriage, and fireworks.
Catering: Buffets from £12.50. Sit down from £26.50

ALSO LICENSED
Hertford County Hall 01992 555550

Manor of Groves Hotel   01279 600777
Pendley Manor Hotel   01442 891891
Putteridge Bury   01582 489092
The Radlett Centre   01923 852697
Redcoats Farmhouse Hotel   01438 729500
The Sun Hotel   01462 436411

Celebration Hotel
Avenue Road, Shanklin
Isle of Wight   PO37 7BG
T: 01983 862746
Contact: Maggie Newman, Owner

Ceremony

The appropriately named L'Amour Wedding Room is the licensed area of this hotel, and is available on any day of the year.
Price guide: POA

Reception

The hotel specialises in arranging complete intimate wedding and honeymoon packages for small weddings. The theme is carried to the menus, with dishes such as Band of Gold deep fried brie and redcurrant sauce, and Cupid's Chicken Chasseur. This is probably as near to the Las Vegas experience as you can get in the UK. The most romantic details can be arranged, including a tour in a horse drawn carriage around the country lanes, while you sip champagne, or a VIP island tour by Rolls Royce.
Catering: Buffets from £6pp. Sit down from £15pp

Northwood House
Ward Avenue, Cowes
Isle of Wight
T: 01983 299752   F: 01983 823369
Contact: Mrs L Kenrick, Administration Officer

Ceremony

Northwood House stands in about 27 acres. It was originally built as the seat of the Ward family in 1837, but is now used for local meetings and social functions. Many sovereigns and members of the Royal family have been entertained at Northwood and, in more recent years, the Duke of Edinburgh has made regular visits during Cowes week. Three rooms are licensed for ceremonies and are available on any day of the year except New Year's Eve and Bank Holidays.
Price guide: from £50

Reception

The venue holds a public entertainment licence, but the catering contractor needs to apply for a liquor licence if one is required for the reception.
Catering: POA

Swainston Manor Hotel
Calbourne Road
Newport
Isle of Wight PO30 4HX
T: 01983 521121   F: 01983 521406
Contact: Mr Woodward, Managing Director

Ceremony

This Grade II listed building is set in 32 acres of grounds and has three rooms available to hold ceremonies with varying capacities from 12 to 120. Ceremonies are available without receptions but costs are dependent on the size of the party. The hotel has its own church which is available for blessings.

Reception

Catering: from £12pp

ALSO LICENSED
The George Hotel   01983 760331
The Old Park Hotel   01983 852583
Osborne House   01983 200022
Sandringham Hotel   01983 406655
Shanklin Manor   01983 862777

Abbots Barton
36 New Dover Road
Canterbury, Kent   CT1 3DU
T: 01227 760341 F: 01277 785442
Contact: Miss Moore

Ceremony

This is a 17th Century gothic house set in two acres.
Price guide: £80 - 1/2 day/ £140 - day

Reception

Catering: £7 (buffet) to £12.50 (waited)

Alexandra Suite
St Mary's Road
Swanley
Kent BR8 7BU
T: 01322 613900 F: 01322 614998
Contact: Paula Smith, Marketing Manageress

Ceremony

Five suites are available for ceremonies at the Alexandra Suite and The Woodlands. The Alexandra Suite (up to 250 guests) itself and the Clocktower Pavilion (30-70 guests) are on the ground floor below the civic centre. The Woodlands, (in Hilda May Avenue), offers the Poplar Suite (100-160 guests), the Linden Suite (80-100 guests) and the Walnut Lounge (60-90 guests), the latter also featuring a conservatory. Marriages can take place on any day of the week.
Price guide: from £104

Reception

Catering at both buildings is operated by Swanley Banqueting.
Catering: £18pp

Boughton Monchelsea Place
Boughton Monchelsea
Nr Maidstone, Kent ME17 4BU
T&F: 01622 743120
Contact: Ms Terry Stevens, PA

Ceremony

This is a privately owned, battlemented Elizabethan ragstone manor house with Regency alterations. It is set in a deer park, with views over the Weald of Kent, and has its own walled gardens. Ceremonies can take place on any week day, with up to four allowed per day.
Price guide: £375

Reception

Activities which can take place here include standard and laser clay shooting, fishing and quad biking. Firework displays, hot air balloons and entertainers, such as magicians, are also welcome, but all will have to be arranged by the couple themselves. While the venue has no drinks licence, it has an arrangement with local pubs who can arrange for relevant licences and supply alcohol. While the venue has several caterers that can prepare the wedding breakfast, couples may also choose their own caterer. Many other services can be recommended by the venue. Local accommodation list available. To hire the whole of the ground floor of the house for a reception costs £1050. To have a marquee costs £1000, plus the cost of the marquee itself. Weddings here must be finished by 8pm.
Catering: POA

Brandshatch Place Hotel
Fawkham Valley Road
Fawkham, Kent DA3 8NQ
T: 01474 872239 F: 01474 879652
Contact: General Manager

Ceremony

A Georgian country house, set in 12 acres, this listed building can play host to wedding ceremonies on any day of the week.
Price guide: £200

Reception

The Head Chef is Mark Cheeseman who holds two rosettes for his skills in modern English cuisine, and has been nominated for a third. Other facilities at the hotel include an indoor heated pool, snooker, beauty centre, gym, and tennis and squash.
Catering: from £20pp

Bridgewood Manor Hotel
Walderslade Woods
Chatham, Kent ME5 9AX
T: 01634 201333 F: 01634 201330
Contact: Conference & Banqueting

Ceremony

This four star AA and RAC hotel (part of Marston Hotels) offers three marriage rooms: the Hythe Suite, Hogarth Suite and Maidstone Suite, for as few as four guests. Not available on Christmas Day and Boxing Day. No confetti.
Price guide: £200 (£150 with reception)

Reception

In addition to the services listed above, the Bridgewood Manor Hotel will also print special wedding menus for receptions held at the venue. If required, children can be catered for separately. The maximum capacity for both waited and buffet style receptions at the hotel is 130, and the site is not suitable for a marquee.
Catering: from £23.50

Broome Park
The Broome Park Estate
Canterbury, Kent CT1 6QX
T: 01227 831701 F: 01227 831973
Contact: Gwen Willbye,
Food & Beverage Manager

Ceremony

Built in the reign of Charles I, this listed mansion, set in 268 acres, was once the home of Lord Kitchener. It is now a club operated on a time-share basis. Two rooms have been granted a licence for ceremonies: The Green Room, which seats up to 60, and the Gazebo, which is set in the Italian Garden, and seats up to 300. Up to two ceremonies are permitted daily. Wheelchair access is limited.
Price guide: from £50

Reception

The Club has three restaurants including Dizzy's Jazz Bar and Creole Restaurant, and a more formal a la carte restaurant. Other facilities include an 18 hole championship golf course, driving range, tennis courts, squash courts, putting green, outdoor pool and health centre. While accommodation is usually available on site; there are 18 suites in the main building and a further 26 villas in the grounds; availability is variable. The club can recommend numerous services that cannot be offered in-house.
Catering: from £18pp

Chiddingstone Castle
Hill Hoath Road
Nr Edenbridge, Kent TN8 7AD
T: 01892 870347
Contact: Functions Manager

Ceremony

One of the historic houses of Kent, and formerly the home of Denys Eyre Bower, Chiddingstone Castle is now maintained by a private charitable trust. Set in its own grounds, with woods and a cascade, the castle is a particularly tranquil setting for a wedding. The oak panelled Great Hall is the marriage room which can be hired on any day of the week except over the Christmas Bank holiday, with only one ceremony permitted per day. Confetti is not allowed, and it should be noted that stiletto heels are prohibited since they irreparably damage the floors.
Price guide: up to £350

Reception

Receptions can take place in one of several rooms, the smallest of which is the Assembly Room, suitable for up to 40

guests. If a marquee is required this is sited in front of the south entrance, which provides a backdrop of towers and battlements. The castle has a restaurant licence for drinks, but you may also provide your own drinks and pay corkage. Personalised wedding stationery is said to be a speciality of the castle. The castle has its own musician; disco music is not permitted. A dressing room is provided for the bride in the 17th Century wing of the castle.
Catering: from £8pp

Chilston Park Hotel
Sandway, Lenham
Kent ME17 2BE
T: 01622 859803 F: 01622 858352
Contact: Sue Greenwood, Events Manager

Ceremony

This Grade I listed mansion house set in parkland has a marriage licence for its Orangery. The minimum number for a wedding ceremony is six people. Ceremonies cannot be held here on Christmas Day or Boxing Day. Up to three ceremonies are permitted per day.
Price guide: £750

Reception

Catering: from £26.50 (3-course meal)

Cobham Hall, Cobham DA12 3BL
T: 01474 824319 F: 01474 822995
Contact: Sue Anderson, Development Director

Ceremony

This 16th Century mansion, former home of the Earls of Darnley and now a girls' school, is set in 150 acres of landscaped parkland and gardens. Ceremonies can take place on any day of the week, in any of three licensed rooms; The Gilt Hall, The Vestibule and Lady Darnley's Gazebo, which is set in a romantic garden. Confetti is not permitted.
Price guide: £600 + vat

Reception

While there is no accommodation on the premises, a list of local accommodation, with preferential rate agreements with the Hall, can be provided. The Hall has its own helicopter landing area.
Catering: £20pp

Cooling Castle Barn
Cooling, Rochester ME3 8DT
T: 01634 222244 F: 01634 222233
Contact: Mrs S Wightman, Office Manager

Ceremony

This is a 17th renovated barn; a listed building and scheduled ancient monument. The Great Barn and the Fathom Barn are licensed for ceremonies which can take place here from Monday to Thursday, but not on Sundays or Bank Holidays.
Price guide: POA

Reception

Customers may bring their own caterers to this venue.

County Hall
County Road
Maidstone
Kent ME14 1XQ
T: 01622 694151 F: 01622 694158
Contact: Conference Manager

Ceremony

Ceremonies can only take place on a Saturday or Sunday at County Hall (a listed building), and not on any Bank Holidays. Up to four ceremonies are allowed per day, unless couples are also holding their reception at the Hall, in which case their's will be the only wedding that day and no charge will be made for room hire for the ceremony.
Price guide: from £250 or F.O.C.

Reception

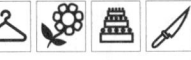

County Hall offers a wedding package, starting at £20.50pp, which includes food and room hire. Drinks packages start at £5 per head. Accommodation is available at Oakwood House, which is also run by Kent County Council.
Catering: from £20.50

Dover Town Hall
Biggin Street
Dover, Kent CT16 1DL
T & F: 01304 201200
Contact: Trevor Jones, GM

Ceremony

This listed building offers a choice of two rooms for ceremonies; The Maison Dieu Hall (up to 400 guests) and the Council Chamber (up to 30 guests).
Price guide: £100

Reception

The Victorian Connaught Hall will accommodate up to 400 guests with room for dancing. Catering and bar services are provided by White Horse Caterers.
Catering: from £15pp

Eastwell Manor
Eastwell Park, Boughton Lees
Ashford, Kent TN25 4HR
T: 01233 219955 F: 01233 635530
Contact: Oriel Stratford, Wedding & Special Functions Co-ordinator

Ceremony

This country house hotel and restaurant offers two marriage rooms: the Bayeaux Room (max 50) and the Rose Garden Room (max 90).
Price guide: £500

KENT

93

KENT

Reception

Catering: £33pp

Finchcocks
Goudhurst, Kent TN17 1HH
T: 01580 211702 F: 01580 211007
Contact: Mrs Katrina Burnett, Director/Owner

Ceremony

Finchcocks, Grade I listed, was built in 1725, and now houses a collection of over 80 historical keyboard instruments. The house stands in 13 acres of grounds including a recently planted walled garden. Period music can be provided free as part of the ceremony. Wheelchair access is good for the marriage room and gardens, but limited for the toilets and restaurant. Confetti is not permitted. Availability for ceremonies varies considerably, please consult Finchcocks directly to enquire about your chosen day.
Price guide: £450 + VAT

Reception

A special feature of the in-house catering at Finchcocks is the choice of Georgian (18th Century) menus. Accommodation is available on the premises by day only, (there is a self-contained flat), but a list of other local accommodation can be provided. Finchcocks has contacts with many musicians who could provide chamber music of all kinds for the wedding.
Catering: from £15

The Garden Hotel
167-169 The Street
Boughton
Faversham
Kent
ME13 9BH
T: 01227 751411 F: 01227 751801
Contact: Karen Carr, Manager

Ceremony

Set in a village location, The Garden Hotel is a 17th Century listed building converted from an antique shop in 1889 and now holds a licence for its Garden Restaurant. This has limited wheelchair access. It is available all days except Christmas Day and Boxing Day.
Price guide: £150

Reception

Catering: Buffets from £12.50pp Sit down from £18.50pp

Groombridge Place
Groombridge, Kent TN3 9QG
T: 01892 861444 F: 01892 863996
Contact: Ryan Whitcut, Functions Co-ordinator

Ceremony

This Grade I listed moated mansion, set in extensive 17th Century gardens, has featured in many films, including Peter Greenaway's The Draughtsman's Contract. Ceremonies can take place in the oak panelled Baronial Hall on any day of the week.
Price guide: £450

Reception

All catering is now on site at Groombridge, and a list of local wedding suppliers is available on request. While there is no overnight accommodation at the house, a list of local hotels, with which Groombridge has arranged preferential rates, can be provided.

Hythe Imperial, Prince's Parade
Hythe CT21 6AE
T: 01303 267441 F: 01303 264610
Contact: Jane Burden, Conference & Banqueting Co-ordinator

Ceremony

The Imperial, built in 1880, is sited on the unspoilt seafront at Hythe. Two rooms are licensed for ceremonies; the Garden Room (max 100) and the Elizabeth Room (max 70). Ceremonies can take place here any day of the week, but not between December 24 and 25, New Year's Eve and New Year's Day or the Easter weekend. Confetti is not permitted.
Price guide: £200

Reception

Catering: from £23pp

Jarvis Great Danes
Hotel & Country Club
Maidstone, Kent ME17 1RE
T: 01622 631163 F 01622 735290
Contact: Wedding Consultant

Ceremony

Originally a manor house, Great Danes has had more recent additions over the years. It is set in 26 acres of landscaped gardens. Wedding ceremonies can take place in one of two rooms (the smaller takes up to 100 guests) on any day of the week. Each wedding is assigned a Wedding Host whose function is to ensure that the event goes smoothly and that all details are taken into account.
Price Guide: £250

Reception

Great Danes has considerable experience of both Greek and Asian weddings, providing traditional fayre. The hotel's wedding package includes free accommodation for bride and groom on their wedding night, plus breakfast, fruit, flowers, champagne and a gift. Other services that can be offered include a free postal service for your invitations, free table fun packs for children, and free

94

cake boxes.
Catering: from £18pp

The Knowle Restaurant
School Lane, Higham
Rochester, Kent ME3 7HP
T: 01474 822262
Contact: Michael Baragwanath, Proprietor

Ceremony

Knowle is a Victorian Gothic-style mansion set in three acres of old English gardens. The proprietor will allow you sole use of the premises for your wedding.
Price guide: £2pp

Reception

Food at Knowle is English and continental style. No charge is usually made for flowers or cake stand and knife. A list of local accommodation, with which the restaurant has preferential rate agreements, is available on request.
Catering: from £24pp

Little Silver Country Hotel
St Michael's
Tenterden, Kent TN30 6SP
T: 01233 850321 F: 01233 850647
Contact: Mrs Lawson, Proprietor

Ceremony

This mock Tudor style hotel has a marriage licence for its Kent Hall (an octagonal shaped room), which can only be hired for wedding ceremonies if the reception is also at the hotel.
Price guide: £175 + vat

Reception

The hotel can also arrange Rolls Royces and video operators.
Catering: £25pp

Lympne Castle
c/o Robert Spicer
52 Lympne Industrial Park
Hythe, Kent CT21 4LR
T: 01303 262398 F: 01303 261810
Contact: Barrie Marshall, Consultant

Ceremony

Price guide: £375

Reception

Catering: from £4.25 (buffet) to £25.50pp

Mount Ephraim Gardens
Hernhill
Faversham
Kent ME13 9TX
T: 01227 751496 F: 01227 750940
Contact: Mrs Lesley Dawes, Events Manager

Ceremony

This Victorian country mansion, a member of the Historic Houses Association, is set in 9 acres of gardens, within a 300 acres estate. Ceremonies are possible here at any time of the year except Bank Holidays.
Price guide: POA

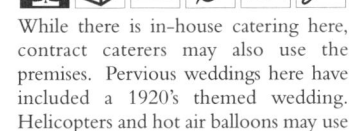

Reception

While there is in-house catering here, contract caterers may also use the premises. Pervious weddings here have included a 1920's themed wedding. Helicopters and hot air balloons may use the site.
Catering: Buffets from £8pp. Sit down from £10pp

Nizel's Golf Club
Nizel's Lane
Hildenborough
Kent TN11 8NX
T: 01732 833138 F: 01732 833764
Contact: Catering Manager

Ceremony

The recently refurbished Queen Anne House at Nizel's is adjacent to formal rose gardens and a summer marquee. The house overlooks an 18 hole golf course in the heart of the Kentish Weald.
Price guide: POA

Reception

Catering: from £25pp

Oakwood House Training Centre, Oakwood Park
Maidstone, Kent ME16 8AE
T: 01622 764433 F: 01622 763704
Contact: Conference Manager

Ceremony

This Victorian house, run by Kent County Council, is set in mature parkland, and is about a mile from the centre of Maidstone. It is only available for ceremonies on Saturdays and Sundays, with only one ceremony permitted per day. Ceremonies here must be followed by reception at Oakwood.
Price guide: See below

Reception

Oakwood offers a comprehensive package, starting at £36 per head, which includes room hire, wedding breakfast, sherry on arrival, a glass of wine with the meal and a glass of wine for toasts. Children under 12 are charged at half price, and children under 4 are catered for free.
Catering: from £36pp

KENT

95

Penshurst Place
Penshurst, Kent TN11 8DG
T: 01892 870307 F: 01892 870866
Contact: Terri Scott, Banqueting

Ceremony

Dating from the 16th Century and set in extensive grounds with formal gardens, Penshurst Place is a privately owned house with two rooms licensed to hold wedding ceremonies. The smaller of these seats up to 80 guests. Ceremonies can take place on any day of the week and are restricted to one per day. There is limited wheelchair access.
Price guide: from £300

Reception

While no accommodation is available on the premises, a list of local accommodation can be provided.
Catering: from £30pp

Philpots Manor, Philpots Lane
Hildenborough, TN11 8PG
T & F: 01732 833047 or 0378 658793
Contact: Helen Garvey, Events Manager

Ceremony

This 15th Century Grade II listed manor house was affiliated to Anne Boleyn's estate. It features minstrel's galleried landing, oak panelled rooms, log fire and a four poster wedding suite. There is also a decorative orangery suitable for photo sessions. The Ceremonial Tudor Hall is licensed for ceremonies which can take place here on any day except Christmas Day and Boxing Day.
Price guide: from £500

Reception

All kinds of cuisine is offered. Tudor costumed and themed weddings have taken place here. Other services can be provided such as string quartets, classic cars, hairdressers and even bridesmaids!
Catering: from £20pp

Quex House & Gardens
Quex Park
Birchington-on-Sea CT12 4AG
T: 01843 842168 F: 01843 346661
Contact: Mrs Sarah Vale, Banqueting Manager

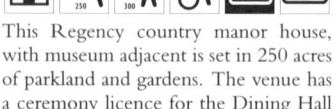

Ceremony

This Regency country manor house, with museum adjacent is set in 250 acres of parkland and gardens. The venue has a ceremony licence for the Dining Hall and the Banqueting Hall. These are available on any day of the year.
Price guide: £250

Reception

The range of buffets available includes a hot fork buffet of homemade spicy and oriental dishes. Helicopters and hot air balloons may use the grounds.
Catering: Buffets from £4.95pp Sit down from £16pp

Read's Restaurant, Painters Forstal
Faversham, Kent ME13 0EE
T: 01795 535344 F: 01795 591200
Contact: Mrs RC Pitchford, Owner

Ceremony

The restaurant is set in a rural location with gardens and views. The restaurant itself is licensed for weddings and ceremonies can take place here on any day of the year, but must be followed by reception at the restaurant.
Price guide: POA

Reception

Read's is the only Michelin starred restaurant in Kent. Helicopters and hot air balloons may use the grounds.
Catering: from £18pp

The Roffen Club
41 New Road, Rochester
Kent ME1 1DY
T: 01634 404770 F: 01634 817664
email: roffen@pipex.dial.com
Contact: Brian Henslow, MD

Ceremony

This private member club has a license for its Roffen Suite, which is available all year except for Christmas and Boxing Day.
Price guide: £1.50pp

Reception

Cake stand and knife, dance area and piped music are all provided free at the Club which offers complete wedding packages with drinks included.
Catering: £27.50pp (package including drinks)

Rowhill Grange
Wilmington
Kent DA2 7QH
T: 01322 615136 F: 01322 615137
Contact: Banqueting Co-ordinator

Ceremony

Extensively refurbished in 1994, Rowhill Grange is a thatched house dating from 1868 and set in 9 acres of woodland and landscaped garden with lake. While ceremonies can take place here any day of the week, these must be followed by reception at the venue. There is an administration cost for the ceremony, then a room hire fee from £500 which covers the reception through to midnight. Two rooms have ceremony licences. Confetti is not permitted.
Price guide: £1.50pp

Reception

While there are 18 bedrooms at the grange, only six of these are allocated to each wedding party.
Catering: from £29.95pp

**Royal Wells Inn
Mount Ephraim
Tunbridge Wells
Kent TN4 8BG**
T: 01892 511188 F: 01892 511908
Contact: Deana Short, Wedding Co-ordinator

Ceremony

Price guide: £200

Reception

Catering: from £15pp

**St Augustines
125 Canterbury Road
Westgate-on-Sea
Kent CT8 8NL**
T: 01709 1000 926 F: 01709 1000 924
email: otani@ndirect.co.uk
Contact: Mass Otani, General Manager

Ceremony

This Grade II listed building set in 11 acres of grounds, is only one mile from the beach. A chapel for up to 400 guest is also on site, and available for blessings. Some Bank Holidays may not be available.
Price guide: £350 + vat

Reception

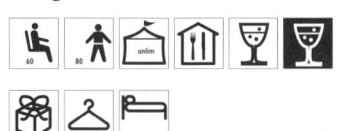

Liquor licences are currently being sought for at this venue. While accommodation is not currently available on the premises, this should be available by the end of 1998.
Catering: from £25pp

**Salomons Centre
David Salomons Estate
Broomhill Road
Tunbridge Wells
Kent TN3 0TG**
T: 01892 515152 F: 01892 539102
Contact: Dawn Ellingham, Sales & Marketing Manager

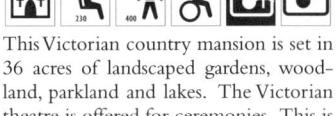

Ceremony

This Victorian country mansion is set in 36 acres of landscaped gardens, woodland, parkland and lakes. The Victorian theatre is offered for ceremonies. This is said to have a cathedral like atmosphere (and even has an organ), and is claimed to be the largest licensed room in Kent. For smaller ceremonies (up to 70), the Gold Room is offered.
Price guide: from £350

Reception

Catering: from £24.45pp

**Sevenoaks Town Council Offices
Bradbourne Vale Road
Sevenoaks, Kent TN13 3Q9**
T: 01732 459953 F: 01732 742577
Contact: Ann White, Admin Asst

Ceremony

The town council offices are newly built. The Chamber is licensed for weddings, and is available on Saturdays and Sundays only.
Price guide: POA

Reception

Receptions cannot be held at the premises, but are held at the community centre nearby. Outside caterers can be used for receptions; hence no price guide.

**Sharsted Court
Newnham, Nr Sittingbourne
Kent ME9 0JU**
T: 01795 890343 F: 01795 890713
Contact: Mrs Judith Shepley, Owner

Ceremony

This stately home is Grade I and II listed and dates from the 12th Century. It features ornamental brick and flint walls, gazebos, and clipped yew trees (including a maze). Ceremonies are held in the Ballroom.
Price guide: £500

Reception

Three rooms are available for receptions: the Ballroom, the Billiard Room and the Front Hall. Couples have a complete choice of caterer; the following prices are offered as a guide to regular caterers at the house.
Catering: Buffets from £7.50pp
Sit down from £20pp

**The Shurland
81 High Street
Eastchurch, Sheppey ME12 4EH**
T: 01795 881100 F: 01795 880906
Contact: Miss Kerry Brown, Manager

Ceremony

This leisure club, hotel and public house offers its Anne Boleyn Suit for ceremonies which can take on any day of the year.
Price guide: £150

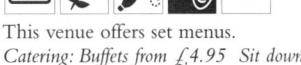

Reception

This venue offers set menus.
Catering: Buffets from £4.95 Sit down from £12.95

Somerhill
Five Oak Green Road
Tonbridge, Kent TN11 0NJ
T: 01732 352124/01732 368398
Contact: Sarah Byrne, Events Manager

Ceremony

This Grade I Jacobean mansion, set in its own gardens, is now a school. It is available for weddings on Saturdays and Sundays and some week days throughout the year. It is not possible to hold ceremonies without a wedding breakfast here. There are two marriage rooms; the Salon and the Grand Hall. The hire charge is for exclusive use of the mansion and grounds.
Price guide: £995 (Summer) £695 (Winter)

Reception

Catering: £21.95pp - £25.99pp

The Spa Hotel
Mount Ephraim
Tunbridge Wells, Kent TN4 8XJ
T: 01892 520331 F: 01892 510575
Contact: David Collier, James Pritchard

Ceremony

Price guide: £250

Reception

Catering: POA

Swallows Leisure Centre
Central Avenue
Sittingbourne, Kent ME10 4NT
T: 01795 420420 F: 01795 431324
Contact: Food & Beverage Manager

Ceremony

The modern Swallows Leisure Centre is situated in the heart of Sittingbourne and offers all round family leisure as well as a suite of function rooms.
Price guide: from £100

Reception

The Centre's Maitre'D has considerable experience of catering for large functions and has catered for the Queen and the Princess of Wales.
Catering: Buffets from £3.50pp Sit down from £12.95pp

Swarling Manor
Petham, Canterbury
Kent CT45 5QW
T & F: 01227 700377
Contact: C Lamb, Owner

Ceremony

This private manor house, dating from 1750 is located in a rural setting with its own 12 self catering cottages. Interestingly, the licensed room here is the Kitchen, which is available any day of the year except Bank Holidays.
Price guide: £250

Reception

There are no reception facilities on site, but couples may appoint their own caterer, with the reception in a marquee.

Tenterden Town Hall
24 High Street
Tenterden
Kent TN30 6AN
T: 01580 762271 F: 01580 765647
Contact: Mrs CA O'Neill, Town Clerk

Ceremony

This Grade II listed 18th Century building is available for an unrestricted number of wedding ceremonies on any day of the week. Confetti is not permitted. There is a £50 price reduction on ceremony facilities for residents.
Price guide: from £150

Reception

Couples need to arrange their own catering at this venue, but suitable function rooms are available. A list of local accommodation can be supplied.

Tonbridge Castle
Castle Street, Tonbridge
Kent TN9 1BG
T: 01732 876333 F: 01732 770449
Contact: Sheila Kostyrka, Tourism and Customer Services Manager

Ceremony

This is a motte and bailey castle, with a 13th Century gatehouse. It is local authority owned and an ancient monument. The marriage room is the Mansion House adjoining the Gatehouse. Ceremonies can take place on any day of the week.
Price guide: £250

Reception

The marriage room can also be used for receptions, but couples must arrange their own catering. There is no accommodation on the premises, but a list of local establishments with which the castle has preferential rate agreements is available on request.

Vale Mascal, 128 North Cray Road, Bexley DA5 3NB
T: 01322 524429
Contact: Roy Grant, Proprietor

Ceremony

This is a 1745 George II manor house in five acres of landscaped grounds which feature a river, ornate bridges, a marble gazebo, swans, etc.. Ceremonies can currently take place here on Saturdays only, but other days will soon become available. There are no reception facilities on the premises
Price guide: £350

**The White Lodge, Loddington Lane, Linton, Maidstone
Kent ME17 4AG**
T & F: 01622 743129
Contact: Merrilyn Boorman, Owner

Ceremony

The White Lodge is a private guest house set in a country house within parkland. Two rooms are licensed for ceremonies and are available any day of the year.
Price guide: £250

Reception

Catering: POA

ALSO LICENSED
*Ashford International Terminal
01233 618501
The Chaucer Hotel   01227 464427
The Coniston Hotel   01795 472131
The County Hotel   01227 766266
Windyridge   01227 263506
Yotes Court   01622 814488*

**The Cornmill Hotel
Mount Pleasant
Holderness Road
Hull HU9 1LA**
T: 01482 589000 F: 01482 586447
Contact: The Duty Manager

Ceremony

This converted mill, situated in the heart of the business community and commercial areas of the city, offers ceremonies seven days a week from 9am to 5pm with no restrictions on the number held per day. No confetti.
Price guide: £250

Reception

The Alexandra Restaurant features original timber beams and cast iron columns. In addition to buffets and special menus, the hotel will strive to meet the religious or dietary requirements of wedding guests. Other services available include room decorations, the provision of stationery, cars, a beautician, balloons and children's entertainment.
Catering: Buffets from £5.75 Sit down from £30pp

**Forte Posthouse Hull Marina
Castle Street
Hull HU1 2BX**
T: 01482 225221   F: 01482 228926
Contact: Xanthe Carmichael, Meetings and Conference Manager

Ceremony

The hotel is based on the marina and has ceremonies available seven days a week with no restrictions on Bank Holidays. The hotel offers a maximum of four ceremonies per day depending on availability, and must be followed by reception at the hotel.
Price guide: £50

Reception

Catering from £22.50

ALSO LICENSED
Quality Royal Hotel   01482 323172

**The Albert Halls
Victoria Square
Bolton BL1 1RU**
T: 01204 543267/8 F: 01204 399928
Contact: Sue Wilkinson, Rene Hall, Sales Executives

Ceremony

The Albert Halls is a Victorian Grade I listed building with two rooms licensed for ceremonies. The smaller of these accommodates 60 people.
Price guide: £100 - £250

Reception

The Halls are a popular venue for Asian weddings.
Price guide: Buffets from £5.75pp. Sit down from £14.50pp

**The Ashton Memorial
Williamson Park
Lancaster LA1 1UX**
T: 01524 33318 F: 01524 33318
Contact: Elaine Charlton, General Manager

Ceremony

The Ashton Memorial, a Grade I listed building, sits within the landscaped gardens of Williamson Park, on the hill overlooking Lancaster. The Ground Floor is licensed for ceremonies and is available on all days except Bank Holidays. A disabled lift was recently installed to facilitate access to the upper floors. Confetti is not permitted.
Price guide: £150 + vat

Reception

Catering: Buffets from 3.50pp

**Astley Hall
Astley Park
Off Hall Gate
Chorley, Lancs PR7 1NP**
T: 01257 515555 F: 01257 232441
Contact: Laura Morris, Administrator

Ceremony

This Grade I listed house dates back to the Elizabethan period, and is set in parkland. The Great Hall and the Dining Room hold licences for weddings which can be held here on any day of the year. Confetti is not permitted.
Price guide: from £150

Reception

Reception facilities are not available on site.

KENT - KINGSTON UPON HULL - LANCASHIRE

LANCASHIRE

Bartle Hall Country Hotel
Lea Lane
Bartle, Nr Preston
Lancs PR4 0HA
T: 01772 690506 F: 01772 690841
Contact: General Manager

Ceremony

Bartle Hall is a Grade II listed building set in 16 acres of landscaped gardens and woodland. Up to three ceremonies are permitted per day.
Price guide: £300

Reception

Bartle Hall's wedding package includes free overnight accommodation for bride and groom as well as full English breakfast, plus a reduced accommodation rate for guests.
Price guide: £8 - £30pp

Beaufort Hotel
High Lane
Burscough
Lancs L40 7SN
T: 01704 892655 F: 01704 895135
Contact: Mike Thompson, General Manager

Ceremony

This is a modern, purpose-built hotel situated in open countryside. The Priory Suite is available for ceremonies on any day except Sundays.
Price guide: £200

Reception

Catering: Buffets from £7.95 Sit down from £14.95

Blackburn Rovers
Ewood Park, Blackburn BB2 4JF
T: 01254 691919 F: 01254 671042
Contact: Carmel Dillon, Conference & Banqueting Manager

Ceremony

The Centenary Suite at the club's stadium is available on any day of the year. Ceremonies here must be followed by reception at the Club. Helicopters and hot air balloons can use the site.
Price guide: £100

Reception

Catering: Buffets from £5.95 Sit down from £15.95

Blackpool Tower Ballroom
Promenade, Blackpool
T: 01253 22242
Contact: Mel Verren

Ceremony

Probably the major landmark in Blackpool, Blackpool Tower is now a Grade I listed building. The Ballroom is licensed for wedding ceremonies for a minimum of 50 guests. In keeping with the ambience of the building, an organist can be provided if required.
Price guide: POA

Reception

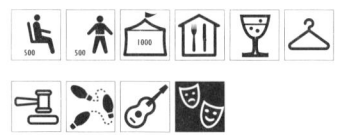

Catering: POA

Blackpool Town Hall
PO Box 77
Blackpool
Lancs FY1 1AD
T: 01253 477150 F: 01253 477101
Contact Mr I Fenton, Senior Administrative Officer

Ceremony

Wedding ceremonies are held in the council chamber of this listed building. The chamber is available from Monday to Friday, but not on Bank Holidays. Confetti is only allowed outside.
Price guide: £50

Reception

No reception facilities are available on site, but a list of local accommodation can be provided.

The Crazy Horse Saloon
Frontierland Theme Park
Marine Road West
Morecambe Bay LA4 4DG
T: 01524 410024 F: 01524 831399
Contact: Sharon Leeson, Marketing Manager

Ceremony

The Crazy Horse Saloon is a western style saloon bar sited in an American theme park. Ceremonies can take place here on any day of the year.
Price guide: from £100

Reception

In keeping with the theme, outdoor barbecues are a speciality at the Saloon. The venue can also provide themed characters such as cowboys and Indians for a truly western style wedding.
Catering: Buffets from £5pp Sit down from £10pp

The Dunkenhalgh Hotel
Blackburn Road
Clayton-le-Moors
Accrington
Lancs BB5 5JP
T: 01254 398021 F: 01254872230
Contact: Gill Sith, Conference Director

Ceremony

The Dunkenhalgh Hotel is a Grade II listed building offering five ceremony rooms. These are available on any day of

100

the year, but ceremonies here must be followed by reception at the hotel.
Price guide: £50

Reception

Several all-inclusive menus are offered, with choices within each price bracket. Wedding guests are offered discounts on overnight accommodation.
Catering: Buffets from £7pp Sit down from £24.50pp

The Farington Lodge
Stanifield Lane
Farington, Leyland
Lancs PR5 2QR
T: 01772 421321 F: 01772 455388
Contact: Steph Brewer,
Events/Banqueting Manager

Ceremony

The Farington Lodge is a listed building set in gardens. The Victoria Room, Royal Room and Garden Room are all available for ceremonies on any day of the year. They have limited wheelchair access. Ceremonies here must be followed by reception at the Lodge.
Price guide: £150

Reception

Catering: POA

Fence Gate Inn
Wheatley Lane Road
Fence, Burnley BB12 9EE
T: 01282 618101 F: 01282 615432
Contact: Mr Kevin Berkins, MD

Ceremony

Two licensed rooms are available in this listed building. Ceremonies here must be followed by reception on the premises.
Price guide: POA

Reception

Catering: Buffets from £6pp. Sit down from £16pp.

Foxfields Country Hotel
Whalley Road
Billington
Clitheroe, Lancs BB7 9HY
T: 01254 822556 F: 01254 824613
contact: Mike G Hill, GM

Ceremony

This is an AA 4-star hotel and part of the Lyric Hotel group. Ceremonies can take place in the Pendle Suite or the boardroom on any day of the year, but must be followed by reception at the hotel.
Price guide: FOC

Reception

Helicopters and hot air balloons may use the hotel grounds.
Catering: from £19.25pp

Gibbon Bridge Hotel
Forest of Bowland
Nr Chipping, Preston
Lancs PR3 2TQ
T: 01995 61456 F: 01995 61277
Contact: Janet Simpson, MD

Ceremony

The Gibbon Bridge Hotel is set in award-winning grounds overlooking the Longridge Fells in the heart of the Forest of Bowland. Ceremonies can be held in the Garden Room or in the Garden Bandstand. Both seat up to 25 seated guests, and have patio areas for further guests to congregate. The hotel also offers honeymoons suites.
Price guide: £250

Reception

Catering: from £20pp

Harris Park Conference Centre
253 Garstang Road, Preston
Lancs PR2 9XB
T: 01772 717621 F: 01772 787243
contact: Roz Goodwin, Asst Manager or Jacqui Hateley, Manager

Ceremony

The conference centre is a Victorian building set in 15 acres of grounds. The Main Hall and Conservatory Bar are licensed for ceremonies which can take place here on any day of the year.
Price guide: £200

Reception

In addition to the above services, the centre can provide decorative balloons.
Catering: Buffets from £5.99pp sit down from £15pp

Higher Trapp
Country House Hotel
Trapp Lane
Simonstone
Lancs
T: 01282 772781 F: 01282 772782
Contact: Warren Marsh, Banqueting

Ceremony

Price guide: P.O.A.

LANCASHIRE

101

LANCASHIRE

Reception

Catering: P.O.A.

Horncliffe Mansions
Bury Road
Rawtenstall
Lancs
BB4 6JS
T: 01706 213093 F: 01706 222929
Contact: Owner

Ceremony

Price guide: P.O.A.

Reception

Catering: P.O.A.

Inn at Whitewell
Forest of Bowland
Nr Clitheroe
Lancs
BB7 3AT
T: 01200 448222
F: 01200 448298
Contact: Jonty Haighton, Partner

Ceremony

Price guide: £100

Reception

Catering: £17.50 - £22pp

Leigh Town Hall
Market Street
Wigan, Lancs
T: 01942 672421
Contact: Halls Manager

Ceremony

Price guide: P.O.A.

Reception

Unfortunately, there are no reception facilities available at Leigh Town Hall. However, wedding receptions can be held nearby at the adjacent Derby Rooms, although separate arrangements will have to be made for ceremony and reception.
For full details of the reception packages that are available at The Derby Rooms, you should telephone 01942 244991.
Catering: P.O.A.

Leyland Masonic Hall
Wellington Park
Burlington Gardens
Church Road
Leyland, Lancs
T: 01772 432881 F: 01772 453151
Contact: General Manager

Ceremony

This modern building, dating from the late 1980s, has four licensed rooms, which are available seven days per week. Ceremonies and receptions must both be held at the hall. Confetti is allowed. A local accommodation list is available, including preferential rates.
Price guide: F.O.C. (with reception)

Reception

Price guide: from £12.75pp (package)

Mains Hall
Mains Lane
Little Singleton
Poulton-le-Fylde, Lancs FY6 7LE
T: 01253 885130 F: 01253 894132
Contact: R Yeomans, Proprietor

Ceremony

This was once the home of Prince Regent George IV and is a Grade II listed house built in 1536. It is set in five acres of grounds, with private access to the River Wyre. There are formal walled gardens, featuring old walnut trees, orchards and an ornamental fountain. Two rooms are available for ceremonies: the oak panelled hall, with room for 40 guests, and the Royal Garden Room, which can accommodate up to 150.
Price guide: from £60

Reception

The house has a recently refurbished dining room overlooking the river. For the catering, a discount of 50% is offered for children under 12 years old, while no charge is made for children under 2 years old. A complimentary four-poster suite is offered if all the hotel rooms are booked for the wedding guests.
Catering: from £28pp

Mawdesley's Eating House
Hall Lane, Mawdesley
Nr Ormskirk, Lancs L40 2QZ
T: 01704 822552 F: 01704 822096
Contact: Michael Gilroy, GM

Ceremony

This former basket works is set in the village of Mawdesley which was recently voted Lancashire's Best Kept Village. Two rooms are licensed for ceremonies and are available any day of the year.
Price guide: £50

Reception

Catering: Sit down from 14pp

102

LANCASHIRE

The Mill at Croston
Moor Road, Croston, Lancs
T: 01772 600110 F: 01772 601623
Contact: Max Pierce, GM

Ceremony

The Mill was originally a farm building that has now been converted to a 46 bedroom hotel with restaurant, bar and banqueting complex. Two suites are licensed for ceremonies.
Price guide: £100

Reception

Catering: Sit down from £14.95pp

Mytton Fold Farm Hotel
Whalley Road
Blackburn
Lancs
BB6 8BE
T: 01254 240662 F: 01254 248119
Contact: Mrs Lillian Hargreaves, owner

Ceremony

Set in its own grounds with gardens, featuring a gazebo, and 18 hole golf course Mytton Fold Farm is a privately owned hotel which allows only one ceremony at a time on any day of the week.
Price guide: £150

Reception

The hotel has five rooms suitable for wedding receptions, but will only accept two wedding parties at any one time; these could be for parties as small as 10 guests. The wedding package includes complimentary bridal suite for the wedding night. Flowers, cake stand and knife, piped music and a stage can all be provided free of charge; other services extra.
Catering: £16

North Euston Hotel
The Esplanade
Fleetwood, Lancs
T: 01253 876525
Contact: Hilary Johns, Partner

Ceremony

Price guide: P.O.A.

Reception

Catering: P.O.A.

Northcote Manor
Northcote Road
Langho
Lancs BB6 8BE
T: 01254 240555 F: 01254 246568
Contact: Craig J Bancroft, GM

Ceremony

This is a small country house hotel, and winner of the Good Hotel Guide's Country Hotel of the Year for 1995. It has been owned and run by Craig Bancroft and Nigel Haworth since 1983. The Northcote Hotel, which is situated in the Ribble Valley, limits ceremonies to one a day, on any day except Christmas Day and Boxing Day.
Price guide: £200

Reception

Northcote's Chef Patron, Nigel Haworth won Egon Ronay's Chef of the Year for 1995. His cuisine is described as 'British cookery with modern tones', and includes many Lancashire specialities.
Catering: £25-£30pp

Oaks Hotel
Colne Road, Reedley
Burnley
Lancs BB10 2LF
T: 01282 414141 F: 01282 33401
Contact: Tina Ostler, Banqueting Manager

Ceremony

The Oaks is a Victorian style Grade II listed building featuring a stained glass window in the main lounge. The hotel stands in four acres at the foot of Pendle Hill. Two ceremonies are allowed per day on any day of the week.
Price guide: £150

Reception

While accommodation is available on the premises, the hotel also has preferential rate agreements with other hotels.
Catering: from £6.50

Olde England Kiosk
Sunnyhurst Wood
Darwen BB3 0LA
T: 01254 701530
Contact: Mr B Winder, Owner

Ceremony

This curiously named venue is a listed building built in the mock Tudor style. It is situated in 25 acres of woodland with ornamental lakes and waterfalls. The Tudor Rom is licensed and available on any day except Christmas Day, Boxing Day and New Year's Eve. Ceremonies here must be followed by reception at the venue.
Price guide: POA

Reception

Catering: Buffets from £4.25pp. Sit down from £12pp

Park Hall Hotel, Charnock Richard, Chorley PR7 5LP
T: 01257 452090 F: 01257 451838
Contact: Alison Wilcock, Wedding Co-ordinator

103

LANCASHIRE

Ceremony

Park Hall is set in 137 acres of grounds featuring a scenic lake. A wedding licence is held for the medieval banqueting hall, and ceremonies can be held here on any day except Sunday. Ceremonies must be followed by reception at the hotel.
Price guide: £120

Reception

Helicopters and hot air balloons may use the hotel grounds. For those looking for a period feeling, however, the hotel can offer a full medieval banquet with full entertainment.
Catering: Buffets from £9.95pp Sit down from £14.95pp.

Pickering Park Country House
Catterall, Garstang
Preston PR3 0HD
T: 01995 600999 F: 01995 602100
email: hotel@pickeringpark.demon.co.uk
Contact: Jim Farrimond, Partner

Ceremony

This country house is set in two acres of rural Lancashire parkland. Two rooms are licensed for ceremonies.
Price guide: P.O.A.

Reception

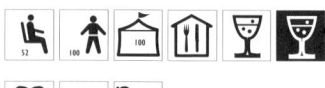

This venue offers the 'finest world wide cuisine, classically prepared'.
Catering: Buffets from £9pp. Sit down from £23pp

Pines Hotel
Preston Road, Chorley PR6 7ED
T: 01772 338551 F: 01772 629002
Contact: Clare Seefus, General Manager

Ceremony

Price guide: P.O.A.

Reception

Catering: P.O.A.

The Preston Marriott
Garstang Road
Broughton
Preston PR3 5YB
T: 01772 864087 F: 01772 861327
Contact: Jane Jameson, Executive Meetings Manager

Ceremony

The Marriott is set in 11 acres of gardens and woodlands and has a Victorian facade. Three rooms are licensed for ceremonies and are available any day of the year.
Price guide: £175 - £300

Reception

Catering: £12.50 - £31

The Priory Wood Beefeater
Orrell Road, Orrell
Wigan, Lancs WN5 8HQ
T: 01942 211516 F: 01942 215002
Contact: Colin Broadhurst, General Manager

Ceremony

This Beefeater is housed in a listed building. Ceremonies can take place in the Orrell Suite on any day of the year.
Price guide: FOC with reception

Reception

Catering: Buffets from £7.50pp. Sit down from £14.95pp.

Queen Elizabeth Hall
PO Box 66 West Street
Oldham OL1 1YT
T: 0161 911 4071 F: 0161 911 3094
Contact: Shelagh Malley, Systems and Administration Manager

Ceremony

This civic building is located in the centre of town, only five minutes from the M62 and 20 minutes from the centre of Manchester. The Chadderton Suite is available for ceremonies on any day except Christmas Day and Boxing Day.
Price guide: £POA

Reception

Numerous services can be recommended.
Catering: £12.50 - £31

Rosehill House Hotel
Rosehill Avenue
Burnley
Lancs BB11 2PW
T: 01282 453031 F: 01282 455628
Contact: Jacky Doherty, Proprietor

Ceremony

This listed stone mansion features ornate architecture, including highly decorative ceilings. The two restaurants have ceremony licences. While the maximum capacity in these is currently 50, this will double by Spring this year. Weddings can take place here on any day except Sundays, but must be followed by reception at the hotel.
Price guide: FOC

LANCASHIRE

Reception

Reception capacities will also double from Spring 1997, when live music and entertainment will also be a possibility at this venue.
Catering: Buffets from £7.50pp Sit down from £19.50pp

Savoy Hotel
Queens Promenade
Blackpool FY2 9JS
T: 01253 352561 F: 01253 500735
Contact: Lisa Maunder, Sales Manager

Ceremony

The Savoy is currently the only hotel on the Promenade to hold a wedding licence. Four rooms are licensed and are suitable for a minimum capacity of 50 guests.
Price guide: from £50 - £250

Reception

If a minimum of £7.50 per head is spent on catering, the ceremony room hire fee is waived.
Catering: Buffets from £5.95pp Sit down from £14.95pp

Scaitcliffe Hall Hotel
Burnley Road
Todmorden OL14 7DQ
T: 01706 818888 F: 01706 818825
Contact: Hugh Carruthers, Manager

Ceremony

The Garden Room is licensed in this 17th Century listed country house set in 16 acres of landscaped grounds. Ceremonies can take place here on any day except Sunday.
Price guide: £40

Reception

Brass bands are a speciality at this hotel, which also offers 'the best of modern British cuisine'.
Catering: Buffets from £4.95pp Sit down from £16.95pp

Shaw Hill Hotel
Preston Road, Whittle Le Woods
Chorley PR6 7PP
T: 01257 269221 F: 01257 261223
Contact: Mrs B Welding, Conference & Banqueting Co-ordinator

Ceremony

This is a Georgian mansion set in 92 acres of parkland. The Vice-President's Lounge and the Penina Suite are licensed and are available any day of the year.
Price guide: POA

Reception

The restaurant here was recently awarded Lancashire Life Restaurant of the Year Award for 1997.
Catering: Buffets from £7pp Sit down from £17pp

The Shireburn Arms Hotel
Hurst Green, Clitheroe BB7 9QY
T: 01254 826518 F: 01254 826208
Contact: Steven Alcock, General Manager/Director

Ceremony

The Shireburn Arms is a Grade I listed building dating from the 16th Century, and claims unrivalled views over the Ribble Valley. The Ribble Room and Conservatory are available for ceremonies on any day of the year, but ceremonies here must be followed by a reception at the venue.
Price guide: £85

Reception

Drinks packages start at £5.45pp.
Catering: Buffets from £6.50pp Sit down from £13.95pp

Smithills Coaching House
Smithills Dean Road
Bolton BL1 7NR
T: 01204 840377 F: 01204 844442
Contact: Mrs Fairclough, Office Manager

Ceremony

This Grade I listed building was originally the stables of the nearby Smithills Hall which dates back to the early 17th Century. The Hunting Lodge and the Stables Room are licensed and are available on all days except Saturdays. Ceremonies here must be followed by reception at the venue.
Price guide: POA

Reception

Smithills provides a comprehensive brochure on the venue, including visuals of possible room layouts.
Catering: Buffets from £7.95pp Sit down from £10.95pp

Sparth House Hotel
Whalley Road, Clayton-Le-Moors
Accrington BB5 5RP
T & F: 01254 872263
Contact: Victoria Taylor, PA to owner

105

LANCASHIRE

Ceremony

The Sparth House is a listed building (1740) featuring period interiors and gardens. The Oak Room and Regency Room are licensed and ceremonies may take place here on any day of the year except Christmas Day. Helicopters and hot air balloons may use the grounds.
Price guide: POA

Reception

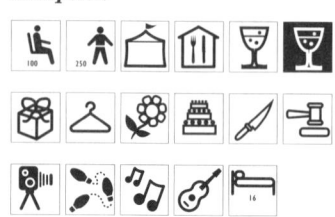

Catering: Buffets from £6pp. Sit down from £16pp.

Springfield House Hotel
Wheel Lane
Pilling, Nr Preston
Lancs PR3 6HL
T: 01253 790301 F: 01253 790907
Contact: Mrs M E Cookson, Proprietor

Ceremony

Two rooms are available for wedding ceremonies in this Grade II listed Georgian building set within walled gardens. Ceremonies are restricted to one per day, on any day except Sunday.
Price guide: £150

Reception

Table decorations form part of the reception package at Springfield. The hotel can also provide a list of other accommodation available locally.
Catering: £18.50pp

Stirk House Hotel
Gisburn, Nr Clitheroe BB7 4LJ
T: 01200 445581 F: 01200 445744
Contact: Mr M Weaving

Ceremony

Originally a 16th Century manor house, Stirk House is located six miles from Clitheroe. The hotel has landscaped gardens to the front. Up to two ceremonies are allowed at the venue per day.
Price guide: £100

Reception

Catering: £12.50 - £31

The Strathmore Hotel
East Parade, Morecambe LA4 5AP
T: 01524 421234 F: 01524 414242
Contact: Christine Poole, Sales Manager

Ceremony

This hotel has a seafront location and boasts views over Morecambe Bay to the Lakeland Fells. Two rooms are licensed and are available any day of the year. Ceremonies here must be followed by reception at the hotel.
Price guide: £100

Reception

Catering: Buffets from £6.25pp. Sit down from £12pp

The Tickled Trout
Preston New Road
Salmesbury PR5 0LJ
T: 01772 877671 F: 01772463
Contact: Rachel Waters, Banqueting

Ceremony

This hotel enjoys a riverside location with grounds featuring a fountain and kissing arch. The Rainbow and Ribble Suites are licensed for ceremonies which can take place here any day of the year.
Price guide: £50

Reception

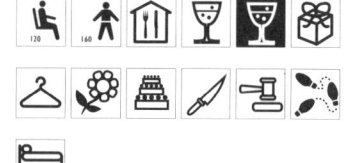

Catering: Buffets from £7.75pp Sit down from £14.95pp

West Tower Country Hotel
Mill Lane, Aughton
Ormskirk L39
T: 01695 423328
Contact: Mrs Brenda Williams, Functions Manager

Ceremony

Once the home of a Liverpool shipping magnate, and built in 1785, West Tower has recently been fully restored and now offers its Talbot Room for ceremonies. Ceremonies can take place here on any day except Bank Holidays.
Price guide: POA

Reception

Drinks packages start at £7.50pp
Catering: Buffets from £6.95pp Sit down from £17.50pp

Whoop Hall Inn
Burrow with Burrow
Kirby Lonsdale
Carnforth
T: 015242 71284 F: 015242 72154
Contact: Elaine Dean, GM

Ceremony

The Inn offers its Lonsdale Suite and Ruskin Room for ceremonies which can take place here on any day of the

year. There is good wheelchair access to the Lonsdale Suite.
Price guide: POA

Reception

Helicopters and hot air balloons may use the grounds.
Catering: Buffets from £5.95pp Sit down from £13pp

STOP PRESS
Bowers Hotel   01995 602120
Burnley Friendly Hotel   01282 427611
Celebrations, Kirkham   01772 671111
Hampson House Hotel   01524 751158
Marine Hall, Fleetwood   01253 771141
The Paradise Room   01253 341033
Seabank Hotel   01253 22717
Whitewalls Restaurant   01524 822768

Barnsdale Country Club
Barnsdale, Exton
Leics LE15 8AB
T: 01572 757901   F: 01572 756235
Contact: Jane Downs (Tel: 01572 722209)

Ceremony

This hotel and restaurant is also a club and time share site. The Club is set in a 60 acre estate of gardens and woodland on the shores of Rutland Water. Wheelchair access is limited.
Price guide: £150

Reception

The Club offers a choice of rooms for receptions, including one that overlooks Rutland Water.
Catering: from £13.50pp

Barnsdale Lodge Hotel
The Avenue, Rutland Water
Oakham, Leics LE15 8AH
T: 01572 724678   F: 01572 724961
Contact: John Farrington   GM

Ceremony

The hotel offers two marriage rooms: the Barn Suite (max 220 seated) and the Conservatory (max 50 seated). Weddings can take place here any day of the year.
Price guide: £100 + vat

Reception

Catering: from £15pp

Beaumanor Hall
Woodhouse, Loughborough
Leics LE12 8TX
T: 01509 890119   F: 01509 891021
Contact: Liz Funnell, Accommodation Officer

Ceremony

The Hall was originally built in the 1840s for a wealthy landowner. It was purchased by Leicestershire County Council in 1974 as a training and conference centre for council employees. Features include ornate ceilings, wood carvings and elaborate stone and plaster work. There is also a galleries central hall with sweeping staircase and stained glass windows. Ceremonies and receptions are usually packaged.

Reception

While there is no accommodation available on the premises, a list of local establishments with which the Hall has preferential rate agreements can be supplied on request.
Catering: Buffets from £4.70pp sit down from £15.50pp

Belmont House Hotel
De Montfort Street
Leicester LE1 7GR
T: 0116 2544773
Contact: Sally Summerscales, Conference & Banqueting

Ceremony

Several rooms at this Best Western Hotel are licensed for ceremonies taking from 6 to 75 guests. Weddings can take place here on any day except Sundays and Bank Holidays. Ceremonies must be followed by a reception at the hotel.
Price guide: from £150

Reception

Catering: from £20pp

The Castle Hotel
Main Street, Kirby Muxloe
Leicester LE9 2AP
T: 0116 239 5337   F: 0116 238 7868
Contact: Mr T Doblander, GM

Ceremony

The Castle Hotel is set in a quiet village, just four miles from Leicester city centre. At the back of the hotel is the remains of a 14th Century castle, with wooden bridge (a suitable location for photographs). The hotel also has large award-winning gardens. Helicopters and hot air balloons may use the grounds. Ceremonies can take place in the Hastings Suite on any day except Sunday, Christmas Day and New Year's Day. At weekends, ceremonies should be followed by a reception at the hotel.

Reception

Cuisine at the hotel is described as 'English/Continental'.
Catering: From £19.50pp

LANCASHIRE - LEICESTERSHIRE

107

LEICESTERSHIRE

Charmwood Arms Hotel
Beveridge Lane
Bardon, Coalville
Leics LE67 2TB
T: 01530 813644 F: 01530 815425
Contact: Jim Conway GM

Ceremony

This modern, recently refurbished, hotel and public house offers wedding ceremonies on any day of the week, but limits these to one per day. It is not possible to hold the ceremony here without the reception.
Price guide: FOC (with wedding breakfast and evening function)

Reception

Catering: from £15pp

Hambleton Hall
Hambleton
Oakham, Rutland
Leics LE15 8TH
T: 01572 756991 F: 01572 724721
Contact: Sue Perkin, House Manger

Ceremony

Hambleton has a starred Michelin restaurant and is a member of the Relais & Chateaux collection of exclusive hotels. It was originally built in 1881 as a hunting box, and has views over Rutland Water. Three rooms are licensed for ceremonies; The Study (max 12 people), the Private Dining Room (max 20 people) and The Restaurant (max 40 people).
Price guide: from £250

Reception

The head chef here is Aaron Patterson. Professional service and an interesting selection of wines are boasted as top priorities at this friendly hotel.
Catering: from £35pp

Hotel St James
Abbey Street
Leicester LE1 3TE
T: 0116 251 0666 F: 0116 575 183
Contact: Heather Doldie

Ceremony

This modern city centre hotel offers one marriage room; the French Suite. Weddings can take place here on any day except Christmas Day, with only one ceremony per day.
Price guide: £100

Reception

A complimentary room is provided for bride and groom to change in during the day.
Catering: from £12.50pp

Leicester City Football Club
City Stadium
Filbert Street
Leicester LE2 7FL
T: 0116 291 5000 F: 0116 247 0585
Contact: Nickie Howard,
Conference Development Manager

Ceremony

Team supporters will be delighted that the Club is now licensed for wedding ceremonies. These can take place in the Boardroom or the Bradgate Suite on any day except when matches are played at home. Photos can, of course, be taken on the pitch, and the Club can arrange for a player to be present.
Price guide: £180

Reception

The Club has established banqueting facilities, and says it can be very flexible, depending upon requirements.
Catering: from £15pp

Leicester Town Hall
Town Hall Square
Leicester
T: 0116 254 9922 F: 0116 285 5681
Contact: Andrew Bubb, Administration Buildings Manager

Ceremony

Whilst the City Council holds a licence to hold civil wedding ceremonies at Leicester Town Hall, bookings for wedding are not currently being taken as possible building and refurbishment worked is planned. Contact the property services division for an update.

Leicestershire Museum
& Art Gallery
New Walk, Leicester LE1 1EA
T: 0116 255 4100 F: 0116 247 3005
Contact: Mrs Helene Kelly, Commercial Services Officer

Ceremony

This is a major regional museum and art gallery featuring local and national collections including many romantic Victorian fine art pieces. Ceremonies can take place in the Victorian Gallery on any day except Sunday, and Bank Holidays. Confetti is not permitted.
Price guide: £155

Reception
There are no reception facilities on site.

Melton Mowbray Council Offices
Nottingham Road
Melton Mowbray
Leics LE12 8TX
T: 01664 67771 F: 01664 410283
Contact: Chief Technical Officer

Ceremony

Three marriage rooms are offered for weddings at the council offices; the

Council Chamber (up to 250), the Egerton Room (up to 80) and the Warwick Room (up to 40). Weddings can take place on any day except Bank Holidays.
Price guide: POA

Reception
There are no reception facilities at the offices.

Normanton Park Hotel
Rutland Water, South Shore
Oakham, Leics LE15 8RP
T: 01780 720315   F: 01780 721086
Contact: General Manager

Ceremony

The hotel was originally the stable block to the Georgian Normanton Manor House. It is only 50 yards from the edge of Rutland Water and set in five acres of parkland. Weddings can take place here on any day of the year.
Price guide: £100

Reception

A late night drinking licence can be applied for if required. Catering arrangements are flexible.
Catering: from £32pp

Noseley Hall
Billesdon LE7 9EH
T: 0116 259 6487   F: 0116 259 6989
Contact: Mr A G Hazlerigg

Ceremony

This Grade II listed building has been home to the Hazlerigg family since 1419. It has its own 12th Century chapel in the grounds which can be used for blessings. Ceremonies, in the Drawing Room or the Library, can take place on any day except Sundays and certain Saturdays between November 1st and February 1st.
Price guide: no charge at present

Reception

Catering: From £25pp

Oakham Castle
Market Place
Oakham, Leics LE15 6JW
T: 01572 732654   F: 01572 757576
Contact: Mr Tim Clough, Keeper

Ceremony

This 12th Century scheduled ancient monument is Grade I listed and houses the Court of Justice on a Monday - hence no ceremonies allowed on this day. Christmas Day, Boxing Day and New Year's Day are also not available. Two rooms have marriage licences; The Great Hall, adorned with over 200 presentation horseshoes!, and the Court Room (30 people max). While there is reasonable disabled access, there are no disabled toilet facilities. Confetti is not permitted.
Price guide: Tues-Sat £145 Sunday or Bank Holiday £175.

Reception
There are no reception facilities at the Castle.

The Olde Stocks Restaurant
Main Street, Grimston
Melton Mowbray LE14 3BZ
T: 01664 812255   F: 01664 813800
email: http://www.country-focus.co.uk
Contact: Penni Harrison, Owner

Ceremony

This Ackerman Guide recommended restaurant has a licence for its lounge, which is available on any day of the year for ceremonies.
Price guide: £100

Reception

Bride and groom often arrive at this venue by horse and carriage, and have also arrived by helicopter. Wedding parties can take over the whole of the restaurant and be entertained to a seven course meal and wine from a selection of over 60 bins.
Catering: Buffets from £15pp. Sit down from £20pp

Prestwold Hall
Prestwold
Loughborough
Leics LE12 5SQ
T: 01509 880236   F: 01636 812187
Contact: Annabel Weldon, GM

Ceremony

Prestwold Hall was largely remodelled in 1843 and has been in the Packe family for 350 years. It is now a conference centre, still owned by a descendant of the Packe family and not open to the general public. Ceremonies take place on any day except Christmas Day and must be followed by a reception at the house.
Price guide: £150

Reception

The Hall offers home-made food using home grown ingredients where possible.
Catering: from £21pp

Quality Friendly Hotel
New Ashby Road
Loughborough,
Leics LE11 0EX
T: 01509 211800 F: 01509 21868
Contact: Conference & Banqueting Manager

Ceremony

This modern hotel offers weddings in the Beaumanor Suite, which comprises four rooms. It is not possible to hold ceremonies here without also booking the reception facilities. Confetti is not permitted. Outdoor photography is limited.
Price guide: no charge at present

LEICESTERSHIRE

109

LEICESTERSHIRE

Reception

A late night drinking licence can be applied for if required. Kosher and Asian caterers can be permitted on discussion with the hotel.
Catering: buffets from £6.75pp Sit down from £14.45pp

Quorn Country Hotel
66 Leicester Road, Quorn
Loughborough, Leics LE12 8BB
T: 01509 415050 F: 01509 415557
Contact: Debby Robinson, Sales Manager or Heather Brewin, Sales Executive

Ceremony

This hotel and restaurant permits one ceremony per day on any day.
Price guide: POA

Reception

The hotel has been awarded two AA Rosettes for the quality of its cuisine.
Catering: POA

Sketchley Grange Hotel
Sketchley Lane
Burbage
Hinckley
Leics LE10 3HU
T: 01455 251133 F: 01455 631384
Contact: Sales Manager

Ceremony

The hotel permits up to two ceremonies per day on any day of the year.
Price guide: £300

Reception

Several rooms are available for receptions, including the Bradgate Suite, with its own bar, lounge and foyer; the Willow Room (up to 100 guests), overlooking the garden; and the Warwick Room (up to 50 guests). The catering has recently received an AA Rosette.
Catering: from £16pp

Stage Hotel
299 Leicester Road
Wigston Fields LE18 1JW
T: 0116 288 6161 F: 0116 281 1874
Contact: Michelle Warner, Sales Manager

Ceremony

The Stage Hotel is situated south of the city centre near to the ring road. Two rooms are licensed; the Knighton Suite (up to 50 guests), and the Oadby Suite (up to 100 guests). The price guide allows for one hour's use. There is an additional charge of £50 per half hour for any extra time required. Ceremonies can take place on any day except Sunday.
Price guide: POA

Reception

Asian weddings can be catered for at the hotel. A 10% discount is given for all Monday to Friday, or Sunday wedding receptions.
Catering POA

Stapleford Park Country House Hotel, Stapleford
Melton Mowbray
Leics LE14 2EF
T: 01572 787522 F: 01572 787332
Contact: Mrs Annabel Eley, Wedding & Banqueting Co-ordinator

Ceremony

This well-known Grade II listed build-

---

ing, is set in grounds designed by Capability Brown. The Drawing Room (max 50) and the Morning Room (max 20) are available for ceremonies on any day of the year except Christmas and New Year. Receptions at the hotel must follow ceremonies here. Confetti is not permitted.
Price guide: from £250 + vat

Reception

Helicopters and hot air balloons may use the grounds of the hotel.
Catering: from £35pp

The Three Swans Hotel
High Street
Market Harborough
Leics LE16 7NJ
T: 01858 466644 F: 01858 433101
Contact: General Manager

Ceremony

Up to two ceremonies per day are permitted at this 16th Century coaching inn. These can take place in the Cygnet Room on any day except Good Friday and Christmas Day. Some assistance would be required with wheelchairs.
Price guide: from £85

Reception

The hotel can offer a selection of well-presented banqueting menus. As well as the above service, the hotel can offer personalised menus, a 'good luck' token and bedrooms with four poster beds.
Catering: from £16.85pp

ALSO LICENSED
Donnington Manor Hotel 01332 810253
Fernie Lodge Hotel 01858 880551
Hermitage Park Hotel 01530 814814
Quorn Grange Hotel 01509 412167

Brackenborough Arms Hotel
Cordeaux Corner
Brackenborough
Louth, Lincolnshire LN11 0SZ
T: 01507 609169   F: 01507 609413
Contact: Rosemary, Duty Manageress

Ceremony

The hotel is situated in the heart of the Lincolnshire Wolds in its own landscaped grounds. Ceremonies are available seven days a week.
Price guide: £175

Reception

Catering is in-house and the hotel prides itself on 35 years of cuisine experience. Although the hotel can not provide the wedding cake and photography themselves, they can organise them externally.
Catering: from £12pp

Comfort Friendly Inn
Bicker Bar Roundabout
Boston, Lincolnshire PE20 3AN
T: 01205 820118   F: 01205 820228
Contact: Chris Crowfoot

Ceremony

This modern building built in 1993 is situated in limited grounds and is available to hold ceremonies seven days a week on any day of the year excluding Christmas Day and New Year's Eve. It is possible to hold your wedding ceremony without a reception at the Comfort Friendly Inn.
Price guide: POA

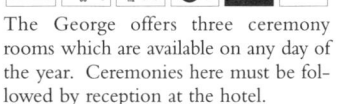

Reception

Catering is in-house and, although there is no area available to display wedding gifts, there is a room for the bride and groom to change in.
Catering: from £7pp.

Elsham Hall Barn Theatre
Elsham Hall Country Park
Brigg, Lincs DN20 0QZ
T: 01652 688698   F: 01652 688240
Contact: Mr R Elwes, Manager

Ceremony

Elsham Hall Barn is a medieval banqueting hall set in lakeside gardens. The theatre and two restaurants are licensed and are available on any day except Bank Holidays.
Price guide: £200

Reception

This venue has specialised in Viking and Medieval feasts, but has also held weddings with a Hollywood, country style, English folklore and even a wartime theme.
Catering: from £16.50pp

Fydell House
South Square, Boston PE21 6HU
T: 01205 351520   F: 01205 358363
Contact: David Jones, Christine Wright, Julie Smith

Ceremony

This is a university adult education centre set in a Grade I listed building. The 18th Century house is set in the centre of town and has its own gardens.
Two rooms (American and Green) are licensed for weddings and are available on any day of the year, but booking are usually easier for out of term time.
Price guide: £60

Reception

Couples need to provide their own caterer for this venue, but may use the kitchens on site.

The George Hotel
71 High Street
St Martins, Stamford PE9 2LB
T: 01780 755171   F: 01780 757070
Contact: Wedding Co-ordinator

Ceremony

The George offers three ceremony rooms which are available on any day of the year. Ceremonies here must be followed by reception at the hotel.
Price guide: POA

Reception

Catering: from £16.50pp

The Habrough Hotel
Station Road
Habrough DN40 3AY
T: 01469 576940   F: 01469 577792
Contact: Mrs Wendy Barnbrook, Banqueting Manager

Ceremony

Ceremonies in this hotel can take place in the Conference Suite or the Hotel Lobby on any day of the year.
Price guide: £150

Reception

Catering: From £17pp

Golf Hotel
The Broadway
Woodhall Spa
**Lincolnshire
LN10 6SG**
T: 01526 353535   F: 01526 353096
Contact: Rose Thomson, Deputy Manager

LINCOLNSHIRE

LINCOLNSHIRE

Ceremony

This Tudor-style building is set in seven acres of grounds and features a terraced area to the front of the hotel. Ceremonies are available seven days a week excluding Christmas Day and Boxing Day, with two permitted per day.
Price guide: £150

Reception

Catering costs range from £4.25 to a maximum of £16.95pp. Children under five years of age are catered for free of charge while those aged between five and 12 are half price. The couple is offered a complimentary bridal suite, while special room rates are available for wedding guests. In addition to the services indicated, the hotel is happy to organise celebratory fireworks. The rear lawn is suitable to act as a helicopter landing pad.
Catering: Buffets from £4.25pp Sit down from £23pp

The Judge's Lodgings
Castle Hill, Lincoln LN1 3AA
T: 01522 511068 F: 01522 512150
Contact: Peter Allen, Manager

Ceremony

This historic building, located between Lincoln Castle and the Cathedral, is still used as the Judge's lodging when the Judge is sitting at the Crown Courts. The Sitting Room is licensed for ceremonies and is available every day of the year.
Price guide: £200

Reception

Catering: From £18.50pp

Kenwick Park
Hotel & Leisure Club
Kenwick Park, Louth
Lincolnshire LN11 8NR
T: 01507 608806 F: 01507 608027
Contact: Craig Dowie, GM

Ceremony

This country house is set in 500 acres of grounds and allows a maximum of three ceremonies per day.
Price guide: £250

Reception

Catering costs average between £15 and £40pp. The hotel offers a full honeymoon package including accommodation in the luxury suite at an additional cost of £65 providing the reception is also held at the hotel.
Catering: from £15pp.

North Shore Hotel
North Shore Road
Skegness PE25 1DN
T: 01754 763298 F: 01754 761902
Contact: Mr Nigel Dorman, General Manager

Ceremony

The hotel is by the seaside and surrounded by a golf course. The Braid Bar and St Andrews Suite Restaurant are licensed.
Price guide: POA

Reception

Children can be catered for separately if required.
Catering: Buffets from £5.25pp. Sit down from £8.95pp

The Oaklands
Country House Hotel
Barton Street
Laceby, Grimsby DN37 7LF
T: 01472 872248 F: 01472 878143
Contact: Karina Ellis, Conference & Banqueting Co-ordinator

Ceremony

This country house was built about 120 years ago as a small family estate. It is set in five acres of parkland and features a terrace which overlooks the lawns and water garden. The Garden Restaurant and Blue Room are licensed, but ceremonies here must be followed by reception on site.
Price guide: £150

Reception

Numerous packages are on offer.
Catering: Buffets from £5.75pp. Sit down from £18pp

Petwood House Hotel
Stixwold Road, Woodhall Spa
Lincolnshire LN10 6QF
T: 01526 352411 F: 01526 353473
Contact: Linda Chalmers, Conference & Banqueting Co-ordinator

Ceremony

The House is set in 30 acres of woodland with extensive lawns and was built at the turn of the century for Lady Weighall. It was also the war-time home of 617 Squadron, the "Dambusters", and features extensive oak panelling with a carved main staircase. Ceremonies are not available on Christmas Day and New Year's Eve.
Price guide: £150

Reception

112

CONTENTS

(ii)   Bindon Country House Hotel
       Powderham Castle
       Tutu L'Auberge

(iii) Epsom Downs Racecourse

(iv)   The Bowes Museum
       Carlton House
       May Fair Inter-Continental

(v)   Thurning Hall
       The Pump House
       Newick Park

(vi)   Longleat

(vii) Kingswood House

(viii) Pittville Pump Rooms
       Elmbridge Civic Centre
       Combermere Abbey

(ix)   Leigh Court
       The Lawn
       Lancashire County Cricket Club

(x)   The New Mill Hotel

(xi)   Stoke Park
       Greystoke Castle
       Grafton Manor

(xii) Amberley Castle
       Haldon Belvedere
       Gedling House

(xiii) Le Gothique
       Osterley Park

(xiv) Chilford Halls
       The Falcon Hotel
       Chelsea Old Town Hall

(xv)   Trent College
       Ripley Castle

(xvi) Lynford Hall
       Vale Mascal
       Brickwall House

(xvii) Donington Park Hotel
       Allt Yr Ynys
       St Augustines'

(xviii) Davenport House
        Eastnor Castle
        Mains Hall

(xix) Polhawn Fort

(xx)   Phyllis Court Club

(xxi) Leez Priory

(xxii) The Roof Gardens
       The Roffen Club
       The Richmond Gate Hotel

(xxiii) The Lanesborough

(xxiv) The Mill House Restaurant

Top left: Bindon Country House Hotel, Langford Budville, Somerset. See p156.
Top right: Powderham Castle, Exeter, Devon. See p54.
Above: TuTu LAuberge, South Godstone, Surrey. See p172.

Above: The Queen's Stand, Epsom Downs Racecourse, Epsom, Surrey. See p169.

Top left: The Bowes Museum, Castle Barnard, Co Durham. See p59.
Top right: The Carlton Lodge Hotel, Helmsley, North Yorkshire. See p144.
Above: The May Fair Intercontinental Hotel, London W1. See p121.

Top left: Thurning Hall, East Dereham, Norfolk. See p138.
Top right: The Pump House, Battersea Park, London SW18. See p122.
Above: Newick Park, Newick, East Sussex. See p64.

Above: Longleat, Warminster, Wiltshire. See p196.

Above: Kingswood House Centre, London SE21. See p120.

Top left: Pittville Pump Rooms, Cheltenham, Gloucestershire. See p73.
Top right: Elmbridge Civic Centre, Esher, Surrey. See p169.
Above: Combermere Abbey, Whitchurch, Shropshire. See p154.

- Top left: Leigh Court, Abbots Leigh, North Somerset. See p10.
  Top right: The Lawn, Rochford, Essex. See p66.
  Above: Lancashire County Cricket Club, Old Trafford, Manchester. See p131.

Top & Above: The New Mill Restaurant, Eversley, Berkshire/Hampshire borders. See p15.

GREYSTOKE CASTLE

Greystoke Castle provides Cumbria's foremost venue for weddings, celebration dinners & private parties. There is an extensive list of wines and our caterer, Dinah Scott-Harden will prepare any special dish to suit the occasion.

Licensed for Civil Marriages

Greystoke Castle, Greystoke, Penrith, Cumbria CA11 0TG
Tel. 017684 83722   Fax 017684 83072

Top left: Stoke Park, Stoke Poges, Buckinghamshire. See p19.
Top right: Greystoke Castle, Penrith, Cumbria. See p41.
Above: Grafton Manor, Bromsgrove, Worcestershire. See p83.

Top left: Amberley Castle, Amberley, West Sussex. See p183
Top right: Haldon Belvedere (Lawrence Castle), Higher Aston, Devon. See p52.
Above: Gedling House, Nottingham. See p149.

Top left and top right: Le Gothique, London SW18. See p118
Above: Osterley Park, Isleworth, London TW7. See p122

xiii

Top left: Chilford Hall, Linton, Cambridgeshire. See p21.
Top right: The Falcon Hotel, Bude, Cornwall. See p38.
Above: Chelsea Old Town Hall, London SW3. See p115.

xiv

Top: Trent College, Nottingham. See p150
Above: Ripley Castle, Near Harrogate, North Yorkshire. See p147

xv

Top left: Lynford Hall, near Thetford, Norfolk. See p137.
Top right: Vale Mascal, Bexley, Kent. See p98.
Above: Brickwall House, Northiam, East Sussex. See p62.

Top left: Donington Manor Hotel, Castle Donington, Derby. See p46.
Top right: Allt Yr Ynys, Walterstone, Hereford & Worcester. See p82.
Above: St Augustines', Westgate-on-Sea, Kent. See p97.

xvii

Top left: Davenport House, Bridgnorth, Shropshire. See p154
Top right: Eastnor Castle, Ledbury, Herefordshire. See p83.
Above: Mains Hall, Poulton-le-Fylde, Lancashire. See p102.

Above: Polhawn Fort, Torpoint, Cornwall. See p37.

Top & Above: The Phyllis Court Club, Henley on Thames, Oxon. See p152

CLEARWELL CASTLE

Above: Clearwell Castle, Coleford, Gloucestershire. See p71.

Top left: The Roof Gardens, London W8. See p125.
Top right: The Roffen Club, Rochester, Kent. See p96.
Above: The Richmond Gate Hotel, Richmond, Surrey. See p124.

Above: St George's at The Lanesborough Hotel, London, SW1. See p120.

Above: The Mill House Restaurant & Hotel, near Reading, Barkshire. See p15.

A late night drinking licence is held for residents only. The House also operates preferential rate agreements with local hotels and guest houses.
Price guide: from £20pp.

Stoke Rochford Hall
Stoke Rochford, Grantham
Lincolnshire NG33 5EJ
T: 01476 530337 F: 01476 530534
Contact: Conference Department

Ceremony

This Grade I listed Victorian mansion house is set in 28 acres of gardens and over 1,000 acres of parkland. The Hall has five rooms licensed to hold ceremonies with varying capacities from 30 to 160. Although the Hall will consider holding ceremonies any day of the week, it prefers to hold them at weekends only. Ceremonies can only be held in conjunction with receptions.
Price guide: £150

Reception

The Hall offers a reception package costing £32pp which includes all food and drink but not an evening function. Included in the package is an overnight stay for the couple, with a champagne breakfast.
Catering: Buffets from £5.95pp. Sit down from £18.25pp

Stragglethorpe Hall
Lincoln
LN5 0QZ
T: 01400 272308 F: 01400 273816
Contact: Mrs Michael Rook, Proprietor

Ceremony

This former monastic building is Grade II listed and set in gardens. The Great Hall and Dining Room are both licensed for weddings which can take place here on any day except Christmas Day and Easter.
Price guide: £400

Reception

Discos and live modern music are only feasible in a marquee. Helicopters and hot air balloons can use the grounds.
Catering: from £18pp

Tattershall Castle
Lincoln LN4 4LR
T & F: 01526 342543
Contact: C R Watson, Custodian

Ceremony

Tattershall is owned by the National Trust and is a scheduled ancient monument. It is a brick built 15th Century castle, reminiscent of Hampton Court. Th ground floor Parlour is licensed and is available for ceremonies on Thursdays and Fridays from April to October. It is available from November to March by special arrangement only. The castle and its grounds will be available for two and half hours for your ceremony, and additional rooms can be hired for serving reception drinks.
Price guide: £200

Reception

There are sadly no reception facilities at the castle

ALSO LICENSED
Branston Hall Hotel 01522 793305
Fantasy Island 01754 872030
Lady Anne's Hotel 01780 481184
Northope Hall 01724 764848

Alexandra Palace
Alexandra Palace Way
Wood Green, London N22 4AY
T: 0181 365 2121 F: 0181 883 3689
Contact: Sarah Freds, Sales Co-ordinator

Ceremony

This impressive Victorian Palace can accommodate even the largest of weddings in style. Only one room, The Londesborough Room, is available seven days a week for marriage ceremonies, with one wedding permitted per day. Confetti is permitted indoors only.
Price Guide: £950

Reception

Reception facilities are available in several rooms including The Palm Court (with seating for 170), The Palace Restaurant (seating 300), The West Hall (seating 2,000) and The Great Hall (seating 5,500 or accommodating 6,500 for a buffet style reception). A marquee of unlimited capacity can be sited in nearby parkland. Catering is provided in-house. Accommodation at local hotels, at preferential rates, can be arranged.
Catering: approx £29.50pp

BAFTA
195 Piccadilly, London W1V 0LN
T: 0171 734 0022 F: 0171 734 1009
Contact: Julie Chadwell, Corporate Events Manager

Ceremony

The headquarters of The British Academy of Film & Television Arts is housed in a Grade II listed building in the heart of London. Ceremonies here must be followed by a reception on the premises.
Price Guide: NA

Reception

Roux Fine Dining are the caterers for this site. House wines start at £11.50 per bottle.
Catering: From £23.25pp

The Barn Hotel
West End Road
Ruislip HA4 6JB
T: 01895 636057 F: 01895 638379
Contact: Clive Richards, GM

LINCOLNSHIRE - LONDON

113

LONDON

Ceremony

The Barn Hotel is a 17th Century listed building set in two acres of landscaped rose gardens. The Leaning Barn is licensed for ceremonies which can take place here on any day except Sunday.
Price guide: £350

Reception

The hotel offers a honeymoon suite with double sunken whirlpool bath, as well as four poster suites with Jacuzzis.
Catering: Buffets from £8.50pp Sit down from £19.95pp

Berkeley Hotel
Wilton Place
London SW1
T: 0171 235 6000 F: 0171 823 1743
Contact: Rosemary Russell, Banqueting

Ceremony

The Berkeley Hotel in Knightsbridge is an ideal choice for a prestigious wedding. Ceremonies are currently permitted on any day, though the hotel is restricted to one wedding per day. Three rooms are available for the reception, namely the Waterloo Room, which seats 20, the Belgravia Room (40) and the Ballroom (250).
Price Guide: POA

Reception

The Berkeley Hotel, member of the Savoy Group, boasts five red stars and two rosettes. The hotel can cater for up to 450 guests for a buffet style reception, and 120 for a seated dinner. Both in-house and contract catering from an approved list is offered and the hotel is able to provide a wide variety of cuisines, including Kosher.
Catering: from £18.50pp

The Bridge
Kangley Bridge Road
Lower Sydenham
London SE26 5AQ
T: 0181 778 7158 F: 0181 659 2680
Contact: Manager

Ceremony

The Bridge is the community leisure centre of Lower Sydenham, and has three licensed rooms for wedding ceremonies, seating 110, 70 and 25 people respectively. A perfect choice for sports enthusiasts, who can even tie the knot in the centre's Training Room. Availability is subject to demand only, as the centre is open every day of the week and is not restricted to a maximum number of ceremonies per day. Confetti is permitted outside the building only.
Price Guide: from £50

Reception

Three rooms are available for the reception, namely the Sports Hall (with a seated capacity of 200), the Functions Room (100) and the Conference Room (40). Both in-house and contract catering is available, and self-catering facilities are also offered.
Catering: from £4- £15pp

Burgh House
New End Square
Hampstead NW3 1LT
Tel: 0171 431 0144
Contact: Pauline Pleasance, Administrator

Ceremony

This Grade I listed Queen Anne house (1703) is run by an independent trust, and is a popular venue for meetings, concerts and exhibitions. Its garden was designed after the style of Gertrude Jekyll. The panelled Music Room is licensed for ceremonies and is available Wednesday to Saturday inclusive.
Price guide: £125

Reception

Catering here is generally finger buffet or fork buffet, with Scandinavian food a speciality.
Catering: £10-£20pp

Cafe de Paris
3-4 Coventry Street
London W1V 7F
T: 0171 734 7700 F: 0171 287 4861
Contact: Gillian Davis, Functions Manager

Ceremony

Sited near Leicester Square, the exclusive Cafe de Paris is glamourously decorated in the style of the ship Lucitania. Ceremonies can take place here any day except Sunday and Monday. The restaurant is situated on the balcony and features the 'VIP table' where diners are apparently presented with a minimum bill of £1000.
Price Guide: POA

Reception

Catering: POA

Cambridge Cottage
37 Kew Green
Royal Botanic Garden
Kew, Richmond TW9 3AB
T: 0181 332 5616 F: 0181 332 5632
Contact: Sarah Corser, Events Manager

Ceremony

Cambridge Cottage, a Grade II listed 18th century building, is set in over 300 acres of the famous Kew Gardens. The Lounge is licensed to hold the wedding ceremony, and can accommodate up to 50 guests, seated or standing. Weddings can be held any day of the week, except between 23rd December and 2nd January. Confetti is not allowed.
Price Guide: POA

Reception

114

The Gallery at Cambridge Cottage can house receptions of up to 80 for a seated dinner and 120 for a buffet. The venue has a list of approved caterers. Guests can enjoy an intimate reception here surrounded by an exhibition of fine botanical paintings.
Catering: P.O.A.

Cannizaro House
West Side, Wimbledon Common
London SW19 4UE
T: 0181 879 1464 F: 0181 879 7338
Contact: Sarah Gammell, Banqueting

Ceremony

Cannizaro House, a Georgian mansion on the edge of Wimbledon Common, claims to be London's first country house hotel. The Queen Elizabeth Room alone is licensed to hold wedding ceremonies, and can seat up to 60 guests. Standing spaces are not allowed by the venue during the ceremony. Weddings are currently permitted every day except Sunday, and are only available in conjunction with a reception.
Price Guide: £800 + vat

Reception

Receptions can be held in the elegant drawing room, which overlooks the terrace and Cannizaro Park. Drinks can be served outside if weather permits. Alternatively, a choice of private dining rooms is available. These can seat up to 100 guests for waited service, or 110 for a buffet reception. Smaller rooms, for around 40 guests, can also be hired. Award winning in-house chefs provide catering.
Catering: approx. £25pp

Central London Golf Centre
Burntwood Lane SW17 0AT
T: 0181 871 2468 F: 0181 874 7447
email: clgc@aol.com
Contact: Jeremy Robson, Manager

Ceremony

The Function Room at this 9-hole golf course is available for ceremonies on any day of the year.
Price Guide: £100

Reception

A Rock 'n Roll wedding and a Line-Dancing wedding have both been hosted by this venue.
Catering: From £15pp

Chelsea Football Club
Fulham Road, London SW6 1HS
T: 0171 385 5545 F: 0171 381 4831
Contact: Debra Ware

Ceremony

The perfect wedding site for fans, Chelsea FC even offers tours of the ground for interested wedding visitors. Two rooms are licensed to hold ceremonies. Weddings are not permitted on match days and Sundays.
Price Guide: £300

Reception

Chelsea FC can cater for 200 guests for a seated banquet and up to 350 for a seated buffet. A marquee, seating up to 200, is also available. The Leith's trained chef can provide catering for any type and scale of event, from basic buffets and pub-style food to a five course silver service dinner.
Catering: £10 - £35pp

Chelsea Old Town Hall
Kings Road, London SW3 5EE
T: 0171 361 2220 F: 0171 938 3468
Contact: Maxine Howitt, Sales Conference Executive

Ceremony

The Main Hall can seat up to 480 guests in theatre style, whilst the Small Hall is suitable for smaller weddings, seating 120. Marriages can be held on any day except Christmas Day.
Price Guide: from £400

Reception

The Main Hall can cater for up to 400 guests for a cocktail style reception, or 250 for a seated dinner. Likewise, the Small Hall is suitable for 150 and 100 respectively.
Catering: P.O.A.

Chiswick House
English Heritage
Historic Properties London
23 Saville Row
London SW1X 1AB
T: 0171 973 3494 F: 0171 973 3470
Contact: Alice Ogilvie, Sales & Events Manager

Ceremony

The Domed Saloon at this English Heritage listed property is licensed for ceremonies which can take place on any day of the week. 4pm ceremonies are preferred. Only two ceremonies can be permitted per month as this property is open to the public. Ceremonies here must be followed by reception on the premises.
Price Guide: £500 for ceremony + £1500 - £3000 for reception

Reception

You may choose the caterer for the reception from an approved list.

Churchill Intercontinental Hotel
Portman Square W1A 4ZX
T: 0171 486 5800 F: 0171 299 2200
email: inter-conti.com
Contact: George Brown, Conference & Banqueting Manager

Ceremony

LONDON

115

This central London five-star hotel has access to the private gardens of Portman Square. The Library and Chartwell Suites are licensed for ceremonies which can take place here on any day of the year. Ceremonies here must be followed by reception on the premises.
Price Guide: POA

Reception

The Churchill boasts chef Idris Caldora heading its team. Perhaps one of the most usual events which has taken place here was the indoor Fun Fair, which included Velcro-suited human flying men, bucking Broncos and side shows.
Catering: from £34pp

Claridge's Hotel
45/57 Brook Street
London, W1A 2JQ
T: 0171 629 8860 F: 0171 872 8092
Contact: Louise Clarke, Deputy Banqueting Manager

Ceremony

One of London's most famous hotels, Claridge's has eight rooms which are licensed for wedding ceremonies: the Royal Suite (25), the Ballroom (125), the Drawing Room (100), The French Salon (75) and The Mirror Room (75). They all boast superb interiors, some with original Art Deco from the 1930s. Weddings can be held every day of the week.
Price Guide: from £1,200

Reception

Claridge's offers the same selection of rooms for wedding receptions, capable of seating up to 240 for a silver service dinner, or 400 for a cocktail party. Catering is in-house, but Claridge's use contract caterers to provide for special requirements such as Kosher.
Catering: from £25pp(canapes) from £30pp (lunches)

Dorchester Hotel
Park Lane
London W1A 2HJ
T: 0171 629 8888 F: 0171 317 6363
Contact: Victoria Bolden, Conference Administration Manager

Ceremony

Built in 1931, the hotel's accolades include Egon Ronay 'Hotel of the Year'. Seven rooms are licensed including the Orchid room, the Ballroom and the Pavilion. Ceremonies are available seven days a week. No confetti.
Price guide: from £400+VAT

Reception

The hotel features in-house catering although contract caterers may be brought in providing they are from an approved list.
Catering: from £34pp

Duke's Hotel
St James's Place SW1
T: 0171 491 4840 F: 0171 493 1264
Contact: Nicky Glynn, Private Dining Co-ordinator

Ceremony

Duke's Hotel, almost adjacent to St James's Palace, is a traditional London hotel. It has recently undergone extensive restoration and now offers its Marlborough Suite for wedding ceremonies.
Price Guide: £300 (with reception)

Reception

The Marlborough Suite is also available for wedding receptions. The room can cater for up to 60 guests for dinner or 75 for a buffet. Guests can enjoy the benefit of complete privacy with their own bar. Alternatively, The Dining Room may be used.
Catering: from £30pp

Dulwich College
Dulwich, London SE21 7LD
T: 0181 299 9284 F: 0181 693 6319
Contact: Julia Field, Enterprise Manager

Ceremony

Dulwich College was built in 1866. Today, it is an elegant combination of classical, mediaeval and contemporary architecture, with spacious grounds. Weddings can be held any day of the week outside school hours.
Price Guide: from £190

Reception

A number of rooms is available for the wedding reception, including the Great Hall, the Lower Hall, the Pavilion Salle, the Cloisters and the Christison Hall which seats a maximum of 300 guests. The majority of catering is undertaken by the in-house team. Wheelchair access is limited.
Catering: £9 - £25pp

Fairfield Halls
Park Lane, Croydon
Surrey CR9 1DG
T: 0181 681 0821 F: 0181 760 0835
Contact: Gary Barnes, Food and Beverage Manager

Ceremony

Fairfield Halls in Croydon offers four rooms including The Concert Hall, complete with balcony, tiered seating and oak panelling (up to 1,800). Smaller rooms are The Maple Room, (120), and The Arnhem Suite (500).
Price Guide: £200 to £2,000 (reduced

rate or FOC if reception held here)

Reception

The Halls can cater for parties of up to 400 for a formal dinner and up to 600 for a buffet. Own caterers allowed for a fee of £2,300+ vat
Catering: from £10pp

The Firs
**890 Green Lanes
Winchmore Hill
London N21 2RS**
T: 0181 360 6788 F: 0181 364 2446
Contact: John Thorpe, GM

Ceremony

Weddings may be held every day of the week, but may only be held in conjunction with a reception. Confetti is allowed.
Price Guide: from £120

Reception

Two rooms, The Grovelands Room, and the larger Winchmore Room, can house 130 guests for a seated dinner, and 170 for a buffet. European-style catering is in-house. There are preferential rate agreements with local hotels.
Catering: from £26.95pp (inclusive package)

Four Seasons Hotel
**Hamilton Place, Park Lane
London W1A 1AZ**
T: 0171 499 0888 F: 0171 499 5572
Contact: Graham Parsons, Banqueting Manager

Ceremony

The Four Seasons offers a choice of four rooms for the ceremony: the newly refurbished Pine Room with its painted ceiling, the Oak Room, the Garden Room and the Ballroom for up to 400 seated or 750 standing.
Price Guide: POA

Reception

Receptions can be held in one of the remaining three rooms, depending on the number of guests. Summer weddings may also wish to enjoy the Garden Room, which opens out on to the patio. In-house catering is provided by executive chef Eric Deblonde, who won the 1995 Banqueting Award from the Craft Guild of Chefs.
Catering: POA

Fulham Town Hall
**Fulham Road
London SW6 1HS**
T: 0181 576 5008 F: 0181 576 5459
Contact: Dee Little, Civic Facilities Manager

Ceremony

Fulham Town Hall is a late Victorian, early Edwardian, listed building, which has recently been completely refurbished. Internally the building is highly decorative with stained glass panels and marble painted columns. There is no wheelchair access to Fulham Town Hall. The ceremonies rooms are available any day of the year except Christmas Day and Good Friday. Confetti is not permitted.
Price guide: from £192

Reception

Catering Buffets from £4pp. Sit down from £12.50pp

The Golden Hinde Sailing Ship
**St Mary Overie Dock
Cathedral Street
London SE1 9DG**
T: 0171 403 0123 F: 0171 407 5908
Contact: Patrick Owen, Marketing Manager

Ceremony

This is a full scale replica of the original Elizabethan galleon, The Golden Hinde. It is located on near London Bridge. The Officers' Cabin and Ship's Hold are licensed and are available every day except Christmas Day.
Price guide: £150

Reception

The ship has hosted Elizabethan themed weddings. Costume suppliers can be recommended, along with other services.
Catering: from £8pp

Goring Hotel
**Beeston Place
London SW1W 0JW**
T: 0171 396 9000 F: 0171 834 4393
Contact: David Morgan Hewitt, Hotel Manager

Ceremony

This is one of the best known, and well respected, privately owned and family run hotels in London. (The hotel holds many accolades from hotel guides and individuals) Set in the centre of London, the hotel enjoys a peaceful location with its own gardens. The Drawing Room and Garden Lounge are licensed for weddings which can take place here on any day of the year. Ceremonies here must be followed by reception at the hotel. Confetti is not permitted.
Price guide: £250

Reception

The Goring offers traditional British cui-

LONDON

117

sine, and is one of a handful of hotels in London to have a Michelin Red Turret.
Catering: from £25pp

**Le Gothique
The Royal Victoria Patriotic Building
Fitzhugh Grove, off Trinity Road
Wandsworth Common SW18 3SX**
T: 0181 870 6567
Contact: Mark Justin, Proprietor

Ceremony

This English Heritage property is Grade II listed and features an award-winning garden. Three areas are licensed including the Cloistered Garden, and are available Fridays, Saturdays and Sundays. Ceremonies here must be followed by reception on the premises. Confetti is not permitted.
Price guide: £100

Reception

Le Gothique has a French chef and recently featured in the 1998 Good Food Guide.
Catering: from £20pp

**Grosvenor House Hotel
Park Lane
London W1**
T: 0171 499 6363 F: 0171 493 3341
Contact: Hugh Harris,
Conference and Banqueting Sales Manager

Ceremony

This is one of the oldest and largest hotels on Park Lane, with facilities to accommodate up to 1500 people. Numerous rooms hold ceremony licences allowing for wedding for 10 to 1500 people. These rooms are available on all days of the year except Christmas Day. Ceremonies here must be followed by a reception at the hotel. Confetti is not permitted.
Price guide: POA

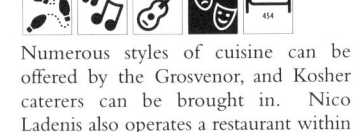

Reception

Numerous styles of cuisine can be offered by the Grosvenor, and Kosher caterers can be brought in. Nico Ladenis also operates a restaurant within the building.
Catering: from £30pp

**Hammersmith Town Hall
King Street, London W6 9JU**
T: 0181 576 5008 F: 0181 576 5459
Contact: Dee Little, Civic Facilities Manager

Ceremony

Hammersmith Town Hall dates from the 1930s and is a listed building. The Hall's Assembly Hall is claimed to be one of the largest halls in west London and features a Canadian sprung dance floor which has been meticulously maintained. Weddings can take place here on any day of the year except Christmas Day and Good Friday.
Price guide: from £192

Reception

Catering: Buffets from £4pp Sit down from £12.50pp

**Hammersmith & Fulham Irish Centre
Blacks Road, Hammersmith
London W6 9DT**
T: 0181 563 8232 F: 0181 563 8233
Contact: Pat Daly, Irish Centre Assistant

Ceremony

The Irish Centre is housed in a modern building. The Main Hall is licensed and available any day of the year. Ceremonies here must be followed by reception at the Centre. Confetti is not permitted.
Price Guide: POA

Reception

All catering must be provided by those hiring the Centre.

**Harrow School
5 High Street
Harrow on the Hill HA1 3HP**
T: 0181 426 4638 F: 0181 864 7180
email: harrow-es@compuserve.com
Contact: Graham Ridgway, Functions Co-ordinator

Ceremony

The Old Harrovian Room in this school is available for ceremonies on most days of the week except during term times. Confetti is not permitted.
Price Guide: £350 + vat

Reception

Catering: Buffets from £18pp. Sit down from £25pp

**Highgate School
Cholmeley House
3 Bishopswood Road
Highgate N6 4PL**
T: 0181 342 8323 F: 0181 342 8225
Contact: Mr Bob Jones, Lettings Manager

Ceremony

This public school is housed in listed buildings. Ceremonies take place in the Undercroft, while the big school is used for functions. It is available on Saturdays and Sundays during term time. Wheelchair access is limited.
Price Guide: from £150

Reception

Clare's Kitchen, who also cater at the Houses of Parliament, provide the catering here. A Bouncy Castle can be provided if required.
Catering: £25pp

**Holiday Inn London - Nelson Dock
265 Rotherhithe Street
London SE16 1EJ**
T: 0171 231 1001 F: 0171 231 0599
Contact: Mr Gary England, Conference & Banqueting Manager

Ceremony

This purpose-built hotel and conference centre incorporates original wharf buildings, as well as Nelson Dock itself; the only dry dock left in London, now housing a full size replica of a 3-masted French barque. The hotel enjoys views over the Thames. Five rooms are licensed, and these are available on any day of the year except Christmas Day.
Price guide: from £250

Reception

Couples can arrive and depart from this venue by boat.
Catering: from £25pp

**The Howard Hotel
Temple Place WC2R 2PR**
T: 0171 836 3555 F: 0171 379 4547
Contact: Mr Erten Sanjack, Banqueting Manager

Ceremony

Situated in the heart of the West End, The Howard Hotel is glamourously decorated with pillars of Italian marble and glittering chandeliers.
Price guide: from £325

Reception

The Howard claims the finest French haute cuisine and wines. Wines start at £11.50 a bottle.
Catering: Buffets from £20pp. Sit down from £25pp.

**Hyatt Carlton Tower
2 Cadogan Place
London SW1X 9PY**
T: 0171 235 1234 F: 0171 823 1708
Contact: Rachel Saunderson, Banqueting Sales Manager

Ceremony

The Hyatt Carlton Tower, a five star hotel in the centre of Knightsbridge, offers its Drawing Room, Boardroom and Ballroom for wedding ceremonies. The Drawing Room, which seats 50 theatre style, offers excellent views of the gardens. The Ballroom is more suitable for large weddings and can host up to 400 guests.
Price Guide: from £150

Reception

The hotel offers to arrange any form of entertainment, themeing and room decoration for wedding receptions, in either The Drawing Room or The Ballroom (which has recently been refurbished). Children can be catered for separately.
Catering: £38pp

**Hyde Park Hotel
66 Knightsbridge
London
SW1X 7LA**
T: 0171 235 2000 F: 0171 235 4552
Contact: Mr Knut Ketterman, Banqueting Manager

Ceremony

This well known hotel located in the heart of Knightsbridge offers four rooms for ceremonies, including the Ballroom, which overlooks Hyde Park. All rooms have natural daylight. Ceremonies can take place here on any day of the year.
Price guide: from £500

Reception

Not only does the hotel offer all the above services, it can also provide printing, room themeing, and even baby-sitting.
Catering: from £35pp

**Kensington Town Hall
Hornton Street
London
W8 7NX**
T: 0171 361 2220 F: 0171 938 3468
Contact: Maxine Howitt, Sales Conference Executive

Ceremony

Kensington Town Hall offers two rooms for wedding ceremonies. The Small Hall can seat up to 190, theatre style, while The Great Hall is suitable for up to 600 guests. Weddings can be held every day of the year except Christmas Day.
Price Guide: from £422

Reception

For many the ideal solution is a wedding in The Small Hall followed by the reception in The Great Hall. Kensington Town Hall has preferential rates with local hotels.
Catering: from £22pp

LONDON

119

LONDON

Kingswood House Centre
Seeley Drive
Dulwich SE21 8QF
T: 0181 761 7239 F: 0181 766 7339
Contact: Yvonne Witter,
Facility Manager

Ceremony

This English Heritage Centre is Grade II listed and set in enclosed grounds. The nucleus of the house was built in the 18th Century, while the greater part of the building dates from the 19th Century. The Great Hall of the house is now used as an adult lending library Confetti is not permitted.
Price guide: POA

Reception

You may choose your own caterer for this venue.

The Lambourne Room
Ilford Town Hall
High Road
Ilford
Greater London
IG1 1DD
T: 0181478 9071 F: 0181 478 9190
Contact: Halls Lettings Officer

Ceremony

The Lambourne Room is in the same complex as Ilford Town Hall, which also has a ceremony licence. The Lambourne Room has a maximum capacity for 180, while the Town Hall itself has room for over 590. Wheelchair access is limited to the Lambourne Room. Both rooms are available on Saturdays and Sundays only. Confetti is not permitted.
Price guide: POA

Reception

Catering: POA

The Landmark London Hotel
222 Marylebone Road
London NW1 6JQ
T: 0171 631 8000 F: 0181 630 8097
Contact: Michael Flatter, Conference & Banqueting Manager

Ceremony

Dating from 1899, this Grade II listed Edwardian hotel has many original features including the clock tower. It offers several rooms for wedding ceremonies: The Ballroom (seating 400), The Music Room (330), The Empire Room (200) the Drawing Room (200) and The Tower Suite (30). .
Price Guide: from £550

Reception

The same set of five rooms is also available for the reception, and can comfortably cater for parties from around 30 to 360 guests for a seated dinner, and up to 500 for a standing buffet. Small receptions in the 5th floor Tower Room are afforded views of the clock tower through its glass roof.
Catering: from £36.95pp

The Lanesborough
Hyde Park Corner
London SW1X 7TA
T: 0171 259 5599 F: 0171 259 5606
email: info@lanesborough.co.uk
Web Site: www.lanesborough.co.uk
Contact: Louise Heron, Director of Private Dining

Ceremony

The Lanesborough, a listed building close to Hyde Park Corner, provides a traditional setting for a London wedding. The hotel offers five rooms for wedding ceremonies. The largest of these, The Belgravia, seats 100 (250 standing). Other rooms are The St. George's, The Wellington, The Westminster and The Wilkins which seats 35. All, except the St George's, are located on the lower ground floor of the hotel.

Price Guide: from £125

Reception

The same suite of five rooms are also available for reception purposes. The largest capacity for a waited service dinner is 100, and the hotel can cater for up to 150 with a fork buffet.
Catering: Buffets from £24pp Sit down from £43pp

The Langham Hilton
1 Portland Place
Regent Street
London W1 3AA
T: 0171 636 1000 F: 0171 436 7418
Contact: Melina Becket, C & B Manager

Ceremony

Opened by the Prince of Wales in 1865, but badly damaged during the war, the hotel was painstakingly restored by Hilton in the 1980s. From the marble floor and pillars of the lobby upwards, the Langham is once again one of the finest places to dine and stay in the capital. Full details of the services were not made available to the guide.
Price Guide: from £1200

Reception

Catering: from £35pp

Lee Valley Leisure Centre
Picketts Lock Lane
Edmonton, London N9 0AS
T: 0181 345 6666 F: 0181 884 4975
Contact: Rick Garvey

Ceremony

120

The Great Hall at Lee Valley Leisure Centre can seat up to 1,900 guests. Weddings can be held every day except Christmas Day and New Year's Day but only with a reception.
Price Guide: POA

Reception

Other than The Great Hall, which can cater for 1,500 for a formal dinner and 2,000 for a buffet, other rooms at the venue are The Sports Hall, catering for 1,000 and 1,200 respectively (weekends only), The Bowls Hall (600 and 1,000), The Golf Bar (60 and 200) and the smaller Conference Room (40 and 60).
Catering: P.O.A.

May Fair
Inter-Continental Hotel
Stratton Street
London W1
T: 0171 629 7777 F: 0171 629 1459
email: mayfair@interconti.com
Web Site: http://www.interconti.com
Contact: David Gibbons,
Conference & Banqueting Manager

Ceremony

The May Fair Hotel offers an extensive range of facilities including a ballroom with magnificent chandeliers. The building itself dates from 1927 and became part of the Inter-Continental Group in 1982 (now part of Bass). Six rooms, including The May Fair Theatre (seating 292), The Crystal Room (320) The Danziger Suite (120), The Berkeley Suite (45) and The Curzon Room (40) are licensed.
Price Guide: P.O.A.

Reception

The May Fair Hotel (previously listed as the London Mayfair Hotel) can cater for receptions of up to 250 for a seated dinner and 350 for a buffet in one of the five rooms listed above. All catering is undertaken in-house under the supervision of Michael Coaker, Executive Chef. Michael has won two gold medals at Hotelympia and is a member of the Academie Culinaire de France.
Catering: from £28pp

Leith's At London Zoo
The Outer Circle
Regents Park, London NW1 4RY
T: 0171 586 3339 F: 0171 722 0388
Contact: Sales Manager

Ceremony

London Zoo is a wedding location with a difference. The ceremony can be held in either The Prince Albert Suite, which seats a maximum of 240 guests, or The Raffles Suite which seats around 100. The bride and groom can arrive at London Zoo by canal boat and travel to the wedding by pony and trap. The Raffles Suite only is accessible for wheelchairs. Both the ceremony and the reception must be held at the venue.
Price Guide: P.O.A.

Reception

Receptions at London Zoo can also be held in either The Prince Albert or The Raffles Suite, although afternoon weddings are able to enjoy evening reception drinks in one of the Zoo's animal houses. A marquee for up to 1,000 guests is a possibility. Catering is provided by Leith's.
Catering: £30pp

Middx and Herts Country Club
Old Redding
Harrow Weald
Harrow
HA3 6SD
T: 0181 954 7577 F: 0181 954 3466
Contact: Banqueting Manager

Ceremony

Price Guide: £250

Reception

Catering: from £30pp

Mosimann's
11b West Halkin Street
London SW1X 8JL
T: 0171 235 9625 F: 0171 245 6354
Contact: Charles Morgan, Club Manager, or Saskia Phillips

Ceremony

Ceremonies must be held with a reception.
Price guide: All-in price with reception

Reception

Availability is on request. Late night licence can be obtained if required. The club's main claim to fame is the renowned cooking of celebrity chef Anton Mossimian. The opportunities for outdoor photography are limited.
Catering: £85pp

New Connaught Rooms
Covent Garden Exhibition Centre
Great Queen Street WC2B 5DA
T: 0171 405 7811 F: 0171 831 1851
Contact: Tracey Worrall, Mekala Ambrose, or Robert Minott

Ceremony

This listed building in the centre of Covent Garden was once a Masonic house. The Drawing Room is licensed, and this takes a minimum of 30 guests. It is available any day of the year. Outside photography is approximately five minutes walk away at Garden Square.
Price guide: POA

LONDON

121

LONDON

Reception

A choice of caterer is offered at this venue.
Price guide: buffets from £24pp. Sit down from £27.50pp.

Oak Lodge Hotel
80 Village Road
Enfield, London EN1 2EU
T: 0181 360 7082
Contact: John Brown, Proprietor

Ceremony

Weddings can be held every day of the week except for the Christmas and New Year period.
Price Guide: £100

Reception

Catering: from £20pp

One Whitehall Place
Westminster SW1A 2HD
T: 0171 839 3344 F: 0171 839 3366
email: whitehallplace@cixcompulink.co.uk
Contact: Alun Roberts, Business Development Manager

Ceremony

This Victorian building, designed by Alfred Waterhouse for the National Liberal Club, is now Grade I listed. The building boasts Europe's largest unsupported marble staircase, an elegant site for wedding photographs. All rooms are licensed except the reception area, and are available for ceremonies on any day of the year. The Reading & Writing Room has a balcony overlooking Whitehall Gardens with views across to the Thames. Many of the rooms have natural daylight. Charing Cross Pier is very close to this venue. Ceremonies here must be followed by a reception on the premises.
Price Guide: POA

Reception

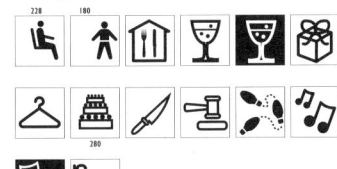

One Whitehall Place is immediately adjacent the The Royal Horseguards Hotel. House wine starts at £18 a bottle.
Catering: Buffets from £37.50pp. Sit down from £45pp.

Osterley Park House
Jersey Road
Isleworth TW7 4RB
T & F: 0181 568 7714
Contact: Keren Manley, Visitor Services

Ceremony

This stately home, now National Trust, is an 18th Century neo-classical villa, designed by Robert Adam and surrounded by 300 acres of landscaped park, farmland and ornamental trees. The Grand Hall is licensed and available on all days except Bank Holidays. Confetti is not permitted.
Price Guide: £1000 + vat

Reception

Reception facilities are not available at Osterley Park.

Park Lane Hotel
Piccadilly, London W1A 4UA
T: 0171 499 6321 F: 0171 499 1965
Contact: Mr Gareth Bush, Banqueting

Ceremony

The hotel has five rooms licensed to hold ceremonies including the Drawing Room, Orchard Room and Tudor Rose Room, which have varying capacities from a minimum of 25 to a maximum of 500 guests. Ceremonies are available seven days a week with a maximum of two a day. The price guide to hold the ceremony is dependent upon the number of guests in the party, the size of the room booked and the time of year; on some occasions there may be no charge. Wheelchair access is limited and the hotel stresses that Green Park proves a popular choice for outdoor photography.

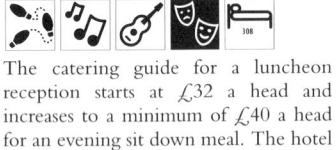

Reception

The catering guide for a luncheon reception starts at £32 a head and increases to a minimum of £40 a head for an evening sit down meal. The hotel holds a Kosher licence and offers a room for the bride and groom to change in which may be subject to a charge. The hotel also charges for the services listed above.
Catering: from £32pp

The Pump House
Battersea Park
London SW18 4NJ
T: 0171 871 7572 F: 0171 228 9062
Contact: Kristine Scarff, Manager (0171 350 0523)

Ceremony

This Grade II listed building was recently restored by English Heritage and Wandsworth Borough Council and serves as a gallery and function rooms. Set in parkland with views of the lake and surrounding greens, the house has a seated ceremony capacity of 120, with the option to adjoin marquees. Ceremonies are available daily, outside of opening hours, but not on Christmas Day, or Sundays in Summer. The price quoted below excludes the Registrar's fee. There is wheelchair access to the ground floor only.
Price guide: £415

Reception

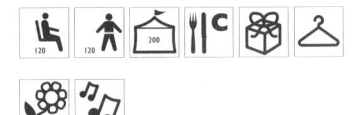

The Pump House offers a list of tried and tested caterers, or clients are welcome to engage their own. For this reason it is not possible to give a catering price guide. Although accommodation is not available on the premises, the house provides a list of local hotels and guest houses. The house states it can provide names of suppliers of any service required, from a horse and carriage to a laser show. Please note the Pump House has a no smoking policy.

Queen Elizabeth II Conf Centre
Broad Sanctuary, Westminster
London SW1P 3EE
T: 0171 798 4017 F: 0171 798 4200
Contact: Marketing Department

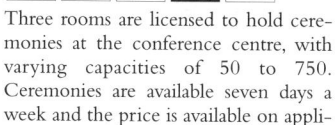

Ceremony

Three rooms are licensed to hold ceremonies at the conference centre, with varying capacities of 50 to 750. Ceremonies are available seven days a week and the price is available on application. Confetti is permitted.

Reception

Catering is undertaken on a contract basis by Leith's and the price per head is available on application. Although accommodation is not available on the premises, a list of local hotels is available. The centre also operates preferential rates agreements with a selection of local hotels. In addition to the services indicated above the centre provides videos, lighting and themed weddings.

The Queen's House
National Maritime Museum
Romney Road
Greenwich SE10 9NF
T: 0181 858 4422 F: 0181 312 6632
Contact: Anna Kingsley-Curry

Ceremony

The Queen's House was designed in 1616 by Inigo Jones as a small Palace for royal entertainment. It has recently been restored to its original glory. It is set next to the Maritime Museum and backs onto Greenwich Park. The ceremony room is the south west parlour in the Van de Velde Suite and this is available any day of the year except 24th - 26th December. Ceremonies here must be followed by a reception at the venue. Confetti is not permitted.
Price guide: from £1000

Reception

Couples can arrive or depart from Greenwich pier which is five minutes walk away.
Catering: Dependent on caterer chosen.

Radisson Edwardian Hotel
140 Bath Road
Hayes, Middx
T: 0181 759 6311 F: 0181 759 4559
Contact: Gavin Sanders, Director of Conference & Banqueting

Ceremony

Voted 'The Best New Business Hotel in the World' by Business Traveller Magazine, the hotel offers ceremonies seven days a week with a maximum of three per day. Ceremonies are not available without reception facilities, and the price guide below indicates the cost of the room hire based on 100 guests being present.
Price guide: £2,000

Reception

Although catering is in-house, contract catering is also available providing it is from an approved list. The hotel's health spa is open to all guests, and offers sauna, gymnasium, steam rooms with spa and plunge pools and solarium; beauty treatments are also available. Of the 459 bedrooms at the hotel, 17 are suites, 62 are executive King size doubles, and 54 are King size doubles.
Catering: £30pp

Raddisson SAS Portman Hotel
22 Portman Square
London W1H 9FL
T: 0171 208 6000 F: 0171 208 6001
Contact: Helmut Polt, Banqueting

Ceremony

The Raddisson SAS Portman Hotel, located in Portman Square close to Marble Arch and Oxford Street, offers a choice of six rooms for either the wedding ceremony or the reception. The largest of these, The Ballroom, seats 400 theatre style or 700 standing. The smallest room, The Bryanston Suite, is more suitable for weddings with less than 100 guests.
Price Guide: POA

Reception

Catering is generally provided by the in-house chef, although approved contract caterers may also be used by arrangement. Guests can easily be accommodated overnight in the hotel's 279 rooms.
Catering: from £50pp

Ravens Ait
Portsmouth Road
Surbiton
London KT6 4HN
T: 0181 390 3554 F: 0181 399 7475
Contact: Keith Hartog, MD

Ceremony

Being an island situated on the Thames, Ravens Ait is a charming setting to hold a wedding. There are two rooms licensed to hold ceremonies; the Thames Suite which holds a minimum of 35 and a maximum of 120, and the Lambourne Room which holds a maximum of 40 and a minimum of five for a more intimate wedding.
It is possible to hold a ceremony without reception facilities although a reduction of £60 will be made if the reception is also held on the island. The guide below includes a complimentary drink.

LONDON

123

Price guide: £250

Reception

Accommodation on the island takes the format of 10 twin bedrooms and six bedded cabins which each sleep six. In addition to the services indicated above, the island may provide decorating services including floral arrangements and balloons, and a registered child minder for attending children during the formalities.
Catering: £8-£30pp

The Regent Banqueting Suite
331 Regents Park Road
Finchley, London N3 1DP
T: 0181 343 3070 F: 0181 343 3010
Contact: Susan Damary, Banqueting Manager or Lynda Scrinminger, Conference Events Manager

Ceremony

This banqueting suite was built at the turn of the century, and still retains all its original features including decorative ceilings and chandelier. The Regency Suite is licensed for ceremonies and is available any day except Saturday and Jewish religious holidays.
Price guide: £250

Reception

The prices below are for a fully inclusive package. This venue employs a Thai chef who prepares reception food, hors d'oeuvres and fruit carvings.
Catering: from £55pp

The Rembrandt Hotel
11 Thurloe Place SW7 2RS
T: 0171 589 8100 F: 0171 225 3363
Contact: Sarah Cox, Banqueting

Ceremony

Built in 1906 as Harrods apartments, the hotel features Georgian architecture and ornate pillars. Ceremonies are available seven days a week excluding Christmas Eve, Christmas Day, and New Year's Day. Confetti is permitted.

Reception

In addition to the services indicated the hotel has full banqueting facilities.
Catering: from £25pp

The Richmond Gate Hotel
Richmond TW10 6RP
T: 0181 940 0061 F: 0181 332 0354
Contact: Samantha Price, Conference Banqueting & Sales Co-ordinator

Ceremony

The hotel is a country house overlooking the Royal Park and is RAC and AA recommended. Three private rooms are available for ceremonies each featuring period furnishings and decor. These rooms are available seven days a week.

Reception

Catering is in-house and the hotel boasts a speciality of international cuisine and vegetarian dishes. It has recently been awarded an AA Rosette. Over 100 world wines are also on offer.
Catering: £42pp

Richmond Hill Hotel
Richmond TW10 6RW
T: 0181 940 2247 F: 0181 940 5424
Contact: Jane Smeeton or Sue Roberts, Conference & Banqueting

Ceremony

This Grade II listed building has original Georgian remains forming the central part of the hotel, which date back to 1726. The Georgian decor and much of the original architecture has been conserved. There are four rooms licensed to hold ceremonies with fees from £300 for the smallest to £3,000 for the largest (the Ballroom). The hotel is also RAC and AA recommended.
Price guide: from £300

Reception

The hotel's Chef de Cuisine, Jean-Claude Seraille, insists that the finest, freshest foods from around Britain are used in the restaurant. Although there is no specifically allocated area for indoor photography, the terrace opposite the hotel with views of the river and the city proves to be ever-popular.
Catering: £35- £47pp

Richmond Theatre
The Green, Richmond, TW9 1QJ
T: 0181 940 0220 F: 0181 948 3601
Contact: Kate Littlewood, Theatre Manager

Ceremony

The theatre was built in 1899 and restored in 1991. Both the Auditorium (max 850) and the Matcham Room (max 20) are licensed for ceremonies which can only take place here on a Friday..
Price guide: from £300

Reception

Catering is buffet style.
Catering: from £15pp

Ritz Hotel
150 Piccadilly W1V 0BR
T: 0171 493 8181 F: 0171 499 7487
Contact: Paul Chamberlain, Banqueting Manager

LONDON

Ceremony

The hotel has two rooms licensed to hold ceremonies; the Marie Antoinette Suite which has a sitting capacity of 50 and a standing capacity of 80, and the Trafalgar Suite with a capacity of 20. Ceremonies are available seven days a week with no restriction on the number permitted per day. An area for outside photography is available by arrangement.
Price guide: from £500

Reception

Personalised menus are created for each occasion and complimentary cards and place cards are also provided. A toastmaster and room for the bride and groom to change in are provided by prior arrangement.
Catering: £80pp

The Roof Gardens
99 Kensington High Street
London W8 5ED
T: 0171 937 7994 F: 0171 938 2774
Contact: Peter Insall, General Manager

Ceremony

This Grade I listed English Heritage roof garden club is set in 1.5 acres of landscaped gardens and fountains. Ceremonies are available seven days a week excluding Christmas Day and Thursday and Saturday evenings. Ceremonies are not available without receptions.

Reception

The Gardens pride themselves on their barbecues and buffets and are more than happy to provide marquees, fireworks and themed receptions in addition to the services indicated.
Catering: £40pp

Royal Garden Hotel
2-24 Kensington High Street
London W8 4PT
T: 0171 937 8000 F: 0171 361 1921
Contact: Mr Philip Sacker, Banqueting Manager

Ceremony

This well known hotel situated in the heart of Kensington offers four rooms for ceremonies on any day of the year except Sundays and Bank Holidays. Ceremonies here must be followed by a reception at the hotel.
Confetti is not permitted.
Price guide: £350

Reception

Catering: from £30pp

Royal Society of Arts
8 John Adam Street
London WC2N 6EZ
T: 0171 930 5115 F: 0171 321 0271
Contact: Christine Bond, Conference Manager

Ceremony

The house of the RSA (the Royal Society for the Encouragement of Arts, Manufacture & Commerce) was designed in the 1770s by Robert Adam specifically for the Society. After a complex £4.5 million refurbishment programme, the terrace of five 18th Century vaults are now fully equipped for receptions and private dining. Ceremonies are available seven days a week excluding Bank Holidays.
Price guide: from £500+VAT

Reception

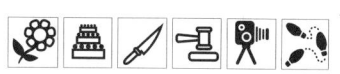

Although the Society does not hold a late night drinking licence, it does have a late supper certificate. All food is prepared in the Society's kitchen by Catering & Allied Services Ltd. Although accommodation is not available on the premises, the Society has a list of local accommodation, with some of whom it operates preferential rate agreements.
Catering: £40 - £60pp (package)

St David's School
Church Road
Ashford TW15 3DZ
T: 01784 248680 F: 01784 248652
Contact: Mrs R Wallace, Bookings Clerk

Ceremony

St David's is an independent school (of which the Queen is patron), set in a Grade II listed building on a 30 acre site with a lake. The main entrance hall is licensed and available on Saturdays and Sundays only.
Price guide: POA

Reception

Helicopters and hot air balloons may use the grounds.
Catering: POA

Savoy Hotel
The Strand
London WC2R 0EU
T: 0171 836 4343 F: 0171 872 8894
Contact: Chris Hamilton, Banqueting

Ceremony

The hotel has 10 rooms licensed to hold ceremonies including the Sorcerer, Iolanthe, Lancaster, Abraham Lincoln, Beaufort, Pinafore, Mikado and Gondoliers suites. These have varying capacities from a minimum of four

125

LONDON

guests to a maximum of 300. Ceremonies are available seven days a week with only one permitted per day. Confetti is not allowed.
Price guide: from £250

Reception

The hotel boasts Anton Edelmann as Maitre Chef des Cuisines. Although the hotel has a total of 202 bedrooms, they would like to point out that it is not possible to hire them all on an exclusive basis.
Catering: from £38pp

Searcy's
Searcy Tansley & Co Ltd
30 Pavilion Road
London SW1X 0HJ
T: 0171 823 9212 F: 0171 823 8694
Contact: James Hickey, GM

Ceremony

30 Pavilion Road was created specifically by Searcy's for the purpose of entertaining, and must be hired on an exclusive basis. The Georgian town house features log fires, antique furniture and chandeliers and is available seven days a week to hold ceremonies excluding the period from Christmas Eve to the 4th of January. As the building is hired on an exclusive basis only, ceremonies are not available without receptions and for this reason no price guide is given as this is part of the overall hire charge.

Reception

The capacity varies from 140 for a seated buffet, 200 for a fork buffet and increases to 250 for a finger buffet. Pavilion Road boasts a speciality in French, English and Oriental cuisine and in addition to the services indicated, is happy to provide a full event management service. At the top of the house there are 12 bedrooms with en-suite facilities.
Catering: POA

Sheraton Skyline Hotel
& Conference Centre
Bath Road, Hayes
Middx UB3 5BP
T: 0181 759 2535 F: 0181 750 9150
Contact: Edwin Wijkhuys,
Food & Beverage Manager

Ceremony

The hotel offers ceremonies seven days a week with a maximum of two held per day. There are no restrictions on Bank Holidays. Confetti is permitted.
Price guide: £500 - £2000

Reception

The hotel prides itself on its chef who has also worked at London's Dorchester Hotel.
Catering: from £15pp

The Stafford Hotel
St James Place   SW1A 1NJ
T: 0171 493 0111 F: 0171 493 7121
email:info@thestaffordhotel.co.uk
Contact: Jeanette Riley, Pat Short, Private Dining Co-ordinators

Ceremony

This elegant town house hotel offers its Sutherland Room and its restaurant for ceremonies on any day of the year except Christmas and Bank Holidays.
Price guide: POA

Reception

Catering: POA

Stakis St Ermins Hotel
Caxton Street   SW1H 0QW
T: 0171 222 7888 F: 0171 222 6914
Contact: Conference & Banqueting Office

Ceremony

This Grade II listed hotel is located between the Houses of Parliament and Buckingham Palace in a quiet corner of Westminster. The Ballroom, which is late Victorian style with a central chandelier, has a balcony surrounding the entire room and is ideal for functions of between 120 and 150 guests. Ceremonies are held in The Balcony Room. Ceremonies here must be followed by a reception on the premises.
Price guide: £300

Reception

For guests staying overnight, St Ermins can offer a special accommodation rate. Car parking is also available.
Catering: from £26pp

Sutton House
2 Homerton High Street
Hackney, London E9 6JQ
T: 0181 986 2264 F: 0181 533 0556
Contact: Carol Mills, Property Manager

Ceremony

This Tudor brick built house, dating back to 1535, is said to be the oldest domestic house in London, built by a courtier of King Henry VIII. It is now National Trust owned, and run as an arts education, cultural centre. Three rooms are licensed to hold ceremonies; the Linen Fold Parlour, which features 16th Century carved panelling and a Tudor fireplace which can be lit, the Wenlock Barn featuring an inglenook fireplace

and balcony, and the Marriage Suite. Ceremonies are available Thursday, Friday and Saturday excluding Bank Holidays and the house is closed in January. There is no wheelchair access to the Marriage Suite. The house does not have gardens but features an enclosed paved courtyard.
Price guide: from £50

Reception

A marquee is available for drinks only, to a capacity of 30, and buffet catering prices range from £10-25 per person and increases to £15-30 per person for a sit down meal. Cuisine is traditional English. Photography is not permitted during the ceremony itself. The Wenlock Barn has a Steinway concert grand piano which may be used for a re-tuning fee of £30. The house has held in the past a Scottish wedding which featured bagpipes at the reception.
Catering: from £10pp

Templeton, 118 Priory Lane
Roehampton, London SW15 5JW
T: 0181 878 1672 F: 0181 876 2753
Contact: Jill Leney, Functions Secretary

Ceremony

This Grade II listed mansion, set in ornate grounds on the edge of Richmond Park, dates back to 1778 and was the home of Winston Churchill in the 1920s. The public room on the ground floor and the formal garden have recently been opened for a wide range of both private and commercial functions. The hire of the premises includes sole use of the complete ground floor and gardens. This comprises an entrance lobby, marble hall, large ballroom, two sitting rooms and a panelled dining room.
Price guide: £180 (£100 with reception)

Reception

The in-house caterer, David Wilson, can advise on any menu requirements from canapes to a banquet. The house also offers a Bride's Room for the day of the wedding from 10am until the event concludes. Hire of the house starts at £1200 (10am to midnight)
Catering: from £25pp

Tower Thistle Hotel
St Katherine's Way
London E1 9LD
T: 0171 481 2575 F: 0171 480 5487
Contact: Rachel Cooper, Conference & Banqueting Manager

Ceremony

The hotel is actually situated in St Katherine's dock and is surrounded by water, with views of Tower Bridge and across the City of London. Two rooms are licensed to hold ceremonies, the Tower Suite with a maximum capacity of 250, and the Neville Suite with a capacity of 60. Ceremonies are available seven days a week and it is possible to hold a ceremony without reception facilities.
Price guide: £600

Reception

Catering prices per head start from £14 for a buffet style reception up to £27 for a sit down meal. A complimentary room is available for the bride and groom to change in and, in addition to the services indicated the hotel features a jetty which allows the bride to arrive by boat if she wishes. The hotel may also provide fireworks on the river. The hotel's restaurant has been RAC and AA recommended.
Price guide: from £49.50pp (including drinks)

Trafalgar Tavern
Park Row
Greenwich
London SE10 9NW
T: 0181 858 2437 F: 0181 858 2507
Contact: Marcus Child, Banqueting Co-ordinator

Ceremony

This riverside pub was the 1996 Evening Standard Pub of the Year. Couples can arrive and depart by boat. The pub is set in a listed building and was once frequented by Dickens, Thackery and Gladstone as well as Dr Crippen! The Nelson room is the ceremony room and this is available any day of the year, but ceremonies here must be followed by reception at the pub.
Price guide: POA

Reception

Whitebait is a speciality of the house!
Catering: from £19pp

TS Queen Mary
Waterloo Pier
Victoria Embankment WC2R 2PP
T: 0171 240 9404 F: 0171 497 8910
Contact: Darren Williams, Functions & Banqueting Manager

Ceremony

Queen Mary is a permanently moored turbine steam ship. The Captain's Quarters and Admiral's Suite are licensed for ceremonies which can take place here on any day except Sundays. Ceremonies here must be followed by a reception on board ship.
Price guide: from £350

Reception

Catering: from £20pp

Waldorf Hotel
Aldwych, WC2B 4DD
T: 0171 836 2400 F: 0171 240 9277
Contact: Kate Signy, Banqueting Manager

Ceremony

LONDON

127

LONDON

This famous hotel, set in the heart of London's theatreland, is a traditional five star Edwardian hotel with authentic decor. The Charter, Adelphi and Palm Court Rooms are licensed for ceremonies and are available any day of the year. Sadly these rooms do not have wheelchair access. Confetti is not permitted.
Price guide: from £3,000

Reception

The minimum number of guests for a wedding reception is 15. Kosher caterers are allowed to use the kitchens if required. Couples can arrive and depart by boat as Charing Cross Pier is five minutes walk away.
Catering: from £26pp

West Lodge Park Hotel
Cockfosters Road
Hadley Wood EN4 0PY
T: 0181 440 8311 F: 0181 449 3698
Contact: Suzanne Glaus, Banq Manager

Ceremony

The hotel offers ceremonies seven days a week excluding Christmas Day with a maximum of two permitted per day. Ceremonies are only available when held in conjunction with receptions and confetti is allowed.
Price guide: £175

Reception

Although the hotel does not hold a late night drinking licence, it does have a late night supper licence. The hotel's head chef, Peter Leggat, is a Chef of the Year semi-finalist.
Catering: POA

West Thames College
London Road, Isleworth TW7 4HS
T: 0181 569 7173 F: 0181 847 2421
Contact: Ian Butlin, Centre Manager

Ceremony

The building housing the West Thames College was originally owned by Captain Cook's botanist, Joseph Banks. The Winter Gardens Room holds the wedding licence, and ceremonies can take place here on any day except Sundays and Bank holidays. Confetti is not permitted.
Price guide: FOC

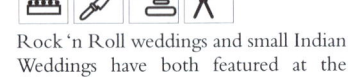

Reception

Rock 'n Roll weddings and small Indian Weddings have both featured at the College.
Catering: from £10pp

White Swan Water
The Pool of Little Venice W9 2PF
T: 0171 266 1100 F: 0171 266 1926
Contact: Emma Hartley, Assistant GM

Ceremony

This permanently moored 1935 Regents Canal barge is situated in the conservation area of Little Venice. Wheelchair access is limited. The barge can host weddings for 4 to 40 guests on any day of the year.
Price guide: POA

Reception

This venue is striving to offer couples a 'truly unique wedding day', and 'aims to meet every culinary requirement'. Space on the barge allows for a two piece band only if live music is required. As a special feature, White Swan can offer Aromastream.
Catering: from £20 - £50pp

York House
Richmond Road TW1 3AA
T: 0181 831 6108 F: 0181 940 7568
Contact: Janet Pattenden, Senior Lettings Officer

Ceremony

York House, a listed civic building which dates from the 17th Century, sits amid gardens overlooking The Thames. Two rooms are offered for wedding ceremonies; The Terrace Room and The Salon. The Salon, an ornate stuccoed room overlooking the driveway, seats 70 guests. The Terrace Room, which opens out onto the Terrace and Gardens, is large enough for 40 seated or 50 standing guests.

Reception

In addition to The Terrace Room and The Salon, York House offers The Hyde Room and Clarendon Hall for receptions. The Hyde Room can cater for 70 seated guests, and up to 100 for a buffet, while Clarendon Hall can cater for 200 and 250 respectively. Contract caterers are used, or self-catering facilities are available.
Catering: negotiated with contract caterers

ALSO LICENSED
Apollonia Restaurant 0181 954 5060
Avenue House 0181 3592000
Belvedere Restaurant 0171 602 1238
Berners Hotel 0171 636 1629
Browns Hotel 0171 493 6020
Cafe Royal 0171 437 9090
Carnarvon Hotel 0181 992 5399
The Comedy Store 0171 839 6642
Excelsior Hotel 0181 759 6611
Grims Dyke Hotel 0181 954 4227
Ham House 0181 940 1950
Heathrow Park Hotel 0181 759 2400
The Lodge 01708 220730
Heathrow Hilton Hotel 0181 759 7755
Hilton on Park Lane 0171 208 4045
Madonna Hayley Hotel 0181 951 5959
Packfords Hotel 0181 504 2642
Prince Regent Hotel 0181 505 9966
Quayside Restaurant 0171 481 0972
Ramada Hotel 0181 897 6363
Regents Park Marriott 0171 722 7711
Royal Geographical Society 0171 589 5466
Scandic Crown Hotel 0171 231 1001
Soho House W1 0171 734 5188
Wandsworth Town Hall 0181 871 6394

MANCHESTER

The Acton Court Hotel
187/189 Buxton Road
Stockport, SK2 7AB
T: 0161 483 6172 F: 0161 483 0147
Contact: Tom McKee, GM

Ceremony

Price guide: F.O.C. (only with reception)

Reception

Catering: POA

The Albany Hotel
87/89 Rochdale Road East
Heywood, Rochdale OL10 1PX
T: 01706 369606 F: 01706 627914
Contact: Peter or Michael Rush

Ceremony

The Albany is an hotel (AA 2 star), restaurant and public house.
Price guide: POA

Reception

The wedding package includes four poster honeymoon suite for the wedding night, plus full English breakfast. The hotel can also offer preferential rate agreements for other local accommodation. The hotel has a resident DJ.
Catering: Buffets from £5pp. Sit down from £10pp

The Belmore Hotel
143 Brooklands Road
Sale, Trafford M33 3QU
T: 0161 973 2538 F: 0161 973 2665
Contact: Carol Deaville, Proprietor

Ceremony

This privately owned Victorian style (1875) hotel is set in mature gardens. As we went to press the hotel was about to undergo extensive refurbishment over nine months after which the details held here will change. Contact the hotel for further information.
Price guide: F.O.C.

Birch Hotel
Manchester Road, Birch
Heywood, Nr Rochdale
T: 01706 366137 F: 01706 621000
Contact: Mrs Purchon, Proprietor

Ceremony

Once a local mill owner's house, this first became an hotel in the early 1970s and is set in over three acres of woodlands and fields.
Price guide: FOC

Reception

Catering: £15

Bolholt Country Park Hotel
Walshaw Road, Bury
Greater Manchester
T: 0161 764 3888 F: 0161 763 1789
Contact: Tracey Whaley, Conference Co-ordinator

Ceremony

Set in its own private estate (of 50 acres), just two miles from Bury, one of the claims to fame for this listed building is that it is the birthplace of the first Dean of Harvard University. The original building has been added to, with a leisure centre and tennis courts completed in 1996.
Price guide: F.O.C. (only with reception)

Reception

Catering: from £13pp

Bolton Moat House
1 Higher Bridge Street, Bolton
Greater Manchester BL1 2EW
T: 01204 879988 F: 01204 380777
Contact: Sue Howell, Banqueting Sales Manager

Ceremony

The Moat House is sited in the centre of town on the former site of the Temperance Hall. The hotel's Cloisters restaurant was formerly St Mary's Catholic church and still features the stained glass windows.

Reception

The hotel offers several rooms for receptions, some providing intimate dining for 10 to 18 guests. For Saturday bookings in the Ashton Suite or Cloisters restaurant there is minimum requirement of 50 guests for the wedding breakfast and 120 for the evening reception. The hotel provides a comprehensive wedding package that includes wine, flowers, changing room, overnight accommodation and breakfast for the bride and groom, plus special overnight rates for guests attending the reception.
Catering: from £14.95

Bramall Hall, Bramall Park
Stockport SK7 3NX
T: 0161 485 3708 F: 0161 486 6959
Contact: Wedding Co-ordinator

Ceremony

This Grade I listed Tudor building is available for wedding ceremonies on Saturdays only.
Price guide: £400 - £500 + VAT

Reception

129

MANCHESTER

While there are in-house catering facilities at the Hall, other caterers are also permitted. A list of local accommodation can be provided by Bramall Hall.
Catering: £25pp - £350pp

Bredbury Hall Hotel
Goyt Valley, Bredbury, SK6 2DH
T: 0161 430 7421 F: 0161 430 5079
Contact: Margaret Anne Stone, Sales

Ceremony

Ceremonies can take place at the hotel on any day except Sundays and Bank Holidays. Up to three are permitted per day. Confetti is not allowed.
Price guide: £75 + VAT

Reception

Catering: from £10.95

Bury Town Hall, Bury
T: 0161 253 5111
Contact: Graeme Ramsden, Superintendent Registrar

Ceremony

This is a 1937 Art Deco civic building with many original features. The marriage room itself, on the ground floor of the building, is also Art Deco in style. Up to eight wedding ceremonies can be performed in a day, mornings and afternoons Monday to Friday, and up to 12.30pm on a Saturday. Ceremonies cannot take place on Christmas Day and other Bank Holidays.
Price guide: F.O.C. (plus registrar's fees)

Reception

The Town Hall has four function suites on the first floor, which can cater for wedding parties of up to 400: the catering for which is operated by Bury Contract Catering. In addition to standard fayre, they are able to provide vegetarian and kosher dishes. While there is no accommodation on the premises, a list of local accommodation is available.
Catering: POA

The Cricketer
Keats Avenue
Poolstock, Wigan WN3 5UB
T: 01942 824555
Contact: Mr Rutter, Manager

Ceremony

Price guide: F.O.C. (with reception)

Reception

Catering: from £2.75pp

Deanwater Hotel
Wilmslow Road
Woodford
Manchester SK7 1RJ
T: 01625 522906 F: 01625 536626
Contact: Jackie Smith

Ceremony

Parts of this hotel, restaurant and public house date back to the 16th Century. The hotel offers two marriage rooms; the Gold Suite (max 120) and the Balmoral Suite (max 250). These are available any day except Sundays and Bank Holidays, with a maximum of four weddings permitted per day.
Price guide: £120-£160

Reception

Catering: from £7pp (buffets) £15pp (waited)

Egerton House Hotel
Blackburn Road
Egerton, Bolton BL7 9PC
T: 01204 307171 F: 01204 593030
Contact: General Manager

Ceremony

Price guide: from £50

Reception

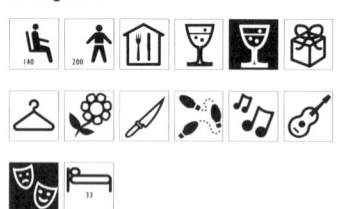

Catering: from £16pp (waited)

Georgian House Hotel
Manchester Road
Blackrod
Bolton BL6 5RU
T: 01942 814598 F: 01942 813427
Contact: Banqueting

Ceremony

The Georgian House (AA 4 star) dates back to to the 1700s, and has been added to more recently. Several rooms are suitable for the wedding ceremony with varying capacities from 50 guests upwards. It is only possible to have ceremonies at the hotel with a reception. There is only a room hire charge made if the ceremony and reception rooms differ. Up to two ceremonies are permitted per day, on any day of the week.
Price guide: from £200

Reception

Reception capacities depend upon the choice of room. The smallest can house a sit down meal for 34 and a buffet for 50. Personalised menu cards, red carpets, and colour co-ordinated table linen can all be provided.
Catering: from £25pp (package)

130

Granada Studio Tours
Bonded Warehouse
Water Street
Manchester M60 9EA
T: 0161 832 9090 F: 0161 834 3684
Contact: Jenny Smith (0161 828 5244)

Ceremony

Ceremonies can take place at the Studios' Baskerville Suite on any day of the year except Christmas Day.
Price Guide: £600 + VAT

Reception

Receptions can take place on the Baker Street set (from Sherlock Holmes), in the Rover's Return and Stables Restaurant, in the Baronial Hall, or the Starlight Theatre - (sadly not in the mock up of the House of Commons). The Studios have a preferential rate agreement with the nearby Victoria & Albert Hotel for those seeking overnight accommodation.
Catering: from £9pp

The Hacienda Club
13 Whitworth Street West
Manchester M1 5WG
T: 0161 236 5051 F: 0161 236 0518
Contact: Jon Drape, Production Manager

Ceremony

This popular live music venue and nightclub features an award winning interior design by Ben Kelly. Up to two ceremonies are permitted here per day, on any day of the year.
Price guide: £200

Reception

In addition to the list of services above, the Club can also design and print your invitations. The club can also supply a list of local accommodation with which it has preferential rate agreements.
Catering: from £2pp

Haigh Hall
Haigh
Wigan WN2 1PE
T: 01942 832895 F: 01942 831081
Contact: Ms Stazicker, Manager

Ceremony

This is a Georgian house overlooking a golf course and the valley of the River Douglas. The Cocktail Bar (up to 35) and the Grand Ballroom (up to 150) are licensed for ceremonies which can take place on any day except Saturday and Sunday.
Price guide: £30-£150

Reception

It is possible for hot air balloons and helicopters to use the grounds, upon discussion. Couples can arrive and depart by boat from the Leeds/Liverpool Canal.
Catering: Buffets from £5pp Sit down from £8pp

Holiday Inn Crowne Plaza Midland Hotel, Peter Street
Manchester M60 2DS
T: 0161 236 3333 F: 0161 932 4100
Contact: Elizabeth Holmes, Conference Network Manager

Ceremony

Built in 1903 and a Grade I listed building, the Crowne Plaza can host wedding ceremonies on any day of the year.
Price guide: from £175

Reception

Catering: from £20pp

Kilhey Court Hotel
Chorley Road
Standish
Wigan WN1 2XN
T: 01257 472100 F: 01257 422401
Contact: Jane Maton, Wedding & Banqueting Co-ordinator

Ceremony

The original part of this hotel is Victorian (1884), but it has since been extended. The hotel is set in its own grounds of around 10 acres. There are no restrictions on the number of ceremonies that can be held per day.
Price guide: £135

Reception

The hotel has a drinking licence extension to midnight, but a further extension could be applied for if required.
Catering: £18

Lancashire County Cricket Club
Old Trafford
Manchester M16 0PX
T: 0161 282 4020 F: 0161 282 4030
Contacts: May Byrom, Senior Sales Co-ordinator, or Tracy Grady or Marie Tunstall, Sales Co-ordinators

Ceremony

This world famous club, which was refurbished in 1997, and is located a few minutes from Manchester's city centre, has a marriage licence for its Members Suite and Lancaster Suite. The smaller of the two (50) has no wheelchair access. Ceremonies are possible here on any day except Sundays and Bank Holidays.
Price guide: £200

MANCHESTER

MANCHESTER

Reception

Nearly all the rooms have a good view of the cricket pitch. Themed events can be arranged, such as sporting themes, a Venetian masquerade or The Caribbean. House wines start at £9.75 a bottle.
Catering: Buffets from £8.50pp. Sit down from £12.50.

Manchester Town Hall
Albert Square, Manchester
Gtr Manchester M60 2LA
T: 0161 234 3039 F: 0161 234 3242
Contact: Rosemary Hayna

Ceremony

This Grade I listed civic building has a wedding licence for seven rooms ranging from the smaller committee rooms (for 50 people) to the Lord Mayor's Parlour, Banqueting Room, Reception Room and Conference Hall (all for 150 people), and The Great Hall (for 500 people). The Great Hall features a 70 foot high ceiling bearing the arms of the principal countries and towns with which Manchester has traded. The walls are adorned with murals by Ford Maddox Brown. Weddings can take place here on any day of the year.
Price guide: from £400

Reception

All catering requests can be provided apart from Kosher cuisine.
Catering: from £10.95

Mash & Air
40 Chorlton Street
Manchester M1 3HW
T: 0161 661 6161 F: 0161 661 6060
Contact: Nicky Pennington, Events Manager

Ceremony

The fourth floor restaurant is licensed for wedding ceremonies which can take place here on any day of the year.
Price guide: £250

Reception

Head Chef here is Jason Whitelock, Executive Chef is Bruno Loubert.
Catering: Buffets from £10pp. Sit down from £25pp

Norton Grange Hotel
Manchester Road
Castleton, Rochdale
Greater Manchester OL11 2XZ
T: 01706 30788 F: 01706 49313
Contact: Conference & Banqueting Manager

Ceremony

Ceremonies can be performed in the Hopwood Suite (max 135 people) and the Restaurant (max 50 people). Up to two ceremonies per day can take place on any day of the week except Sundays. Confetti is not permitted.
Price guide: £75

Reception

Catering: from £22.95

Quaffers Theatre Restaurant
Stockport Road West
Bredbury, Stockport
Greater Manchester SK6 2AR
T: 0161 494 0234 F: 0161 406 6372
Contact: Norma Levy

Ceremony

This well known Northern venue has its own hydraulic stage system, which presents the most unusual and dramatic opportunities for the imaginative staging of wedding receptions, such as bringing the couple's wedding car up on stage. Various rooms at Quaffers have the marriage licence, seating from 50 to 850, but wheelchair access is only available to the Cheshire Suite. The only days that the venue is not available for ceremonies are Sundays and Bank Holidays.
Price guide: £150

Reception

Contract caterers are allowed in to cater for ethnic weddings.
Catering: from £5.75pp

Rochdale Town Hall
The Esplanade
Rochdale
Gtr Manchester OL16 1AB
T: 01706 864797 F: 01706 59475
Contact: The Manager

Ceremony

This Victorian gothic style civic building has three marriage rooms including the Great Hall, the main banqueting hall which has feature stained glass windows and a balcony. Ceremonies can take place here on Saturdays only, and not on Christmas Day or Bank Holidays. It is not possible to hold ceremonies here without also booking the reception at the Town Hall. Confetti is not permitted. While there is nowhere to take outdoor photographs immediately outside the building, there is a park across the road.
Price guide: from £300

Reception

The Town Hall specialises in large scale

banqueting. Outside caterers can only be brought in for Kosher or Halal catering. Recent weddings included one on an American theme.
Catering: from £3.74 (buffet) - £10.20 (waited)

Royal Northern College of Music
124 Oxford Road
Manchester
Gtr Manchester M13 9RD
T: 0161 907 5289 F: 0161 273 7611
Contact: Allan Taylor, Events Manager

Ceremony

This arts centre and college of music has a licence for its main concert hall and can provide use of a Steinway grand piano and organ. Choir balconies and orchestral seating can also be made available. Ceremonies can take place here on Fridays, Saturdays and Sundays, but not during term time. Only one ceremony is permitted per day.
Price guide: £500

Reception

The College can create personalised desserts with the initials of the couple. A red carpet can also be provided in the main venue. While there is no accommodation on the premises, a list of establishments with which the College has preferential rate agreements can be provided on request. Receptions can also take place at Hartley Hall, the college's Victorian style hall of residence situated 10 minutes from the main concert halls.
Catering: from £7 (buffets)

Royals Hotel
Altrincham Rd
Wythenshawe M22 4BJ
T: 0161 998 9011 F: 0161 998 4641
Contact: Amanda Taylor, Conference & Banqueting

Ceremony

This hotel, restaurant and pub has its own private garden. The King Alfred, Windsor and Balmoral rooms are licensed and available for ceremonies on any day of the year. Ceremonies here must be followed by a reception at the hotel.
Price guide: £POA

Reception

Catering: Buffets from £6pp. Sit down from £12pp

Saddleworth Hotel
Huddersfield Road, Delph
Saddleworth, Oldham OL3 5LX
T: 01457 871888 F: 01457 871889
Contact: Anthony, Owner

Ceremony

The Saddleworth Hotel was originally built in 1800 as a pack horse station. It is set in nine acres which includes woodlands and landscaped gardens. The hotel has a marriage licence for one room which has a conservatory at one end. Up to two ceremonies can take place here each day, on any day except Good Friday and Christmas Day.
Price guide: £200

Reception

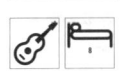

The hotel offers wedding packages, the most basic of which caters for 15 people and includes use of the hotel's Rolls Royce, ceremony, flowers and a three course meal with coffee and toasting drink. This costs £550. Each additional person is charged at £17.50pp. Banqueting is a speciality of the hotel which offers English and French style cuisine.
Catering: £550 (15 people)

Stockport Town Hall
Stockport, Manchester SK1 3XE
T: 0161 474 3259 F: 0161 477 9530
Contact: Ann Cullen, Reception

Ceremony

The Town Hall can cater for between 30 and 350; the latter accommodated in the Large Hall. Ceremonies can take place on any day of the week.
Price guide: P.O.A.

Reception

A late night drinking licence can be applied for. While there is no accommodation on the premises, a list of local establishments can be supplied. The services above can be organised in house or by the wedding party themselves.
Catering: P.O.A.

The Village Leisure Hotel
George Street
Prestwich M25 9WS
T: 0161 798 8905 F: 0161 773 5562
email: village.p@cybase.co.uk
Contact: Amanda Smithers, Conference & Banqueting Co-ordinator

Ceremony

The Village Leisure Hotel is one of a chain of leisure centres. This one has a license for its Norwood Suite which is available on any day except Good Friday and Christmas Day.
Price guide: £50

Reception

The wedding package here includes overnight accommodation for bride and groom, as well as a master of ceremonies, and entertainment or disco A cake stand is also provided. Private bar facilities are inclusive of a midnight extension to the licence. The hotel can also arrange printing of table plans and ordering balloons for tables.
Catering: Buffets from £9.50pp. Sit down from £16pp

MANCHESTER

133

MANCHESTER - MERSEYSIDE

Wythenshawe Hall
Wythenshawe Park
Wythenshawe M23 0AD
T: 0161 234 7780 F: 0161 234 7142
Contact: Rosemary Hamer
Sales Manager

Ceremony

The Library and The Grandfather Room are licensed at this venue, and are available for ceremonies on any day of the year.
Price guide: £350 (discount for locals)

Reception

While there is no accommodation on the premises, this venue has preferential rates with local establishments.
Catering: Buffets from £7.95pp. Sit down from £10pp

ALSO LICENSED
Bowdon Hotel 0161 928 7121
The Bower Hotel 0161 682 7254
Buile Hill Banqueting Suite
0161 737 6277
Cresta Court Hotel 0161 927 7272
East Lancs Masonic Hall 0161 832 6256
Flixton House 0161 912 3000
Last Drop Village Hotel 01204 591131
Longfield Suite 0161 773 3769
Manchester United Football Club
0161 872 3331/7722
The Oaks 0161 703 8694
Pack Horse Hotel 01204 527261
Queen Elizabeth Hall 0161 911 4071
Radcliffe Civic Hall 0161 723 2917
Ramsbottom Civic Hall 0161 253 5894
Worsley Court Hotel 0161 794 5760

The Alicia Hotel
3 Aigburth Drive
Liverpool L17 3AA
T & F: 0151 727 4411
Contact: Brian Bennett, GM

Ceremony

The Alicia has two ceremony rooms, the Park Lounge and the Zodiac Suite. These are available on any day except Christmas Day and Good Friday.
Price guide: from £160

Reception

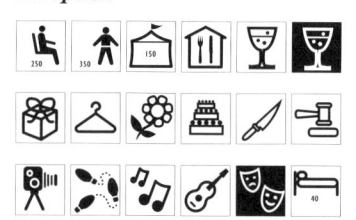

The Alicia has hosted a Somali wedding (which is quite a noisy affair with a lot of whooping) which included themeing the room in Somali style. This demonstrates the hotel's flexibility and puts stock behind their claim that they will cater as required.
Catering: Buffets from £6pp. Sit down from £15pp

Bowler Hat Hotel
2 Talbot Road
Oxton
Birkenhead L43 2HH
T: 0151 652 4931 F: 0151 653 8127
Contact: Greg Ballasty, Gen Manager

Ceremony

The hotel is a Grade II listed building and is set in 1.5 acres of gardens. Three rooms are licensed to hold ceremonies; the Restaurant, the Oxton Suite and the Garden Suite (which are both function rooms). Ceremonies are available without reception facilities but an extra charge of £100 will be made. Confetti is permitted.
Price guide: £150 or £250 (without recep)

Reception

The hotel is AA recommended.
Catering: Buffets from £9.45pp sit down from £16.95

The Cavern
8/10 Matthew Street
Liverpool L2 6RE
T: 0151 236 9091 F: 0151 236 8081
Contact: Dave Jones, Director

Ceremony

A must for all Beatles fans, The Cavern is probably one of the most famous clubs in the country, if not the world. One ceremony room is available here, (with limited wheelchair access), and this is available any day except August Bank Holiday Monday.
Price guide: £300

Reception

Catering here is buffet style.
Catering: from £3.50pp

The Devonshire House Hotel
293-7 Edge Lane
Liverpool L7 9LD
T: 0151 280 3903 F: 0151 263 2109
Contact: Marcia Hughes, Marketing Manager

Ceremony

Devonshire House is a Grade II listed building set in 1.5 acres of landscaped gardens. The Holt Suit is licensed and available any day of the year.
Price guide: £150

Reception

Special dietary requirement can be catered for. The hotel often arranges Bridal Fayres.
Catering: Buffets from £6.55pp. Sit down from £15pp

Hulme Hall
Bolton Road, Port Sunlight Village
Wirral L62 5DH
T: 0151 644 8797
Contact: Mr P Mortimer, Proprietor

Ceremony

This Grade I listed building is home to the banqueting hall which is available to hold ceremonies Monday to Saturday with a maximum of two to be held a day. Ceremonies are only available in conjunction with reception facilities and confetti is permitted.
Price guide: P.O.A.

Reception

The hall states that children may be catered for separately and although no accommodation is offered on the premises, the hall has a list of local accommodation. Preferential rates are available from some of these hotels.
Catering: from £14pp

Huyton Suite
Poplar Bank
Huyton
Merseyside L36 9TP
T: 0151 443 3761 F: 0151 443 3573
Contact: Mrs Jan Scully, Manager

Ceremony

The Huyton Suite is located in the centre of Huyton and offers three rooms for ceremonies: one of which is the Octagon Room with its octagonal dance floor. Ceremonies can take place here on any day except Sundays and Bank Holidays, but must be followed by a reception at the venue.
Price guide: £150

Reception

This venue can offer an all inclusive package, including disco and evening buffet.
Catering: Buffets from £4.50pp. Sit down from £12.45pp

The Kirkby Suite
Cherryfield Drive
Kirkby, Knowsley L32 1TX
T: 0151 442 4063
Contact: Mrs Cathy Weir, Manager

Ceremony

This central Kirkby venue offers two ceremony rooms; the Eagle Room and the Falcon Room, which are available on any days except Sundays and Bank Holidays. Ceremonies here must be followed by a reception at the Suite.
Price guide: £150

Reception

All inclusive arrangements are possible, to include all food and drink, room hire and disco.
Catering: Buffets from £4.50pp. Sit down from £12.45pp

Leasowe Castle Hotel
Moreton, Wirral L46 3RF
T: 0151 606 9191 F: 0151 678 5551
Contact: Mr Carruthers, GM

Ceremony

This listed building is 400 years old and set in five acres of land. One room is licensed to hold ceremonies which are available seven days a week with a maximum of two permitted per day. It is not possible to hold ceremonies without reception facilities.
Price guide: £125

Reception

The catering costs range from £15.50 a head, for a sit down meal; up to a starting price of £19 a head for a buffet style reception, although the hotel does not recommend buffet receptions at weddings.
Catering: from £15.50pp

Liverpool Town Hall
High Street, Liverpool L2 3SW
T: 0151 707 2391 F: 0151 709 2252
Contact: Simon Osborne, Manager

Ceremony

The Town Hall is a listed building and offers ceremonies seven days a week with no restrictions on Bank Holidays.
Price guide: from £50

Reception

Although the Town Hall does not have accommodation on the premises, a list of local hotels is available and preferential rate agreements are operated with selected guest houses.
Catering: £17pp

Raby House Hotel
Benty Heath Lane
Willaston L64 1SB
T & F: 0151 327 1900
Contact: Sean McKenna, Wedding Manager

Ceremony

This is a country house hotel, built in 1867, with lakeside views, fountains, waterfalls and gardens.
Price guide: POA

Reception

Raby House has hosted 16th and 17th Century themed weddings.
Catering: from £15pp

MERSEYSIDE

MERSEYSIDE

The Scarisbrick Hotel
Lord Street
Southport
Merseyside PR8 1NZ
T: 01704 543000 F: 01704 533335
Contact: Carol Taylor, Sales
& Banqueting Co-ordinator

Ceremony

The hotel is a Grade II listed building and is situated in the centre of the famous Lord Street. With the promenade just one minute's walk away, the hotel is also a short distance from the Marine Lake and several top class golf courses. Ceremonies are available seven days a week excluding Christmas Day. Confetti is permitted.
Price guide: £300

Reception

The hotel offers executive bedrooms and four poster mini-suites in addition to its regular rooms.
Catering: £15-20pp

Thornton Hall Hotel
Neston Road
Thornton Hough L63 1JF
T: 0151 336 3938 F: 0151 336 7864
Contact: Sue Rushton,
Conference & Banqueting Co-ordinator

Ceremony

The hotel is a period hall set in three acres of grounds, with a modern accommodation block. Ceremonies only permitted with receptions.
Price guide: POA

Reception

The hotel achieved a Les Routier award in 1995 and although a late night drinking licence is not permanently held, it can easily be obtained. The hotel has 63 bedrooms, all of which are en-suite. 1996 catering prices started at £12pp.
Catering: POA

Tree Tops Country House Hotel
Southport Old Road
Formby, Merseyside L37 0AB
T: 01704 879651 F: 01704 879651
Contact: Ann Marie Jackson

Ceremony

This listed building was the former dower house to Formby Hall and is set in three acres of woodland. Although ceremonies are available Monday to Saturday the hotel would like to stress that Fridays and Saturdays are already proving extremely popular during April to September, but is happy to discuss requirements for 1999 and 2000. One ceremony a day is permitted and it is not possible to hold ceremonies without reception facilities.
Price guide: £25

Reception

The hotel is keen to stress that each wedding is adapted to suit the individual requirements of the couple and every effort is made to tailor reception and ceremony facilities to suit the party. For this reason most services and facilities are open to negotiation. The hotel boasts a speciality in French and traditional English cuisine while the price indicated below is for a weekend reception and may be reduced at other times of the week. A late night drinking licence may be obtained.
Catering: from £25pp

The Village Hotel
Whiston
Fallows Way
Whiston L35 1RZ
T: 0151 449 2341 F: 0151 449 3832
Contact: Kirsten Orr,
Wedding Co-ordinator

Ceremony

This is part of The Village Leisure chain of leisure centres and hotels. Ceremonies here must be followed by reception on site.
Price guide: £150

Reception

Catering: Buffets from £8.50pp. Sit down from £17.50pp

The Village Leisure Hotel
Village Bromborough
Pool Lane
Bromborough L62 4UE
T: 0151 643 1616 F: 0151 643 1420
email: village.b.cybase.so.uk
Contact: Judy Robinson, Conference
& Banqueting Co-ordinator

Ceremony

Another in The Village Leisure chain, this one has two licensed rooms, the Hesketh Suite and the Bryce Suite, which are available on any day of the year.
Price guide: £150

Reception

Catering: Buffet from £8pp. Sit down from £17pp.

ALSO LICENSED
Aintree Racecourse 0151 522 2935
Haydock Thistle Hotel 01942 272000
Liverpool Marina 0151 709 0578
Liverpool Moat House 0151 471 9988
Logwood Mill Hotel 0151 449 2341
Lyceum Library Restaurant 0151 709 7097
Solna Hotel 0151 281 7595

136

The Appleyard
Banham Zoo
The Grove
Norfolk, NR16 2HB
T: 01953 887 384 F: 01953 888 427
Contact: Mr David Barber, Manager

Ceremony

This is one of only two zoos currently registered for ceremonies (the other being London Zoo). The ceremony room here (no wheelchair access) is available on any day except Sunday.
Price guide: POA

Reception

Helicopters and hot air balloons can use the grounds here. Horse drawn carriage and zoo train can be made available to the marriage couple. You can even have your pictures taken by the penguin pool.
Catering: Buffets from £3.75pp. Sit down from £7.50pp

Barnham Broom Hotel
Honingham Road
Barnham Broom NR9 4DD
T: 01603 759393 F: 01603 758224
Contact: Liz Heath, Conference Manager

Ceremony

Barnham Broom is a modern hotel set in 250 acres with two 18 hole golf courses and extensive leisure and conference facilities. Four suites are licensed for ceremonies and are available any day of the year except Christmas Day and Boxing Day. Children can be catered for separately.
Price guide: £75

Reception

Catering: from £24.50pp

Congham Hall Country House
Grimston, King's Lynn
Norfolk PE32 1AH
T: 01485 600250 F: 01485 601191
Contact: Mr Trevor Forecast, Proprietor

Ceremony

This Georgian manor house, situated only six miles from King's Lynn, stands in 40 acres of parkland and formal gardens. One ceremony can take place here per day, on any day except Bank Holidays.
Price guide: £250

Reception

The head Chef, Jonathon Nicholson, has created several menus specially for wedding celebrations. The Hall has an attractive restaurant, the Orangery, with full length windows overlooking the lawns. Large doors open onto the terrace from here. Smaller dinner parties can be catered for in the Board Room.
Catering: £17.50pp - £30pp

The Highwayman
Hermanus Leisure Centre
Winterton on Sea, Gt Yarmouth
T: 01493 393607
Contact Mr Malcolm Lake, Manager

Ceremony

This venue overlooks the beach. The wedding room (with limited wheelchair access) is available on any day of the year. Ceremonies here must be followed by a reception at the venue.
Price guide: POA

Reception

Helicopters and hot air balloons can land on site. Firework displays have also been held here as part of wedding celebrations.
Catering: Sit down from £10pp

King's Lynn Town Hall
Saturday Market Place
King's Lynn
Norfolk PE30 5DQ
T: 01553 692722
Contact: Miss Brenda Hall, Administrative Officer

Ceremony

The Town Hall was built in 1421 and features ornate decoration, portraits and decorative mirrors. Confetti is not permitted here.
Price guide: Ceremony £77 + an hourly rate or £52 with reception + hourly rate

Reception

Couples may use their own choice of caterer for a reception at the Town Hall. A list of local accommodation can be provided.
Catering: P.O.A.

Lynford Hall
Lynford, Thetford
Norfolk IP26 5HW
T: 01842 878351 F: 01842 878252
Contact: Louis Vella or John Good

Ceremony

This is a Grade II listed mansion house (English Heritage), formerly the seat of the Montagu family. The grounds include Italian gardens designed by Nesfield, and an ornamental lake. The park and gardens have been featured in Country Life and on TV. Ceremonies can take place here on any day of the year.
Price guide: £350 + VAT

Reception

NORFOLK

137

NORFOLK

Receptions can be held in either the Main Hall for up to 100 or in the new, purpose-built, Lyne Stephens Function Suite for up to 350 people. Accommodation is available in the Motel, and suites, including the four poster bridal suite, in the Mansion.
Catering: £27pp - £49pp

Norwich City Football Club
Carrow Road
Norwich NR1 1JE
T: 01603 760760 X2290 F: 01603 628373
Contact: Alex Irving
Director of Operations

Ceremony

Undoubtedly the first choice venue for keen Canary fans, the Club has gained marriage licences for four rooms; The Boardroom, The Players Room, The Carvery and the Executive Suite. These are suitable for wedding parties of 75 to 300. Only one ceremony is permitted per day on any day except match days. All ceremonies must be followed by a reception at the Club.
Price guide: P.O.A.

Reception

A list of local accommodation, with which the Club has preferential rate agreements, can be provided.
Catering: from £6.95pp

Sprowston Manor Hotel
Sprowston Park, Wroxham Road
Norwich NR7 8RP
T: 01603 410871 F: 01603 423911
Contact: S Pepworth, Conf Co-ordinator

Ceremony

This 4-star hotel is set in 10 acres of parkland, which can be used by helicopters and hot air balloons. Three rooms are licensed (one has no wheelchair access), and these are available any day of the year.
Price guide: from £150

Reception

Catering: from £18pp

Stakis Norwich
Amsterdam Way
Cromer Road
Norwich, Norfolk NR6 6JA
T: 01603 410544 F: 01603 478801
Contact: Ann Eagle, Conference and Banqueting Sales Manager

Ceremony

The hotel offers its City Penthouse as the ceremony room. This is available on any day of the year, but ceremonies here must be followed by a reception at the venue. Confetti is not permitted.
Price guide: £50 (over 30 guests FOC)

Reception

Catering: from £14.95pp

St Andrews & Blackfriars Hall
S Andrews Plain, Norwich
Norfolk NR3 1AU
T: 01603 628477 F: 01603 762182
Contact: Tim Aldous, Halls Manager

Ceremony

This Grade I, Scheduled Ancient Monument is claimed to be 'The most complete Friary complex in the UK'. Ceremonies can take place in St Andrew's Hall (max 900) or in Blackfriars Hall (max 400). Up to four ceremonies per day, on any day.
Price guide: from £120

Reception

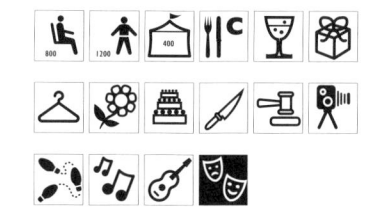

Despite its ability to cater for large numbers, the Hall can also cater for parties with as few as 10 people. A late night drinking licence can be applied for, if required. The Hall can arrange vehicles.
Catering: £5pp - £50pp

Thurning Hall
East Dereham NR20 5QY
T: 01263 587200
Contact: Pauline Harrold, Owner

Ceremony

This private house is a remote mid 18th Century Georgian hall, set in woodland and approached via a tree-canopied drive. It was recently used for the filming of Mill on the Floss. Ceremonies can take place here on any day except Christmas Day, Boxing Day and Good Friday. The two licensed rooms are at the front of the house overlooking the lawns and lake. There are two walled gardens for marquees, and excellent settings for photographs.
Price guide: £150-£200

Reception

Couples may choose their own caterers and marquee. A list of local accommodation can be provided.
Price guide: POA

The Town Hall, Hall Quay
Great Yarmouth NR30 2QF
T: 01493 846324 F: 01493 846332
Contact: Mrs D Fletcher, Admin Officer

Ceremony

This Victorian Town Hall is a listed building located near the river. Four rooms are licensed and are available on any day of the year.
Price guide: £50

Reception

Weston Park Golf Club
Weston Longville
Norwich   NR9 5JW
T: 01603 872363   F: 01603 873040
Contact: Richard Wright, General Manager

Ceremony

The Woodforde Room is licensed for ceremonies and available any day of the year.
Price guide: from £150

Reception

Catering: Buffets from £15pp. Sit down from £20pp.

The Wensum Lodge Hotel
Bridge Street
Fakenham   NR21 9AY
T: 01328 862100   F: 01328 863365
Contact: Dawn Woods, Manageress

Ceremony

The hotel is a former grain store which stands on the banks of the River Wensum by the original mill house.
Price guide: from £120

Reception

The hotel's chef is said to draw his inspiration from the finest seasonal produce sourced locally. The bar offers a wide selection of malt whiskies and cask-conditioned ales. The hotel can also offer a four-poster bedroom.
Catering: P.O.A.

Woodland Comfort Inn
Thetford Road
Northwold   IP26 5LQ
T: 0500 61 62 63   F: 0500 00 5000
Contact: Conference Co-ordinator

Ceremony

This is part of the Friendly Hotels group, and is set in its own 7 acres. Ceremonies here must be followed by a reception at the Inn.
Price guide: POA

Reception

Catering: from £9.95pp

ALSO LICENSED
Caistor Hall   01603 624406
Gissing Hall   01379 677291
Quality Friendly Hotel   01603 744535
Sculthorpe Mill   01328 862726
South Walsham Hall   01603 270378
Taverham Hall School   01603 868206

Castle Ashby House
Castle Ashby
Northampton   NN7 1LQ
T: 01604 696696   F: 01604 696516
Contact: Andrea Fawkes, Sales Manager

Ceremony

Castle Ashby was built in 1574 to entertain Queen Elizabeth I. It is now owned by the Marquess of Northampton, and run as a special event venue with accommodation.
Price guide: P.O.A.

Reception

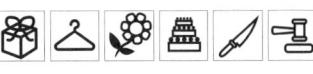

Catering is in-house for smaller receptions, but contract caterers are brought in if the number of guests exceeds 500. This would also mean the erection of a marquee, which can accommodate up to up to 800
Catering: POA

Bentleys
West Park House
Whittlebury
Towcester   NN12 8XW
T & F: 01327 857336
Contact: Mrs Carol Sargeant

Ceremony

Bentleys is a private country house with two rooms licensed: the Main Hall and the Gold Room. These are available on any day of the year.
Price guide: £325

Reception

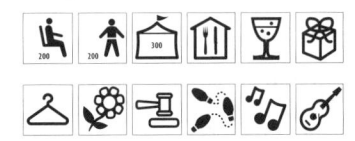

Catering: Buffets from £15pp. Sit down from £17.95pp.

Kettering Park Hotel
Kettering Parkway
Kettering
Northants NN15 6XT
T: 01536 416666   F: 01536 416171
Contact: Janine Thorne, Banqueting

Ceremony

The Kettering Park Hotel offers a price which includes room hire in conjunction with a wedding breakfast.
Price guide: £100 (with breakfast)

Reception

NORFOLK - NORTHAMPTON

139

NORTHAMPTONSHIRE - NORTH EAST LINCOLNSHIRE - NORTH LINCOLNSHIRE

The hotel can cater for any dietary requirements. The maximum capacity for buffets of 200 refers to evening receptions only.
Catering: from £18pp (wedding breakfast)

Rushden Hall
Rushden, Northants
T: 01933 412000 F: 01933 410564
Contact: Mike Bowerman, Rushden Centre Manager

Ceremony

This Grade II listed period building is set in a public park in the town centre. Ceremonies can take place here on any day of the year. Confetti is not permitted.
Price guide: £160

Reception

Catering: POA

Silverstone Circuit
Silverstone, Towcester
Northants NN12 8TN
T: 01327 857271 F: 01327 857663
Contact: Helen Tombs

Ceremony

Home of the RAC British Formula One Motor Racing Grand Prix, Silverstone has licensed its Jimmy Brown Centre for wedding ceremonies. This is available all year except between July 1st and July 15th.
Price guide: POA

Reception

Catering: Buffets from £5.95pp. Sit down from £25pp

Stakis Corby Hotel
Geddington Road
Corby, Northants NN18 8ET
T: 01536 401020
Contact: Steph Bashford, Deputy Conference & Banqueting Manager

Ceremony

The hotel has licences for the Welland and Octagon Suites which are available on Mondays, Fridays and Saturdays, but not on Christmas Day, Boxing Day or New Year's Day.
Price guide: POA

Reception

Catering: Buffets from £7.50pp. Sit down from £18.50pp

Sunley Management Centre
Nene University College
Park Campus
Boughton Green Road
Northhampton
NN2 7AL
T: 01604 791907 F: 01604 712413
Contact: Fiona Waye,
Conference Administrator

Ceremony

The ceremony room at the Centre is the Sir William Shapland Lecture Theatre. This is available on Saturday or Sunday only. Ceremonies here must be followed by reception at the Centre.
Price guide: POA

Reception

Catering: Buffets from £12.95pp. Sit down from £16.25pp

Towcester Racecourse
Easton Neston
Towcester
Northants NN12 7HS
T: 0327 353414 F: 01327 358534
email: towcester-races.demon.co.uk
Contact: Jayne Walker, Special Events and Promotions Manager

Ceremony

Towcester boasts a building of outstanding architectural excellence overlooking one of Britain's most picturesque racecourses. Ceremonies can take place here on any day when there is no racing.
Price guide: POA

Reception

Helicopters can land on site here.
Catering: from £25pp

ALSO LICENSED
The Diamond Centre 01933 650345
Hellidon Lakes 01327 262550
The Hind Hotel 01933 222827
Lamport Hall 01604 686272
The Talbot Hotel 01832 273621

NORTH EAST LINCOLNSHIRE
LICENSED PREMISES
Forte Posthouse 01472 350295
The Oaklands Hotel 01472 872248
Stallingborough Grange Hotel
01469 561302

Wortley House Hotel
Rowland Road
Scunthorpe
North Lincolnshire
DN16 1SU
T: 01724 842223 F: 01724 280646
Contact: Caroline Hutson, Conference Co-ordinator, or James Main, Deputy Manager

Ceremony

This modern hotel is situated in the

middle of town and has three rooms licensed to hold ceremonies; the Sergeant Suite, with a capacity of 250, and the Rolling Mill, with a capacity of 100, and the hotel restaurant for the smaller wedding of 15-30 people. Ceremonies are available seven days a week with no restrictions on the number held per day or on Bank Holidays. Ceremonies are only available with receptions and are free of charge.

Reception

Although no specifically allocated area exists for outdoor photography, the hotel recommends the use of a park, just two minutes walk away.
Catering: £18.50-25.50pp

Bedlingtonshire Suite
Bedlington Community Centre
Front Street, Bedlington NE22 5TT
T: 01670 824141
Contact: Simon Baxter, Manager

Ceremony

This town centre venue is a community centre with function rooms, two of which are licensed, including the Public Bar. Receptions must be on site.
Price guide: £50

Reception

Catering: Buffet from £2.95pp. Sit down from £11.50pp

Chillingham Castle
Chillingham, Nr Alnwick
Northumberland NE66 5NJ
T: 01668 215359 F: 01668 215463
Contact: Joanna Powell, Administrator

Ceremony

This Medieval fortress with Tudor additions, is a gem among the venues for wedding ceremonies. The Castle is set in Italian gardens and grounds featuring a lake and views to the Cheviots. The Castle is open to the public every day in July and August and every day except Tuesdays between May and October. Ceremonies can take place in the tapestried Great Hall on any day of the year.
Price guide: £300

Reception

This is a popular venue for medieval themed weddings. The venue can also arrange horses and carriage if required. Accommodation is in seven apartments, sleeping 15 in total.
Catering: Buffet from £10pp Sit down from £17.50pp

Cragside
Rothbury, Morpeth NE65 7PX
T & F: 01669 620150
Contact: Lesley Carnaby, Assistant to the Property Manager

Ceremony

This National Trust Victorian mansion is open to the public from April to October. Wedding ceremonies are available March to mid December. Recognised as the first house to be lit by hydro-electricity in 1878, this listed building is set in approximately 1,000 acres of grounds. Ceremonies are held in the Gallery and are available on Friday and Saturday mornings during the open season. Only one ceremony per day is permitted.
Price guide: £300+ VAT

Reception
Reception facilities are not available at Cragside.

Embleton Hall
Longframlington
Morpeth
Northumberland NE65 8DT
T: 01665 570249 F: 01665 570056
Contact: Lindsey

Ceremony

Price guide: F.O.C. (with reception)

Reception

Catering: from £16.00pp

Eshott Hall
Morpeth
Northumberland NE65 9EP
T: 01670 787777 F: 01670 787020
Email: eshott@btinternet.com
Contact: Margaret Sanderson

Ceremony

Eshott is a private country house and a listed building. It boasts an exquisite ceiling in its Drawing Room. one of four licensed rooms. These are available every day except Christmas Day.
Price guide: POA

Reception

Discos or dances would take place in a marquee. A list of local accommodation can be provided on request.
Catering: Buffet from £7.50pp. Sit down from £20pp.

Espley Hall
Morpeth
Northumberland NE61 3DJ
T: 01670 513986
Contact: Mr J Kenworthy, Owner

Ceremony

This Victorian merchant's house is available for hire on an exclusive basis only;

141

NORTHUMBERLAND

thereby ensuring total privacy and personal attention. It features 15 acres of lawns and flower beds surrounded by trees. Ceremonies are available seven days a week. Confetti is not permitted.
Price guide: £40 - £125

Reception

There are three types of menus to choose from: a formal hot meal with all courses being served at the table for 90, a finger buffet, a more informal gathering up to a maximum of 120 guests, and a cold fork buffet, whereby guests are seated in a formal arrangement and are shown to the buffet table, to a maximum of 90 guests. The Hall operates preferential rate agreements with other local hotels.
Catering: £28 - £31 (including drinks)

**Kirkley Hall
Ponteland
Northumberland NE20 0AQ**
T: 01661 860808 F: 01661 860047
Contact: Brian Glover, College Services Manager

Ceremony

Kirkley Hall is the mansion house attached to a farming college. It is a listed building set in open countryside and boasts 'magnificent gardens'. Ceremonies here must be followed by a reception on the premises.
Price guide: £25pp

Reception

Catering: from £12pp

**Langley Castle Hotel
Langley on Tyne, Hexham
Northumberland NE7 5LU**
T: 01434 688888 F: 091434 684019
Contact: Anton Phillips, General Manager

Ceremony

This 14th Century castle is a Grade I listed building and has only limited wheelchair access to the ceremony room. Ceremonies are available seven days a week with only one permitted a day.
Price guide: £275

Reception

Catering: from £18pp

**Longhirst Hall
Longhirst, Morpeth NE61 3LL**
T: 01670 791348 F: 01670 791 385
Contact: The Wedding Co-ordinator

Ceremony

This 19th Century building is set in 55 acres of grounds. Now used as a management training and conference centre, the Hall offers ceremonies seven days a week with restrictions over the Christmas period. The capacity of the Joicey room is 45 and standing is discouraged. Ceremonies with receptions only.
Price guide: £50

Reception

Catering: £20 - £27.50pp

**Marshall Meadows Country House Hotel
Berwick upon Tweed TD15 1UT**
T: 01289 331133 F: 01289 331438
Contact: Matthew Rudd, GM

Ceremony

Just a quarter of a mile South of the Scottish border, this Georgian mansion was converted into a country house hotel in 1991 and is set in 15 acres of woodland and matured gardens, bordered by open farmland with sea views.
Price guide: £50-150

Reception

The hotel states that fresh local produce plays an important part when creating its traditional home cooking. This includes fresh fish and shell fish caught daily at the nearby Scottish fishing village of Eyemouth.
Catering: from £5.20pp (buffet) to £14.20pp

**The Ramblers Country House Restaurant
Farnley, Corbridge
Northumberland NE45 5RN**
T: 01434 632424 F: 01434 633656
Contact: Mrs Jennifer Herrmann, Owner

Ceremony

This 19th Century country house is run by husband and wife team Jennifer and Heinrich Herrmann. The restaurant is available to hold ceremonies from Tuesday to Sunday, excluding Bank Holidays, Christmas Day and Boxing Day. During the "wedding season", May to October, the restaurant cannot accept bookings for wedding parties of less than 50 guests on Saturdays. Prices to hold the ceremony range from £50, Tuesday to Friday, up to £100 on Saturday and Sunday.
Price guide: from £50

Reception

Chef/proprietor Heinrich states that menus can be individually planned for each reception. The couple pride themselves on the quality of the in-house

cuisine. Although a late night drinking licence is not held permanently, the restaurant is more than happy to apply for one. Piano music is a feature of the restaurant.
Catering: from £17.35pp

**Tillmouth Park Hotel
Cornhill on Tweed
Northumberland TD12 4UU**
T: 01890 882255 F: 01890 882540
Contact: Charles Carroll, General Manager

Ceremony

This Grade II listed building offers ceremonies seven days a week and holds no restrictions during Bank Holidays or other times of the year. Only one ceremony a day is permitted and confetti is allowed.
Price guide: £150

Reception

Buffet-style catering is available for a maximum of 200 guests. Couples requiring this format must hire a marquee in order to house this number of guests, as the hotel itself can only accommodate up to 70. It may, however, be hired on an exclusive basis and features a portable dance floor. Children can be catered for separately.
Catering: £25pp

**White Swan Hotel
Bondgate Within, Alnick
Northumberland NE66 1TD**
T: 01665 602109 F: 01665 510400
Contact: Sonia Grey, Conference & Banqueting Co-ordinator

Ceremony

The licensed Olympic Suite at this hotel features fittings from the RMS Olympic, the Titanic's little known sister ship. Ceremonies here must be followed by reception on the premises.
Price guide: POA

Reception

Catering: from £21.95 (inc drinks)

**Woodhorn Colliery Museum
QEII Country Park
Ashington
Northumberland NE63 9YF**
T: 01670 856968 F: 01670 810958
Contact: Barry Mead, Museums Officer

Ceremony

This listed building is a converted 19th Century steam winding house. The function rooms is licensed for ceremonies which can take place here Thursday to Sunday, but not on Christmas Day or New Year's Day.
Price guide: from £60

Reception

Reception facilities are not available at the Museum.

ALSO LICENSED
*Anglers Arms   01665 570271
Ashington Leisure Centre   01670 813254
Linden Hall Hotel 01670 516611
Northumberland County Hall
01670 533030
Otterburn Hall   01830 520663
Slaley Hall   01434 673350
Tynedale Farmer Function Suite
01434 605444
Wallington Hall   01670 774691*

**Aldwark Manor Golf Club
Aldwark, York YO6 2NF**
T: 01347 838146 F: 01347 838867
Contact: Richard Harrison, GM

Ceremony

The Club is housed in a listed building, dating back to 1865, and allows only one ceremony per day, but this must be booked in conjunction with the reception.
Price guide: from £50

Reception

The Club offers traditional English fayre, and has a range of complete packages on offer.
Catering: from £29.90

**Allerton Park
Nr Knaresborough
N Yorks HG5 0SE**
T: 01423 330927 F: 01423 330632
Contact: Mike Farr, Administrator

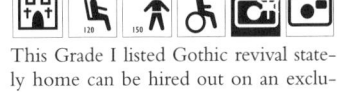

Ceremony

This Grade I listed Gothic revival stately home can be hired out on an exclusive use basis. Only one ceremony is permitted here per day, on any day except Sunday. Confetti is only permitted outside.
Price guide: £2000

Reception

Catering: from £17.50pp + vat

**Beningbrough Hall
Shipton by Beningbrough
York, North Yorks YO6 1DD**
T: 01904 470666 F: 01904 470002
Contact: Assistant Property Manager

Ceremony

This National Trust property is a Georgian hall set in 365 acres. It features many pictures on loan from the National Portrait Gallery, as well as a cantilevered staircase, fine furniture and porcelain. Croquet is available for hire. Ceremonies can take place in the Great Hall on Thursdays, Fridays and Saturdays (after 5pm for exclusive use), but not on Bank Holidays.
Price guide: £350 + VAT

Reception

NORTHUMBERLAND - NORTH YORKSHIRE

143

NORTH YORKSHIRE

Catering: from 18pp

**Bilton House
31 Park Parade
Harrogate HG1 5AG**
T: 01423 506949
Contact: Mrs A Goodwin,
Superintendent Registrar

Ceremony

This is the county register office and has three licensed rooms licensed. These are available on any day of the week except Sundays and Saturday afternoons.
Price guide: £30-£60

Reception
There are no reception facilities.

**The Bridge Inn hotel
Walshford, Wetherby LS22 5HS**
T: 01937 580115 F: 01937 580556
Contact: Anna Piechocki, Business Development Manager

Ceremony

This independently owned, ranch style hotel offers five rooms for ceremonies on any day of the year. Ceremonies must be followed by a reception on the premises.
Price guide: FOC (with reception)

Reception

Catering: Buffets from £6.95pp. Sit down from £14.75pp

**The Carlton Lodge Hotel
Bondgate
Helmsley YO6 5EY**
T: 01439 770557 F: 01439 770623
email: carlton.lodge@dial.pipex.com
Web Site:
http://dspace.dial.pipex.com/carlton.lodge
Contact: Chris Parkin, Director

Ceremony

The Lodge is situated on the edge of 12th Century Helmsley within the North York Moors National Park. Three rooms are licensed for ceremonies and are available any day of the week.
Price guide: from £95

Reception

'Romance is alive in Helmsley' says the hotel. A bespoke service or total packages are available.
Catering: Buffets from £12.50pp Sit down from £13.75pp

**Crathorne Hall Hotel
Crathorne, Yarm TS15 0AR**
T: 01642 700398 F: 01642 700814
email: hotel.reservations@virgin.co.uk
Contact: Sharon West, Conference & Banqueting Co-ordinator

Ceremony

Part of Richard Branson's Virgin group, Crathorne Hall is an Edwardian building which was occupied by Lord Crathorne until 1977.
Price guide: P.O.A.

Reception

Catering: POA

**Croft Spa Hotel
Croft on Tees DL2 2ST**
T: 01325 720319 F: 01325 721252
Contact: Mr Lawrence

Ceremony

Up to two ceremonies per day are permitted in this listed building, on any day of the year.
Price guide: P.O.A.

Reception

Catering: from £8.75

**Crown Hotel
Crown Place, Harrogate
N Yorks HG1 2RZ**
T: 01423 567755 F: 01423 502284
Contact: Laura Isherwood

Ceremony

The Crown has been a hotel since 1740. One of its claims to romantic fame is that Lord Byron wrote his ode "To a beautiful Quaker' whilst staying here. Ceremonies can take place here on any day of the year.
Price guide: from £150

Reception

Catering: P.O.A.

**Crown Hotel
Horse Fair
Boroughbridge YO5 9LB**
T: 01423 322328 F: 01423 324512
Contact: Emma Dunn
Sales Co-ordinator

Ceremony

This former 13th Century coaching inn has licences for several of its rooms (Tancred Restaurant, St Helena, Marston and Lancaster suites) which are available on any day of the year.
Price guide: from £60

144

Reception

Catering: P.O.A.

The Crown Inn at Roecliffe
Nr Boroughbridge
North Yorkshire YO5 9LY
T: 01423 322578 F: 01423 324060
Contact: Philip Barker, Landlord

Ceremony

This 16th Century inn has a license for its Snug Bar and Coach House, which are available any day of the year.
Price guide: FOC (with reception)

Reception

The inn offers 12 bedrooms and a cottage for accommodation and will provide the bridal suite free for the bride and groom. Courtesy cars can also be provided.
Catering: Buffets from £6pp. Sit down from £12pp.

Devonshire Arms Country House Hotel, Bolton Abbey
Skipton, N Yorks BD23 6AJ
T: 01756 710441 F: 01756 710564
Contact: Sarah Graham-Harrison, Sales, Conference & Banqueting Manager

Ceremony

Originally a 17th Century coaching inn, the Devonshire Arms is now owned by the Duke and Duchess of Devonshire and enjoys a splendid setting in the Yorkshire Dales national parkland. Although ceremonies are usually available on any day of the year, they are not available from 24 to 26 December inclusive or on New Year's Eve. Up to four ceremonies can be held per day, depending upon availability. Confetti is only allowed outside
Price guide: £150 - £500

Reception

The Devonshire Arms holds two AA rosettes for its cooking.
Catering: £25 - £32pp

Duncome Park
Helmsley
York YO6 5EB
T: 01439 770213 F: 01439 771114
Contact: Sally Potter, Visitor Co-ordinator

Ceremony

Duncombe Park is a Baroque style stately home, built around 1713 and set in extensive grounds. Three rooms are offered for wedding ceremonies, all of which are richly decorated; The Saloon and The Stone Hall (100 max), and the Ladies Withdrawing Room ((seats 25). Weddings can take place here on any day except event days, and are restricted to one per day.
Price guide: from £450 + vat

Reception

Accommodation is not available on the premises, but a list of local establishments can be supplied.
Catering: £33pp

Dunsley Hall Hotel
Whitby
N Yorks YO21 3TL
T: 01947 893437 F: 01947 893505
Contact: Mr Steven Talbot, Assistant Manager

Ceremony

Dunsley Hall is a country house hotel set in 4 acres of grounds. Three rooms are licensed for ceremonies, with only one ceremony permitted here per day.
Price guide: POA

Reception

Catering: from £12.50pp

Falcon Manor Hotel
Skipton Road
Settle, N Yorks BD24 9BD
T: 01729 823814 F: 01729 822087
Contact: Elizabeth Weatherby
Events Manager

Ceremony

The Falcon Manor is a listed building and is set in its own landscaped gardens. One ceremony is permitted here per day on any day of the year.
Price guide: £175

Reception

Catering: POA

Galtres Centre
Market Place, Easingwold
N Yorks YO6 3AD
T: 01347 822472
Contact: Major RM Crees, Vice Chairman Management Committee

Ceremony

The Galtres Centre is a community centre within a Victorian house, and is run by volunteers. Four rooms have marriage licences; two on the ground floor, for which catering is available, and two

NORTH YORKSHIRE

145

NORTH YORKSHIRE

on the first floor (no catering). The Centre hopes to install a lift to improve disabled access to the first floor. Ceremonies can take place here on any day of the year. Confetti is not encouraged.
Price guide: £50

Reception

Couples may choose their own caterers for receptions, with prices varying accordingly. In addition to the Centre itself, a large leisure hall is adjacent, which will accommodate up to 250 for a disco or dinner dance. Other facilities at the Centre include a rifle range and tennis courts. List of local accommodation is available.
Price guide: P.O.A.

Hanover International Hotel
**Keighley Road
Skipton
North Yorkshire BD23 2TA**
T: 01756 700100 F: 01756 700107
Contact: Sarah Bratley
Events Co-ordinator

Ceremony

One of a chain of seven hotels in the UK, the Hanover International at Skipton has four rooms licensed for ceremonies which can take place here on any day of the year.
Price guide: POA

Reception

Numerous meal and drinks packages have been put together, with meal packages starting at £18.95pp and drinks packages at £5.15pp. Ten bedrooms can be offered to guests at a discounted rate. A Playzone Nursery can be set up to look after the smaller guests.
Catering: from £17pp

Hotel St Nicholas
**St Nicholas Cliff
Scarborough, N Yorks YO11 3EU**
T: 01723 364101 F: 01723 500538
Contact: James Brown, Conference & Banqueting Co-ordinator

Ceremony

The hotel is set overlooking Scarborough's South Bay and is a few minutes walk from the beach itself. Ceremonies can take place here on any day of the year except Christmas Day and New Year's Day, but must be in conjunction with a reception at the hotel.
Price guide: FOC

Reception

Flowers on the tables are provided as part of the wedding package, as is a first anniversary dinner for the happy couple. Wedding guests are also offered special overnight rates.
Catering: from £5.95 (buffet) - £18.50pp (waited)

National Railway Museum
Leeman Road York YO2 4XJ
T: 01904 621261 F: 01904 631319
Contact: Rowena Cunningham, Events Executive

Ceremony

Three ceremony rooms are available at the museum; the Conference Room, the Stephenson Room and the South Hall. Weddings can take place here any day of the week except Sunday.
Price guide: from £275

Reception

A list of local accommodation with which the museum has preferential rates can be supplied if requested,
Catering: £11.50 - £24.50pp

The Old Lodge Hotel
**Old Maltongate
Malton YO17 0EG**
T: 01653 690870 F: 01653 690652
Contact: N Binner

Ceremony

The hotel was built as a gate house to Malton House in around 1604 and is now a listed building. Three rooms are licensed including the Jacobean Main Hall. Ceremonies can take place here on any day of the year.
Price guide: £100

Reception

Recent unusual weddings here have included a Korean marriage.
Catering: Buffets from £6pp. Sit down from £20pp.

The Orangery
**Settrington, Malton
N Yorks YO17 8NP**
T: 01944 768 345 F: 01944 768 484
Contact: Mandy Atkinson, Administrator

Ceremony

This former riding school features a large pillared hall. It is a classical building set in extensive grounds. Ceremonies (only one per day) can take place here on any day of the year, but must be followed by a reception at the venue.
Price guide: £450

Reception

A list of local accommodation can be provided.
Catering: £11 - £15pp

Quality Kimberley Hotel
11-19 Kings Road
Harrogate HG1 5JY
T: 01423 505613 F: 01423 530276
Contact: Martin Wilks, General Manager

Ceremony

This Victorian Town House hotel has a licence for its De Beer Suite which is available on any day of the year.
Price guide: POA

Reception

The hotel can offer a choice of table linen colours, a full wine list and special accommodation rate for wedding guests.
Catering: Buffets from £15pp. Sit down from £17pp.

Ripley Castle
Ripley
Nr Harrogate HG3 3AY
T: 01423 770152 F: 01423 771745
Contact: Chloe Evans, VIP Event and Administration Manager

Ceremony

Ripley Castle itself is a Grade I listed building and a member of the Historic Houses Association. It has been home to the Ingilby family for over 670 years and stands in extensive grounds featuring a Capability Brown landscaped deer park, lakes and valley. Ceremonies can take place here on any day of the year, but must take place after 4.30pm between April and October when the castle is open to the public.
Price guide: £500

Reception

A marquee is available for use all Summer. This is usually used for any events involving dancing. In addition to the above services, the castle can also arrange for a horse and carriage, hot air balloon or helicopter. Exclusive tours of the castle and its walled gardens (home of the National Hyacinth Collection) can also be arranged. Accommodation is available in the Castle's adjacent hotel, the Boar's Head Hotel, a Grade II listed building located in a conservation area.
Catering: Complete packages start at £65pp

Royal Hotel
St Nicholas Street
Scarborough YO11 2HE
T: 01723 364333 F: 01723 500618
Contact: Miss Tessa Maxwell, Wedding Co-ordinator

Ceremony

The Royal Hotel is a Regency building in the centre of Scarborough. It has a fine Regency staircase; a suitable setting for indoor photographs. Outside photographs may be taken in the Town Hall Gardens opposite the hotel. The Gardens have the harbour and sea as a backdrop. The Royal Ballroom and Prince Regent Room are licensed and available any day of the year.
Price guide: from £75

Reception

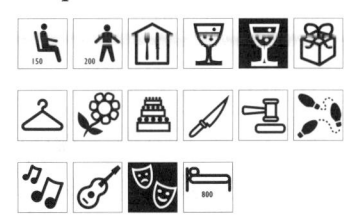

Personalised menus and place cards are included in the packages.
Catering: £14.50pp

Rudding Park House & Hotel
Rudding Park, Follifoot
Harrogate, N Yorks HG3 1JH
T: 01423 871350 F: 01423 844848
Contact: Joanne McBratney, Weddings Co-ordinator

Ceremony

Rudding House is a Grade I listed Regency house, set in 230 acres and designed by Wyatt in 1806. It is now an award-winning residential conference and banqueting centre, with grounds featuring woodlands and ornamental lakes and a herb garden. Ceremonies can take place on any day of the year.
Price guide: from £200

Reception

Accommodation is now available at Rudding Park. Prices are available on request.
Catering: £40 - £50pp

Scotch Corner Hotel
Nr Richmond DL11 6ED
T: 01748 850900 F: 01748 825417
Contact: Alison Boys, GM

Ceremony

The hotel permits wedding ceremonies on any day of the year, allowing only one per day. Confetti is not permitted.
Price guide: from £170

Reception

Catering: from £6.95 - £25pp

Solberge Hall
Newby Wiske DL7 9ER
T: 01609 779191 F: 01609 780472
Contact: Wedding Co-ordinator

Ceremony

NORTH YORKSHIRE

NORTH YORKSHIRE

Once a Victorian country house, Solberge Hall sits in 16 acres overlooking the moors and dales. Ceremonies must be followed by reception at the Hall.
Price guide: F.O.C. (with reception)

Reception

The Hall offers two main function suites; the Garden Suite (max 100) and the Clock Tower Suite (max 120). As part of the wedding package, bride and groom are offered complimentary use of a four-poster bedroom on their wedding night. Reduced rates are offered for children under 10 years old. Personalised menus can also be provided.
Catering: POA

Stephen Joseph Theatre
Westborough
Scarborough YO11 1JW
T: 01723 370540 F: 01723 360506
email: response@sjt.onyxnet.co.uk
Contact: Jaye Lewis,
Functions Organiser

Ceremony

The theatre is a 1930s' Grade II listed building and former Odeon Cinema in the town centre. Several areas are licensed including the theatres themselves, the Atrium and the Restaurant. These are available, subject to theatre performances, on any day of the year. Confetti is not permitted.
Price guide: POA

Reception

Weddings here have included bride and groom and guests in full theatrical costume.
Catering: from £7.50pp

Tan Hill Inn
Keld, Nr Richmond DL11 6ED
T: 01833 628246
Contact: Maureen Keating, Manager

Ceremony

The Tan Hill Inn claims to be the highest pub in Britain (1732ft), and the first pub in the country to hold a wedding (televised). The pub is also a listed building and dates back to the 13th Century. Ceremonies can take place on any day except Bank Holidays, although in high season, Saturdays and Sundays availability can be limited.
Price guide: £75

Reception

Catering: from £4.25pp

Waterford House
Middleham
N Yorks D28 4PG
T: 01969 622090 F: 01969 624020
Contact: Everyl M Madell, Joint Proprietor

Ceremony

This Grade II listed building, with its own walled garden, is set in Middleham, a major racehorse training centre in the Yorkshire Dales. Internally the house features period and antique furnishings and four poster beds. The Dining Room (limited wheelchair access) and Lounge are licensed for ceremonies on any day of the year. Ceremonies must be followed by a reception at the house.
Price guide: £20- £100

Reception

The hotel features in many guides, including the Good Food Guide. Guests can go on a racing stable visit during their stay if requested.
Catering: Buffets from £10pp. Sit down from £19.50pp

Wood Hall Hotel
Trip Lane, Linton LS22 4JA
T: 01937 587271 F: 01937 584353
Contact: Elaine Hardy, Conference & Banqueting Co-ordinator

Ceremony

Four marriage rooms are available in this Grade II listed building. Ceremonies can take place here on any day of the year except Easter Monday. Only biodegradable confetti is permitted.
Price guide: from £100

Reception

Catering: £27pp - £35pp

Wrea Head Country House
Barmoor Lane
Scalby
Scarborough
N Yorks YO13 0PB
T: 01723 378211 F: 01723 371780
Contact: Mike Turner, Sales Director

Ceremony

This Yorkshire country house is set in acres of grounds and gardens, which can be used by helicopters and hot air balloons. The ceremony room is the Library which is available any day of the year. Vintage cars can also be provided by this venue.
Price guide: £200

Reception

The marquee is set up permanently throughout the summer – April to November.
Catering: Buffets from £15pp. Sit down from £20pp

148

ALSO LICENSED
Angel Inn 01845 577237
Ayton Hall 01642 723595
Bedale Hall 01677 423797
Bolton Castle 01969 623981
Bridge Inn 01937 580115
Cairn Hotel 01423 504005
Gateforth Hall Hotel 01757 228225
Grantley College 01765 620259
Larpool Hall, Whitby 01947 602737
Newburgh Priory 01347 868372
Old Swan Hotel 01423 500055
Pavilions of Harrogate 01423 561536
Raven Hall 01723 870235
Ripon Spa Hotel 01705 602172

Blotts Hotel & Country Club
Home Pierrepont
Nottingham NG2 7PD
T: 0115 933 5656   F: 0115 933 4696
Contact: Sandra Heathcote, General Manageress

Ceremony

This banqueting venue is set in five acres of open parkland with car parking for 200 cars. The Crystal Room and Lincoln Suite are licensed and available any day of the year.
Price guide: £50

Reception

Many celebrity weddings have apparently been held at this hotel.
Catering: Buffets from £6.50pp. Sit down from £12.50pp

Cotgrave Place
Golf & Country Club
Stragglethorpe, Notts
T: 0115 9333344   F: 0115 9334567
Contact: Melissa Read, Banqueting

Ceremony

The golf club is set in 250 acres of parkland. The venue is available for ceremonies seven days a week. The Club suggests couples telephone to arrange a visit.
Price guide: £50

Reception

All wedding bookings include a complimentary flower arrangement for the head table.
Catering: from £6pp (buffet)

Gedling House
Wood Lane
Nottingham NG4 4AD
T: 0115 955 2500 F: 0115 953 4144
Contact: Mr V Skitt, Miss C Lacey, Event Managers

Ceremony

This conference and function centre is set in a listed Georgian mansion. Four rooms are licensed and are available any day of the year.
Price guide: from £225

Reception

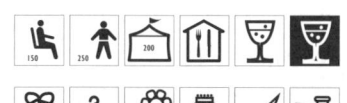

Chinese and Indian food can be provided if required. Helicopters and hot air balloons may use the grounds.
Catering: Buffets from £15pp. Sit down from £22.50.

Indian Community Centre
Rawson Street, New Basford
Nottinghamshire N67 7FR
T: 0115 9785 985 F: 0115 9791 500
Contact: Raj Jogia, Manager

Ceremony

The Indian Community Centre has recently been refurbished and extended. It now offers two halls which are licensed to hold ceremonies. The smaller hall is offered at a rate of £30 for four hours, while the large hall is offered at a cost of £50 for four hours. Each additional hour is charged at an additional £10 per hour. Each of the halls has adjoining rooms for receptions.
Price guide: from £30

Reception

Catering facilities are undertaken on a contract basis, and although the Community Centre can recommend a selection of caterers (specialising in ethnic cuisine), couples are welcome to supply their own contract caterers which will incur a kitchen hire fee. A list of local accommodation which operate rate agreements with the Centre is available.
Catering: from £4.50pp

Kelham Hall, Newark
Nottinghamshire NG23 5QX
T: 01636 708256   F: 01636 708263
Contact: John Underwood, Catering Manager or Bridgette Nice, Administration Officer

Ceremony

Kelham Hall is a very large Victorian Gothic mansion, which includes the later addition of a Byzantine style chapel which is now used as a conference centre. The building is set in 42 acres of gardens and parkland adjacent to the River Trent. The property is now owned by Newark and Sherwood District Council and the Hall is used as its headquarters. Four rooms are licensed for ceremonies and are available any day of the year. Confetti is not permitted.
Price guide: £200

Reception

Catering: Buffets from £7pp. Sit down from £16.50pp

Langar Hall Hotel
Langar
Nottinghamshire
NG13 9HG
T: 01949 860559 F: 01949 861045
Contact: Mrs Imogen Skirving Proprietor/Manager

149

NOTTINGHAMSHIRE

Ceremony

This Grade II listed building offers ceremonies seven days a week excluding Saturday afternoons unless the House is booked as a whole. Only one ceremony per day is permitted and confetti is allowed. The ceremony fee includes the marriage room, private meeting room, changing room for the bride and flowers.
Price guide: £200

Reception

The buffet capacity indicated is on the basis of a plated buffet or finger buffet only. If a seated meal for more than 50 guests is required, the marquee and both dining rooms will need to be used. For weekday lunchtime marriages, a 25% discount will be offered for parties of 15 guests or less.
Catering: POA

**The Manor School of Fine Cuisine
Old Melton Road
Widmerpool
Nottingham NG12 5QL**
T & F: 01949 81371
Contact: Claire Tuttey

Ceremony

This is a private cordon bleu cookery school set in a Georgian manor house with gardens and a duck pond. The Marriage Lounge has the ceremony licence and is available on any day of the year.
Price guide: POA

Reception

Any cuisine is offered including French, Thai, Arabic, Indian and Italian.
Catering: from £12pp

**Mansfield Civic Centre
Chesterfield Road South
Mansfield
Nottinghamshire**
T: 01623 656766 F: 01623 635764
Contact: Ring & Brymer

Ceremony

The Centre has two rooms licensed to hold ceremonies, one of which has a capacity of 600 in a seated, theatre style. Ceremonies are available seven days a week with only one per day permitted in the Banqueting Suite. However, ceremonies can be held as and when required in the Council Chamber. Maximum capacity is 700. All enquiries from combined weddings and receptions should be made to the in-house contract caterers, Ring & Brymer. Contact Carol Grant or Pam Potter, General Manager, on 01623 656766. Anyone interested in holding their ceremony in the Oakham Room or Council Chamber without any catering or reception at the venue, should contact James Spray of Mansfield District Council on 01623 656766.
Price guide: £100

Reception

Catering is in-house and the Centre boasts a speciality in ethnic cuisine. The Centre operates preferential rate agreements with local hotels and guest houses.
Catering: from £9pp

**Newstead Abbey
Linby
Basford, Nottinghamshire**
T: 01623 793557 F: 01623 797136
Contact: Brian Ayres, Custodian

Ceremony

This Grade I listed monument was originally a 12th Century monastery, which later became the country residence of Lord Byron. The Abbey is set in 320 acres of parkland, with 28 acres of Japanese, Rose and French gardens. There is also an orangery, which is the only interior space suitable for wedding photography. Nottinghamshire City Council took over ownership of the Abbey in 1939. A loop system is also offered in the ceremony room for the hard of hearing. Ceremonies are available seven days a week, excluding the period from Christmas Eve until New Year's Day.
Price guide: £350.50

Reception

The Abbey features a separate restaurant, the White Lady Restaurant, which is run by an independent caterer. For further information please contact Mrs Crisp on 01623 797392. The Abbey is keen to stress that various wedding packages are available, including items such as flowers, car, etc.
Catering: P.O.A.

**Norwood Park
Southwell NG25 0PF**
T: 01636 815649 F: 01636 815649
email: starkey@farmline.com
Contact: Sarah Dodd, Events Manager

Ceremony

This is a private Georgian country house, with Edwardian stable block, set in parkland and orchard. The Main Hall is licensed and available for ceremonies on any day except Sundays and Bank Holidays. Confetti is not permitted.
Price guide: £500

Reception

While the venue has no drinks licence, a bar facility can be provided. The venue is happy to organise themed dinners and barbecues in the courtyard. Accommodation is available for honeymooners only.
Catering: Buffets from £5pp. Sit down from £15pp

**Trent College, Derby Road
Nottingham NG8 2NP**
T: 0115 946 2848 F: 0115 946 3284
email: pithsh@trentcollege.nott.sch.uk
Contact: Althea Tomlin, Banqueting

Ceremony

Trent College is an independent school on the outskirts of Nottingham. It was built in 1868 and is set in 45 acres of grounds. Five rooms are licensed and are available at any time during the shcool holidays..
Price guide: £200 (25% discount if reception held here also.)

Reception

The college offers a very reasonable and flexible catering service, and is also able to provide all kinds of music (from disco to string quartet). In addition to accommodation on the premises, a list of local establishments can be provided.
Catering: Buffets from £7pp. Sit down from £15.25

The Village Leisure Hotel
Brailsford Way, Chilwell
Nottingham NG9 6DL
T: 0115 946 4422 F: 0115 946 4428
email: village.n@cybase.co.uk
Contact: Melissa Wroe, Conference & Banqueting Co-ordinator

Ceremony

This is a modern hotel, part of a chain, sited next to a nature reserve. The Nightingale Suite is licensed and available any day of the year. Ceremonies here must be followed by reception on the premises.
Price guide: £175

Reception

Many services can be recommended.
Catering: Buffets from £10pp. Sit down from £16pp.

West Retford Hotel
East Retford
Nottinghamshire
T: 01777 706333 F: 01777 709951
Contact: Craig Dowie, GM

Ceremony

The hotel offers ceremonies seven days a week with a maximum of four permitted a day. Confetti is allowed.
Price guide: £150

Reception

In addition to the hotel's 60 bedrooms, it also operates preferential rate agreements with other local hotels and guest houses. The hotel takes particular pride in its grounds.
Catering: Buffets from £10.50pp. Sit down from £13.95

ALSO LICENSED
The Charnwood Hotel 01909 591610
Clumber Park Hotel 01623 835333
Trent Lock Golf Centre 0115 9464398

Abingdon Four Pillars Hotel
Marcham Road
Abingdon
Oxon OX14 1TZ
T: 01235 553456 F: 01235 554117
Contact: Sue Randall, GM

Ceremony

This modern hotel is set in limited grounds, and has two rooms licensed to hold ceremonies with capacities varying from 30 to 80. Ceremonies are permitted without receptions and confetti is allowed.
Price guide: £150

Reception

Buffet receptions are available from £8.25 with sit down meals increasing to a minimum of £14. A complimentary overnight suite for the couple is offered if the reception is also held at the hotel.
Catering: from £8.25pp

The Corn Exchange
Faringdon SN7 7HQ
T: 01367 240281 F: 01367 240303
Contact: June Rennie, Town Clerk

Ceremony

This civic building is located in the town centre and is available for ceremonies all year round.
Price guide: from £50

Reception

Catering: from POA

The Garth
Launton Road
Bicester, Oxon OX6 0JB
T: 01869 252915 F: 01869 324554
Contact: Mrs A Graham, Town Clerk

Ceremony

The Garth, operated by Bicester Town Council, is available to hold ceremonies seven days a week. Confetti is not permitted.
Price guide: £130

Reception

No reception facilities or accommodation are offered at The Garth, although a list of local hotels and guest houses is available.

Hawkwell House Hotel
Church Way Iffley Village OX4 4DZ
T: 01865 749988 F: 01865 748525
Contact: Lisa Williams, Sales & Conference Co-ordinator

Ceremony

NOTTINGHAMSHIRE - OXFORDSHIRE

152

OXFORDSHIRE

The hotel was originally a family home dating back to 1856 and features two houses on the same site. The hotel is 1.5 miles from the centre of Oxford and is set in three acres of grounds. The hotel has five rooms licensed to hold ceremonies, the smallest of which, the Windrush Suite, accommodates 20 guests, while the largest room, the Ballroom, accommodates a maximum of 200.
Price guide: from £275

Reception

Receptions may be held in the same five rooms as the ceremonies, with the hotel particularly recommending the conservatory room. The hotel specialises in modern English cuisine, and the price indicated below includes a drink for guests on arrival, two glasses of wine with the meal, a glass of Champagne for the toast, and flower arrangements. In addition to the 27 bedrooms, the hotel also has two honeymoon suites available which feature a jacuzzi, champagne, flowers and chocolates.
Catering: £37pp

**Lains Barn, Ardington
Near Wantage
c/o
The Vale and Downland Museum, Church Street
Wantage, Oxon OX12 8BL**
T: 01235 760991 F: 01235 764316
email: lainsbarn@wantage.com
Contact: Howard Hill, Manager

Ceremony

This historic timber-framed building is set in a rural location with adjoining lawns. The Main Barn is licensed and available on any day of the year.
Price guide: £265 - £500

Reception

Anything goes here, they say, and you can provide your own caterer to create your own special event.

**Le Manoir Aux Quat' Saisons
Church Road
Great Milton, Oxon OX44 7PB**
T: 01844 278881 F: 01844 278847
Contact: Julia Saunders, Conference & Banqueting Co-ordinator

Ceremony

Raymond Blanc's 15th Century manor house is a listed building set in 30 acres of grounds with a water garden. The Cromwell Room, the Manor's private dining room, is licensed to hold ceremonies with only one permitted a day. There is no guaranteed area suitable for indoor photography but the Manor's grounds more than make up for this. No confetti.
Price guide: £750

Reception

The Manor's famous restaurant (two Michelin stars, five Egon Ronay rosettes and four AA red stars) offers three menu packages: all on a waited service basis. Buffets are not available. In addition to the services indicated, the Manor can recommend toastmaster, photographer, piped music, live music and other entertainments.
Catering: from £45-£65pp

**Phyllis Court Club
Marlow Road
Henley on Thames
Oxon RG9 2HT**
T: 01491 570500 F: 01491 570528
Contact: Roger Best, Banqueting Manager

Ceremony

This club, with its Grade II grandstand pavilion, stands on the banks of the Thames, opposite the winning post of the Royal Regatta. The Club has a long history dating back as far as 1301, while the re-built part of the building has been nominated for a British Construction Industry Award. Four rooms are licensed with varying capacities of 30 to 300.
Price guide: £100 (Oct - Mar) £150 (Apr - Sep)

Reception

Catering: £28.00pp

**Rivers and Boaters
1 St Helen's Avenue
Benson
Oxon OX10 0PY**
T: 01491 838331 F: 01491 826353
Contact: C J Price, General Manager or Mike Allen, Promotions Manager

Ceremony

Both Rivers (nightclub and restaurant) and Boaters (bar and restaurant) are licensed to hold ceremonies, with capacities ranging from 50 to 400. Available Tuesday to Sunday, inclusive, but not Christmas or New Year's Day.
Price guide: from £175

Reception

Although accommodation is not available on site, a list of local hotels is available.
Catering: from £14pp

**The Stonor Arms Hotel
Stonor
Nr Henley-on-Thames
Oxon RG9 6HE**
T: 01491 638866 F: 01491 638863
Contact: Guy Hodgson, Manager

Ceremony

The 18th Century Stonor Arms is a privately owned country hotel and award winning restaurant, set in the countryside and featuring its own walled garden.
Price guide: £150

Reception

The restaurant has won various culinary awards and claims an 'industry-respected chef'.
Catering: Buffets from £15pp. Sit down from £25pp.

Studley Priory Hotel
Horton cum Studley, Oxon
T: 01865 351203 F: 01865 351613
Contact: Mr Bright, Manager or Mr Parke, Owner

Ceremony

This Elizabethan manor house was converted from a 12th Century nunnery, and is situated in 13 acres of wooded grounds with views, to the West, of the Cotswolds and, to the East, along the line of the Chilterns. The hotel has been awarded three AA stars and is ETB four crown commended and Egon Ronay recommended.
Price guide: from £250

Reception

The hotel has three wedding packages available: The Regal, The Grand and The Traditional; all of which aim to facilitate planning arrangements. These packages may be adapted to suit individual requirements. All include a complimentary overnight stay for the couple on their first wedding anniversary.
Catering: £25pp

Sudbury House Hotel
56 London Street
Faringdon
Oxon SN7 8AA
T: 01367 241272 F: 01367 242346
Contact: Donna O'Sullivan, Events Executive

Ceremony

This listed Regency building offers six licensed rooms, all of which are available on any day of the year. Rooms include The Folly Room which overlooks the walled garden and croquet lawn, and the Garden Room, which opens directly onto the lawns.
Price guide: £95 or £145

Reception

Preferential rates are offered to wedding guests for overnight accommodation, and a complimentary room is offered to the bride and groom for the wedding night. Children under 12 are charged at 50% of the published price.
Catering: Buffets from £8.95pp. Sit down from £29.75pp.

Whately Hall Hotel
Banbury Cross
Banbury, Oxon OX16 0AN
T: 01295 263451 F: 01295 271736
Contact: Vena Arnold, Conference & Banqueting Manager

Ceremony

Whately Hall is a Forte Heritage hotel, with its own resident, authenticated ghost (whatever that means). The hotel offers three marriage rooms which are available any day of the year except Easter, Christmas and New Year. Ceremonies here must be followed by a reception on the premises.
Price guide: from £50

Reception

Bride and groom are offered complimentary accommodation on their wedding night, as well as an MC and cake stand and knife for the day.
Catering: from £22pp

Woodstock Town Hall
The Market Place
Woodstock, Oxon OX20 1SL
T & F: 01993 811216
Contact: Mrs Marian Moxon, Town Clerk

Ceremony

The Town Hall is a Grade II listed building built by William Chambers in 1766. It commands a view over Woodstock market place and is adjacent to Blenheim Palace and estate. The Mayor's Parlour is the marriage room, and is available every day except Sunday, Christmas Day and Boxing Day. Outdoor photography can be taken in the Museum gardens.
Price guide: £125

Reception

Reception at the Town Hall take place in the Assembly Room. This room is also covered by a Public Entertainments Licence. Receptions larger than 60 could use the nearby Community Centre off New Road. Caterers for the reception would be your own choice of contract caterers, the price below is therefore an average price.
Catering: Buffets from £5pp. Sit down from £10pp

Wroxton House
Banbury, Oxon OX15 6QB
T: 01295 730777 F: 01295 730800
Contact: Jessica Pickup, Conference & Banqueting Co-ordinator

Ceremony

The hotel is a thatched, country house, dating back to the 17th Century. Ceremonies are available seven days a week, excluding the Christmas and New Year period.
Price guide: £155

Reception

OXFORDSHIRE

OXFORDSHIRE - SHROPSHIRE

Catering is in-house with a speciality in French and English cuisine. A list of local accommodation with preferential rates is available.
Catering: from £31pp (package)

Albrighton Hall Hotel
Albrighton, Shrewsbury
Shropshire SY4 3AG
T: 01939 291000 F: 01939 291313
Contact: Maria Roberts, Conference & Banqueting Co-ordinator

Ceremony

Albrighton Hall is a listed building, built in 1603. It is set in 14 acres of grounds that include an ornamental lake and a croquet lawn. Ceremonies can take place here on any day except Sundays and Bank Holidays. Ceremonies must be followed by a reception at the hotel.
Price guide: POA

Reception

The wedding package (for over 50 guests) includes complimentary accommodation for bride and groom on their wedding night, choice from a selection of menus, and discounts on accommodation for wedding guests.
Catering: POA

Bourton Manor
Bourton
Nr Much Wenlock
Shropshire TF13 6QE
T: 01746 785531 F: 01746 785683
Contact: Chris Stewart, Manager

Ceremony

Bourton Manor is set in its own grounds and is a listed country house dating from the 16th Century. Internal features include oak panelling and a Queen Anne staircase. Weddings can take place here on any day of the year.

Price guide: £100

Reception

A special overnight rate of £25 per person (B&B) is available for your wedding guests.
Catering: £12pp - £25pp

Buckatree Hall Hotel
The Wrekin, Wellington
Telford, Shrops TF6 5AL
T: 01952 641821 F: 01952 247540
Contact Mr MacKay, General Manager

Ceremony

This Best Western hotel has two rooms with licences: The Champagne Suite and The Terrace Restaurant. These take minimum numbers of 25 and 60 guests respectively. Fall below these numbers and a room charge will be incurred. Otherwise, the room hire for the ceremony is free, although ceremonies can only be held with a reception.
Price guide: FOC (with reception)

Reception

Tailor-made menus will be created on request. Children can be catered for separately, on request. A marquee taking up to 100 can be erected in the gardens, which feature a lake.
Catering: from £16.50pp

Castle Lodge
Castle Square, Ludlow SY8 1AY
T: 01584 878098
Contact: Mr W Pearson, Owner

Ceremony

This is a Grade II listed Tudor mansion style building which features oak panelling and stained glass. Ceremonies can take place on any day except Sunday. Other facilities available for your ceremony include flowers, photography, live or piped music. A list of local accommodation is also available.
Price guide: £100

Reception

Reception facilities are not available.

Combermere Abbey
Nr Whitchurch
Shropshire SY13 4AJ
T: 01948 871637 F: 01948 871293
Contact: Mrs Sue Brookes, Administrator

Ceremony

Weddings can be held in either the Library or the Porter's Hall of this Grade I listed Abbey on the Combermere estate, overlooking the 160 acre lake. Blessings may be conducted outside in the surrounding gardens.
Price guide: £1,000

Reception

Standing receptions in the Abbey until 6.30pm for up to 100 people. Marquees for dinner/dance and larger receptions in the restored Walled Garden. Accommodation for up to 50 can be provided in decorated cottages in the award-winning converted stables.
Catering: from £25pp

Davenport House
Worfield, Bridgnorth WV15 5LE
T: 01746 716221/345
F: 01746 716021
Contact: Roger G R Murphy, Proprietor

Ceremony

This 18th Century Grade I listed country house is privately run. Only one

SHROPSHIRE

wedding party is ever accommodated on one day, so you have the house to yourselves. The emphasis here is on a relaxed, friendly ambience. Ceremonies can take place here on every day of the year, with the exception of Sundays and Bank Holidays. Confetti is not permitted. Physical assistance would be required for wheelchair access.
Price guide: £200

Reception

A small number of guest bedrooms are available, if required.
Catering: from £35pp

**Delbury Hall
Diddlebury, Craven Arms
Shropshire SY7 9DH**
T: 01584 841267 F: 01584 841441
Contact: Patrick Wrigley, Owner

Ceremony

This stately home is a Grade II listed Georgian country house (c1750), with attractive gardens. Only one ceremony is permitted per day, every day except Sunday and Bank Holidays.
Price guide: £150

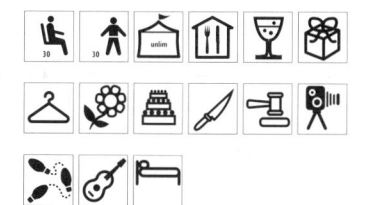

Reception

Receptions will sometimes take place in the house, but usually a marquee is erected. Catering may be in-house or contract depending on the size of party, but there is no choice of caterer.
Catering: £15pp - £25pp

**The Longmynd Hotel
Cunnery Road
Church Stretton SY6 6AG**
T: 01694 722244 F: 01694 722718
Contact: Max Chapman, Manager

Ceremony

Longmynd is a Regency style building, with more recent additions, set in 15 acres of private landscaped grounds, and is set against the backdrop of the South Shropshire Hills. The hotel has two restaurants and its own leisure club including outdoor swimming pool. Ceremonies can take place here on any day of the week.
Price guide: £100

Reception

In addition to the services above, the hotel can also make a Rolls Royce available for use by the wedding couple.
Catering: £12pp - £25pp

**Newport Guildhall
High Street, Newport
Shropshire TF10 7TX**
T: 01952 814338
Contact: Jayne Parnham, Projects Officer

Ceremony

The Guildhall dates from the late 15th Century, with additions made up to 1860. It has been restored with help from English Heritage. Weddings can take place here on all days except Sundays and Bank Holidays. A room can be made available for bride and groom to change in, and a list of local accommodation can also be provided. There are, however, no reception facilities at the Guildhall.
Price guide: £50

**The Parkhouse Hotel
Park Street, Shifnal TF11 9BA**
T: 01952 460128 F: 01952 461658
Contact: Sharon Roberts or Karen Ryder, Banqueting Co-ordinators

Ceremony

The hotel offers three marriage rooms, taking a minimum of 20. The rooms are: The Garden Suite, the Stephen Dobson Suite and the Assac Suite. Ceremonies can take place here any day except Sundays and Bank Holidays. Ceremonies must be followed by a reception at the hotel.
Price guide: POA

Reception

A late night licence can be obtained.
Catering: £17.95pp

**Shrewsbury Castle
Shrewsbury
Shropshire SY1 2AT**
T: 01743 358516
Contact: Mr S J Martin

Ceremony

The Castle is a scheduled ancient monument set in its own grounds in the heart of Shrewsbury. It now houses a regimental museum. Ceremonies can take place here on any day except Sundays. Confetti is not permitted. A list of local accommodation can be provided. There are no reception facilities at the Castle.
Price guide: £100

**The Telford Moat House
Forgegate, Telford Centre TF3 4NA**
T: 01952 429988 F: 01952 292012
Contact: Sally Felton, Banqueting Admin Manager or Sarah Corbett

Ceremony

The Moat House is in the centre of Telford and offers its Ironbridge and Telford Suites as marriage rooms. These are available any day of the year.
Price guide: POA

Reception

155

Catering: from £19.95pp

The Walls
Eating House & Dining Room
Welsh Walls, Oswestry
Shropshire SY11 1AW
T: 01691 670970 F: 01691 653370
Contact: Sarah Oliver, Weddings Organiser

Ceremony

This building is a spacious converted Victorian school. Only one wedding can take place here at any one time, on any day except Sunday.
Price guide: P.O.A.

Reception

As well as the above services, the venue will also print menu cards and name cards for you, and can provide a list of local overnight accommodation if requested.
Catering: £15pp - £25pp

ALSO LICENSED
Adcote School 01939 260202
The Feathers Hotel 01584 875261
The Lion Hotel 01743 353107
Lord Hill Hotel 01743 232601
Madeley Court Hotel and Mill 01952 680068
Radbrook Hall Hotel 01743 236676
Rowton Castle Hotel 01743 884044
The Shropshire 01952 677800
Tern Hill Hall Hotel 01630 638310

Bindon Country House Hotel
Langford Budville, Wellington
Somerset TA21 0RU
T: 01823 400070 F: 01823 400071
Contact: Lynn Jaffa, MD or Jo Greenshields, Wedding Co-ordinator

Ceremony

Bindon is a Grade II listed Baroque style building with an orangery. It is set in seven acres of woodlands and gardens and has four licensed areas, including the Orangery. These are available on all days except Bank Holidays, although ceremonies here must be followed by a reception on the premises.
Price guide: £150

Reception

The hotel boasts a French chef and two rosettes for its cuisine. For overnight accommodation the hotel offers a four poster honeymoon room.
Catering: from £29.95pp

Carnarvon Arms Hotel
Dulverton, Somerset TA22 9AE
T: 01398 323302 F: 01398 324022
Contact: Mrs Jones, Proprietor

Ceremony

The hotel is a Victorian building set in 50 acres. Its features include lounges with log fires and a billiard room. One ceremony per day can take place in one of three marriage rooms. Ceremonies can take place on any day of the year, but must be followed by a reception at the hotel.
Price guide: FOC (with reception)

Reception

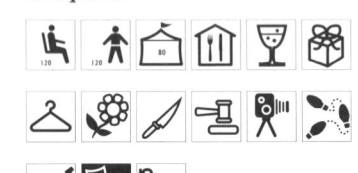

A late night drinking licence can be applied for as required. As well as the above services, the hotel can help couples arrange cars, horse and carriage, helicopters and hot air balloons.
Catering: from £10.50

Curdon Mill
Lower Velloe, Williton TA4 4LS
T: 01984 656522 F: 01984 656197
Contact: Daphne Criddle

Ceremony

Curdon is a sandstone watermill set amidst acres of farmland at the foot of the Quantock Hills. Ceremonies are restricted to one per day on any day of the year except Christmas Day.
Price guide: POA

Reception

The Mill specialises in home made food using local produce. A wide selection of menus is available to help bridal parties choose the ideal food for their function.
Catering: Buffets from £12pp. Sit down from £16.40pp

Dillington House
Ilminster
Somerset
TA19 9DT
T: 01460 52427 F: 01460 52433
Contact: Carol Slinger, Conference Manager

Ceremony

This Grade II listed house was once the home of Lord North, Prime Minister to George III. Somerset County Council took responsibility for Dillington in 1949. The grounds feature a croquet lawn and putting green, while the back terrace looks out across the rose garden to parkland. Ceremonies can take place here on any day of the year. Confetti is not permitted.
Price guide: £120

Reception

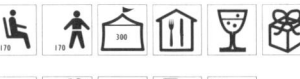

There is a room hire charge of £475 for the use of the appropriate function rooms in the main house. Discounts on food and accommodation are available for children.
Catering: from £9pp (main course dish)

156

Farthings Hotel
Hatch Beauchamp
Taunton
Somerset TA3 6SG
T: 01823 480664   F: 01823 481118
Contact: Marie Barker, Owner

Ceremony

Farthings is a family owned Georgian country hotel set in three acres of gardens, which includes a croquet lawn. Up to two ceremonies can take place here per day on any day of the year. All of the bedrooms are en-suite and feature the usual extras one would expect in a well-appointed establishment.
Price guide: £150

Reception

The hotel's restaurant, specialising in modern English cuisine, is Egon Ronay recommended and has two AA Rosettes.
Catering: £12pp - £22pp

Haynes Motor Museum
Sparkford, Yeovil BA22 7LN
T: 01963 440804   F: 01963 441004
email: mike@gmpwin.demon.co.uk
Contact: Pauline Penn, Administrator

Ceremony

Haynes claims to have Britain's most extensive historic car collection. The marriage ceremony here would take place in front of one of the world's rarest cars (worth £1.5 million) in Exhibition Hall 6. Ceremonies can take place here on any day, except Bank Holidays
Price guide: £250

Reception

There is an extensive choice of cars for your wedding car here. The first wedding held here was for the museums own chief mechanic and receptionist.
Catering: Buffets from £7pp. Sit down from £15pp.

The Holbrook House Hotel
Holbrook
Nr Wincanton BA9 8BS
T: 01963 32377   F: 01963 32681
Contact: Giovanni Cestagrossa, GM

Ceremony

This country house hotel offers two marriage rooms; the Kent Room and the Drawing Room. Ceremonies must be followed by a reception at the hotel, but only one wedding is permitted per day. Ceremonies can take place on any day of the year except the Christmas and New Year's Bank Holidays.
Price guide: £100

Reception

Catering: £12.95pp - £50pp

Hornsbury Mill
Eleighwater, Chard TA20 3AQ
T & F: 01460 63317
Contact: Keith and Sarah Jane Lewin, Proprietors

Ceremony

This is a restored working corn mill and museum set in five acres of water gardens with trout lake and resident ducks. The Conference and Lakeside Suites are licensed for ceremonies which can take place here on any day of the year.
Price guide: £150

Reception

At previous weddings here couples have arrived by helicopter and fire engine, have tied the knot wearing full Japanese costumes and have scuba dived in the lake; this is clearly a flexible venue.
Catering: Buffets from £8pp. sit down from £21pp.

The Lordleaze Hotel
Forton Road, Chard TA20 2HW
T: 01460 61066   F: 01460 66468
Contact: Reception

Ceremony

This is a converted 18th Century farmhouse in a country setting. It has its own gardens and parking and is 4-crown Highly Commended as an hotel. The Meadows Suite is licensed and ceremonies can take place here on any day of the year. Ceremonies must be followed by a reception on the premises.
Price guide: £125

Reception

Catering: from £13.95pp

The Manor Hotel
Hendford, Yeovil BA20 1TG
T: 01935 423116   F: 01935 706607
Contact: Mrs Joanne Clark, Banqueting

Ceremony

The Manor House dates from 1735 and is located in the town centre. It has a conservatory and a small garden for photographs. Three areas are licensed, including the conservatory. Ceremonies can take place here on any day except Christmas Day and Boxing Day
Price guide: £150

Reception

SOMERSET

157

SOMERSET - SOUTH GLOUCESTERSHIRE

Catering: Buffets from £8.95pp. Sit down from £10.95pp

The Old Muncipal Buildings
Corporation Street
Taunton TA1 4AQ
T: 01823 356356 F: 01823 356329
Contact: Peter Cottell, Admin Officer

Ceremony

The Old Muncipal Hall is an ancient monument (1522) and listed building right in the centre of Taunton. The marriage rooms are the Municipal Hall and the Committee Room, and are available on any day except Sundays, Bank Holidays, or when the council offices are normally closed.
Price guide: from £60

Reception

Hirers are to arrange their own caterers at this venue.

The Shrubbery Hotel
Ilminster
Somerset
TA19 9AR
T: 01460 52108 F: 01460 536600
Contact: Stuart Shepherd, Managing Director

Ceremony

This country house hotel and restaurant offers four rooms licensed for civil ceremonies. Weddings can take place here on any day of the year.
Price guide: £125

Reception

Preferential overnight rates can be offered to wedding guests.
Catering: £25-£30pp (Packages)

ALSO LICENSED
The Centurion Hotel 01761 417711
Crewkerne Town Hall, 01460 74001
The Old Rectory 01373 836265
Rumwell Manor Hotel 01823 461902
The Walnut Tree Hotel 01278 662255

Chipping Sodbury Town Hall
57-59 Broad Street
Chipping Sodbury BS17 4UQ
T: 01454 852222 F: 01454 852223
Contact: Mrs Krystyna Brown, Manager

Ceremony

This Grade II listed building is located in the centre of this ancient market town. The Charter Suite is licensed and is available for ceremonies on any day except Sundays and Bank Holidays. Confetti is not permitted.
Price guide: £65

Reception

Catering: Buffets from £4.30pp. Sit down from £10.00pp

The Commodore Hotel
Beach Road, Sand Bay
Weston Super Mare BS22 9UZ
T: 01934 415778 F: 01934 636483
Contact: Steve Goddard

Ceremony

This modern, privately owned, hotel enjoys a beach front location and is set in 17 acres. Two rooms are licensed and are available on any day of the year. Ceremonies here must be followed by a reception on the premises
Price guide: £50 - £100

Reception

Catering: from £13.50pp

Forte Posthouse Bristol
Filton Road, Hambrook BS16 1QX
T & F: 0117 956 4242
Contact: Alison Smith, Banqueting

Ceremony

The hotel is set in its own extensive landscaped grounds which feature two ornamental ponds. It has two rooms with licences to hold weddings, the smaller of which can accommodate up to 25 guests.
Price guide: £250

Reception

The wedding package is an all-inclusive price which includes drinks on arrival, with meal and for toasts, plus flowers and complimentary overnight accommodation for bride and groom. The hotel recently hosted a show business wedding complete with opera singer.
Catering: from £29.50pp

Rangeworthy Court Hotel
Church Lane, Rangeworthy BS37
T: 01454 228347 F: 01454 228945
Contact: Mrs Lucia Gillet, Owner/Director

Ceremony

This old manor house is a 17th Century listed building with gardens and good car parking. Three rooms are licensed including the Garden Room and the Courtyard Room. Ceremonies can take place here on any day except Bank Holidays but must be followed by a reception on the premises.
Price guide: £50 - £100

Reception

The hotel boasts two AA rosettes for its food. Children's entertainment and a creche can be provided if required. The bridal suite features a four poster bed.
Catering: Buffet from 19pp. Sit down from £20pp.

**Thornbury Castle
Thornbury
South Gloucestershire
BS12 1HH**
T: 01454 281182 F: 01454 416318
Contact: Janine Black

Ceremony

This former Tudor castle is now run as an award-winning hotel and restaurant. It still retains a vineyard and walled gardens within its 15 acres. The restaurant has two, baronial style, dining rooms.
Price guide: £175-£250

Reception

The top catering package here includes 8 courses with dishes such as smoked salmon and caviar.
Catering: £24.75 - £58.75pp

*ALSO LICENSED
Park Hotel & Restaurant 01454 260550*

**The Beauchief Hotel
161 Abbeydale Road
Sheffield
South Yorkshire S7 2QW**
T: 0114 262 0500 F: 0114 235 0197
Contact: Beth Coward, Conference & Banqueting Manager or Sarah Nutt, Food and Beverage Manager

Ceremony

The Beauchief, one of the Country Club Hotel Group, describes itself as a 'traditional' hotel. It is set in its own grounds adjacent to a golf course and offers three licensed areas which are available on any day of the year.
Price guide: POA

Reception

Catering: Buffets from £7.95pp. Sit down from £18pp

**Carlton Park Hotel
Moorgate Road
Rotherham S60 2BG**
T: 01709 849955 F: 01709 368960
Contact: Anne Michle, Conference & Banqueting Manager

Ceremony

The Carlton Park offers four licensed rooms on any day of the year.
Price guide: POA

Reception

Catering: from £26.50pp

**The Earl of Doncaster Hotel
Bennetthorpe DN2 6AD**
T: 01302 361371 F: 01302 321858
Contact: Claire Fleetwood, Duty Manager

Ceremony

This hotel is in the centre of town with good car parking facilities. Three rooms are licensed and available all year round. Ceremonies here must be followed by a reception on the premises.
Price guide: £100

Reception

Catering: Buffets from £6.95pp. Sit down from £13pp

**Mosborough Hall Hotel
High Street, Mosborough
Sheffield
South Yorkshire S19 5AE**
T: 01142 484353 F: 01142 477042
Contact: Tracy, Banqueting Manager

Ceremony

This Grade II listed building has two rooms licensed to hold ceremonies; the Stables and the hotel restaurant. These have varying sitting and standing capacities from 75 to 150. Ceremonies are available seven days a week, excluding Christmas Day, with a maximum of two ceremonies permitted per day. The hotel does allow confetti.
Price guide: from £150

Reception

Reception capacities are to a maximum of 150, while the site is also suitable for a marquee with a capacity of 200. Although the hotel has 24 rooms it also operates preferential rate agreements with other local hotels and guest houses.
Catering: £25pp

**Mount Pleasant Hotel
Great North Road, Rossington,
Doncaster DN11 0HP**
T: 01302 868219 F: 01302 865130
Contact: Helen Pitts, Sales & Marketing

Ceremony

The hotel has two rooms available to hold ceremonies, although the conservatory is generally chosen in preference. The conservatory has a maximum capacity of 45 standing, and 35 sitting. Up to 10 ceremonies are available, seven days a week excluding Christmas Day.
Price guide: POA

159

SOUTH YORKSHIRE - STAFFORDSHIRE

Reception

The hotel offers reception catering facilities to a maximum of 120 guests, while the hotel's grounds are suitable for a marquee of a similar capacity.
Catering: from £16pp

Sheffield Wednesday Football Club
Penistone Road
Hillsborough
Sheffield S6 1SW
T: 0114 2212310 F: 0114 12212122
Contact: Lesley Adyer, Facilitator

Ceremony

A must for Wednesdayites, the Club has three marriage rooms, two of which overlook the pitch. These rooms are available on any day except match days. Confetti is not permitted.
Price guide: POA

Reception

Catering: Buffets from £6pp. Sit down from £16pp

Stakis Sheffield Hotel
Victoria Quays
Furnival Road S4 7YA
T: 0114 252 5500 F: 0114 252 5511
Contact: Josie Bunting, Conference & Banqueting Sales Manager

Ceremony

This hotel, part of the Stakis group, enjoys a quayside location. The hotel itself is bult into 130 year old railway arches. Eight areas are licensed and available for ceremonies on any day of the week.
Price guide: from £500

Reception

Couples may arrive or depart by barge at this venue.
Catering: Buffets from £6.95pp. Sit down from £21.50pp

Swallow Hotel
Kenwood Road
Sheffield S7 1NQ
T: 0114 2583811   F: 0114 500138
Contact: Maxine Clark, Sales Manager

Ceremony

The hotel is set in 11 acres of landscaped gardens with its own ornamental lake. Helicopters and hot air balloons may use the grounds. The marriage rooms are the Raffles and Meadow rooms which are available on any day of the year. Ceremonies here must be followed by a reception at the hotel.
Price guide: POA

Reception

Catering: Buffets from £14.70pp. Sit down from £17pp

Tom Cobleigh's Weetwood House
Ecclesall Road South
Sheffield S11 9PL
T: 0114 235 3164 F: 0114 235 3266
Contact: Neil Felton,
Function Co-ordinator

Ceremony

This is a sympathetically restored former library with a function room and private facilities. One room is licensed and receptions must follow ceremonies here.
Price guide: POA

Reception

Catering: Buffets from £4.95pp. Sit down from £13.50pp.

Whitley Hall Hotel
Elliott Lane, Sheffield S30 3NR
T: 0114 245 4444 F: 0114 245 5414
Contact: Ian Davies, General Manager

Ceremony

This Elizabethan manor house is a Grade II listed building and is available to hold ceremonies seven days a week with a maximum of three per day. The price guide to holding ceremonies increases to £325 on a Saturday. Confetti is not permitted. The hotel would like to stress that ceremonies are only available in conjunction with reception facilities.
Price guide: POA

Reception

Catering capacities are to a maximum of 100 guests, while a marquee may be made available to a capacity of 250. The hotel prides itself on the quality of its traditional English cuisine.
Catering: POA

The Bass Museum
PO Box 220
Horninglow Street
Burton on Trent,
Staffs DE14 1YQ
T: 01283 511000 F: 01283 513509
Contact: Mrs S Stokes

Ceremony

The Bass Museum of Brewing is housed

STAFFORDSHIRE

in brewery buildings dating from 1835. Shire horse stables are also on the site. The museum's Worthington Suite (max 170) and Charrington Room (max 120) are licensed for ceremonies, which can take place on any day of the year, and are restricted to one per day.
Price guide: POA

Reception

Catering is by contract caterers from an approved list. A list of local accommodation with which the museum has rate agreements can be provided on request.
Catering: P.O.A.

Biddulph Town Hall
High Street, Biddulph
Staffs ST8 6AE
T: 01782 297836 F: 01782 297846
Contact: Mrs K Thacker, Administrator

Ceremony

Biddulph Town Hall is located in the town centre and holds a licence for ceremonies in its Council Chamber. This is available any day of the year except Sundays and Bank Holidays. Confetti is not permitted.
Price guide: £25

Reception

A list of local accommodation can be provided.
Catering: POA

The Borough Arms Hotel
King Street
Newcastle Under Lyme ST5 1HX
T: 01782 629421 F: 01782 712388
Contact: Mr S N Sheikh, GM

Ceremony

The Borough Arms is an English Heritage, listed, building which offers two marriage rooms. These are the King Room (max 100) and the Baker Room (max 45). These are available for ceremonies on any day of the year, but ceremonies must be followed by a reception at the hotel.
Price guide: £50 - £125

Reception

Vegetarian menus are available on request. The hotel can also cater for ethnic cuisine, such as Indian and Pakistani food, if required.
Catering: £8pp - £16pp

Britannia Stadium
Stanley Matthews Way
Stoke on Trent
Staffs ST4 4EG
T: 01782 592234/36 F: 01782 846422
Contact: Chris Lucas/Michael Flock

Ceremony

Five marriage rooms are available at the stadium: the Wadington Suite; Vice President's Suite; Gordon Banks Suite; Reception Lounge and an Executive Box. These will accommodate from 5 to 350 guests. Ceremonies must be followed by a reception at the stadium. The venue has ample free parking as well as easy access from all major road and rail links.
Price guide: £152.50

Reception

Marquees can be the 'size of a football pitch' if required! Players and management may also be available for your wedding, as may celebrities such as Frank Bruno.
Catering: from £12pp (sit down)

The Comfort Friendly Inn
Liverpool Road
Cross Heath
Newcastle Under Lyme
Staffs ST5 9DX
T: 01782 717000 F: 01782 713669
email: admin@gb617.v.net.com
Contact: Sian Hughes, General Manager

Ceremony

The Hotel, part of the Choice Hotels Europe group, is a mile out of the town centre. It claims to be a 2-star plus with the facilities of a 3-star hotel. One suite is licensed and available any day except Christmas Day, Boxing Day and New Year.
Price guide: Registrar fees only

Reception

Catering: Buffets from £5pp. Sit down from £10.75pp

Dovecliff Hall Hotel
Stretton
Burton upon Trent
Staffs DE13 0DJ
T: 01283 531818 F: 01283 516546
Contact: Mr Leigh Frost
Restaurant Manager

Ceremony

This Georgian listed building set in seven acres features gardens overlooking the River Dove. The Lounge is licensed for ceremonies and is available on all days except Sunday, Monday and Bank Holidays.
Price guide: POA

Reception

Helicopters and hot air balloons may use the grounds.
Catering: POA

161

STAFFORDSHIRE

Ford Green Hall
Ford Green Road
Smallthorne
Stoke on Trent ST6 1NG
T: 01782 233195 F: 01782 233194
email:
judith.franklin@stoke01.stokecc.gov.uk
Contact: Judith Franklin, Manager

Ceremony

This is a timber framed farmhouse built in 1624 and fully furnished as a 17th Century home. It is a listed building and features a period garden. It is currently owned by Stoke-on-Trent City Council and is licensed for ceremonies in The Hall, where many ceremonies would have taken place over the centuries. Ceremonies can take place here on Fridays and Saturdays. Confetti is not permitted.
Price guide: from £300 + vat

Reception

There are no reception facilities at Ford Green Hall. Drinks and light refreshments only are possible.

The Forge Inn
Bottomhouse, Nr Leek ST13 7QN
T & F: 01538 304249
Contact: Mr I M Bacon, Proprietor

Ceremony

The Forge is situated in the Staffordshire Moorlands on the edge of The Peak District. The Restaurant is licensed and available for ceremonies on any day except Mondays.
Price guide: £40 with reception

Reception

Catering: Buffets from £10pp. Sit down from £18.50pp

Haydon House Hotel
Haydon Street, Basford ST4 6JD
T: 01782 711311 F: 01782 717470
Contact: Ken Machin, Assistant GM

Ceremony

The Library here is licensed and available any day of the year.
Price guide: FOC with reception

Reception

Catering: Buffets from £5pp. Sit down from £16pp

Hotel Rudyard, Lake Road
Rudyard, Nr Leek ST13 8RN
T & F: 01538 306208
Contact: Mr R W Lloyd, Owner

Ceremony

The hotel is licensed to hold ceremonies in the Lake Carvery Room and the Rudyard Room. These are available on any day except Sunday.
Price guide: from £50

Reception

Catering: Buffets from £7.50pp. Sit down from £16pp

Keele Conference Park
Darwin Building
Keele University, Keele ST5 5BG
T: 01782 584025 F: 01782 713058
Contact: Anne Nicholls, Events Organiser

Ceremony

This Grade II listed building featuring lakes and Italian gardens, was originally owned by the Sneyd family. The Great Hall and the Old Library are both licensed for ceremonies.

Price guide: £150

Reception

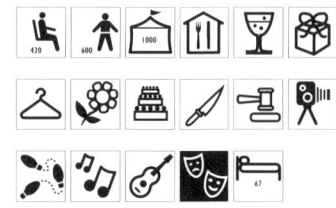

Catering: POA

The Moat House Hotel
Festival Way, Festival Park
Stoke on Trent, Staffs ST1 5BQ
T: 01782 609988 F: 01782 284500
Contact: Tracy Grocott, Wedding Co-ordinator

Ceremony

The hotel is a listed building (in part) and was the former family home of Josiah Wedgwood. Up to two ceremonies a day can take place here on any day except Bank Holidays.
Price Guide: from £120

Reception

Catering: from £28.95 (including drinks)

The Moat House Restaurant
Lower Penkridge Road
Acton Trussell
Nr Stafford, Staffs ST17 0RQ
T: 01785 712217 F: 01785 715344
Contact: Christopher Lewis, Manager

Ceremony

The Moat House was formerly the home of the de Trussell family and is a listed building. It is set in six acres of landscaped grounds. The moat flanks the Colin Lewis Suite, and the restaurant overlooks the Staffordshire and Worcestershire Canal. Ceremonies can take place here on any day except Monday and Sunday.

Price guide: £200 (F.O.C. with reception)

Reception

The Colin Lewis Suite is an oak beamed room that dates from 1480. It has its own bar and is suitable for parties of up to 66. The Trussell Room and Restaurant, meanwhile, has a Victorian style conservatory overlooking the gardens and canal, and can take parties of up to 86. For receptions, children can be eligible for discounts. A list of local accommodation with which the restaurant has negotiated special rates is available on request.
Catering: £16pp - £25pp

Pendrell Hall College
Codslall Wood
Nr Wolverhampton WV8 1QP
T: 01902 434112 F: 01902 434113
email: pendrell.college@staffordshire.gov.uk
Contact: David Evans, Principal

Ceremony

This residential college for adult education is based in a Victorian country house in a rural setting with 12 acres of grounds. It is a member of the South Staffs Tourism Association. Three rooms (all with ornate wooden fireplaces) are licensed and are available to fit around the working college.
Price guide: POA

Reception

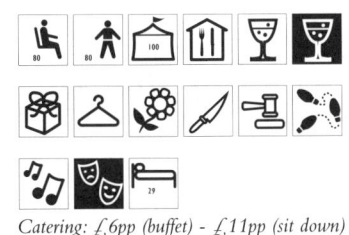

Catering: £6pp (buffet) - £11pp (sit down)

Port Vale Football Club
Vale Park, Burslem ST6 1AW
T: 01782 835524 F: 01782 836875
Contact: Rebecca Wood

Ceremony

Five new function rooms are available for hire on any day except Bank Holidays.
Price guide: £300

Reception

A late night drinking licence can be applied for if required. While there is no overnight accommodation on the premises, the Club has a list of local establishments with which it has preferential rate agreements.
Catering: Buffets from £5pp. Sit down from £11pp

The Queens Hotel
One Bridge Street
Burton upon Trent DE14 1SY
T: 01283 564993 F: 01283 517556
Contact: Colin Roberts, Managing Director

Ceremony

This is a traditional 16th Century coaching inn in the town centre. It has a 3-star RAC comfort award and is Grade II listed.
Price guide: £75- £120

Reception

Couples can arrive and depart from this venue by brewery dray.
Catering: Buffets from £5.95pp. Sit down from £15.95pp.

The Riverside Hotel
Riverside Drive, Branston DE14 3EP
T: 01283 511234 F: 01283 511441
Contact: Duty Manager

Ceremony

The Riverside hotel is situated in a garden setting overlooking the River Trent. Only one ceremony is permitted here per day.
Price guide: POA

Reception

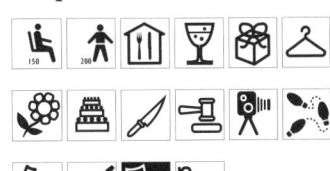

Catering: from £15pp

Seedy Mill Golf Club
Elmhurst, Lichfield
Staffs WS13 8HE
T: 01543 417333 F: 01543 418098
Contact: Craig Rogers, Marketing

Ceremony

The Clubhouse derives from an old seed mill, and its surrounding buildings are Grade II listed. The Millcroft Suite is licensed for ceremonies which can take place here on any day of the year. Ceremonies here must be followed by a reception at the venue.
Price guide: FOC

Reception

The prices below are for packages which include drinks on arrival, cake stand, menu, etc. Apparently grooms have, in the past, managed to get in 18 holes of golf before the ceremony - perhaps the ultimate in relaxation!
Catering: Buffets from £6pp. Sit down from £28pp

Shugborough Estate
Shugborough, Milford ST17 0XB
T: 01889 881388 F: 01889 881323
Contact: Anne Wood, Events Manager

STAFFORDSHIRE

163

STAFFORDSHIRE - SUFFOLK

Ceremony

Shugborough is a National Trust property, and is the 900 acre seat of the Earls of Lichfield. One wedding can take place here per day and on any day except Sunday. Confetti is not permitted, nor is indoor photography. Lists of both entertainers and other services can be provided.
Price guide: £600 + vat

Reception

Reception facilities are not available at Shugborough.

Trentham Gardens
Trentham Leisure Ltd
Stone Road, Trentham
Stoke on Trent ST4 8AX
T: 01782 657341 F: 01782 644536
Contact: Karen Nixon, Sales Co-ordinator

Ceremony

This conference and leisure centre is set in a 750 acres estate featuring Italian gardens. Three rooms are available (from 50 to 1,000 guests), on any day of the year.
Price guide: from £100

Reception

Helicopters and hot air balloons may use the grounds.
Catering: Buffets from £6pp. Sit down from £15pp

Uttoxeter Racecourse
Wood Lane
Uttoxeter
Staffs ST14 8BD
T: 01889 562561 F: 01889 562786
Contact: Janet Womby, Marketing Manager

Ceremony

The racecourse offers views across the Dove Valley. The Staffordshire Room is licensed for ceremonies which can take place here on any day, although there are certain restrictions on race days. The venue says there are many areas suitable for outdoor photography.
Price guide: £300

Reception

The racecourse offers 'extreme flexibility of menus and numbers' and can even provide a behind the scenes tour. Helicopters and hot air balloons can also use the site.
Catering: Buffets from £7.50pp. Sit down from £12pp

Uttoxeter Town Hall
High Street
Uttoxeter ST14 7HN
T: 01889 564085 F: 01889 568426
Contact: Mrs A M Clare, Town Clerk

Ceremony

The Town Hall is right in the town centre and has been redecorated recently. The Alan Dean Suite is licensed and available on any days except Sundays and Bank Holidays.
Price guide: £25

Reception

Catering: POA

ALSO LICENSED
Blakelands 01384 221464
Fox Hotel 01260 226692
Garth Hotel 01785 256124
Haling Dene Centre 01785 714157
Hatherton Country Hotel 01785 712459
Queens Hotel 01283 564993
Red Lion Inn 01538 300325
Stone House Hotel 01785 815531
Swinfen Hall Hotel 01543 481494
Upper House 01782 373790

The Angel Hotel
Angel Hill, Bury St Edmunds
Suffolk IP33 1LT
T: 01284 753926 F: 01284 750092
Contact: Mrs Adi Ellis, Conf & Banq

Ceremony

This 14th century, creeper-clad listed building, was immortalised by Dickens as the hostelry where Mr Pickwick enjoyed an evening meal. The hotel allows two ceremonies per day and is situated opposite the award winning Abbey Gardens, which provides a picturesque location for photography.
Price guide: approximately £150

Reception

Catering is in-house with prices ranging from £7.50 to £25 per head. The hotel prides itself on its English and French cuisine. Special accommodation rates are offered to wedding guests staying overnight.
Catering: from £7.50

Belstead Brook Manor Hotel
Belstead Road, Ipswich IP2 9HB
T: 01473 684241 F: 01473 681249
Contact: Karen Smith,
Sales Development Manager

Ceremony

This manor house has four rooms licensed for ceremonies, which are available on any day except Christmas Day.
Price guide: POA

Reception

Catering: Buffets from £12.50pp. Sit down from £21.50pp

The Brook Hotel
Orwell Road, Felixstowe IP11 7PF
T: 01394 278441 F: 01394 670422
Contact: Peter Whalley, Functions

SUFFOLK

Ceremony

This 4-Crown Victorian-style hotel offers ceremonies free of charge if in conjunction with a waited service reception. Ceremonies cannot be at Christmas or the New Year holiday.
Price guide: FOC (with waited reception)

Reception

Catering is in-house and Chinese cuisine is available. Waited meals start at around £15 per head.
Catering: POA

The Courtyard by Marriott
The Havens, Ransomes Europark Ipswich IP3 9SJ
T: 01473 272244 F: 01473 272484
Contact: Lucy Westaway,
Executive Meetings Manager

Ceremony

The hotel, owned by Whitbread, is able to offer two licensed areas. The Gippeswick Suite has its own bar and self-contained dance floor, while the Bucklesham Room, on the first floor, is more suited to the smaller wedding.
Price guide: £115 - £175

Reception

The wedding package includes menus, red carpet, special overnight rates for guests, toastmaster, use of cake stand and knife, linen napkins (choice of colours) and, overnight accommodation for bride and groom, and an opportunity to sample your chosen menu in the Priory Restaurant.
Catering: Buffets from £7.35pp. Sit down from £17.65pp

Heath Court Hotel
Moulton Road, Newmarket Suffolk CB8 8DY
T: 01638 667171 F: 01638 666533
Contact: Alexandra Price, Sales Manager

Ceremony

The York Room is licensed at this hotel, and is available on any day of the year.
Price guide: £100

Reception

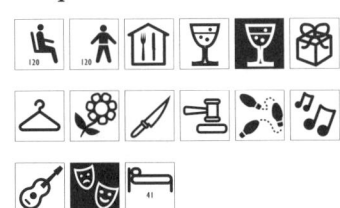

Catering rates are based on a fully inclusive package.
Catering: from £23pp

Hill Lodge Hotel
8 Newton Road Sudbury, Suffolk CO10 6RL
T: 01787 377568 F: 01787 373636
Contact: Jim or Anita French, Owners

Ceremony

The original part of the hotel is 70 years old and has a sympathetic modern extension. Set in nearly two acres of grounds, the hotel has two rooms licensed to hold ceremonies which are free of charge if in conjunction with receptions. Ceremonies are available without receptions upon discussion only. Ceremonies can be performed on any day of the year except Christmas Day.
Price guide: POA

Reception

Catering is in-house with a capacity of 80, whether for a formal seated meal or a buffet-style. Although formal wheelchair access is not available assistance is at hand. The hotel has 17 bedrooms. Its garden is a suitable site for wedding photography or the erection of a marquee.
Catering: POA

Hintlesham Hall
George Street, Hintlesham Ipswich, Suffolk IP8 3NS
T: 01473 652268 F: 01473 652463
Contact : Function Co-ordinator

Ceremony

This Grade I listed Manor House features a Georgian façade and has Tudor origins. The Carolean Room is licensed to hold ceremonies for up to 50. It features plasterwork ceilings dating from the end of the 17th Century. The Hall is also available for hire on an exclusive basis. Ceremonies must be held in conjunction with receptions.
Price guide: £450

Reception

Catering facilities are extended from the Carolean Room into the dining room up to a capacity of 120. A room will be offered for the bride and groom to change in, subject to availability.
Catering: from £27.50pp.

Hatfield Hotel
The Esplanade Lowestoft NR33 0QP
T: 01502 565337 F: 01502 511885
Contact: Ibrahim Mohammed, GM

Ceremony

The hotel stands next to the 'best beach in Britain' for 1995 and 1993. The hotel has four rooms licensed for ceremonies with capacities ranging from 4 to 200.
Price guide: £150 - £200

Reception

165

SUFFOLK

Catering: from £14.50pp

Ipswich County Hotel
London Road
Copdock, Ipswich IP8 3JD
T: 01473 209988 F: 01473 730801
Contact: Danny Jarvis

Ceremony

The Constable Suite and the Lucas Room are licensed for ceremonies which can take place here on any day of the year.
Price guide: POA

Reception

Helicopters and hot air balloons may use the site.
Catering: from £10pp

Ipswich Guildhall
Hadleigh, Ipswich, IP7 5DT
T: 01473 823884
Contact: Mrs J Townsend, Bookings Clerk/Mr R Stevens, Clerk to the Charity

Ceremony

This 15th Century Grade I listed building is situated just off Hadleigh High Street, and contains many of its original architectural features. It has three licensed rooms.
Price guide: £75

Reception

Catering: POA

Marlborough Hotel
Henley Road, Ipswich
Suffolk IP1 3SP
T: 01473 257677 F: 01473 226927
Contact: Karen Gough, Owner

Ceremony

This small, family owned and family run hotel, is set in it own secluded floodlit garden, and may be hired for weddings on an exclusive basis. Ceremonies are not permitted without reception facilities also.
Price guide: from £100

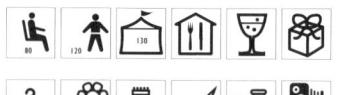

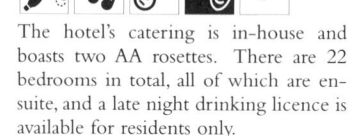

Reception

The hotel's catering is in-house and boasts two AA rosettes. There are 22 bedrooms in total, all of which are en-suite, and a late night drinking licence is available for residents only.
Catering: £15 - £30pp

Orwell Park
Nacton, Ipswich IP10 0ER
T: 01473 659140, F: 01473 659140
Contact: Mrs Ungate

Ceremony

Orwell Park was originally a Georgian stately home and now acts as a preparatory school which overlooks the river Orwell and is set in 80 acres of grounds. There are four rooms licensed to hold ceremonies with varying capacities of 50 (in the Headmaster's drawing room) to 200. Although the school is interested in enquiries throughout the year, ceremonies would be more convenient during holiday time.
Price guide: from £250

Reception

Catering capacities vary from a waited service of 110 to 150 for a stand up buffet, while children are offered reduced catering rates. Orwell Park prides itself on the quality of its chef's cuisine.
Price guide: £31.50-50pp.

Priory Barn, Priory Farm
Preston St Mary, Sudbury, CO10 9LT
T: 01787 247251
Contact: Mr and Mrs Adrian Thorpe, Owners

Ceremony

Preston Priory Barn, a renovated traditional Suffolk timber-framed barn, featured in BBC's Lovejoy. It is available for hire for a three-day period.
Price guide: £1,000 (3 days)

Reception

The Barn features a large caterer's kitchen. A list of local accommodation can be provided.
Catering: POA

Ravenwood Hall
Country Hotel & Restaurant
The Pavilion
Rougham
Bury St Edmunds
Suffolk IP30 9JA
T: 01359 270345 F: 01359 270788
Contact: Richard Clayfield, Conference & Banqueting Manager

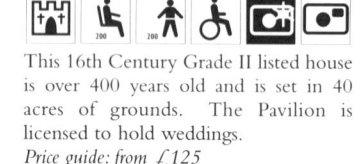

Ceremony

This 16th Century Grade II listed house is over 400 years old and is set in 40 acres of grounds. The Pavilion is licensed to hold weddings.
Price guide: from £125

Reception

The Pavilion at Ravenwood Hall specialises in traditional English food and will cater for children separately.
Catering: from £16.95pp

166

The Smoke House
Beck Row
Mildenhall
Suffolk IP28 8DH
T: 01638 713223 F: 01638 712202
Contact: Matthew Cooke
Restaurant Manager

Ceremony

The Sunderland Lounge holds the licence.
Price guide: FOC with reception

Reception

Catering: from £7.50

Somerleyton Hall & Gardens
Somerleyton NR32 5QQ
T: 01502 730224 F: 01502 732143
Contact: Ian Pollard, Administrator

Ceremony

This stately home and historic house is a member of the Historic Houses Association and is set in 12 acres featuring a maze. Helicopters may use the grounds. Four rooms are licensed with capacities from 56 to 120. Ceremonies can take place here on any day except over Christmas and New Year. Bahai faith weddings have also taken place here, in the gardens.
Price guide: from £400

Reception

Wedding reception drinks can be served at the centre of the 150 year old maze - guests have to find their way to the champagne! Formerly part of the Victorian Winter Garden, the Hall also boasts a Loggia which serves as a function room and is used for evening dancing and extra guests. The Loggia leads out into the sunken garden on one side. Evening receptions should be concluded by midnight.
Catering: POA (Venue fee from £1,100)

Stoke By Nayland Golf Club
Keepers Lane, Leavenheath
Nr Colchester, Suffolk CO6 4PZ
T: 01206 262836 F: 01206 263356
Contact: Duty Manager

Ceremony

Just one ceremony permitted per day, and only when the reception is also at the club.
Price guide: POA

Reception

A list of local accommodation is available, including preferential rate agreements with hotels and guest houses. The club also boasts a trained florist as part of the wedding package.
Price guide: from £12pp.

Tarantella Hotel & Restaurant
Sudbury Hall, Melford Road
Sudbury CO10 6XT
T & F: 01787 378879
Contact: Mr Domenico Gargiulo, Proprietor

Ceremony

This is a Georgian house set in a secluded position overlooking the River Stour. The hotel is further enhanced by terrace statues and mature landscaped gardens. Ceremonies here must be followed by a reception on the premises.
Price guide: £100

Reception

This venue is very experienced in hosting weddings. Past events have included Greek weddings, Jewish weddings, Scottish weddings, military weddings and Italian weddings (non-stop eating and dancing). The chef here is Agnello Gargiulo.
Catering: from £13.25pp

Thorpeness Country Club
The Benthills, Thorpeness
Suffolk IP16 4NU
T: 01728 454704 F: 01728 453868
email: 106414.100@compuserve.com
Contact: Jenny Loyd
Events Manager

Ceremony

This is a light and airy venue overlooking the sea and with its own garden. It has a 30ft ceiling and sprung dance floor. Two rooms are licensed and are available any day of the year.
Price guide: POA

Reception

Accommodation is available at the Golf Club next door or in Aldeburgh just over a mile away. Couples could arrive by sea to this venue.
Catering: from £15pp

Tuddenham Mill
Inn & Restaurant
Tuddenham St Mary
Newmarket IP28 6SQ
T: 01638 713552
Contact: Mr Richard Clayfield, General Manager

Ceremony

This is an 18th Century working water mill set in 12 acres of mature gardens and riverside walks. The site apparently dates back to the Domesday Book of 1086.
Price guide: from £125

Reception

SUFFOLK

167

SUFFOLK - SURREY

Catering: from £16.95pp

Ufford Park Hotel, Golf & Leisure
Yarmouth Road, Ufford
Woodbridge IP12 1QW
T: 01394 383555 F: 01394 383582
email: uffordparkltd@btinternet.com
Contact: Mr S Thurlow, Managing Director or Mrs C Hayter, Sales & Marketing Coordinator

Ceremony

This is a Best Western AA/RAC 3-star hotel with a licence for its Debden Suite. Ceremonies can take place here any day of the year, but must be held in conjunction with a reception at the venue on Saturdays between May and November.
Price guide: £160

Reception

Catering: Buffets from £12pp. Sit down from £19.50pp.

The Westerfield House Hotel
Humber Doucy Lane
Ipswich, Suffolk IP4 3QG
T: 01473 231344 F: 01473 213709
Contact: Frank Howard, MD

Ceremony

Ceremonies must be held with a reception.
Price guide: £150

Reception

Catering: £16.50pp + vat

Woodbridge Town Council
Shire Hall, Woodbridge
Suffolk IP12 4LU
T: 01349 383599
Contact: Y Schofield

Ceremony

This listed building is available any day and permits a maximum of four ceremonies a day.
Price guide: £50 for local residents (£100 others).

Reception
Reception facilities are not available.

ALSO LICENSED
Cornwallis Arms   01379 870326
Swan Hotel   01787 247477

Anugraha Hotel
Wick Lane, Englefield Green
Surrey TW20 0XN
T: 01784 434355 F: 01784 430596
Contact: Conference & Banqueting Department

Ceremony

This hotel and conference centre is housed in a Grade II listed building set in attractive grounds. Ceremonies can take place here on any day of the year.
Price guide: £350

Reception

Catering: from £28pp

Bookham Grange Hotel
Little Bookham Common
Bookham KT23 3HS
T: 01372 452742 F: 01372 450080
Contact: Mr Perry, Proprietor

Ceremony

Ceremonies can take place here in the Wedgewood and Eastwick Rooms of this Victorian country house hotel, but must be followed by reception on the premises. The hotel is set in 2.5 acres of gardens and says it blends modern with traditional facilities.
Price guide: POA

Reception

Catering: from £19.75pp

Bourne Hall
Spring Street, Ewell
Epsom, Surrey KT171UF
T: 0181 393 9571 F: 0181 786 7265
Contact: Sandra Dessent, Facilities Manager

Ceremony

Bourne Hall is a restaurant, museum and library which can offer several marriage rooms. Only one ceremony is permitted here per day on any day of the year.
Price guide: £60 - £100

Reception

A list of local accommodation can be provided on request.
Catering: P.O.A.

Clandon Park
West Clandon, Guildford
Surrey GU7 7RQ
T: 01483 224912 F: 01483 223479
Contact: Sonia Ashworth,
Events Manager

Ceremony

This 18th Century stately home, is set in parkland and gardens which include a parterre, grotto, Dutch garden and Maori House. Clandon is available for ceremonies on any day of the week when the house is closed to the public (except Sundays, Easter, January or February). Only one ceremony is allowed per day. No confetti is allowed.

168

Price guide: from £350 - £1350 + vat

Reception

Receptions take place in the vaulted undercroft or in a marquee on the lawn. Carriages before midnight. There is no accommodation on the premises, but a list of local accommodation can be provided. The grounds are suitable for a helicopter to land if desired.
Catering: £8.95 - £32.50 + vat

Elmbridge Borough Council
Civic Centre
High Street, Esher KT10 9SD
T: 01372 474474 F: 01372 474972
Contact: Tina Bailey, Civic Centre Manager

Ceremony

The Civic Centre is in a secluded location off the High Street, and offers two rooms for ceremonies on any day of the year.
Price guide: £115 - £175

Reception

Reception facilities are available here at the weekends only.
Catering: POA

Epsom Downs Racecourse
Epsom Downs
Surrey KT18 5LQ
T: 01372 726311 F: 01372 748258
Contact: Marilyn Watkinson, Sales & Marketing

Ceremony

The two marriage rooms at Epsom are in the Queen's Stand. Weddings may take place here Monday to Saturday, but not during Christmas, New Year's or Easter Holidays, or race days.
Price guide: £400 (£350 with reception) + vat

Reception

The Epsom wedding package (and price guide shown below) includes drinks, floral table arrangements and room hire for the day. Evening room hire starts at £200. The Racecourse has its own helipad, and hot air balloons can also take off from here (all with permission). The venue will be holding a Wedding Fair on 4th October 1998, which will include a wedding exhibition and fashion show. A list of local accommodation can be provided, if required.
Catering: from £37pp

Frensham Heights
Rowledge
Farnham
Surrey GU10 4EA
T: 01252 850089/792299
F: 01252 794369
Contact: Margaret Grimwood

Ceremony

This Edwardian, neo-Elizabethan style, country house (now a school) stands in 100 acres on the Heights of Frensham, looking south towards the Blackdown Hills. Ceremonies can be held in the Ballroom, Jacobean Gallery, Blue Drawing Room or Old Orangery. The suite of rooms, as well as terrace and lawns, is available 7 days a week, with or without reception.
Price guide: £450 without reception
£350 with reception

Reception

Menus of your choice are provided by a specialist firm and up to 150 can be seated in the Ballroom. Sole occupation is guaranteed, with full drinks licence.
Catering: from £16pp

Guildford Forte Posthouse
Egerton Road
Guildford GU2 5XZ
T: 01483 574444 F: 01483 506890
Contact: Tabby Talbot or Debbie Bedford, Conference & Banqueting Sales Managers

Ceremony

This Forte hotel offers three licensed rooms, available any day of the year. Ceremonies here must be followed by reception on the premises.
Price guide: POA

Reception

Wedding packages here include complimentary overnight accommodation for bride and groom, toastmaster, printed menu and table plan and a celebration meal on your first anniversary. Several menu packages are offered and drinks packages start at £10.50pp. House wine is £12.55 a bottle.
Catering: from £24.50pp

The Hawker Centre
Lower Ham Road
Kingston Upon Thames KT2 5BH
T: 0181 296 9747 F: 0181 296 9759
Contact: Malcolm North, Facilities Manager

Ceremony

This sport and leisure facility enjoys a riverside location with large car park and licensed bar on site. The main hall, small hall and studio are all licensed for ceremonies.
Price guide: from £20

Reception

Couples need to organise their own catering at this venue.

e Lake
oad, Godalming
U7 1RH
5575 F: 01483 860445
nes Ginders, GM

Ceremony

The Inn on the Lake (which claims to be an inn, not a hotel) is a part Tudor building with a listed Georgian frontage. It is set in two acres of landscaped grounds overlooking is own lake. The building has limited wheelchair access. Ceremonies can take place here on any day of the year.
Price guide: POA

Reception

The venue has a lakeside restaurant as well as a bar which features a log fire and real ale.
Catering: from £32pp

Jarvis Thatcher's Hotel
Epsom Road, East Horsley
Nr Leatherhead KT24 6TB
T: 01483 284291 F: 01483 284222
Contact: Corinne Hall, Conference & Banqueting Manager

Ceremony

This is a Tudor style building set in its own landscaped gardens. Ceremonies can take place here on any day except Christmas Day and New Year's Day, with up to five ceremonies permitted per day.
Price guide: £275

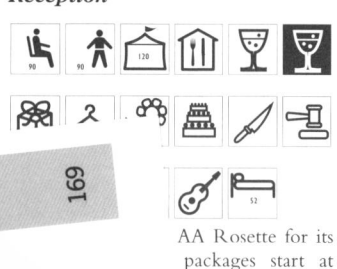

Reception

AA Rosette for its packages start at £22pp, which includes a three course meal, toastmaster, invitations sent out for you, table plan and cards, cake boxes and a double room at any Jarvis hotel for the wedding night. Drinks packages start at £10.50pp. Other packages offered by the hotel have also been well thought out and include things such as fun packs for children, 'favours' for all the ladies, and a dinner for two at Thatcher's on your first anniversary.
Catering: from £8.50pp - £22pp

Leatherhead Golf Club
Kingston Road, Leatherhead
Surrey KT22 0EE
T: 01372 843958 F: 01372 843966
Contact: Terry

Ceremony

The club allows one ceremony per day on any day of the week, but not on Bank Holidays. No confetti is allowed.
Price guide: from £250

Reception

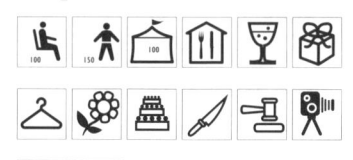

Catering: POA

The Long Hall, Ramster
Chiddingford, Surrey GU8 4SN
T: 01428 654167 F: 01428 658345
Contact: Mrs M Gunn, Owner, or Mrs N Chandler, Wedding Services Manager

Ceremony

The Long Hall is beamed and panelled and dates from 1604. It lies in the seclusion of a private estate and has central heating and inglenook fireplaces which can be used for log fires. The Great Drawing Room, adjoining the Log Hall, is licensed for ceremonies and has a grand piano and a music system.
Price guide: POA

Reception

Outside caterers of the couple's own choice can be employed at this venue. A list of local accommodation can be supplied if required.

Loseley Park, Guildford
Surrey GU3 1HS
T: 01483 304440 F: 01483 302036
Contact: Vicky Owen, Corporate Affairs Manager

Ceremony

This estate features a 2.5 acre walled garden and an Elizabethan mansion. Three areas are licensed; The Great Hall (100), The Drawing Room (50) and The Tithe Barn (160). Ceremonies can take place here on any day when the house is not open to the public. It is open to the public 2pm-5pm in June, July and August. Confetti is not permitted.
Price guide: from £600 - £1200

Reception

Alexander Catering Events provide the catering for this venue.
Catering: POA

Lythe Hill Hotel
Petworth Road, Haslemere
Surrey GU27 3BQ
T: 01428 651251 F: 01428 644131
Contact: K Lorimer, General Manager

Ceremony

Three rooms are available for ceremonies within this cluster of buildings, the oldest of which dates from 1475. The hotel's 20 acres of grounds includes a lake, a floodlit tennis court, a croquet lawn, games room and even a jogging track. Two ceremonies are permitted per day at the Lythe Hill Hotel, and can be held on any day of the week.
Price guide: from £50.

Reception

The hotel's wedding package includes a room to use during the day, and a complimentary room for the night. An accommodation discount is offered to all wedding guests. For the reception the hotel specialises in traditional English and French cuisine. Children under 10 are charged at half price.
Catering: £45.50 (wedding package)

The Manor
Newlands Corner
Guildford, Surrey GU4 8SE
T: 01483 222624 F: 01483 211389
Contact: David Hill, GM

Ceremony

The Manor is a country house hotel set in nine acres of parkland, and within easy reach of Heathrow and Gatwick airports. Three rooms are available for weddings, but ceremonies can only take place Sunday to Friday throughout most of the year. Saturdays are only available in November, January and February. Only one ceremony per day is permitted at The Manor. As part of its standard wedding package, The Manor offers a complimentary room for the bride and groom, or transport for the couple to their evening destination within the local area
Price guide: Registrar's fees only

Reception

The Manor has a late night drinking licence for Thursday, Friday and Saturday only. For the reception, children under 12 are charged at half price, while those under 4 are free.
Catering: from £23pp

The Market House
Market Place
Kingston upon Thames
Surrey
T: 0181 296 9747 F: 0181 296 9759
Contact: Malcolm North, Facilities Manager

Ceremony

This is the old Kingston town hall and is a Grade II listed building. The main hall and ante chamber are licensed for ceremonies which can take place here on any day of the year.
Price guide: from £40

Reception

There is currently no catering on site, so couples may arrange their own.

Oatlands Park Hotel
Oatlands Drive
Weybridge
Surrey
KT13 9HB
T: 01932 847242 F: 01932 821413
Contact: Barbara Harris, Sales & Marketing Manager

Ceremony

Three marriage rooms are available in this Grade II listed building which is set on the original estate where Henry VIII built a palace for Anne of Cleves. The rooms are The York Suite (120-220 people), The Broadwater Restaurant (80-160 people), and the Drawing Room & Garden room (up to 60 people). Ceremonies can take place here on any day of the year.
Price guide: £200

Reception

Cake stand and knife, and typed menus are provided free for the day, and a complimentary changing room is offered for the bride and groom. Overnight accommodation is also offered free of charge for the newlyweds.
Price guide: from £26pp

Runnymede Hotel & Spa
Windsor Road, Egham
Surrey TW20 0AG
T: 01784 436171 F: 01784 436340
email: info@runnymedehotel.com
Contact: Gillian Bramley, Conference & Banqueting Sales Manager

Ceremony

Runnymede Hotel has a splendid riverside setting with gardens on the banks of the Thames. It holds a licence for the Earl of Warren Suite, where ceremonies may be held on any day of the week. Confetti is allowed and there are areas available for both indoor and outdoor photography. Ceremonies need not be followed by a reception at the venue. The wedding couple can arrive or depart from the hotel by boat, and the site is also suitable for helicopters.
Price guide: £450 for Earl Warren Suite

Reception

All catering at Runnymede is in house. Children can be catered for separately and the hotel has 180 rooms to offer plenty of accommodation on site for guests.
Price guide: Buffets from £26pp. Sit down from £26pp

Sandown Park
Portsmouth Road, Esher
Surrey KT10 9AJ
T: 01372 464790 F: 01372 465205
Contact: Banqueting Co-ordinator

Ceremony

Opened as a racecourse in 1875 Sandown Park offers a choice of seven suites in its main building for receptions; and three suites for ceremonies.
Price guide: from £250

Reception

SURREY

SURREY

Sandown has a marquee erected from May to August. Accommodation is offered in the Ostler's Lodge, a modern hotel set in the grounds of the Park. The park also has a golf centre, a squash club and three artificial ski slopes.
Catering: from £19pp

Stanhill Court Hotel
Charlwood
Horley, Surrey RH6 0EP
T: 01293 862166 F: 01293 862773
Contact: Leonie Hudson, Manager

Ceremony

This Victorian country house was built in 1881 in the Scottish Baronial style. It is set in 35 acres of ancient wooded countryside. Its grounds feature an open-air ampitheatre and a walled garden. The Morning Room is licensed for ceremonies, which must be followed by a reception at the venue.
Price guide: £150

Reception

Stanhill holds English Tourist Board Awards (1995/96) for food, hospitality and service.
Catering: from £22pp

TuTu L'Auberge
Tilburstow Hill, South Godstone
Surrey RH9 8JY
T: 01342 892318 F: 01342 893435
email: HR36@Dial.Pipex.Com
Contact: Antoine Jalley, Director & Proprietor

Ceremony

This privately owned Victorian manor house is set in 14 acres with a lake. There are two marriage rooms, The Garden Room and the Zazou Suite, which can be used only if the reception is to follow at the restaurant. They are available any day (Bank Holidays are only available by prior arrangement). Two ceremonies only per day. Confetti is allowed.
Price guide: from £115

Reception

The restaurant specialises in classical French and modern English cuisine. Receptions are tailor-made around the client's requirements and the venue has recently introduced a range of ideas based on themes. Children can be catered for separately. Helicopters and hot air balloons may use the grounds of the restaurant, and it is possible to have use of a gondola on the lake. Fireworks can also be organised.
Catering: Buffets from £12.50. Sit down from £22.50

Waverley Borough Council
The Burys, Godalming
Surrey GU7 1HR
T: 01483 861111 F: 01483 426337
Contact: Brian Sewrey, Office Services & Borough Hall Manager

Ceremony

Three rooms hold licenses at this town centre, civic, venue: The Council Chamber (100), The Borough Hall (247) and The Court Room (50). Ceremonies can be held on any day of the year, excluding Christmas Day, Boxing Day and New Year's Day; with up to three ceremonies per day. Ceremony and reception package price is £458.
Price guide: £206 (ceremony only)

Reception

Receptions here have included an Indian wedding which the venue claims was "most unusual and very interesting." The reception-only room hire rate is £252. A late night licence can be arranged, if required. A list of local accommodation is available.
Catering: from £22pp

Woodlands Park Hotel
Woodlands Lane
Stoke D'Abernon KT11 3QB
T: 01372 843933 F: 01372 842704
Contact: Judy Watts, Conference & Banqueting Office Manager

Ceremony

A member of the Arcadian Hotels group, Woodlands Park is a Victorian mansion set in 10 acres of grounds. Its interior features original oak panelling, a minstrel's gallery and a stained glass roof. Four rooms are licensed: the Sitting Room, the Drawing Room, the Cornhall Suite and the Leicester Suite. Weddings may take place on any day of the week except Saturday, but not on Christmas Day, Easter or Good Friday.
Price guide: POA

Reception

The hotel offers modern British cuisine. Both hot air balloons and helicopters can land on the site by prior arrangement.
Catering: Buffets from £29.50pp. Sit down from £23.50pp

ALSO LICENSED
Airport House 0181 781 1234
Bramley Grange Hotel 01483 893434
The Bush Hotel 01252 715237
Copthorne Effingham Park Hotel 01342 714994
Coulsdon Manor Hotel 0181 668 0414
Croydon Clock Tower 0181 760 5400
Ewell Court House 0181 939 9571
Fairfield Halls 0181 681 0821
Farnham House Hotel 01252 716908
Frimley Hall Hotel 01276 28321
Great Fosters, Egham 01784 433822
Lingfield Park 01342 834800
Nonsuch Mansion 0181 393 4922
Nutfield Priory Hotel 01737 822066
Preston Cross Hotel 01372 456642
Ravens Ait 0181 390 3554

Reigate Manor Hotel 01737 822066
Russ Hill Hotel 01293 862171
Saville Court Hotel 01784 434355
St David's School 01784 240680
The Wentworth Club 01344 842201
Winter Garden 0181 654 4404

Close House Mansion
Heddon on the Wall
Newcastle upon Tyne NE15 0HT
T: 01661 852255 F: 01661 853322
Contact: Jane Thompson

Ceremony

This conference and banqueting centre is an English Heritage, Grade II listed building, set in 179 acres of wooded grounds and parkland. It features an 18 hole private golf course and helipad. Just 10 minutes from Newcastle city centre, the mansion dates back to 1779 and was once the property of a former Mayor of Newcastle. Ceremonies are permitted seven days a week, but only one is allowed per day.
Price guide: £300

Reception

The Bolbec and Bewicke Rooms are considered spacious and light and ideal for larger wedding breakfasts. The Bewicke Room features a marble fireplace and a bay window which opens out on the the east lawn. The Rococo Room, decorated in the Italian Rococo style, features a marble fireplace as a centrepiece and is suitable for smaller wedding parties. The mansion's grounds and lawns provide excellent surroundings for exterior photography. Pre-arranged wedding packages include, amongst other services, menu and drinks of your choice, table plans, hire of the function room and a private changing room for the bride and groom. Although bedrooms are not available on the premises, a list of local accommodation is available which operate preferential rate agreements with the mansion.
Catering: from £16pp

County Thistle Hotel
Neville Street, Newcastle NE99 1AH
T: 0191 232 2471 F: 0191 232 1285
Contact: Mary Thornton, GM

Ceremony

The hotel has three rooms licensed to hold ceremonies, which are not available on Bank Holidays or over the period 24th - 27th December. Ceremonies are free of charge when held in conjunction with receptions, while the price without a reception is available upon application, depending on the room required and the time of year.
Price guide: POA (FOC with reception)

Reception

A buffet style reception can hold a maximum of 200 standing guests, while the price guide below includes a sit down luncheon, red carpet, drinks for the reception, wine with the meal, sparkling wine for the speeches, flowers, and overnight accommodation for the bride and groom.
Catering: £23pp

Dissington Hall, Dalton
Newcastle Upon Tyne NE18 0AD
T: 01661 886063 F: 01661 886896
Contact: Michael Brown, Proprietor

Ceremony

This Georgian mansion was designed in 1794 and is set in 18 acres of grounds. Three rooms are licensed to hold ceremonies, the Garden Room which features a sweeping staircase and has a seated capacity of 90 people; the Old Library, which features a large book case and fireplace, and seats 50; and the Billiards Room which is the main banqueting room and has a seated capacity of 100. Ceremonies are not available during the Christmas and New Year holidays and are only available with reception facilities. There is wheelchair access to the ground floor.
Price guide: POA

Reception

The Hall takes pride in its high standard of cuisine and specialises in home-made food. If required, children can be catered for separately. The Admiral's bedroom is available for the bride and groom to change in, and the Hall can also provide a list of local hotels and guest houses. However, there are no preferential rate agreements with any of these establishments. The grounds are suitable for a marquee for up to 200 guests.
Catering: from £21pp

Jarrow Town Hall
Grange Road, Jarrow
Newcastle upon Tyne NE32 3LE
T: 0191 489 1141 F: 0191 455 0208
Contact: Mr Graham Jarvis, Assistant Director (Administration)

Ceremony

The Town Hall is a listed building and is licensed to hold ceremonies in the Council Chamber, on Saturdays and Sundays only. Confetti is permitted.
Price guide: £225

Reception

Although no reception facilities are offered at the Town Hall, a list of local accommodation is available and background music can be provided.

Newcastle United Football Club
St James' Park
Newcastle upon Tyne NE1 4ST
T: 0191 201 8525 F: 0191 201 0611
Contact: Conference & Banqueting

Ceremony

Newcastle United FC, established over 100 years ago, now play in one of the world's most modern sporting arenas. Situated in the heart of Newcastle, St James' Park offers panoramic views over the River Tyne and the City, and has extensive parking facilities. Four rooms are licensed; the St James' Suite, the Boardroom Club, the Centenary Suite and the United Suite. These rooms offer varying capacities from between 80 to 180. Ceremonies are available seven

173

days a week, excluding match days of course.
Price guide: POA

Reception

Although it is not possible to hold the ceremony or take photographs actually on the pitch, the grounds are available to take outside photography. The club boasts a speciality in Northumbrian cuisine in the Magpie Room, thanks to chef, John Blackmore of Alnwick, and Barry Johnson is featured as head chef. There are a total of eight function rooms in which to hold receptions and although accommodation is not available on the premises, the Club does operate preferential rate agreements with local hotels.
Catering: from £9pp

Ormesby Hall
Ormesby TS7 9AS
T: 01642 324188 F: 01642 300937
Contact: Deborah Osborne
PA to Estate Manager

Ceremony

Surrounded by beautiful gardens and parkland, Ormesby Hall is an imposing and elegant mid 18th Century mansion. The Palladian-style Main Hall is licensed to host ceremonies, which can take place on Fridays and Saturdays only. Up to two ceremonies are allowed per day, and they do not have to be followed by a reception at the Hall. Confetti is not permitted.
Price guide: £300

Reception

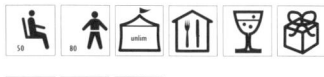

The tea rooms are able to accommodate receptions for up to 30, while the Victorian kitchen can seat 50. Buffets can be provided for up to 80 guests. Larger groups can be accommodated in a marquee, where catering is contracted out, as are other services such as entertainment, music, etc. Otherwise, catering is in-house.
Catering: Buffets from 10.50pp. Sit down from £18.50pp

Quality Friendly Hotel
Witney Way, Boldon NE35 9PE
T: 01691 519 1999 F: 0191 519 0655
Contact: Julie Corbyn, Conference & Banqueting Co-ordinator

Ceremony

Three rooms are licensed: The Monkton Suite, Cleadon and Westoe. Ceremonies can take place any day of the week excluding Bank Holidays. Only one ceremony is permitted per day, but these can be held without a reception at the venue. Confetti is allowed.
Price guide: POA

Reception

Children can be catered for separately.
Catering: Buffets from £5.50pp. Sit down from £16.50pp

South Shields Town Hall
Westoe Road, South Shields
Newcastle upon Tyne NE33 2RL
T: 0191 427 1717 F: 0191 455 0208
Contact: Mr Graham Jarvis, Assistant Director (Administration)

Ceremony

The Town Hall has four rooms licensed to hold ceremonies, with varying capacities; the Reception Room is the largest with a capacity of 145, the Ante-room to the Council Chamber seats 50, while the two Committee rooms each seat 30. Ceremonies are available on Saturday and Sunday only. Confetti is permitted.
Price guide: £225

Reception

Although accommodation is not available on the premises, the Town Hall can provide a list of local hotels and guest houses. In addition to the services indicated above, the Hall provides background music, if requested.
Catering: £9.50 - £15pp

Temple Park Centre
John Reid Road, South Shields
Tyne & Wear NE34 8QN
T: 0191 456 9119 F: 0191 456 6621
Contact: Anne Addison
Contracts Administration

Ceremony

The leisure centre has not renewed its license to hold wedding ceremonies.
Price guide: NA

Reception

Temple Park Centre is a large leisure centre with a variety of function facilities suitable for any size of event, including wedding receptions. The Function Suite seats approximately 150 people and, with its own bar, is ideal for any average size wedding party, both for the reception itself and for an evening function. In addition, the centre can offer a separate, good size bar which seats 100. The Main Hall can cater for up to 600. A range of menu and drinks packages are offered. Although accommodation is not available on the premises, the centre offers a list of local hotels and guest houses. In addition to the services indicated, the centre provides champagne for the guests on arrival. Past weddings have featured a horse and carriage for the bridal party.
Catering: £4.00 - £20.00pp

Tuxedo Royale
Hillgate Quay, Gateshead
Tyne & Wear NE8 2QS
Tel: 0191 477 8899 Fax: 0191 477 3297
Contact: Thelma Barnes

Ceremony

The Tuxedo Royale is actually a ship that has been berthed on the Tyne for

approximately seven years. The room licensed to hold ceremonies is the Commodore Suite which has a minimum capacity of four guests for a more intimate wedding. Although it is possible to hold a ceremony without reception facilities, ceremonies are free of charge if held in conjunction with receptions. Confetti is permitted.
Price guide: £500

Reception

Catering is in-house and children can be catered for separately. Although accommodation is not available on the premises, preferential rate agreements are operated with local hotels and guest houses.
Catering: Buffets from £10.95pp

Tyne Theatre & Opera House
Westgate Road
Newcastle upon Tyne NE1 4AG
T: 0191 232 1551 F: 0191 230 1407
Contact: Regan Old, Wedding Co-ordinator

Ceremony

This Grade I listed Victorian theatre features an auditorium in the classical Victorian style based on La Scala opera house in Milan. Two rooms hold licences; the Auditorium and the Upper Rehearsal Room. While the venue is theoretically available seven day a week throughout the year, actual availability is dependent upon the theatre's season. While no limit is set upon the number of ceremonies that can be held per day, it is the venue's policy to offer sole use of the premises if the reception is also to be held at the theatre.
Price guide: POA

Reception

Both in-house caterers or contract caterers can provide catering services. A wide range of differently priced menus is available. Indeed, the theatre claims to be able to tailor a wedding package to suit any budget. The first wedding held at the venue was between two of theatre's employees who actually met at the venue.
Catering: POA

Washington Old Hall
The Avenue, Washington Village
District 4, T&W NE38 7LE
T: 0191 416 6879
Contact: Kate Gardner, Wedding Co-ordinator

Ceremony

Owned by the National Trust, the Hall is fine example of a small 17th Century manor house. It incorporates the medieval remains of the dwelling lived in by the direct ancestors of the first President of the USA, George Washington. The house is furnished with contemporary paintings, delftware and richly carved oak furniture. Ceremonies take place in the Great Hall, which has a total capacity of 60 (30 seated). They can be held on Fridays or Saturdays throughout the year and on Sundays before 10am. From November to March, the hall is available seven days a week. Smoking is not permitted in the building. Hire of the hall for a ceremony only costs £150, which allows its use for a maximum of 90 minutes. For £500, you can hire the hall for both ceremony and reception, in total no more than five hours.
Price guide: £100 - £500

Reception

The hall has three approved contract caterers on its list. The hall tailors each wedding to the couple's exact specification, helping with flowers, catering etc. However, the hall does not have a drinks license, although it will allow couples to supply guests with wines and spirits of their own choice and do not charge corkage. The hall does not insist on daytime receptions. Evening receptions are allowed, provided that they are completed within the allotted time, which allow three hours for a reception on its own and five hours for a ceremony followed by a reception.
Catering: from £9 - £25pp

ALSO LICENSED
Civic Hall, Wallsend
Grand Hotel, Tynemouth 0191 293 6666
Marriott Hotel, Metro Centre
Park Hotel, Redcar 01642 491233
Park Hotel, Tynemouth 0191 257 1406
Pulman Lodge Hotel, Seaburn 0191 529 2020
Rushpool Hall Hotel 01237 624111
Swallow Gosforth Park
Swallow Hotel, Stockton 01642 679721
Tall Trees Hotel, Yarm 01642 781050
Theatre Royal, Grey Street, Newcastle

007 Bond Street
Bond Gate
Nuneaton
Warwickshire
CV11 4DA
T: 01203 347563 F: 01203 352458
Contact: Heather Clelland, Wedding Co-ordinator

Ceremony

This is a themed venue based on the James Bond character. Ceremonies are available seven days a week with one permitted per day. Although there is no specific area for outdoor photography, the venue is only five minutes walk away from a park.
Price guide: £215

Reception

The venue prides itself on the ability to provide any service the couple may require, from videos and horse and carriages to organising the honeymoon for them. As an extra special touch, the venue can organise a James Bond lookalike for the reception. The venue operates special rate agreements with local hotels and guest houses. The price guide indicates the cost per head of a buffet reception, which rises to £12.50 for a sit-down meal.
Catering: from £7.50pp

WARWICKSHIRE

**The Alveston Manor
Stratford-upon-Avon
Warwicks CV37 7HP**
T: 01789 204581 F: 01789 414095
Contact: Pat Hollis Business Development Manager

Ceremony

This riverside hotel and restaurant offers ceremonies seven days a week with a maximum of two to be held per day.
Price guide: £150

Reception

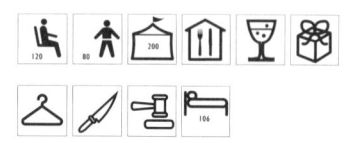

The grounds are suitable for a marquee with a capacity for accommodating up to 200 people.
Catering: from £27pp

**Ansty Hall Hotel
Main Road
Ansty, Coventry CV7 9HZ**
T: 01203 612222 F: 01203 602155
Contact: Melissa Fell, Sales Coordinator

Ceremony

Ansty Hall is a Grade II listed Georgian house, set in eight acres of private gardens and located near a canal and the golf course. The Drawing Room is licensed and available on Fridays, Saturdays and Sundays only.
Price guide: £100

Reception

The marquee is set up here for 11 months of the year. Cusine is French. Helicopters can land on site, and the nearby canal is navigable. Numerous services can be organised or recommended including fireworks. The Hall will add a further 40 bedrooms in 1999.
Catering: Buffets from £8.75pp. Sit down from £19.95pp

**The Arden Thistle Hotel
44 Waterside
Stratford upon Avon CV37 6BA**
T: 01789 294949 F: 01789 415874
Contact: Jeremy Mason or Claire Gale, Conference & Banqueting Administrators

Ceremony

This Regency built hotel is opposite the Royal Shakespeare & Swan theatres and is available seven days a week.
Price guide: £195

Reception

The hotel has 63 bedrooms, some of which are executive rooms and two of which feature four poster beds. The hotel's Bard's restaurant features traditional English and continental cuisine, while the terrace is a relaxing location to enjoy drinks with guests.
Catering: £25.50-£36.50pp

**The Ardencote Manor Hotel
Lye Green Road, Claverdon
Warwickshire CV35 8LS**
T: 01926 843111 F: 01926 842646
Contact: Mrs D Sale, Conference & Banqueting Manager

Ceremony

This hotel and country club, originally a Victorian manor house residence, is set in 40 acres of grounds, gardens and lakes. Three rooms are licensed at the hotel with varying capacities; the Palms Conservatory which overlooks the gardens, fountain and maze, the Henley Suite and the Oak Room, which is a classical dining room with oak panelling and has a capacity of 46.
Price guide: £170

Reception

The hotel prides itself on a modern European approach to cuisine and offers special accommodation rates for wedding guests.
Catering: from £35pp (wedding package)

**The Belfry
Lichfield Road, Wishaw
N Warwickshire B76 9PR**
T: 01675 470301 F: 01675 470178
Contact: Rita Cooper, Sales Manager

Ceremony

The Belfry is a four star hotel set in 500 acres of north Warwickshire countryside and offers ceremonies seven days a week with a maximum of two to be held per day.
Price guide: from £250 - £1,500

Reception

The hotel prides itself on the ability to meet any catering requirements the couple may have. In addition to the services indicated, the hotel stresses that any request may be arranged.
Catering: from £40pp (package including drinks). From October 1998 £45pp.

**The Brandon Hall Hotel
Main Street
Brandon
Warwickshire
CV8 3FW**
T: 01203 542571 F: 01203 545771
Contact: Penny Parke, Conference Manager

Ceremony

This is a county house hotel set in 17 acres of gardens and woodland. Ceremonies can take place in the Brandon Suite on Fridays, Saturdays and Sundays, and not over Christmas and New Year Confetti is not permitted.
Price guide: from £200 (with reception)

WARWICKSHIRE

Reception

Catering: Buffets from £8pp. Sit down from £18.75pp.

Courtyard by Marriott Hotel
London Road
Ryton On Dunsmore CV8 3DY
T: 01203 301585   F: 01203 301610
Contact: Des Richardson, Conference & Banqueting Manager

Ceremony

The hotel is RAC and AA recommended. A maximum of one ceremony a day is permitted, on any day of the week.
Price guide: from £475

Reception

The hotel stresses that however formal or informal your reception requirements may be, they will provide the necessary arrangements. The price guide indicates the starting price of a standing finger buffet. Of the services indicated, the cake stand, toastmaster and piped music are all provided free of charge, a fee will be charged for the remaining services.
Catering: from £7pp

De Montfort Hotel
The Square, Kenilworth CV8 1ED
T: 01926 855944   F: 01926 857830
Contact: Kerry Holmes, Conference & Events Manager

Ceremony

This modern hotel is situated in the town centre and has recently undergone a £2 million refurbishment. The hotel does not feature any gardens but has parking for up to 70 cars. Four rooms are licensed to hold ceremonies with varying capacities from 20 to 130. De Montfort has exclusive use of the ruins of Kenilworth Castle for photographs. No charge is made by the hotel for the hire of the ceremony room but a fee of approximately £135 will be made by the registrar.

Reception

The hotel has a lounge area suitable for indoor photography and offers a complimentary overnight suite for the bride and groom on the night of the wedding. Wedding breakfast prices start at approximately £17 per person, reducing to £7 a head for an evening buffet reception. The hotel operates preferential rate agreements with local guest houses for wedding guests.
Catering: from £17pp

Eathorpe Park Hotel
The Fosse
Leamington Spa
Warwickshire
CV33 9DQ
T: 01926 632632   F: 01926 632481
Contact: Carol or Rodney Grinnell, Directors

Ceremony

Ceremonies are available any day of the week with no cap on the number held per day.
Price guide: FOC

Reception

In addition to the hotel's 16 bedrooms, it also operates special rate agreements with other local hotels and guest houses.
Catering: POA

Falstaff Hotel
16-20 Warwick New Road
Leamington Spa CV32 5JQ
T: 01926 312044   F: 01926 450574
Contact: John Seeger, GM

Ceremony

This 18th Century building, converted into three Regency mansions, is now home to this 63 bedroom hotel. One room is available to hold ceremonies, with a capacity of 46. Ceremonies are not available without reception facilities.
Price guide: £150

Reception

The hotel features traditional English and continental cuisine with a focus on fresh produce. The charge for the changing room for the bride and groom is included in the price of the evening reception.
Catering: from £11.25pp

Kingsbury Country Club
Coventry Road
Kingsbury, Tamworth B78 2LP
T: 01827 872404
Contact: Martin Shakespeare, Manager

Ceremony

This modern building is surrounded by a public recreation area with gardens and is available to hold ceremonies seven days a week. Ceremonies are only permitted when held in conjunction with receptions.
Price guide: FOC (with reception)

Reception

The club prides itself on home cooked, traditional cuisine.

177

WARWICKSHIRE

Catering: Buffets from £4.95pp Sit down from £12.50pp

Lea Marston Hotel
Haunch Lane, Lea Marston
Warwickshire B76 0BY
T: 01675 470468 F: 01675 470871
Contact: Sharon Smith, Sales Co-ordinator

Ceremony

The hotel is set in 20 acres of grounds and features a nine hole golf course. Three rooms are licensed at the hotel: the Atrium Room, which is in the hotel's conservatory, has a marble floor and holds 80 guests; the Octagon Suite, which overlooks the golf course, has a capacity of 100; and the Perry-Barton room, which has a capacity of 80 people. Ceremonies are permitted without reception facilities, although the room hire charge rises to £100 in these circumstances.
Price guide: from £75 (£150 without reception)

Reception

There is a reception room hire fee of £195.
Catering: Buffets from £6.95pp. Sit down from £19.95pp

The Manor House Hotel
Avenue Road
Leamington Spa CV31 3NJ
T: 01926 423251 F: 01926 425933
Contact: Jan Deeming, Banqueting

Ceremony

Said to be home of the first Lawn Tennis Club, this listed building features smooth landscaped lawns and was opened in 1847. Included in the wedding package for a minimum of 45 guests, the hotel includes amongst other things, afternoon room hire, table posies, changing room and overnight accommodation for the bride and groom.

Price guide: from £80

Reception

The hotel offers special overnight rates to wedding guests including a traditional English breakfast. Of the services indicated, the hotel includes the flowers and cake stand in the reception price.
Catering: from £12.90pp. Drinks packages from £5.55pp

Millers Hotel
Twycross Road, Sibson
Nuneaton CV13 6LB
T & F: 01827 880223
Contact: Tracy, Functions & Restaurant Manager

Ceremony

This hotel, restaurant and public house features a waterwheel in the bar. The restaurant is licensed for ceremonies and is available on any day of the year.
Price guide: £45

Reception

Catering: Buffets from £7.50pp. Sit down from £16pp

Nuthurst Grange Country House Hotel & Restaurant
Nuthurst Grange Lane
Hockley Heath B94 5NL
T: 01564 783972 F: 01564 783919
Contact: Karen J Seymour, Manager

Ceremony

The hotel has been awarded four ETB Crowns, three AA Red Stars and three Rosettes for its restaurant. Ceremonies are available any day of the week with only one permitted per day.
Price guide: £195

Reception

The hotel prides itself on using only the freshest foods in its award winning restaurant.
Catering: from £29.90pp

Salford Hall Hotel
Abbotts Salford
Evesham WR11 5UT
T: 01386 871300 F: 01386 871301
Contact: Sally Pearce, General Manager

Ceremony

This Tudor manor is a Grade I listed building, restored six years ago. Up to two ceremonies are permitted per day, on any day except Christmas Day. Confetti is not permitted.
Price guide: £100 (FOC with reception)

Reception

The Hotel has two AA Rosettes for its cuisine. It is also possible to take over the whole hotel, including a minimum of 30 bedrooms.
Catering: from £27.50pp.

Welcombe Hotel & Golf Course
Warwick Road
Stratford upon Avon CV37 0NR
T: 01789 295252 F: 01789 414666
Contact: Miss Denise Elliot
Sales & Marketing Manager

Ceremony

The hotel is housed in a period building in a rural location with gardens and a golf course. The West Lounge is licensed for ceremonies which can take place here, if followed by reception at the hotel on any day except Christmas and New Year.
Price guide: from £350

Reception

The hotel has its own health and beauty salon and can offer a beauty package if required. Wedding breakfasts are also in packages at £60 per head.
Catering: Packages £60pp

ALSO LICENSED
Billesley Manor Hotel 01789 279955
Brownsover Hall Hotel 01788 546100
Charlecote Pheasant 01789 279954
Marston Farm Hotel 01827 872133
Moxhull Hall Hotel 0121 329 2056
Riverside Hotel 01926 858331
Southam Community Hall, Southam 01926 813933
Woodhouse Hotel 01926 632131

Aston Villa Football Club
Villa Park
Birmingham B6 6HE
T: 0121 327 5308 F: 0121 328 1351
Contact: Carol Deakin, Sales & Marketing Co-ordinator

Ceremony

This famous football club and restaurant is licensed to hold ceremonies in the McGregor restaurant seven days a week excluding match days. Two ceremonies per day are permitted and confetti is allowed.
Price guide: £250

Reception

Although accommodation is not available on the premises, the football club has a list of local hotels and guest houses, some of which operate preferential rate agreements with the club. In addition to the services indicated, the club allows photographs to be taken on the pitch and prides itself on offering a full wedding package. The price guide indicated below is for a sit down meal.
Catering: from £15pp

The Chace Hotel
London Road
Toll Bar End
Coventry CV3 4EQ
T: 01203 303398 F: 01203 301816
Contact: Trisha Hennessy-Cooper, Room Sales Manager

Ceremony

The hotel dates back to the late 19th Century and features traditional wood panelling, a large open fireplace and an imposing foyer. The foyer leads to a sweeping staircase which features stained glass windows. One room is licensed to hold ceremonies at the hotel which is available seven days a week with no restrictions on Bank Holidays. Ceremonies are free when held in conjunction with receptions. The hotel also has the Abbey Room, a luxury bedroom complete with four-poster bed and spa bath, which is popular for both newly weds and anniversary couples. All bedrooms have colour TV and other amenities.
Price guide: FOC (with reception) or £100

Reception

Of the 66 bedrooms, 17 are located in the original building. The hotel boasts traditional English cuisine but is willing to discuss any specific catering requirements. Children can be catered for separately.
Catering: from £16.95pp

The Chamberlain Hotel
Alcester Street
Birmingham B12 0PJ
T: 0121 627 0627 F: 0121 627 0628
Contact: Jacqueline A Perkins, Banqueting Sales Executive

Ceremony

This Grade II listed building has four rooms licensed to hold ceremonies, one of which, the Rowton Suite, features Victorian skylights, ornate pillars and specially imported wood panels. The Suite also includes an extensive sound and light system and a dance floor at no extra cost. Ceremonies are not available on Good Friday or Christmas Day. Confetti is not permitted.
Price guide: from £150

Reception

The hotel is happy to discuss any special dietary requests and, in addition to the reception services indicated, the hotel provides a car service, video photography and a contact for stationery.
Catering: Buffets from £7pp. Sit down from £24pp

The Clarendon Suites
2 Stirling Road
Edgbaston B16 9SB
T: 0121 454 2918 F: 0121 455 0859
Contact: Maureen Hadley, Operations Manager

Ceremony

This conference and banqueting centre is located five minutes from New Street Station and just ten minutes from Birmingham city centre. It holds a licence for six dining rooms, plus the Concourse. The centre is available for hire seven days a week throughout the year, including Bank Holidays. Two ceremonies are allowed per day; only with a reception. Confetti is allowed.
Price guide: £200

Reception

Children can be catered for separately. There is no accommodation on site, but there are many hotels nearby.
Catering: Buffets from £5.95pp. Sit down from £15.00pp

WEST MIDLANDS - WARWICKSHIRE

179

WEST MIDLANDS

Coombe Abbey Hotel
Coombe Abbey Park
Brinklow Road, Binley CV3 2AB
Tel: 01203 450450 Fax: 01203 635101
Contact: Paul Gossage, Wedding Co-ordinator

Ceremony

This 12th Century Abbey, which is set in 550 acres of grounds, has been tastefully restored into a luxury hotel, which has medieval, 18th Century and Victorian features. Two rooms are licensed to hold ceremonies: the De-Canville room, which has a capacity of 23 guests; and the Abbeygate room, with a capacity of 138. The hotel prides itself as being "no ordinary hotel" and consequently plans "no ordinary weddings".
Price guide: £200 - £400

Reception

The hotel offers the finest English cuisine, with a touch of European flair. In addition to the services indicated, the hotel offers a complimentary overnight stay for the bridal couple and may also provide medieval themed weddings and in-house opera singers for the reception. There is a room hire fee if only a buffet is required.
Catering: from £24.50pp

Coventry City Football Club
Highfield Road Stadium
King Richard Street
Coventry CV5 4FW
Tel: 01203 234000 Fax: 01203 630318
Contact: Raj Athwal or Val Wright

Ceremony

The club has a total of 30 hospitality and conference rooms which are capable of catering for as few as two to up to 24,000 people. There are six rooms licensed to hold ceremonies, one of which is the restaurant, which actually overlooks the pitch. Ceremonies are available seven days a week, including match days, and are available without reception facilities, if required. Outdoor photography includes the use of the pitch.
Price guide: FOC

Reception

The site is suitable for a marquee which may be constructed on the pitch itself upon discussion. During our initial research, we were quoted buffets from £10pp, with wedding breakfasts starting at £15pp. The Club is now keen to state that catering prices vary according to requirements, which demonstrates their flexibility. The club operates preferential rate agreements with various local hotels and offers a limousine service for the bride and groom to travel to their hotel. A late night licence may be obtained.
Catering: POA

Edgbaston Conference &
Banqueting Centre
County Ground, Edgbaston
B5 7QU
T: 0121 440 0747 F: 0121 440 0116
Contact: Vikki Steel, Conference & Banqueting Co-ordinator

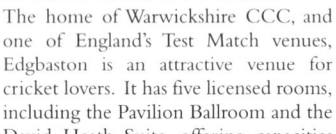

Ceremony

The home of Warwickshire CCC, and one of England's Test Match venues, Edgbaston is an attractive venue for cricket lovers. It has five licensed rooms, including the Pavilion Ballroom and the David Heath Suite, offering capacities from 30 up to 380. Up to two ceremonies can be held per day on every day of the year except Christmas Day.
Price guide: from £100

Reception

Catering is provided by Letheby & Christopher, one of the UK's leading sporting, social and corporate caterers. While there is no accommodation on site, Edgbaston can provide a list of local establishments with which it has special rate agreements.
Catering: Buffets from £10.00pp. Sit down from £16.00pp

Friendly Hotel
20 Wolverhampton Road West
Bentley, Walsall WS2 0BS
T: 01922 724444 F: 01922 723148
Contact: Mandy Chagger, Banqueting Co-ordinator

Ceremony

This modern hotel has two rooms licensed for ceremonies; the Oliver Cromwell Suite and the King Charles Suite, both of which can be divided into three sections and used individually or as a whole. Each section has a capacity for approximately 50 people seated, which rises to a maximum of 180 when using all three sections.
Price guide: £100 - £360

Reception

The hotel arranges special themed receptions which have, in the past, included an Indian theme and a Halloween theme. A late night drinking licence may easily be obtained and a complimentary overnight room is available for bride and groom.
Catering: Buffets from £5.95pp

Grange Hall
Coventry Road
Southam CV33 0ED
T: 01926 813933
Contact: Fenella Nudd, Administrator

Ceremony

This civic building has two licensed rooms; the Foyer and the Main Hall. They are available every day of the week

except Sunday. Seating capacities range from 56 to 300.
Price guide: POA

Reception

Catering: POA

Hagley Hall
Hagley, Stourbridge DY9 9LG
T: 01562 882408 F: 01562 882632
Contact: Lesley Haynes, Events Manager

Ceremony

Hagley Hall is a stately home with four licensed rooms; the White Hall, the State Dining Room, the Crimson Drawing Room and the Gallery. Ceremonies can only be held when the reception is also at the Hall. Hire of the Hall involves a facility fee of £1,100, plus £200 if you want the hire period to exceed six hours; with an additional £250 for the ceremony, excluding the Registrar's fees. All prices exclude VAT. Wheelchair access is limited and confetti is not allowed.
Price guide: from £1,100

Reception

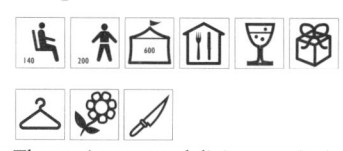

The maximum seated dining capacity in a single room is 140, although buffets for 200 can be provided across two rooms. Children can be catered for separately.
Catering: from £17pp

Highbury
Yew Tree Road
Moseley B13 8GJ
T: 0121 449 6549 F: 0121 442 4782
Contact: Mrs J Tanner

Ceremony

Highbury enjoys a secluded parkland setting three miles from Birmingham city centre. Originally built as the home of Joseph Chamberlain MP in 1878, it features a central Hall with a first floor Minstrel's Gallery. The Drawing Room, which is licensed, looks out over the house's south-facing terrace, grounds and surrounding parkland. Ceremonies can only be held with a reception at the venue.
Price guide: POA

Reception

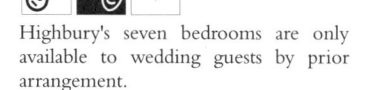

Highbury's seven bedrooms are only available to wedding guests by prior arrangement.
Catering: from £17pp

Jarvis International Hotel
The Square, Solihull
West Midlands B91 3RF
T: 0121 711 2121 F: 0121 711 3374
Contact: Amanda Hillier
or Helen Wallace

Ceremony

English Tourist Board recommended, this hotel specialises in wedding packages. Of its three specific packages, the cheapest is the Sandringham at £29 to £42pp. There are three rooms licensed to hold ceremonies, with capacities varying from 25 to 100. Ceremonies are available seven days a week, with discounts available on Sundays, Fridays and Bank Holidays.
Price guide: £50 - £200

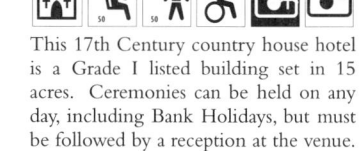

Reception

The Sandringham wedding package includes room hire charges for the reception, a drink for wedding guests on their arrival, a choice of three menus, 1.5 glasses of wine for guests with their meal, a glass of sparkling wine for the toast, top table flowers, a changing room for the couple on the day, and a town house overnight suite for the bride and groom.
Catering: packages from £29pp

Nailcote Hall Hotel
Nailcote Lane, Berkswell
Coventry CV7 7DE
T: 01203 466174 F: 01203 470720
Contact: Karen Bentley, Conference Manager

Ceremony

This 17th Century country house hotel is a Grade I listed building set in 15 acres. Ceremonies can be held on any day, including Bank Holidays, but must be followed by a reception at the venue.
Price guide: £50 - £200

Reception

The hotel offers complimentary overnight accommodation for the bride and groom.
Catering: packages from £35.50pp

Pine Lodge Hotel
Kidderminster Road
Bromsgrove B61 9AB
T: 01527 576600 F: 01527 878981
email: pinelodge@bromsgrove.telme.com
Contact: Claire Cardinal, Conference & Banqueting Manager

Ceremony

This hotel has two licensed rooms; the Europa Suite and the Belbroughton Suite. Up to two ceremonies can be held per day, on any day of the year. Confetti is allowed.
Price guide: £125 (including flowers)

Reception

Children can be catered for separately.
Catering: Buffets from £6.95pp. Sit down from £17.50pp

WEST MIDLANDS

WEST MIDLANDS

Quality Cobden Hotel
166 Hagley Road, Edgbaston
Birmingham B16 9NZ
T: 0121 454 6621 F: 0121 456 2935
Contact: Debbie Baker, Conference
& Banqueting Manager

Ceremony

This hotel boasts attractive gardens. It has three licensed rooms: the Acorn, the Calthorpe and the Arden, offering seated capacities up to 50. Wheelchair access is limited but confetti is allowed.
Price guide: £200

Reception

Catering: Buffets from £7.50pp. Sit down from £13.50.

Quality Norfolk Hotel
157-267 Hagley Road
Edgbaston B16 9NA
T: 0121 454 8071 F: 0121 455 6149
Contact: Lynn Evans, Conference
& Banqueting Manager

Ceremony

Situated two miles west of the city centre in its own grounds, the hotel offers ceremonies seven days a week, excluding Good Friday and Christmas Day.
Price guide: POA

Reception

The hotel claims to be a well-known wedding and function venue. Its services also include contacts with cake suppliers, photographers and musicians. A complimentary bedroom is offered to the bride and groom.
Catering: from £10pp

Solihull Conference
& Banqueting Centre
Homer Road, Solihull B91 3QW
T: 0121 704 0088 F: 0121 711 3157
Contact: Paula Perla, Conference
& Banqueting Administration Manager

Ceremony

This town centre conference venue features tree-lined lawns. Its Aylesford and Shenstone rooms are licensed for ceremonies, which can be held on any day of the year.
Price guide: £100 - £200

Reception

The centre is able to provide Asian cuisine, if required.
Catering: Buffets from £6.50pp. Sit down from £12.50pp

St Mary's Guildhall Complex
Bayley Lane, Coventry CV1 5RR
T: 01203 833327 F: 01203 833329
Contact: Roma Stone, Conference
& Banqueting Manager

Ceremony

This Grade I listed medieval Guildhall has four rooms licensed with a minimum capacity of four guests.
Price guide: £60 - £255

Reception

While there is no accommodation on site, The Guildhall is situated near to a hotel, which can arrange suitable accommodation for the bride and groom and their guests.
Catering: from £7.20pp

Stakis Birmingham Metropole
NEC, Birmingham B40 1PP
T: 0121 780 4242 F: 0121 782 1685
Contact: Darren Bailey, Assistant
Food & Beverage Manager

Ceremony

This large hotel, which caters for exhibitors at the National Exhibition Centre, has its own leisure and business centres. It offers a range of licensed function rooms catering for parties from 50 up to 2,000. Ceremonies can be held on any day of the year, but only with a reception at the hotel.
Price guide: FOC with reception

Reception

The hotel offers a wide variety of cuisines and will cater for children separately, if required. The hotel's wedding package includes a sherry reception, three-course wedding breakfast, one glass of wine per person, sparkling wine for the toasts, room hire, cake stand and knife, background music, linen napkins in a choice of colours, matching candelabra and candles, a luxury suite for the bride and groom with complimentary fruit and champagne; plus a complimentary suite for the couple's First Wedding Anniversary.
Catering: Buffets from £12.25. Sit down from £31.50

Sutton Coldfield Town Hall
Upper Clifton Road
Sutton Coldfield B73 6AB
T: 0121 355 8990 F: 0121 355 8255
Contact: Lynette Skinner, Manager

Ceremony

Three rooms are licensed to hold ceremonies at the Town Hall; the Council Chamber, the Vesey Lounge and the Vesey Suite. Ceremonies are available throughout the year, excluding Christmas Day or Good Friday.
Price guide: £100 - £200

Reception

Although the Town Hall does not hold a late night drinking licence, one can be applied for, if required. Ethnic cuisine is a speciality. A list of local accommodation is available, some with preferential rate agreements.
Catering: from £12.50pp

Sutton Court Hotel
**60-66 Lichfield Road
Sutton Coldfield B74 2NA**
T: 0121 355 6071   F: 0121 355 0083
email: reservations@sutton-court-hotel.co.uk
Contact: Peter Bennett, Proprietor

Ceremony

This Victorian building is set in its own grounds with a gazebo featured in the garden; providing an ideal backdrop for romantic wedding photographs. Three rooms are licensed: the Wyvern Room, decorated in brick-effect with stained glass windows; the Wallace Room, the hotel's main function room; and the restaurant, PJs, which is lit by chandeliers. There is wheelchair access to the Wallace Room only. Up to three ceremonies can be held per day on any day of the year. Confetti is allowed.
Price guide: £200

Reception

Bride of the Year 1996, in association with Xtra FM, won a complete wedding at the hotel, plus honeymoon. The proprietor, Peter Bennett, was the first person to be married by civil ceremony at Sutton Court Hotel for 158 years when he tied the knot in 1995. The hotel boasts a wide selection of three-course meals and a speciality gourmet buffet. Children can be catered for separately.
Catering: Buffets from £7.50pp. Sit down from £16.95pp

Westmead Hotel
**Reddich Road
Hopwood B48 7AL**
T: 0121 445 1202   F: 0121 445 6163
Contact: Tracy Murphy, Conference & Banqueting Co-ordinator

Ceremony

This hotel offers ceremonies seven days a week, but these must be followed by a reception at the venue. Wheelchair access is limited.
Price guide: £100

Reception

Catering: Buffets from £6.25pp. Sit down from £20pp

ALSO LICENSED
*Avoncroft Museum   01527 831363
Bescot Stadium, Walsall   01922 22791
Birmingham Botanical Gardens
0121 454 1860
Birmingham Grand Moat House
0121 607 9988
Dunstall Park Centre, Wolverhampton
Fairlawns Hotel, Walsall   01922 55122
Hyatt Regency Birmingham 0121 643 1234
Jarvis Penns Hall Hotel 0121 351 3111
Moor Hall Hotel 0121 308 3751
The Westley Hotel 0121 706 4312
West Bromwich Moat House 0121 609 9988*

Alexander House Hotel
**East Street
Turners Hill
West Sussex RH10 4QD**
T: 01342 714914   F: 01342 717328
Contact: Kate Hargreave, Deputy Manager

Ceremony

This property was previously owned by the Bysshe family (of the poet Shelley fame), and is set in 135 acres of gardens and parkland. Ceremonies can take place here in th South Drawing Rom or the Library on any day of the year.
Price guide: £400

Reception

Catering: from £28pp

Amberley Castle
**Country House Hotel
Amberley, Nr Arundel
BN18 9ND**
T: 01798 831992   F: 01798 831998
Contact: Emma Pearson
Front of House Manager

Ceremony

Stunning is the only word to describe this 12th Century castle nestling in the lee of the South Downs. Through the portcullis and 60ft thick walls lie ornamental gardens and dramatic medieval architecture, plus an atmosphere of intimacy and privacy. The scope for creative wedding photography is limitless. The Great Room is licensed (48 seated, 60 standing). Other function rooms include the King Charles Room (12 seated) and the Queen's Room (48 seated, 60 standing). Ceremonies can be held on any day of the week, but must be followed by a reception at the venue.
Price guide: from £650

Reception

Extra services co-ordinated by the venue can include speciality cakes, wedding photography, dress design, horse-drawn carriages, floral design, marquee hire, music consultancy, harpists, string quartets, event management, helicopter flights and fireworks.
Catering: Buffets from £16.50pp. Sit down from £24.50

The Angel Hotel, North Street
Midhurst GU29 9DN
T: 01730 812421   F: 01730 815928
Contact: Caroline Stevens, Front Office Manager

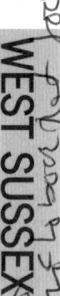

WEST SUSSEX

Ceremony

This hotel, a former coaching inn which overlooks the Cowdray estate, is located in the centre of Midhurst and has three acres of gardens. The Court Room is licensed and available on any day of the year.
Price guide: from £190

Reception

The hotel boasts three AA rosettes for its food.
Catering: Buffets from £28.50pp. Sit down from £21.50pp

Bailiffscourt Hotel, Climping
Littlehampton BN17 5RW
T: 01903 723511   F: 01903 723107
Contact: Amanda Cox, Banqueting Man

Ceremony

This listed building is a recreation of a medieval manor house and features oak beams, log fires and four poster beds. It is set in 22 acres adjacent to the sea and has two tennis courts and an outdoor swimming pool. The hotel is available every day, except Christmas Day.
Price guide: POA

Reception

Reception facilities include a walled courtyard filled with climbing roses which is suitable for al fresco dining. The hotel has also been awarded three AA rosettes for its French/English style cuisine. As well as the above services, a harpist can be arranged, if required. There is also a 12th Century chapel on site, which is available for blessings.
Catering: from £25pp

Chatsworth Hotel
Steyne, Worthing BN11 3DU
T: 01903 236103   F: 01903 823726
Contact: Jon Walpole, General Manager

Ceremony

This town centre hotel is situated on the seafront with gardens opposite. Ceremonies can take place here on any day of the year, but must be followed by a reception on the premises.
Price guide: £250

Reception

Catering: Buffets from £10.50pp. Sit down from £15.95pp

Dolphin & Anchor Hotel
West Street, Chichester
West Sussex PO19 1QE
T: 01243 785121   F: 01243 533408
Contact: Tim Scargill, General Manager

Ceremony

The Dolphin & Anchor (a Forte Heritage hotel) is situated in the heart of Chichester, directly opposite the Cathedral. Ceremonies can take place here any day of the year except 24th to 26th December and 31st December.
Price guide: from £150

Reception

Reception facilities at the hotel also include printing of menus and supplying place cards, discounted menus for children under 10 years old, overnight accommodation for the bride and groom, and special overnight rates for wedding guests.
Catering: packages from £25pp

East Court
College Lane
East Grinstead RH19 3LT
T: 01342 323636   F: 01342 327823
Contact: Mrs Rudin, Facilities Manager

Ceremony

East Court Mansion is an 18th Century Grade II listed manor house to which the Meridian Hall was a fairly recent addition. The Mansion's Cranston Suite (max 40) and the Meridian Hall (max 100) have views over East Court's gardens and the Ashdown Forest. Meridian also has its own private patio. Confetti is permitted outside only. Ceremonies can take place on any day of the year, except Christmas Eve, Christmas Day, Boxing Day and Good Friday.
Price guide: from £60

Reception

Couples may bring in their own caterers for a reception at East Court, so no catering price guide is quoted here. A list of local accommodation is available.

Goodwood House
Goodwood
Chichester PO18 0PX
T: 01243 774107   F: 01243 774313
Contact: Sally Lower, Sales Executive

Ceremony

This famous stately home is only available on an exclusive use basis. Three marriage rooms are licensed, and ceremonies must be followed by a reception. Neither confetti, nor stiletto heels, are permitted.
Price guide: from £1,500

Reception

Goodwood does not have a set menu,

184

but will tailor each meal to the client's specific requirements. Helicopters can use the grounds, if required.
Catering: from £45pp

Goodwood Racecourse
Goodwood, Chichester PO18 0PS
T: 01243 755022   F: 01243 755025
Contact: Sarah Edgar, Events & Leisure

Ceremony

This is one of the UK's most attractive racecourses, with views of the Sussex Downs and Chichester Harbour. The Charlton Suite and Charlton Boxes are licensed and are available any day except Christmas Day.
Price guide: from £150

Reception

Catering: Buffets from £18pp. Sit down from £28pp.

Horsham Museum
9 The Causeway
Horsham RH12 1HE
T: 01403 254959
Contact: Gill Graham, Admin Assistant

Ceremony

The museum is a timber-framed former medieval merchant's house in the town centre. It has a walled garden which is available for photographs. Ceremonies can take place in the Georgian Marriage Room on any day except Sundays and Bank Holidays.
Price guide: from £10 (garden £10 extra)

Reception
There are no reception facilities.

Le Meridien London Gatwick
North Terminal RH6 0PH
T: 01293 567070   F: 01293 569137
Contact: John Angus, F&B Manager

Ceremony

Probably one of the most convenient locations for those wanting to make a quick getaway by air. The hotel has three licensed rooms which are available on any day of the year.
Price guide: £100 - £450

Reception

Drinks packages start at £12.95pp. The hotel can offer you car parking for up to 15 days, plus use of the VIP Airport lounge to make to start of your trip away a bit special.
Catering: Buffets from £19.50pp. Sit down from £23.95pp.

Little Thakeham
Merrywood Lane
Storrington
West Sussex RH20 3HE
T: 01903 744416   F: 01903 745022
Contacts: Fiona Watson or Jenny Ratcliff

Ceremony

This Grade I listed house was designed by Edwin Lutyens, as were the five acres of gardens. One room is available for marriage ceremonies. While wheelchair access around the house is not difficult, there are steps up to the house itself. Confetti is not permitted. Ceremonies can take place on any day, except Christmas Day and New Year's Day.
Price guide: from £250

Reception

Little Thakeham is most suited to small dinner party style receptions in the house itself. A pianist can be arranged, and the grounds are suitable for hot air balloons and helicopters. The house has an outdoor swimming pool and tennis courts, and can arrange a spit roast in the gardens. A horse and carriage is available. The house regrets that reception facilities for children are limited.
Catering: Buffets from £21.50pp

The Mansion House
High Down Towers
Littlehampton BN12 6PF
T: 01903 700152   F: 01903 245387
Contact: Tracy Cotton, Manager

Ceremony

The Mansion House, originally owned by the Lyon family, features famous chalk gardens. The Edward Suite is licensed for ceremonies (limited wheelchair access), which may take place on any day of the year. Ceremonies must be followed by a reception at the venue.
Price guide: £100

Reception

Catering: from £10.30pp

Marle Place
Leylands Road
Burgess Hill RH15 8JD
T: 01444 248275   F: 01444 871269
Contact: Heather Williamson Administrator

Ceremony

Marle Place is an Edwardian house set in a quiet location near Burgess Hill. Among its prominent features is an sweeping staircase. Wedding ceremonies are conducted in the ground floor Hall, which is south facing and therefore makes the most of natural light. It also has French doors that lead directly onto the verandah and well-stocked garden. Up to four ceremonies are permitted here per day on any day of the year.
Price guide: £250 (including Registrar's fees)

Reception

This venue offers a wedding breakfast, including ceremony and finger buffet

WEST SUSSEX

WEST SUSSEX

reception for up to 70 people, for under £1,000. A sit-down reception can be catered for in a marquee in the grounds. Stationery can also be arranged by the venue.
Catering: from £6.95 (finger buffet)

Marriott Goodwood Park Hotel
Goodwood
Chichester
West Sussex PO1
T: 01243 775537 F: 01243 520125
Contact: Paul Goldthorpe, Executive Meetings Manager

Ceremony

The hotel is set in the 12,000 acre Goodwood estate, ancestral home to the Dukes of Richmond.
Price guide: £350

Reception

Price guide: Buffets from £21.95pp. Sit down from £22.50pp.

Millstream Hotel & Restaurant
Bosham, Chichester PO18 8HL
T: 01243 573234
Contact: Aris Tzonis, Restaurant Manager

Ceremony

The original building of this hotel and restaurant dates back to 1701. Only one ceremony is permitted here per day, on any day of the year.
Price guide: £150

Reception

The restaurant holds an AA Rosette for its cuisine, and is said to be famous for its buffets.
Catering: £18pp

Ockenden Manor Hotel
Ockenden Lane
Cuckfield RH17 5LO
T: 01444 416111 F: 01444 415549
Contact: Mr K Turner, Manager or Mrs C Webster, Banqueting Manager

Ceremony

Ockenden is set in nine acres of grounds with views of the countryside towards the South Downs. It features open fireplaces, crystal chandeliers and antique furniture. It is 15 minutes drive from Gatwick Airport. Ceremonies can take place in one of two rooms.
Price guide: £350

Reception

Catering: from £20pp

The Ravenswood
Horsted Lane, Sharpthorne
RH19 4HY
T: 01342 810216 F: 01342 811393
Contact: Stephen McArthur, Owner

Ceremony

Ravenswood is a manor house dating from the 15th Century, set in grounds and gardens, and overlooking its own lake. Inside the house has minstrel's galleries and a panelled baronial hall. Weddings can be held here on any day of the year, and their numbers are not restricted. Confetti is allowed, but only in certain areas.
Price guide: £200

Reception

Two rooms are available for receptions, ranging from the smallest gathering up to to 350.
Price guide: £18 - £25

Southdowns Hotel & Restaurant
Trotton Rogate
Petersfield GU31 5JN
T: 01730 821521 F: 01730 821790
Contact: Dominic Vedovato, Owner

Ceremony

This country hotel is set in spacious grounds, with its own croquet lawn and leisure club.
Price guide: £250

Reception

The restaurant has an AA Rosette for its cuisine. Wedding guests are offered a 10% discount on a two- or three-day break.
Catering: £15pp - £25pp

Spread Eagle Hotel
South Street, Midhurst GU29 9NH
T: 01730 816911 F: 01730 815668
Contact: Karen Edgington, Conference & Banqueting Manager

Ceremony

This is a Grand Heritage Hotel, dating from 1430. Period features include Flemish stained glass windows, inglenook fireplaces, tudor bread ovens and four-poster beds. The hotel's Edward VII Room is licensed to hold wedding ceremonies for up to 30, on any day of the year. Ceremonies must be followed by a reception at the hotel.
Price guide: £550

Reception

Catering: from £21pp

Tottington Manor Hotel
Edburton
Nr Henfield BN5 9LJ
T: 01903 815757 F: 01903 879331
Contact: Mrs K Miller, Proprietor

Ceremony

This Grade II listed building dates from the 16th Century. It is set in its own grounds with views of the South Downs and Sussex Weald. Two rooms are licensed, for on any day except Sundays.
Price guide: £175

Reception

The proprietor/chef here is the ex Head Chef of the Ritz in Piccadilly.
Catering: Buffets from £16pp. Sit down from £17.50pp

Wiston House
Steyning BN44 3DZ
T: 01903 815020 F: 01903 815931
Contact: Roger Barr, General Manager

Ceremony

Wiston House is a Grade I listed conference centre. The Library is licensed for marriages. Ceremonies are restricted to one per day on any day of the year, and must be followed by a reception.
Price guide: POA

Reception

Catering: from £30pp

ALSO LICENSED
Cathedral Clubhouse 01243 536666
Copthorne Hotel 01342 714971
Great Ballard School 01243 814236
Highley Manor 01444 811711
Inglenook Hotel 01243 262495
South Lodge Hotel 01403 891711
Wimpole Hotel 01273 846028

Alder House Hotel
Towngate Road, Batley WF17 7HR
T: 01924 444777 F: 01924 442644
Contact: Clive Sowler, GM

Ceremony

This privately-owned Georgian house hotel, set in over 2 acres, holds a license for its York Suite. Wheelchair access is limited. Ceremonies can take place on any day of the year, except Bank Holidays. Saturday weddings must be followed by a reception at the hotel.
Price guide: £125-£175

Reception

Catering: Buffets from £6.95pp. Sit down from £15.95pp

Bagden Hall Hotel
Wakefield Road, Scissett
Huddersfield HD8 9LE
T: 01484 865330 F: 01484 861001
Contact: Charles Storr, General Manager

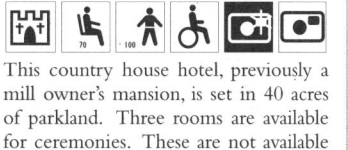

Ceremony

This country house hotel, previously a mill owner's mansion, is set in 40 acres of parkland. Three rooms are available for ceremonies. These are not available on Sundays, and a maximum of one ceremony is permitted per day. A minimum of 45 guests is permitted for Saturday ceremonies.
Price guide: £225

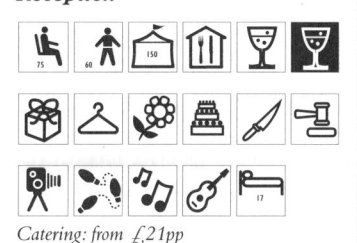

Reception

Catering: from £21pp

Batley Town Hall
Market Place, Batley
T: 01484 442019 F: 01484 446842
Contact: Julia Robinson, Senior Development Officer

Ceremony

Batley Town Hall is also a concert hall and council chamber. Ceremony capacity is between 10 and 300. Ceremonies

WEST YORKSHIRE

are permitted Monday to Saturday inclusive.
Price guide: from £100

Reception

Catering may be provided either in-house or from the Town Hall's list of approved contract caterers. A late night liquor licence is available upon application and a list of local accommodation is available.
Catering: P.O.A.

Bertie's Banqueting Rooms
Brook Street, Elland, Halifax
HX5 9AW
T: 01422 371724 F: 01422 372830
Contact: Brett Woodward, Proprietor

Ceremony

This stone-built, listed and converted chapel, offers ceremonies seven days a week with no restrictions. Confetti is permitted and an unlimited number of ceremonies can be held each day.
Price guide: £250 (FOC with reception)

Reception

Catering: POA

Bradford City Football Club
The Pulse Stadium
Valley Parade
Bradford BD8 7DY
T: 01274 773355 F: 01274 773356
Contact: Mrs C Gilliver, Sales Manager

Ceremony

The stadium is in the town centre and has three rooms licensed including the Board Room and the Director's Suite. Ceremonies can take place here on any day except match days.
Price guide: POA

Reception

Catering: Buffets from £7pp. Sit down from £13pp.

Bretton Hall
West Bretton, Wakefield WF4 4LG
T & F: 01924 832044
Contact: Lesley Entwhistle, Wedding Co-ordinator

Ceremony

Bretton Hall is a University College and 18th Century Palladian mansion. It is set in 500 acres of lakes, woods and parkland and has a licence for its Music Room. Ceremonies can take place here at weekends, or on weekdays during student vacations.
Price guide: POA

Reception

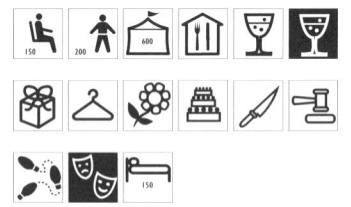

Accommodation is only available during vacation time.
Catering: Buffets from £12.50pp. Sit down from £21pp

Cartwright Hall
Lister Park, Bradford
BD9 4NS
T: 01274 493313 F: 01274 481045
Contact: Administration Assistant

Ceremony

This Grade II listed Edwardian baroque art gallery in a parkland setting was opened by the Prince and Princess of Wales in 1904. Situated roughly one mile from the centre of Bradford, ceremonies are only possible on Saturdays; with a maximum of three per day.
Price guide: £250

Reception

Reception facilities are not available, although local hotels can offer both accommodation and reception services.

Cedar Court Hotel
Denby Dale Road
Calder Grove, Wakefield EF4 3QZ
T: 01924 261294 F: 01924 261016
Contact: Jeannette Morgan, Conference Sales Manager

Ceremony

Cedar Court is a large modern private hotel with its own private gardens. Several rooms are licensed and are available for ceremonies on any day of the year. Receptions must also take place at the hotel.
Price guide: from £50

Reception

The wedding package here includes red carpet, changing room for bridesmaids, liquor licence extension until 12.30am, master of ceremonies and honeymoon suite with fruit, chocolate and English breakfast.
Catering: Buffets from £10pp. Sit down from £15pp.

Cleckheaton Town Hall
Bradford Road, Cleckheaton
T: 01484 513808 F: 01484 446842
Contact: Julia Robinson, Senior Devt Officer

Ceremony

The Town Hall also acts as a concert hall and has a ceremony capacity of between 10 and 500. Ceremonies are permitted Monday to Saturday inclusive, with a maximum of two ceremonies allowed per day.
Price guide: from £100

Reception

Catering may be provided either in-house or from the Town Hall's list of approved contract caterers. A late night liquor licence can be applied for and a list of local accommodation is available.
Catering: POA

Craiglands Hotel
Cowpasture Road, Ilkley
LS29 8RQ
T: 01943 430001 F: 01943 430002
Contact: Joanna Stoke, Conference & Events Manager or Frank Moss, GM

Ceremony

Set amidst spectacular scenery, this Victorian building stands adjacent to the famous Ilkley Moor. Up to five ceremonies can be held per day: seven days a week. Confetti is permitted.
Price guide: from £125

Reception

Receptions for as few as a dozen to as many as 400. Specialities include French cuisine. There are 70 en-suite bedrooms, with discounts available for wedding party guests.
Catering: from £17.50pp

Dewsbury Town Hall
Wakefield Road, Dewsbury
T: 01484 226300 F: 01484 446842
Contact: Julia Robinson, Senior Devt Officer

Ceremony

This Grade II listed Victorian building is also a concert hall and old courthouse with cells. Up to two ceremonies are permitted per day, Monday to Saturday inclusive. Confetti is permitted by arrangement.
Price guide: from £100

Reception

Catering may be provided either in-house or by an approved list of contract caterers. A late night liquor licence is available upon application. A list of local accommodation is available.
Catering: POA

East Riddlesden Hall
Bradford Road, Keighley BD20 5EL
T: 01535 607075
Contact: Liz Houseman, Assistant Property Manager

Ceremony

East Riddlesden is a National Trust property, one mile from Keighley. The manor house was built in 1640. The adjoining Airedale Barn was also built in the 17th Century but was substantially rebuilt in the 19th Century. The Great Hall and the Airedale Barn are licensed for ceremonies and are available on Fridays and Saturdays only. Confetti is not permitted.
Price guide: from £185

Reception

The canal is nearby so couples can arrive and depart by boat.
Catering: Buffets from £7.95pp. Sit down from £15.95pp

Forte Posthouse Leeds/Bradford
Bramhope LS16 9JJ
T: 01977 682711
Contact: Julie Clark, Venue Guarantee

Ceremony

With a ceremony seated capacity of 120 and standing capacity of 150, the hotel offers ceremonies seven days a week throughout the year.
Price guide: from £185

Reception

As part of the wedding package, a complimentary overnight suite is provided for the bride and groom.
Although the hotel has 124 bedrooms of its own, a list of alternative local accommodation is also available. All catering at the hotel is carried out in-house. Children can be catered for separately, on request.
Catering: £13.75pp

The George Hotel
St George's Square
Huddersfield HD1 1JA
T: 01484 515444 F: 01484 435056
Contact: June Thompson, Sales Manager

Ceremony

This Grade II listed Victorian building offers ceremonies seven days a week, with a maximum of four per day. No area is available for outdoor photography, but confetti is permitted.
Price guide: £150

Reception

Reception facilities include a waited service capacity of 150, with 200 for a buffet-style reception. The hotel has 60 bedrooms and also operates preferential rate agreements with other local hotels and guest houses.
Catering: £15pp

WEST YORKSHIRE

189

WEST YORKSHIRE

The Glenmoor Centre
Wells Road, Ilkley LS29 9JF
T: 01943 430270 F: 01943 436273
Contact: Marianne Cairns, Manager

Ceremony

This Victorian building is a residential training and conference centre that allows one ceremony to be held per day on any day of the week, excluding Sundays and Bank Holidays.
Price guide: £120

Reception

Catering is in-house, with specialities including halal, vegetarian and vegan options.
Catering: from £16.50pp

The Guide Post Hotel
Common Road, Low Moor
Bradford BD12 0ST
T: 01274 607866 Fax: 01274 671085
Contact: Mr Day, Owner

Ceremony

The hotel has two licensed rooms available; one with a sitting capacity of 80, and one with a capacity of 100. Ceremonies are available seven days a week, excluding Christmas and New Year.
Price guide: FOC (with reception)

Reception

Catering: from £13.95pp

Haley's Hotel, Shire Oak Road
Headingley, Leeds LS6 2DE
T: 0113 278 4446 F: 0113 275 3342
Contact: Pauline Cowie, Conference Co-ordinator

Ceremony

Set in the Headingley conservation area, just two miles from Leeds city centre, Haley's claims to have been the first hotel in Leeds to be granted a licence. Ceremonies may be held in the hotel's Bramley Room, Library or Restaurant. One ceremony only allowed per day, any day of the week.
Price guide: POA

Reception

Haley's Hotel & Restaurant is a member of the Virgin Collection and won the Good Food Guide County Restaurant of the Year in 1994. The late night drinking licence is permitted for residents only.
Catering: from £20pp

Hanover International Hotel
Penistone Road, Kirkburton
Huddersfield HD8 0PE
T: 01484 607788 F: 01484 607961
Contact: Treda Shotton, Admin Manager

Ceremony

The hotel is a former textile mill. The Burton Suite is licensed and is available on any any except Christmas Day and Boxing Day. Ceremonies must be followed by reception on the premises.
Price guide: POA

Reception

Catering: Buffets from £10pp. Sit down from £16pp.

Hilton National, Wakefield Road
Garforth, Leeds LS25 1LH
T: 0113 286 6556 F: 0113 286 8326
Contact: Jean Gray, Conference and Banqueting Services Manager

Ceremony

The hotel has four rooms licensed to hold ceremonies. The Magnet room holds a maximum of 120 seated guests, the Yorkshire room 80, the Stamford room 40, and the Boardroom 15. Ceremonies are possible seven days a week.
Price guide: from £180

Reception

Reception facilities vary in capacity from 60 to 200 for both waited service and buffet options.
Catering: from £16.95pp

Holdsworth House
Holdsworth
Halifax
West Yorkshire HX2 9TG
T: 01422 240024 F: 01422 245174
Contact: Sue Pickles, Conference and Banqueting Co-ordinator

Ceremony

This 17th Century Jacobean manor house is set in its own grounds, and has two rooms licensed to hold ceremonies. Ceremonies are possible seven days a week, with one permitted per day. The hotel is closed for a couple of days over the Christmas period.
Price guide: Available only as part of a reception package.

Reception

This three star hotel features a two AA rosette restaurant. The bride and groom are offered a complimentary suite for the night, while wedding guests are offered preferential room rates.
Catering: from £20pp

WEST YORKSHIRE

Hoyle Court
**Otley Road, Baildon
Shipley BO17 6JS**
T: 01274 584110
Contact: Mr & Mrs D T Blair

Ceremony

This is a Grade II Edwardian Baroque house with a south facing terrace and stone steps leading to a sunken garden. The house was once owned by one of Bradford's successful mill owning families. Two rooms are licensed; the Lounge and the Dining Room. They are available on Saturdays only. Ceremonies must be followed by a reception at the house. This venue claims to be one of the UK's most prestigious Masonic premises.
Price guide: £125

Reception

A traditional Danish wedding is among events staged here in recent years.
Catering: from £15.45pp

Huddersfield Town Hall
**Ramsden Street
Huddersfield HD1 2TA**
T: 01484 442019
Contact: Julia Robinson, Senior Devt Officer

Ceremony

The Town Hall has three rooms available to hold ceremonies: the largest, the Concert Hall, has a capacity of 400. Ceremonies are available Monday to Saturday inclusive.
Price guide: from £100

Reception

Jarvis Bankfield Hotel
Bradford Road, Bingley BD16 1TU
T: 01274 567123 F: 01274 551331
Contact: Helen Kirk, Conference and Events Sales Manager

Ceremony

Catering may be provided either in-house or by an approved list of contract caterers. A late night liquor licence and a list of local accommodation are available on request.
Catering: POA

The hotel offers two ceremony rooms, which are available on any day of the year. Ceremonies must be followed by a reception at the hotel.
Price guide: £175

Reception

Helicopters and hot air balloons may use the site.
Catering: Buffets from £8.50pp. Sit down from £16pp

Leeds Civic Hall, Leeds LS1 1UR
T: 0113 247 4055 F: 0113 247 4772
Contact: Steven Mason, Lord Mayor's Secretary

Ceremony

This is a Grade I listed building, claimed to be one of the finest civic buildings in the country. Four rooms are licensed, which can take place on any day of the year except Christmas Day.
Price guide: POA

Reception

All types of cuisine are available.
Catering: Buffets from £5pp. Sit down from £12pp

Linton Springs Hotel
**Sicklinghall Road, Wetherby
LS22 4AF**
T: 01937 585353 F: 01937 587579
Contact: Linsey Rowbury, Wedding Co-ordinator

Ceremony

Set in 14 acres of park and woodland, the hotel offers three ceremony rooms. Ceremonies are not available on Saturdays and Sundays, or Christmas Day. One ceremony only is permitted per day.
Price guide: £150

Reception

Catering: £23pp

Marsden Mechanics Hall
Peel Street Marsden HD7 6BW
T: 01484 844587
Contact: Janet Maude, Bookings Officer

Ceremony

This listed building in the centre of this Pennine village is situated close to the river and the village stocks. The Main Hall is licensed and is available on any day of the year, although Bank Holidays cost more. Confetti is not permitted.
Price guide: from £60

Reception

Catering: POA

Newsholme Manor Hotel
Slaymaker Lane, Keighley BD22
T: 01535 642964 F: 01535 645629
Contact: Mr CT Sexton, Owner

WEST YORKSHIRE

Ceremony

This country manor is available for ceremonies on any day of the week.
Price guide: POA

Reception

Catering: POA

**Oakwell Hall Country Park
Nutter Lane, Birstall WF17 9LG**
T: 01924 326240   F: 01924 326249
Contact: Karen Jewell, Administrative Officer

Ceremony

This 17th Century Elizabethan Manor (with Brontë connections) is Grade I listed. Furnished to the year 1690, it also features a period garden. The Great Hall is licensed. Ceremonies can take place on any day except Bank Holidays and Sundays.
Price guide: from £100

Reception

Receptions take place in the Oakwell Barn, which is a separate building. This must be arranged separately by the hirer.

**The Queens
City Square, Leeds LS1 1PL**
T: 0113 243 1323   F: 0113 242 5154
Contact: Julia Robinson, Senior Devt Officer

Ceremony

The Queens hotel is situated in the centre of Leeds, adjacent to the main railway station. The Ark Royal Suite and the Ballroom are licensed for ceremonies, which can take place here on any day of the year. Ceremonies must be followed by a reception at the hotel.
Price guide: from £425

Reception

Catering: Buffets from £4.50pp. Sit down from £14.95pp

**The Rock Inn Hotel
Holywell Green
Halifax HX4 9BS**
T: 01422 379721   F: 01422 379110
Contact: Robert Vinsen, Proprietor

Ceremony

Set in four acres of breathtaking Yorkshire countryside, The Rock is situated in its own serene rural valley close to Brontë country. Dating back to the 17th Century, the Rock has been extensively refurbished in recent years. Special areas are available for outdoor photography.
Price guide: from £50

Reception

A special bridal suite is available for the bride and groom, with reduced accommodation rates for guests. A dance floor and a disco are also available.
Catering: from £14.00pp

**Rogerthorpe Manor Hotel
Thorpe Lane, Badsworth
Pontefract WF9 1AB**
T: 01977 643839   F: 01977 641571
Contact: Laeley Denton

Ceremony

This Jacobean Grade II listed building has been restored to create a hotel of 12 bedrooms, an oak-panelled restaurant and large function room. An unlimited number of ceremonies is permitted per day, seven days a week; excluding Christmas Day.
Price guide: £250

Reception

In addition to buffets and special menus, the hotel will strive to meet the religious or dietary requirements of wedding guests. Sample menus are readily available. The hotel also operates preferential rate agreements with local guest houses and other hotels. Other services offered include room decorations, fireworks, stationery, cars, balloons and children's entertainment.
Price guide: from £5.75pp

**Sacha Court
Park Road, Elland
West Yorkshire
HX5 9HP**
T: 01422 377232   F: 01422 310408
Contact: Andrea Allen, Wedding Co-ordinator

Ceremony

The Sacha Court hotel and restaurant is actually an extended and fully renovated Victorian mill owner's house and is English Tourist Board four crown commended. Ceremonies are available seven days a week.
Price guide: from £50

Reception

The reception facilities include a large purpose-built disco area and free car parking for up to 90 cars.
Catering: from £6.95pp

WEST YORKSHIRE

Springfield Park Hotel
Penistone Road
Kirkburton HD8 0PE
T: 01484 607788 F: 01484 607961
Contact: Treda Shotton, Sales Co-ordinator

Ceremony

Ceremonies are available seven days a week.
Price guide: £200

Reception

The hotel has preferential rate agreements with local guest houses and hotels.
Catering: £15pp

Under the Clock Tower
The Town Hall, Wood Street
Wakefield WF1 2HQ
T: 01924 305121 F: 01924 305293
Contact: Simon Hartley, General Manager

Ceremony

'Under the Clock Tower' is actually the banqueting and restaurant complex within Wakefield Town Hall. The Victorian Town Hall was first opened in 1880 and is now a Grade I listed building. All 11 rooms within the Town Hall may be used for marriage ceremonies, with the rich wood panelling, ornate plasterwork and chandeliers making it an attractive venue. Ceremonies may be held on any day of the year, excluding Bank Holidays.
Price guide: from £70.00

Reception

Fully inclusive reception packages are offered, with a 50% discount on room hire if the reception is also held here. Alternatively, the Clock Tower Restaurant may be used for the smaller party to celebrate after the ceremony.
Catering: from £14.50pp

Waterton Park Hotel
Walton Hall, Walton
Wakefield WF2 6PW
T: 01924 257911 F: 01924 240082
Contact: Debbie Taylor, Conference and Banqueting Manager

Ceremony

This Georgian listed mansion is situated on an island surrounded by 26 acres of lake and is accessed by an iron bridge. Ceremonies are available all days of the week, excluding Saturdays, apart from January-March when Saturdays are also available.
Price guide: £175

Reception

Maximum buffet capacity is 150, increasing to 175 during evening buffets, while a marquee is suitable for a maximum of 175 seated guests. A complimentary honeymoon suite is available for the bride and groom.
Catering: from £21pp.

Weetwood Hall
Otley Road, Far Headingley
Leeds LS16 5PS
T: 0113 230 6000 F: 0113 230 6095
Contact: Maxine Porter, Business Administration Manager

Ceremony

Set in 9 acres of wooded seclusion on the outskirts of Leeds, this purpose-built centre has been developed around a Grade II listed Tudor manor house. One ceremony per day is permitted, seven days a week. Confetti is not permitted.
Price guide: from £180

Reception

In addition to the 108 en-suite bedrooms, Weetwood Hall offers 14 deluxe rooms and a four-poster honeymoon suite.
Catering: from £17.00pp

Woolley Hall
Course & Conference Centre
New Road, Woolley
Wakefield WF4 2JR
T: 01226 382500/382509
F: 01226 386638
Contact: Maxine Wilson, Conference Coordinator

Ceremony

This listed building features Italian gardens. Three rooms are licensed and are available on any day except Bank Holidays.
Price guide: £150

Reception

Catering: from £15pp

ALSO LICENSED
Baildon Masonic Hall 01274 584110
Bradford City Hall 01274 752222
Briar Court Hotel 01484 519902
Clay House 01422 378586
The Grove 01977 642159
Hilton National 0113 244 2000
Hollings Hall Hotel 01274 530053
Leeds Forte Posthouse 0113 243 1323
Leeds Marriott Hotel 0113 2366366
Leeds United FC 013 226 1166
Moorland Lodge 01484 843398
Oakwood Hall Hotel 01274 564123
Stakis Bedford Hotel 01274 734734
Swallow Hotel 01924 372111
Todmorden Town Hall 01706 813597
Wentbridge House Hotel 01977 620444

WILTSHIRE

Blunsdon House Hotel
Blunsdon, Swindon SN2 4AD
T: 01793 721701 F: 01793 721056
Contact: Philip Dodds, Sales and Marketing Manager

Ceremony

Three rooms are licensed within the hotel to hold wedding ceremonies, with seated capacities varying from 60 to 250 and standing capacities from 70 to 300. Ceremonies are available seven days a week with no restrictions on the number permitted per day.
Price guide: £150

Reception

Waited service reception facilities are to a maximum of 250 with buffet service offering a maximum of 300. The site is also suitable for a marquee.
Catering: from £11.50pp

Bowood Golf & Country Club
Derry Hill, Calne SN11 9PQ
T: 01249 822228 F: 01249 822218
Contact: Liz Schofield, Marketing Manager

Ceremony

This Grade I listed building is part of the Bowood Estate, which covers 2,000 acres in total. The park itself was designed by Capability Brown. Three rooms, with limited wheelchair access, are licensed. Ceremonies can take place on any day of the year except Christmas Day.
Price guide: £150

Reception

Receptions can take place in the Fitzmaurice Room (up to 50) or in the club's marquee.
Catering: from £15.00pp

Box House
Bath Road, Box SN13 8NR
T: 01225 744447 F: 01225 744333
Contact: The Manager

Ceremony

The Box House is a Grade II Georgian Manor set in nine acres of grounds and situated next door to the village church. Ceremonies are available seven days a week, with a maximum of two permitted per day. Confetti is allowed.
Price guide: £150

Reception

Reception catering facilities vary from finger buffets to sit down banquets with prices adjusted accordingly. The manor house now has 20 bedrooms, following recent improvements. A 1950's vintage bus is available for the exclusive use of the manor house's guests.
Catering: from £6.50pp

Chiseldon House Hotel
New Road, Chiseldon SN4 0NE
T: 01793 741010 F: 01793 741059
Contact: Jan Capaldi, General Manager

Ceremony

This Grade II listed building offers ceremonies from Monday to Saturday.
Price guide: £80

Reception

The hotel offers themed weddings and receptions which, in the past, have included a Medieval theme and a Caribbean wedding featuring a steel band around the hotel's swimming pool. In addition to the services indicated below, the hotel can organise cars, stationery, balloons and a video. Some of the bedrooms feature four-poster beds.
Price guide: from £12.50pp

Cricklade Hotel & Country Club
Common Hill, Cricklade
SN6 6HA
T: 01793 750751 F: 01793 751767
Contact: Mrs Kearney, General Manager

Ceremony

This Cotswold manor house, set in its own grounds, features a nine hole golf course. There are five rooms available to hold ceremonies at the hotel, with capacities from 30 to 80.
Price guide: from £100

Reception

The main function room features views of a walled garden and a gazebo. The hotel includes flowers in the price of the ceremony.
Catering: from £18.50pp

Crudwell Court Hotel & Restaurant
Crudwell SN16 9EP
T: 01666 577194 F: 01666 577853
Contact: Nick Bristow, Joint Proprietor

Ceremony

This 17th Century rectory has three rooms available to hold ceremonies, seven days a week. The hotel is situated in three acres of garden and features a heated outdoor swimming pool for use during the summer. The restaurant and ceremony room, but not the bedrooms, have wheelchair access. No fee is charged for the ceremony if the reception is also held at the hotel.

194

WILTSHIRE

Price guide: FOC (with reception)

Reception

Reception facilities feature a waited service capacity of 90, finger buffets for up to 120 and a seated buffet capacity of 90 also. The site is suitable for a marquee with a capacity of between 150 and 200. The hotel has, in the past, held a Scottish theme wedding, featuring tartan decorations and Scottish music.
Catering: from £15.50pp

Cumberwell Park
Bradford-on-Avon
Wiltshire BA15 2PQ
T: 01225 863322   F: 01225 868160
Contact: Ron Smith, Manager

Ceremony

Cumberwell Park is a club with two licensed rooms which are available every day, except Bank Holidays. Ceremonies here must be followed by a reception on the premises.
Price guide: £200

Reception

Catering: Buffets from £6.50pp. Sit down from £14.50pp.

Grasmere House Hotel
Harnham Road, Salisbury
Wiltshire SP2 8JN
T: 01722 338388   F: 01722 333710
Contact: Dale Naug, Manager

Ceremony

This Victorian hotel and restaurant, set in 1.5 aces of gardens, offers four licensed rooms on any day of the year except Sundays. Confetti is not permitted.
Price guide: £200

Reception

Catering: Buffets from £8.50pp. Sit down from £16.50pp

Grittleton House
Grittleton, Chippenham
Wiltshire SN14 6AP
T: 01249 782434   F: 01249 782669
Contact: Adrian Shipp, Owner

Ceremony

Situated in its own grounds, this Grade II listed building is available to hold up to two ceremonies, seven days a week. The price is just £25 if the reception is also held at the venue.
Price guide: £150 (without reception)

Reception

Reception facilities include a marquee, with a maximum capacity of 1,000. A list of local accommodation is available.
Catering: from £15pp

Guyers House
Guyers Lane, Pickwick
Corsham SN13 0PS
T: 01249 713399   F: 01249 712801
Contact: Martin Bevis, Manager

Ceremony

This Grade II listed building is now operating as a training and conference centre. Seating capacity for ceremonies is 50 in one room and a further 65 in adjoining rooms. Ceremonies are available on Saturdays only, with a maximum of one per day. The price guide for ceremonies is £175 plus the hire of the house at £1,000. Confetti is restricted to inside the building only.
Price guide: £1,750 + VAT

Reception

Reception catering may be in-house or from an approved list of contract caterers. The ballroom features a sprung dance floor.
Catering: from £18.00pp

Kington Manor
Kington St Michael
Chippenham   SN4 6JA
T: 01249 750655   F: 01249 750651
Contact: Peter Le Grys, Manager

Ceremony

Kington Manor stands in 15 acres of parkland, featuring grounds terraced with fountains and herbaceous borders leading to a large lake. The standing capacity for the ceremony is in excess of 180. Ceremonies may be held every day of the week, but only be held in conjunction with receptions.

Reception

The Manor offers buffet receptions for over 400, and specialises in home cooking.
Catering: £20pp

Leigh Park Hotel
Leigh Road West
Bradford on Avon BA15 2RA
T: 01225 864885 F: 01225 862315
Contact: Pamela Duckett, Assistant Manager

Ceremony

195

WILTSHIRE

This Georgian country house hotel stands in five acres of grounds, with its own walled garden and vineyard. Three rooms are available to hold ceremonies, all with varying capacities, from 20 to 120. Ceremonies are available throughout the week excluding Sundays, Christmas Day, Boxing Day and other Bank Holidays.
Price guide: from £75.00

Reception

The hotel offers a complimentary overnight stay for the bride and groom in an executive room on the night of the wedding; while special rate overnight accommodation is available for wedding guests.
Catering: from £26.95pp (package)

Longleat
The Estate Office, Warminster
Wiltshire BA12 7NW
T: 01985 845415 F: 01985 844885
Contact: Clare Hopkinson, Marketing & Events Manager

Ceremony

The Orangery is licensed at Longleat which is set informal gardens, with the highly appropriate Maze of Love and a secret garden. Ceremonies can take place here at any time other than Bank Holidays.
Price guide: £500

Reception

Receptions take place in a marquee at Longleat, but you can choose your own caterer. Numerous service suppliers can be recommended, including hot air balloon suppliers, as a company regularly operates from Longleat.

Lucknam Park Hotel
Colerne
Wiltshire SN14 8AZ
T: 01225 742777 F: 01225 743536
Contact: James Gormley

Ceremony

This imposing Palladian mansion was built in 1720 and is set in 500 acres of grounds. While wedding ceremonies can be held at the Lucknam Park Hotel seven days a week, only one ceremony is permitted per day. The price guide shown below indicates the cost of hiring the ceremony room. This is a package price that also includes the charge for hiring the room in which the wedding reception is held.
Price guide: £1,000

Reception

Catering capacities are to a maximum of 50, although the site is suitable for a marquee with a capacity of 100. A late night drinking licence is held for residents only.
Catering: from £24.50pp

The Manor House
Castle Combe
Chippenham SN14 7HR
T: 01249 782206 F: 01249 782159
Contact: Lynne Lawton, Sales

Ceremony

This Grade II listed building is set in 26 acres of grounds, with an additional 200 acres of golf course. Two rooms are licensed to hold ceremonies with capacities varying from 30 to 90. Ceremonies are available seven days a week, with only one ceremony permitted per day. The price guide increases to £500 for use of the larger room.
Price guide: from £200

Reception

Although a room is available for the bride and groom to change in, an extra charge will be made.
Catering: from £26.00pp

Milford Hall Hotel
206 Castle Street
Salisbury, Wilts SP1 3TE
T: 01722 417411 F: 01722 419444
email:
Milfordhallhotel@compuserve.com
Contact: Alison Drew, Conference & Function Manager

Ceremony

This is a Grade II Georgian house which is now a family-run hotel. Three areas are licensed and are available every day except Sundays and Bank Holidays.
Price guide: £100

Reception

The hotel claims to have the only AA two rosette restaurant in Salisbury.
Catering: Buffets from £10pp. Sit down from £14.50pp.

The Pear Tree at Purton
Church End, Purton
Swindon SN5 9ED
T: 01793 772100 F: 01793 772369
Contact: Francis Young, Proprietor.

Ceremony

This Cotswold stone hotel, set in 7.5 acres of grounds, has achieved the RAC's highest award: The Blue Ribbon. Ceremonies are available seven days a week, with only one permitted per day. Confetti is allowed.
Price guide: £200

Reception

The hotel's chef, Catherine Berry, has been awarded two AA rosettes.
Catering: from £30pp

The Royal Oak
Wootton Rivers
Marlborough SN8 4NQ
T: 01672 810322 F: 01672 811267
Contact: Mr and Mrs Jones, Proprietors or G Lewis, Administration Manager

Ceremony

This thatched 16th Century free house is available to hold ceremonies seven days a week, with a maximum of two per day. No charge is made for the ceremony providing the reception is also held at The Royal Oak.
Price guide: FOC (with reception)

Reception

Reception catering is in-house although the proprietors would be happy if couples preferred to organise their own contract catering. The pub features three self-contained cottages for wedding guests, providing a total of nine rooms.
Catering: from £10.00pp

Rudloe Hall Hotel
Hinton Grange, Leafy Lane
Nr Corsham
Wiltshire SN13 0PA
T: 01225 810555 F: 01225 811412
Contact: Melanie Crick, Assistant Manager.

Ceremony

This listed Gothic building is situated in four acres of award-winning gardens and features oak panelling and high corniced ceilings. It offers a choice of 11 bedrooms. Ceremonies are available seven days a week.
Price guide: £200

Reception

Catering is in-house with a buffet capacity of 100. Subject to availability, a room will be provided for the bride and groom to change in.
Catering: from £19.50pp

Whatley Manor
Nr Easton Grey
Malmesbury SN16 0RB
T: 01666 822888 F: 01666 826120
Contact: Peter Kendall, General Manager

Ceremony

This Grade II listed building dates back to the 17th Century and is set in extensive gardens. Ceremonies are available seven days a week, excluding Christmas Day, Boxing Day and the New Year holiday. Only one ceremony per day is permitted and confetti is not allowed. There is no charge for the ceremony if the reception is also held at the Manor.
Price guide: FOC (with reception)

Reception

There are 18 bedrooms in the Manor House and Tudor and Terrace Wings; with a further 11 rooms in the Court House situated 70 yards across the courtyard. The waited service capacity for the reception is 80, although the Manor may consider a stand-up finger buffet for a maximum of 100. Dancing and live music are possible when guests take exclusive use of the whole hotel.
Catering: from £18pp

ALSO LICENSED
Bishipstrow House Hotel 01985 212312
De Vere Hotel 01973 878785
Limpley Stoke Hotel 01225 723333
Marlborough Golf Club 01672 512147

Moormead Country Hotel 01793 814744
Old Bell 01666 822344
Salisbury Guildhall 01722 412144
Wiltshire County Hall 01225 713097

Grange Hotel
1 Clifton, York YO3 6AA
T: 01904 644744 F: 01904 612453
Contact: Shara Ross, General Manager

Ceremony

The Grange is a Regency townhouse with two marriage rooms; the Green Room and the Library (which do not have wheelchair access). Ceremonies can take place any day except Christmas Day.
Price guide: £200 (£100 with reception)

Reception

The Library and Drawing Room with french windows, or the Green Room with small dance floor, can be used for receptions. Alternatively, guests may have exclusive use of the Restaurant.
Catering: from £10.50pp

Knavesmire Manor Hotel
302 Tadcaster Road, York YO2 2HE
T: 01904 702941 F: 01904 709274
Contact: Karne Smith, Manageress

Ceremony

This Georgian house (1833) was once home to the Rowntree family. Ceremonies here must be followed by a reception on site.
Price guide: POA

Reception

Catering: from £15pp

WILTSHIRE - YORK

197

YORK - BRIDGEND - CAERPHILLY

Merchant Adventurers' Hall
Fossgate, York YO1 2XD
T/F: 01904 654818
Contact: Mr Wheatley, Clerk
to the Company

Ceremony

This medieval building is situated right in the centre of York, within the city walls, and has its own garden with river frontage. This means that the bride and groom can arrive or depart by boat. Wheelchair access to the ground floor only. Weddings can take place here on any day of the year. No confetti.
Price guide: from £75

Reception

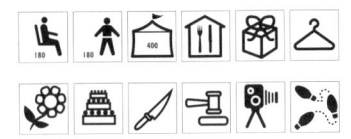

There is a choice of caterers. Themes may include a medieval banquet in keeping with the setting. Drinking licences can be applied for as required. Local accommodation can be recommended.
Catering: from £5pp

National Railway Museum
Leeman Road, York YO2 4XJ
T: 01904 621261 F: 01904 611112
Contact: Mandy MacGrath, Events Executive

Ceremony

Three ceremony rooms are available at the museum; the Conference Room, the Stephenson Room and the South Hall. Weddings can take place here any day of the week except Sunday. Confetti is not permitted.
Price guide: £175

Reception

A list of local accommodation with which the museum has preferential rates can be supplied if requested.
Catering: Buffets from £9.95. Sit down from £24.50pp

Swallow Hotel York
Tadcaster Road
York YO2 2QQ
T: 01904 412204 F: 01904 702308
Contact: Business Development Manager

Ceremony

The hotel allows only one ceremony per day on any day of the year.
Price guide: POA

Reception

Catering: POA

ALSO LICENSED
Forte Posthouse   01904 707921
Merchant Taylor's Hall   01904 608218

WALES

Coed-y-Mwstwr Hotel
Coychurch, Nr Bridgend
CF35 6AF
T: 01656 860621 F: 01656 863122
Contact: Andrea Scholefield
Conference & Banqueting Co-ordinator

Ceremony

Ceremonies can take place here on any day of the year.
Price guide: £150

Reception

The Head Chef at the hotel is Scott Morgan, who will cater to your exact requirements. This could include catering separately for children or developing a menu to suit your budget and dietary or religious requirements.
Catering: from £1,300 (sit down reception)

Court Colman Hotel
Court Colman, Penyfai
T: 01656 720212 F: 01656 724544
Contact: June Davies, General Manager

Ceremony

Court Coleman is set in six acres of grounds, and was the seat of the Llewellyn family at the turn of the century. Internally, the hotel features a wide sweeping staircase, oak panelled walls, and a fireplace in the hall that is a replica of one in the Doges Palace in Venice. The Ballroom is modelled on the Crystal Room in the Palace of Versailles. Ceremonies can take place here on any day except Sunday.
Price guide: £50 - £150

Reception

The hotel offers several rooms for receptions: The Ballroom and Garden Room (up to 200), The Llewellyn Room (up to 75) and the Priory Suite (up to 120).
Catering: Buffets from £4.95. Sit down from £17.50

Caerphilly Castle
Caerphilly CF8 1JL
T: 01222 500200 (bookings)
F: 01222 500300 (bookings)
Contact: Philip Stallard, Site Facilities Officer
T: 01222 883143 (monument)
Contact: Mr D Radford, Head Custodian

Ceremony

198

This Medieval castle is said to be the largest in Wales and is now operated by Cadw Welsh Historic monuments. The Great Hall is licensed for wedding ceremonies, which can take place on Saturdays and Sundays only, but must be followed by a reception at the castle. Caerphilly Castle is not available on Bank Holidays.
Price guide: £100 + VAT

Reception

Catering and bar facilities must be organised by the hirer.

Cardiff Castle
Castle Street, Cardiff CF1 2RB
T: 01222 878100   F: 01222 231417
Contact: Mrs Jean Brown, Tours & Functions Co-ordinator

Ceremony

Cardiff Castle is a Grade I listed building and an ancient monument. Ceremonies (for parties of 16 to 100) can take place in one of three rooms on any day of the week, but not on Bank Holidays, or before 6pm from April to September. Confetti is not permitted.
Price guide: POA

Reception

Catering: POA

Cardiff City Hall
**Cathays Park
Cardiff
CF1 3ND**
T: 01222 872000   F: 01222 871695
Contact: Ivor Mallett, Function Manager

Ceremony

Up to two ceremonies per day are permitted at this listed building. These can take place on any day of the week, but not on the Christmas Day, Boxing Day or New Year's Day.
Price guide: POA

Reception

Catering: POA

Castell Coch
Tongwynlais, Cardiff CF4 7JS
T: 01222 500200 (bookings)
F: 01222 500300 (bookings)
Contact: Philip Stallard, Site Facilities Officer
T: 01222 810101 (monument)
Contact: Ms A M Peterson, Head Custodian

Ceremony

Castell Coch is described as a fairytale Victorian folly and is operated by Cadw Welsh Historic Monuments. The banqueting Room and the Drawing Room are licensed for ceremonies, which can take place on any day of the year except Bank Holidays.
Price guide: £120 + VAT

Reception

There are no reception facilities at Castell Coch.

Quality Friendly Hotel
**Merthyr Road
Tongwynlais
Cardiff
CF4 7LD**
T: 01222 529988 F: 01222 529977
Contact: Claire Watkins, Conference & Banqueting Co-ordinator

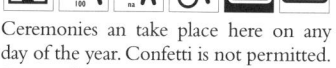

Ceremony

Ceremonies an take place here on any day of the year. Confetti is not permitted.
Price guide: POA

Reception

Catering: from £16.00pp

Manor Parc Hotel & Restaurant
**Thornhill Road
Cardiff CF1 5UA**
T: 01222 693723 F: 01222 614624
Contact: Mr Salvatore Salimeni or Mr Efisio Cinus, Partners

Ceremony

The Manor Parc can offer ceremonies on any day of the week except Saturdays, with a maximum of two ceremonies per day.
Price guide: POA

Reception

Catering: £18pp - £35pp

New House Country Hotel
**Thornhill Road
Cardiff CF4 5UA**
T: 01222 520280 F: 01222 520324
Contact: Stephen Banks, General Manager

Ceremony

This country hotel is housed in a Grade II listed building with views of Cardiff and the Bristol Channel. Only one ceremony is permitted here per day, on any day of the year.
Price guide: £150

Reception

The hotel has two AA Rosettes for its cuisine. A complimentary room is offered to the bride and groom.
Catering: from £16pp

ALSO LICENSED
Cardiff International Arena 01222 234500
Park Hotel, Cardiff 01222 383471

CARMARTHENSHIRE - CEREDIGION - CONWY

Ashburnham Hotel
Ashburnham Road, Pembrey
Llanelli SA16 0TH
T: 01554 834343 F: 01554 834483
Contact: Susan Thomas, Manager

Ceremony

This hotel, restaurant and public house is set in its own grounds overlooking the Ashburnham Championship Golf Links and the Gower Peninsula. Ceremonies can take place here on any day except Sunday.
Price guide: FOC (with reception)

Reception

The hotel's restaurant, Rebecca's, offers Welsh cuisine, while the Conservatory Bar offers a choice of local ales.
Catering: from £13.95pp

Diplomat Hotel
Felinfoel, Llanelli SA15 3PJ
T: 01554 756156 F: 01554 751649
Contact: Mr J B Jenkins, Managing Director

Ceremony

Up to two ceremonies per day can take place at The Diplomat, on any day of the year.
Price guide: POA

Reception

The hotel can also offer beauty and leisure facilities.
Catering: £12.50pp - £18pp

ALSO LICENSED
Gwellian Court Hotel 01554 890217
Gwesty Plas Plant-Yr-Athro 01267 241515

Ty Penlan, Llandelio 01558 822644
Undercliff, Ferryside 01267 267270

Tyglyn Aeron
Ciliau Aeron, Lampeter
T/F: 01570 470625
Contact: Mrs Thomas, Proprietor

Ceremony

One ceremony per day is permitted at this hotel, on any day except Christmas Day.
Price guide: £30

Reception

Catering: from £15pp

ALSO LICENSED
The Cliff Hotel 01239 613241
Falcondale Hotel 01570 422910
Ynyshir Hall Hotel 01654 781209

Conwy Council Offices
Bodlondeb, Conwy LL32 8DU
T: 01492 574000 F: 01492 592114
Contact: Gwenda Ells, Superintendent Registrar on 01492 592407

Ceremony

The council offices building was constructed in 1877 as a private residence and is located in a public park. The areas registered to hold ceremonies include the Council Chamber, an adjoining Committee Room and the Members' Room.
Price guide: £70

Reception

Reception facilities are not available.

Gwydir Castle
Llanrwyst
LL26 0PN
T: 01492 641687
Contact: Judy Corbett or Peter Welford, Owners

Ceremony

This historic, 16th Century castle is set in Grade I listed gardens. The Solar Hall is licensed for ceremonies (limited wheelchair access), on any day of the year.
Price guide: POA

Reception

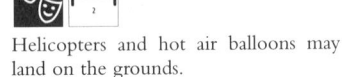

Helicopters and hot air balloons may land on the grounds.
Catering: POA

Hopeside Hotel
West End, Colwyn Bay
LL29 8PW
T: 01492 533244 F: 01492 532850
Contact: Paul Cliffe, Proprietor

Ceremony

This three star AA and RAC hotel offers two marriage rooms, the Penrhos Suite (50 guests) and the Prince's Suite (100 guests). Ceremonies can take place here any day except between December 27th and January 10th.
Price guide: from £65

Reception

Cuisine at the hotel is French/English in style and holds an RAC award.
Catering: from £12.95pp

Plas Maenan
Country House Hotel
Conwy Valley
Llanwrst
T: 01492 660232 F: 01492 660551
Contact: James Graham Turner, Proprietor or Marsha Kendall, Manager

200

Ceremony

Ceremonies are available seven days a week throughout the year. Although there is no formal wheelchair access, hotel staff members are always willing to help.
Price guide: £65

Reception

The hotel has a buffet capacity of 175. Unfortunately children cannot be catered for separately.
Catering: from £8.50pp

**St Georges Hotel
The Promenade
Llandudno LL30 2LG**
T: 01492 877544 F: 01492 878477
Contact: Judy Window or Karen Burns, Conference & Banqueting

Ceremony

This period seafront building, dating from 1854, features a protected classic facade. The Conwy Suite is licensed for ceremonies, which may take place here on any day of the year. Wheelchair access is limited.
Price guide: £200 (£100 with reception)

Reception

Couples may arrive and depart from this venue by boat. Receptions may also feature Welsh-themed menus.
Catering: Buffets from £6.50pp. Sit down from £14.95pp.

ALSO LICENSED
*Colwyn Bay Hotel 01492 516555
Grand Hotel, Llandudno 01492 876245
Imperial Hotel, Llandudno 01492 877466*

*Kinmel Manor Hotel 01745 832014
Priory Hotel 01492 660247
Taylor's Restaurant 01492 533360*

**Bodidris Hall
Llandegla, Wrexham LL11 3AL**
T: 01978 790434 F: 01978 790335
Contact: Tudor Williams, Manager

Ceremony

This venue allows only one ceremony per day, on any day of the year except Sundays and Bank Holidays.
Price guide: £50

Reception

Catering: From £20pp

**Chainbridge Hotel
Llangollen LL20 8BS**
T: 01978 860215 F: 01978 861841
Contact: Mr V N Baker, Proprietor

Ceremony

The hotel sits on the banks of the River Dee and is about three minutes walk from the Horseshoe Falls. The hotel takes its name from the bridge which spans that river at this point. The hotel is also surrounded by the Berwyn and Eglwysig mountains. Only one ceremony is permitted here per day on any day of the year.
Price guide: £100 (FOC with reception)

Reception

The hotel's honeymoon suite is included with all reception reservations, subject to availability.
Catering: from £6.50pp

**Ruthin Castle
Ruthin LL15 2NU**
T: 01824 702664 F: 01824 705978
Contact: Mr Clayton, Manager

Ceremony

Ruthin Castle offers two ceremony rooms, which are available on any day of the week except Sunday. Ceremonies here must be followed by a reception at the castle. Confetti is not permitted.
Price guide: £50 - £95

Reception

Catering: £10pp - £30pp

ALSO LICENSED
*Bryn Howel Hotel 01978 860331
Bryn Morfydd Hotel 01745 890280
Faenol Fawr Hotel 01745 591691
Tyddyn Llan Hotel 01490 440264
White House Hotel 01745 582155*

**All Seasons Lodge Hotel
Northop Hall
CH7 6HB**
T: 01244 550011 F: 01244 550763
Contact: Ms Jennifer Smith, General Manager

Ceremony

Up to two ceremonies can be held on any day of the week at the All Seasons Lodge.
Price guide: £125

Reception

Catering: Buffets from £6.95. Sit down from £15.95

CONWY - DENBIGHSHIRE - FLINTSHIRE

FLINTSHIRE - GWYNEDD - ISLE OF ANGLESEY

The Cornist Hall
Flint CH6 5RA
T: 01352 733241 F: 01352 731710
Contact: Mrs S Napier, Proprietor or Paula Williams, Wedding Co-ordinator

Ceremony

The Cornist Hall is a Jacobean mansion set in parkland and featuring an original walled rose garden. One ceremony per day can take place here, on any day of the year.
Price guide: £75

Reception

In addition to the above services, the Hall can provide cars, Daimler, Rolls Royce or Mercedes, at special rates. While accommodation is not available on the premises, a list of local accommodation can be provided.
Catering: Buffets from £6pp. Sit down from £12.00pp

Highfield Hall Hotel
Northop CH7 6AX
T/ F: 01352 840221
Contact: Virginia Smith or Molly Millar, Owners

Ceremony

This Georgian Grade II listed building is set in nine acres of mature gardens. The hotel was established in 1982, is family owned, and specialises in weddings. Up to two ceremonies are permitted here per day on any day of the year except Christmas Day.
Price guide: £150

Reception

Plas Hafod Country House Hotel
Gwenymynydd, Mold CH7 5JS
T: 01352 700177 F: 01352 755499
Contact: Mrs Buckley, Manager

Ceremony

Hafod Hall was built in the 1730s and features an imposing entrance and stone staircase, and a romantic garden setting of around nine acres. Only one ceremony is permitted per day, on any day of the year.
Price guide: £120

Reception

Catering: from £16.95pp

Soughton Hall
Country House Hotel
Northop CH7 6AB
T: 01352 840811 F: 01352 840382
Contact: Rosemary Rodenhurst, Event Banqueting Manager

Ceremony

This Georgian country house hotel is set in parkland with a half mile long, 150 year old, lime tree avenue, which can feature in wedding photographs. The house retains many original period fittings, and is full of antiques assembled for generations. Surprisingly, then, the owners of Soughton Hall welcome young children. The hotel offers a video of its wedding services. Only one wedding is permitted here per day.
Price guide: POA

Reception

The hotel's wedding package includes flowers for each table, a decorated cake table, a cake stand and knife, and a changing room for the day. Corkage is charged if you bring your own wine.
Catering: from £16.50pp

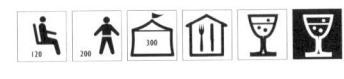

As well as the above, services offered by the hotel include menu printing, stationery, and personalised serviettes.
Catering: from £23pp

ALSO LICENSED
Kinsale Hall, Holywell 01745 560001
Springfield Hotel 01352 780503
St Davids Park Hotel 01244 520800

LICENSED PREMISES IN GWYNEDD
Bontddu Hall Hotel 01341 430661
Castell Cidwn Hotel 01286 650243
Hotel Maes-y-Neuadd 01766 780200
Penmaenuchaf Hall Hotel 01341 422129
Royal Victoria Hotel 01286 870253
Seiont Manor Hotel 01286 673366

Tre-ysgawen Hall
Capel Coch, Anglesey LL77 7UR
T: 01248 750750 F: 01248 750035
Contact: Neil Rowlands, Asst. Manager

Ceremony

This restored country mansion dates from 1882. Three rooms are available for ceremonies, ranging in capacity from 35 to 150. These are available every day of the year, except the Christmas and New Year's holidays. Ceremonies must be followed by a reception at the Hall.
Price guide: £100

Reception

The Hall offers European cuisine, and is Egon Ronay recommended.
Catering: Buffets from £6.95pp. Sit down from £16.95

Victoria Hotel, Menai Bridge
Anglesey LL59 5DR
T: 01248 712309 F: 01248 716774
Contact: Anne Smeaton, Proprietor or Simon Owen, Manager

Ceremony

This Grade II listed Victorian building overlooks the Menai Straights and has two rooms licensed to hold ceremonies with capacities of 80 and 120. Ceremonies are permitted without receptions.
Price guide: £50

Reception

The hotel offers a complimentary overnight stay for bridal couples, and will arrange special rates for wedding guests.
Catering: Buffets from £5.50pp. Sit down from £12.00pp

ALSO LICENSED
Bulkeley Hotel 01248 810146
Bwyty Glantraeth Restaurant 01407 840401
Henllys Hall Hotel 01248 810412
Trearddur Bay Hotel 01407 860301

Cwrt Bleddyn Hotel
Llangybi, Nr Usk
T: 01633 450521 F: 01633 450220
Contact: Adrian Puckey, General Manager

Ceremony

The hotel offers three ceremony rooms, which are available seven days a week with restrictions on Christmas Day and New Year's Day.
Price guide: £100 - £150

Reception

The hotel boasts accolades including Welsh Chef of the Year 1994 and Young Welsh Chef of the Year 1994 and 1995.
Catering: from £19pp

Glen-Yr-Afon House Hotel
Pontypool Road
Usk NP5 1SY
T: 01291 672302 F: 01291 672597
Contact: Mrs J A Clarke, Proprietor or Mr A Brown, Manager

Ceremony

The hotel was built in 1868 as a private residence and is set in its own grounds, with plenty of space for parking. Two rooms are licensed to hold ceremonies with varying capacities from 30 to 100. The hotel will consider booking ceremonies without receptions upon application.
Price guide: £100

Reception

Children cannot be catering for separately. The hotel holds a late night drinking licence until midnight.
Catering: from £21.95pp

ALSO LICENSED
Caldicot Castle 01291 424447

Glyn Clydach Hotel
Longford Road, Neath SA10 7AJ
T: 01792 813701 F: 01792 815612
Contact: Rico Rabaiotti, Manager

Ceremony

The hotel is set in its own grounds and features a nine hole golf course. Two rooms are licensed to hold ceremonies, seven days a week excluding Christmas Day. A maximum of two ceremonies per day are permitted. Confetti is allowed.
Price guide: £50

Reception

Three course wedding breakfasts start at approximately £18.50 a head, while buffets, which include the room hire, DJ and an overnight bridal suite, start at £8.50 per person. Of the hotel's seven bedrooms, five are en-suite, and a 10% discount is offered to wedding guests staying overnight at the hotel.
Catering: Buffets from £8.50pp. Sit down from £18.50pp

Margam Orangery
Margam, Port Talbot SA13 2TJ
T: 01639 881635 F: 01639 895897
Contact: Rosemary Lloyd

Ceremony

This award-winning orangery, set in acres of ornamental gardens, was originally built in 1786 and is the biggest of its kind in Britain. Following extensive restoration work the orangery was opened by the Queen in 1977. Ceremonies are available any day of the year, excluding Christmas Day and Good Friday, and are only available when held in conjunction with receptions.
Price guide: FOC (with reception)

Reception

All catering is in-house, undertaken by the Orangery's own contract caterers, West Glamorgan Catering Services. A list of local hotels and guest houses is provided, some of which operate preferential rate agreements with the Orangery.
Catering: £10 - £30pp

Celtic Manor Hotel
Coldra Woods, Newport NP6 2YA
T: 01633 413000 F: 01633 412910
Contact: Nicola Chatham, Wedding Co-ordinator

Ceremony

ISLE OF ANGELSEY - MONMOUTHSHIRE - NEATH PORT TALBOT

203

This former manor house offers two ceremony rooms; one of which has only limited wheelchair access. Ceremonies can be held on any day of the year, but only if followed by a reception at the hotel.
Price guide: from £100

Reception

Helicopters and hot air balloons may use the grounds.
Catering: Buffets from £14.95pp. Sit down from £20.70pp

ALSO LICENSED
St Mellons Hotel 01633 680355
Tredegar House 01633 815880

Canolfan Pentre Ifan
Felindre Farchog
Crymych   SA41 3XE
T: 01239 820317   F: 01239 820317
Contact: Carol Owen, Development Officer

Ceremony

This Tudor gatehouse, dating from 1485, is a listed building. Ceremonies are restricted to one per day, on any day of the year except Bank Holidays.
Price guide: £125

Reception

At Canolfan Pentre Ifan you may supply your own alcohol for the wedding reception but it cannot be sold on the premises. Children cannot be catered for separately. In true Welsh musical tradition, a harpist can be provided if required.
Catering: £5.50pp - £10pp

Cwmwennol Country House
Swallowtree Woods
Saunderfoot   SA69 9DE
T: 01834 813430   F: 01834 813430
Contact: Tony Smiles, Owner

Ceremony

Cwmwennol has a woodland setting, just 300 yards from the beach. The original building dates back to 1870s. The current owners took over the hotel in 1989 and have been making improvements over recent years, including the refurbishment of the restaurant in Laura Ashley designs.
Price guide: £100

Reception

The hotel uses local produce wherever possible, and fish landed on the harbour. Barbecue weddings are a speciality.
Catering: Buffets from £5.50pp. Sit down from £10pp

St Brides Hotel
St Brides Hill
Saundersfoot   SA69 9NH
T: 01834 812304   F: 01834 813303
Contact: Ian Bell, Managing Director

Ceremony

St Brides is set right by the sea, and has its own outdoor pool. Ceremonies can take place here on any day of the week except Sundays. Confetti is not permitted.
Price guide: £50 - £200

Reception

Catering: Sit down from £15.00

Warpool Court Hotel
St Davids   SA62 6BN
T: 01437 720300   F: 01437 720676
Contact: Rupert Duffin, GM

Ceremony

The AA and RAC Three Star, WTB Four Crown, Warpool Court Hotel enjoys sweeping views across its lawns to the coast of St Brides Bay and the offshore islands. Inside, the hotel is embellished by 3,000 hand painted tiles decorated by the lady who lived here in the early 1900s. Only one ceremony is permitted here per day on any day of the year. Confetti is not permitted.
Price guide: POA

Reception

The hotel offers an extensive range of fish dishes, with smoked salmon a speciality. A choice of vegetarian dishes is always available and special diets can be catered for.
Catering: Sit down from £18pp

Ynys Hewel Centre
Cwmfelinfach
Crosskeys   NP1 7JX
T: 01495 200113   F: 01495 200658
Contact: Mrs Deborah Haylock, General Manager

Ceremony

This conference centre is in a rural location in the heart of the Sirhowy Valley Country Park. Three rooms are licensed and available any day except Christmas Day. Ceremonies must be followed by reception here.
Price guide: POA

Reception

Catering: Buffets from £5.50pp. Sit down from £14.95pp.

ALSO LICENSED
Castell Malgwyn   01239 682382
Druidstone Hotel 01437 781221
Foncroft Hotel   01834 842886
Holyland Hotel   01646 681444
Nantyffin Motel   01437 563423
Penally Abbey   01834 843033

Caer Beris Manor
Builth Wells
T: 01982 552601
F: 01982 552586
Contact: Peter & Katharine Smith

Ceremony

This former home of Lord Swansea, set in 27 acres of parkland, offers wedding ceremonies on any day of the week except Sunday.
Price guide: £50 (FOC with reception)

Reception

Cuisine at the Manor is international in style.
Catering: from £10.95pp

Castle of Brecon Hotel
The Castle Square
Brecon
LD3 9DB
T: 01874 624611
F: 01874 623737
Contact: Duty Manager

Ceremony

The Castle of Brecon is a listed building with its own gardens and excellent views. It has three marriage rooms, ranging in seated capacity from 35 to 150, and in standing capacity from 45 to 200. Ceremonies can take place here on any day of the year. The Castle of Brecon Hotel has set no limit on the number of ceremonies that can be held each day.
Price guide: £25

Reception

Catering: Packages from £19pp

Lake Country House Hotel
Llangammarch Wells LD4 4BS
T: 01591 620202 F: 01591 620457
Contact: Mr J P Mifsud, Proprietor

Ceremony

The Lake is a Victorian Welsh country house set in 50 acres, with sweeping lawns, rhododendron lined pathways, riverside walks and a large trout lake. This is a homely sort of hotel that serves Welsh teas in front of the log fire in the drawing room every afternoon. Ceremonies can take place here any day of the year, but only one is permitted per day.
Price guide: POA

Reception

The hotel claims an award winning restaurant which uses fresh produce and herbs from its own gardens.
Catering: Sit down from £22.50pp

Lake Vyrnwy Hotel
Lake Vyrnwy, Powys
T: 01691 870692 F: 01691 870259
Contact: Jim Talbot

Ceremony

This country house hotel sits overlooking the six mile long Lake Vyrnwy. The hotel offers two marriage rooms; The Drawing Room (max 65) and the Tower Suite (max 200). Ceremonies can take place here on any day except Sundays and religious holidays, with up to four permitted per day.
Price guide: £150 - £200

Reception

The hotel holds two AA Rosettes for its restaurant.
Catering: from £17pp

Llangoed Hall
Llyswen, Brecon LD3 0YP
T: 01874 754525 F: 01874 754545
Contact: Helen Pugh, General Manager

Ceremony

Llangoed Hall is a listed building that sits on the banks of the river Wye and was designed by Sir Clough Williams-Ellis. The atmosphere of the house is designed to be that of your own home, and is delightfully presented in the Hall's literature. Only one wedding is permitted here at any one time, and that must be followed by a reception at the Hall.
Price guide: £200

Reception

The Hall can accommodate up to 50 guests in The Orangery and a maximum of 14 in the Whistler Room. Carriages should be arranged before 6pm. Should you want to party on into the evening, it would be necessary to take the Hall on an exclusive use basis. The Hall's restaurant has three AA Rosettes and four red pavilions from Michelin.
Catering: £17.50pp - £39pp

Nanteos Mansion
Rhydyfelin
Aberystwyth SY23 4LU
T: 01970 624363 F: 01970 626332
Contact: Graham or Sue Hodgson-Jones

Ceremony

Nanteos is a Grade II listed mansion with connections with Wagner and the Holy Grail. It is now operating as an hotel and restaurant. The Roccoco style music room (claimed to be the finest in Wales) is the licensed room and is available on any day of the year.
Price guide: £100 - £200

Reception

POWYS

POWYS - RHONDDA CYNON TAFF

Catering: Buffets from £15pp. Sit down from £22pp.

Plas Dolguog Hotel
Machynlleth   SY20 8UJ
T: 01654 702244   F: 01654 702530
Contact: Mrs Pritchard, Proprietor

Ceremony

This is a listed 16th Century country house set in nine acres of garden and woodland. Ceremonies can take place here on any day, except Sunday and Easter Saturday.
Price guide: £50

Reception

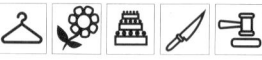

There is a site available for a large marquee.
Catering: from £12.95pp

Powis Castle
Welshpool
SY21 8RF
T: 01938 554338   F: 01938 554336
Contact: Mr H N Williams, Administrator

Ceremony

The ancestral home of the Herbert family since 1587, Powis Castle is perhaps best known for its wonderful gardens, which are laid out in 17th Century Italian and French styles. The Castle is now run by The National Trust, which has elected the Castle's Ballroom as the marriage room. Just one ceremony is permitted per day, and only when the Castle is closed to the public, i.e. Monday and Tuesday in April, May, June, September and October, and Mondays only in July and August (not Bank Holiday Mondays). Marriages may be held on any day during the closed season.
Price guide: £500

Reception

In-house catering is available at the Castle, but your own choice of contract caterer may be appointed.
Catering: POA

Swan at Hay Hotel
Church Street, Hay on Wye
T: 01497 821188   F: 01497 821424
Contact: Mrs RG Vaughan, Proprietor

Ceremony

Ceremonies at this listed Georgian building are limited to one per day on any day of the year except the 10 days over the Whitsun holiday. Wheelchair users must negotiate one step.
Price guide: £120

Reception

The hotel holds an AA Rosette for its food. Children cannot be catered for separately.
Catering: £12pp - £25pp

ALSO LICENSED
Elephant & Castle Hotel   01686 626271
Garthmyl Hall   01686 640550
Gliffaes Hotel   01874 730371
Greenway Manor Hotel   01597 851230
Llanidloes Council Chamber
01686 412353
Maesmar Hall Hotel   01686 688255

Heritage Park Hotel
Coed Cae Road
Trehafod   CF37 2NP
T: 01443 687057   F: 01442 687060
Contact: Victoria Williams, General Manager

Ceremony

The modern Heritage Park is situated 10 miles from the centre of Cardiff. Ceremonies can take place here on any day of the year.
Price guide: £50

Reception

The bride and groom are offered a complimentary room to change in during the day, as well as overnight accommodation on their wedding night. Children under 12 years old are catered for at half price.
Catering: Sit down from £13pp

Miskin Manor
Pendolyn Road, Groesfaen
Pontyclun   CF7 8ND
T: 01443 224204   F: 01443 237606
Contact: Joanna Kocker, Conference & Banqueting Manager

Ceremony

This four star hotel is housed in a Grade II listed building set in 20 acres of gardens. It has a Wales Tourist Board Five Crowns Highly Commended Award. There are four marriage rooms: Meisgyn, the Garden Room, the Cedar Room, and the Drawing Room and Terrace Suite. These cater for a minimum of 10 guests. Ceremonies can take place here any day except New Year's Day and Good Friday, and must be followed by a reception at the hotel.
Price guide: £275

Reception

The hotel is able to offer menus to suit your requirements, including special Welsh menus. All the above services are offered in the hotel's standard wedding package, but other services can be provided. The hotel offers wedding guests

a special overnight rate.
Catering: from £21.50pp

ALSO LICENSED
The Visitors Centre, Aberdare
01685 874672

Daw-Yr-Ogof Caves
Abercave, Swansea SA9 1GT
T: 01639 730049 F: 01639 730203
Contact: Sara Reynolds, Event manager

Ceremony

Weddings can take place in the Cathedral Cave at this popular tourist attraction. Wheelchair access is limited. Ceremonies can be held every day, except Bank Holidays. Confetti is not permitted.
Price guide: £200

Reception

There are no reception facilities at the site, although five bedrooms are available for overnight stays.

Langland Court Hotel
31 Langland Court Road
Langland, Swansea SA3 4TD
T: 01792 361545 F: 01792 362302
Contact: Chris Hamilton-Smith, Wedding Manager

Ceremony

This Tudor-style house is set in award winning gardens in a quiet residential area and boasts sea views. The Adam Lounge is licensed to hold ceremonies which can take place throughout the year excluding Christmas Day and Boxing Day.
Price guide: £55 (with reception only)

Reception

Welsh dishes and menus are a special feature of the hotel.
Catering: Buffets from £12.25pp.
Sit down from £15.95pp

ALSO LICENSED
Fairyhill Hotel, Gower 01792 390139
Swansea Marriott Hotel 01792 642020

Parkway Hotel
& Conference Centre
Cwmbran Drive, Cwmbran
T: 01633 871199 F: 01633 869160
Contact: Teresa Langton, Conference & Banqueting Co-ordinator

Ceremony

This privately owned hotel has AA/RAC four star status and has a five crown award from the Wales Tourist Board. Three rooms are available to hold ceremonies.
Price guide: £105

Reception

As part of the day-reception package, the hotel offers amongst other things, a choice of 12 menus and a complimentary honeymoon suite for the couple.
Catering: from £22.90pp

The Egerton Grey Hotel
Porthkerry, Nr Barry CF62 3BZ
T: 01446 711666 F: 01446 711690
Contact: Anthony Pitkin, Proprietor

Ceremony

This former 19th Century rectory, 10 miles from Cardiff, was opened as a small luxury hotel in 1988. It is set in seven acres of gardens, with croquet lawn and tennis court, with views down to Porthkerry Park and the sea. Weddings may take place in the Drawing Room, with views over the gardens, or in the mahogany-panelled Dining Room. Ceremonies may take place here on any day, except Christmas Day.
Price guide: £100

Reception

At Egerton Grey, an alternative to the formal sit-down meal is offered: a buffet luncheon. Guests are served in the main Dining Room, but may then be seated at tables throughout the house; in the Library, the two halls, the Private Dining Room, the Drawing Room or outside.
Catering: from £17.50pp

The Boat Inn
Erbistock, Wrexham LL13 0Dl
T: 01978 780143
Contact: General Manager

Ceremony

This restaurant and public house is a Grade II listed building. One ceremony is permitted per day here, on any day of the week except Sundays and public holidays.
Price guide: £100 (£75 with reception)

Reception

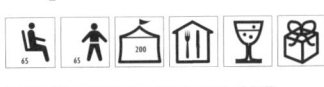

The restaurant serves British/French style cuisine and has two AA Rosettes.
Catering: Buffets from £8pp. Sit down from £12.00pp

Hanmer Arms
Hanmer
Nr Whitchurch SY13 3DE
T: 01948 830532 F: 01948 830740
Contact: General Manager

Ceremony

The Hanmer Arms is a privately owned village hotel and restaurant. Ceremonies can take place here any day of the year. Disabled access is to the ground floor only, this room having a capacity for 40 people.
Price guide: £100

Reception

RHONDDA CYNON TAFF - SWANSEA - TORFAN - VALE OF GLAMORGAN - WREXHAM

207

Rossett Hall Hotel
Chester Road, Rossett
Wrexham   LL12 0DE
T: 01244 571000   F: 01244 571505
Contact: David Craven, Partner

Ceremony

Rossett Hall is a Grade II listed building, built in 1750. Up to two ceremonies per day are permitted here, on any day of the year.
Price guide: £500

Reception

Catering: £16pp - £25pp

ALSO LICENSED
Cross Lanes Hotel   01978 780555
The Hand Hotel, Chirk   01691 773472

Catering: from £11pp

STOP PRESS - LATE ENTRIES

Hertford Castle
Hertford SG14 1HR
T: 01992 552885   F: 01992 505876
Contact: Mrs Lynne Saunders, Functions Secretary

Ceremony

This is a Grade I listed building, dating from the 13th Century, set in tranquil riverside gardens. Two rooms are licensed and available on any day except Christmas and New Year.
Price guide: £350

Reception

Couples may appoint their own caterers for this venue.

The Lund Pavilion
Derbyshire County Cricket Club
County Ground
Nottingham Road
Derby DE21 6DA
T: 01332 383211   F: 01332 290251
Contact: Louise Holloway, Pavilion Manager

Ceremony

Rooms in the Pavilion overlook the cricket ground. Three are licensed for ceremonies and are available any day of the year except match days.
Price guide: £100

Reception

Summer barbecues are popular here.
Catering: Buffets from £3./95pp. Sit down from £10pp

Waltham Court Hotel
Kake Street
Petham, Canterbury
Kent CT4 5SB
T: 01227 700413   F: 01227 700127
email: sgw.chives.waltham@dial.pipex.com
Contact: Steve Weaver, Director

Ceremony

This was originally an 18th Century poor house and is now a Grade II listed building with two acres of gardens, situated in a conservation area. The Restaurant and Garden Room are licensed for ceremonies which can take place here on any day of the year.
Price guide: POA

Reception

Quality fresh cuisine is boastED by this venue. Helicopters and hot air balloons may use the grounds if required.
Catering: Buffets from £14pp. Sit down from £18.50pp.

INDEX

A
Abbey Hotel, Great Malvern...81
Abbey House Hotel, Barrow...39
Abbots Barton, Canterbury...91
Abingdon Four Pillars Hotel, Oxfordshire..151
Abington Hall, Cambridgeshire...24
Acton Court Hotel, Stockport...129
Adcote School, Shropshire...156
Aintree Racecourse, Liverpool...136
Airport House, Surrey...172
Alban Arena Civic Centre, St Albans...86
Albany Hotel, Rochdale...129
Albert Halls, Bolton...99
Albrighton Hall Hotel, Shrewsbury...154
Alder House Hotel, Batley...187
Alderley Edge Hotel, Cheshire...24
Aldwark Manor Golf Club, Aldwark...143
Alexander House Hotel, Turners Hill...183
Alexandra Palace, London N22...113
Alexandra Suite, Swanley...91
Alicia Hotel, Liverpool...134
All Seasons Lodge Hotel, Flintshire...201
Allerton Park, Knaresborough...143
Allt Yr Ynys, Walterstone...82
Allt Yr Ynys, Walterstone...XVII
Alton House Hotel, Alton...74
Alverton Manor, Truro...35
Alveston Manor, Stratford-upon-Avon..176
Amberley Castle, West Sussex...183
Amberley Castle, West Sussex...XII
Anchor Inn, Barcombe...61
Angel Hotel, Bury St Edmunds...164
Angel Hotel, Midhurst...183
Angel Inn, North Yorkshire...149
Anglers Arms, Northumberland...143
Anne of Cleves House, Lewes...61
Ansty Hall Hotel, Coventry...176
Anugraha Hotel, Englefield Green...168
Apollonia Restaurant, London...128
Appleby Castle, Cumbria...45
Arden Thistle Hotel, Stratford upon Avon...176
Ardencote Manor Hotel, Claverdon...176
Arley Hall, Northwich...24
Armathwaite Hall Hotel, Keswick...39
Ascot Racecourse, Berkshire...16
Ashburn Hotel, Fordingbridge...75
Ashburnham Hotel, Llanelli...200
Ashford International Terminal, Kent...99
Ashington Leisure Centre, Northumberland...143
Ashton Court Mansion, Bristol...9
Ashton Memorial, Lancaster...99
Assembly Rooms, Bath...9
Astbury Water Park, Congleton...24
Astley Hall, Chorley...99

Aston Villa FC, Villa Park...179
Atlantic Hotel, Newquay...35
Aurora Garden Hotel, Windsor...11
Avenue House, London...128
Avon Gorge Hotel, Bristol...17
Avoncroft Museum, Bromsgrove...82
Avoncroft Museum, West Midlands...183
Avonmouth Hotel, Dorset...58
Aylestone Court Hotel, Hereford...82
Ayton Hall, North Yorkshire...149

B
BAFTA, London W1...113
Bagden Hall Hotel, Huddersfield...187
Baildon Masonic Hall, West Yorkshire...193
Bailiffscourt, Climping..184
Banham Zoo, Norfolk...137
Barley Town House, Royston...86
Barn Hotel, Bedford...10
Barn Hotel, Ruislip...113
Barnham Broom Hotel, Norfolk...137
Barnsdale Country Club, Exton...107
Barnsdale Lodge Hotel, Oakham...107
Barnsgate Manor Vineyard, Uckfield...61
Barrowfield Hotel, Newquay...35
Bartle Hall Country Hotel, Bartle...100
Bartley Lodge Hotel, Cadnam...75
Barton Hall, Torquay...50
Bass Museum, Burton on Trent...160
Bassetsbury Manor, High Wycombe...17
Bath Spa Hotel, Bath...9
Batley Town Hall, Batley...187
Beadlow Manor, Shefford...10
Bear at Hungerford, Hungerford...11
Bear of Rodborough Hotel, Stroud...70
Beauchief Hotel, Sheffield...159
Beaufort Hotel, Burscough...100
Beaulieu Hotel, Hampshire...81
Beaumanor Hall, Loughborough...107
Beauport Park Hotel, Hastings...62
Bedale Hall, North Yorkshire...149
Bedlington Community Centre, North Lincolnshire...141
Beech Hill Hotel, Cumbria...45
Beeches, Bristol...16
Beehive, Gloucestershire...74
Bel & Dragon, Berkshire...16
Belfry Hotel, Handforth...24
Belfry, Wishaw...176
Bell Inn, Stilton...20
Bell's Hotel, Coleford...70
Bella Vista Hotel, Cornwall...38
Belmont House Hotel, Leicester...107
Belmore Hotel, Sale...129
Belstead Brook Manor Hotel, Ipswich...164
Belverdere Restaurant, London...128
Benington Hall, Shipton by Beningborough...143
Bentley Museum, Lewes...62
Bentleys, Whittlebury...139
Berkeley Hotel, London SW1...14

Berners Hotel, London...128
Berrington Hall, Leominster...82
Bertie's Banquetting Rooms, Halifax...188
Berystede Hotel, Ascot...12
Bescot Stadium, Walsall...183
Bickleigh Castle, Devon...55
Biddulph Town Hall, Staffordshire...161
Bididris Hall, Wrexham...201
Big Lock, Middlewich...35
Billesley Manor, Warwickshire...179
Bilton House, Harrogate...144
Bindon Hotel, Langford Budville...156
Bindon Hotel, Langford Budville...II
Birch Hotel, Heywood...129
Birmingham Botanical Gardens...183
Birmingham Grand Moat House...183
Bishop Auckland Town Hall, Durham...58
Bishops Court Hotel, Torquay...50
Bishopstrow House Hotel, Wiltshire...197
Bitton House, Teignmouth...51
Blackpool Tower Ballroom, Lancashire...100
Blackpool Town Hall, Lancashire...100
Blakelands, Staffordshire...164
Blotts Hotel, Holmepierrepoint...149
Blunsden House Hotel, Swindon...194
Boat Inn, Wrexham...207
Boltholt Hotel, Bury...129
Bolton Castle, North Yorkshire...149
Bolton Moat House, Bolton...129
Bontddu Hall, Gwynedd...202
Bookham Grange Hotel, Surrey...168
Boringdon Hall Hotel, Colebrook...51
Borough Arms Hotel, Newcastle under Lyme...161
Boship Farm Hotel, East Sussex...65
Botleigh Grange Hotel, Hedge End...75
Boughton Monchelsea Place, Maidstone...92
Boulters Lock Hotel, Maidenhead...12
Bourne Hall, Surrey...168
Bourton Manor, Much Wenlock...154
Bowdon Hotel, Manchester...131
Bower Hotel, Manchester...134
Bower House Inn, Cumbria...45
Bowers Hotel, Lancashire...107
Bowes Museum, Barnard Castle...59
Bowes Museum, Barnard Castle...IV
Bowler Hat Hotel, Birkenhead...134
Bowood Golf & Country Club, Calne...194
Box House, Box...194
Brackenborough Arms Hotel, Louth...111
Bradford City FC, Valley Parade...188
Bradford City Hall, West Yorkshire...193
Bramhall Hall, Stockport...129
Bramley Grange Hotel, Surrey...172
Brandon Hall Hotel, Brandon...176
Brandshatch Place Hotel, Fawkham..92

209

Branston Hall Hotel, Lincolnshire...113
Breadsall Priory, Morely...45
Bredbury Hall Hotel, Bredbury...130
Brereton Hall, Sandbach...24
Bretton Hall, Wakefield...188
Briar Court Hotel, West Yorkshire...193
Brickwall House, Northiam...62
Brickwall House, Northiam...XVI
Bridge Hotel, Macclesfield...25
Bridge House Hotel, Longham...55
Bridge Inn Hotel, Wetherby...144
Bridge Inn, North Yorkshire...149
Bridge, London SE26...114
Bridgewood Manor Hotel, Chatham...92
Briggens House Hotel, Stanstead Abbots...86
Britannia Stadium, Stoke on Trent...161
Broad Oaks, Windermere...39
Brook Hotel, Felixstowe...164
Brook House Motel, Soham...20
Brookfield Hall, Buxton ...45
Broome Park, Canterbury...92
Broughton Craggs Hotel, Cockermouth...39
Browns Hotel, London...128
Brownsover Hotel, Warwickshire...179
Bryn Howel Hotel, Denbighshire...201
Bryn Morfydd Hotel, Denbighshire...201
Buckatree Hall Hotel, Wellington...154
Buckerell Lodge Hotel, Devon...55
Buckland-Tout-Saints Hotel, Kingsbridge...51
Bude Castle, Bude...36
Budock Vean Hotel, Falmouth...35
Buile Hill Banqueting Suite, Manchester...134
Bulkeley Hotel, Anglesey...203
Bull Inn, Bisham...12
Bull's Head Hotel, Congleton...25
Bullers Arms Hotel, Marhamchurch...35
Burford House, Tenbury Wells...82
Burgh House, Hampstead NW3...114
Burgh Island Hotel, Bigbury on Sea...51
Burley Manor Hotel, Ringwood...75
Burnham Beeches Hotel, Burnham...18
Burnley Friendly Hotel, Lancashire...107
Burnside Hotel, Bowness...39
Bury Town Hall, Bury...130
Bush Hotel, Surrey...172
Busketts Lawn Hotel, Hampshire...81
Buxted Park Hotel, Uckfield...62
Bwyty Glantraeth Restaurant, Anglesey...203

C
C I M, Berkshire...16
Cadbury House Country Club, Bristol...16
Caer Beris Manor, Builth Wells...205
Caerphilly Castle, Caerphilly...198
Café de Paris, London W1...114

Café Royal, London...128
Cairn Hotel, North Yorkshire...149
Caistor Hall, Norfolk...139
Calcot Hotel, Reading...12
Calcot Manor Hotel, Calcot...70
Caldicot Castle, Monmouthshire...203
Cambridge Cottage, Kew Gardens...114
Cannizaro House, London SW19...115
Canolfan Pentre Ifan, Crymych...204
Cantley House Hotel, Wokingham...12
Carbis Bay Hotel, Cornwall...38
Carden Park Hotel, Carden...25
Cardiff Castle, Cardiff...199
Cardiff City Hall, Cardiff...199
Cardiff International Arena...199
Careys Manor Hotel, Hampshire...81
Carlton Hotel, Bournemouth...55
Carlton Lodge Hotel, Helmsley...144
Carlton Lodge Hotel, Helmsley...IV
Carlton Park Hotel, Rotherham...159
Carlton Towers, Goole...60
Carlyon Bay Hotel, St Austell...35
Carnarvon Arms Hotel, Dulverton...156
Carnarvon Hotel, London...128
Cartwright Hall, Bradford...188
Castell Cidwn Hotel, Gwynedd...202
Castell Coch, Cardiff...199
Castell Malgwyn, Newport...205
Castle Ashby House, Northamptonshire...139
Castle Green, Cumbria...45
Castle Hotel, Kirby Muxloe...107
Castle Inn Hotel, Bassenthwaite...39
Castle Lodge, Ludlow...154
Castle of Brecon Hotel, Brecon...205
The Castle, Cambridgeshire...24
Cathedral Clubhouse, West Sussex...187
Cavendish Hotel, East Sussex...65
Cavern, Liverpool...134
Cedar Court Hotel, Wakefield...188
Celebration Hotel, Shanklin...91
Celebration Plaza, Southampton...75
Celebrations, Kirkham...107
Celtic Manor Hotel, Newport...203
Central London Golf Centre, London SW17...115
Centurion Hotel, Somerset...158
Chace Hotel, Coventry...179
Chainbridge Hoel, Llangollen...201
Chamberlain Hotel, Birmingham...179
Charingworth Manor, Chipping Camden...70
Charlecote Pheasant, Warwickshire...179
Charleston Manor, East Sussex...65
Charnwood Arms Hotel, Coalville...108
Charnwood Hotel, Nottinghamshire...151
Chase Hotel, Cumbria...45
Chase Hotel, Ross on Wye...86
Chatsworth Hotel, East Sussex...65
Chatsworth Hotel, Worthing...184

Chaucer Hotel, Kent...99
Chelsea FC, Stamford Bridge London SW6...115
Chelsea Old Town Hall, London SW3...115
Chelsea Old Town Hall, London SW3...XIV
Cheltenham Park Hotel, Gloucestershire...74
Cheltenham Racecourse, Gloucester...70
Cheshunt Marriott Hotel, Broxbourne...86
Chester Grosvenor, Chester...25
Chester Moat House, Cheshire...35
Chester Racecourse, Chester...31
Chester Town Hall, Chester...25
Chestergate Banqueting Suite, Stockport...26
Chewton Glen Hotel, New Milton...76
Chiddingstone Castle, Kent...92
Chigwell Manor Hall, Essex...65
Chilford Halls, Linton...21
Chilford Halls, Linton...XIV
Chillingham Castle, Alnwick...141
Chilston Park Hotel, Lenham...93
Chilworth Manor, Chilworth...76
Chimney House Hotel, Sandbach...26
China Fleet Country Club, Saltash...36
Chipping Sodbury Town Hall, South Gloucestershire...158
Chisledon House Hotel, Chisledon...194
Chiswick House, London SW1...115
Churchgate Manor Hotel, Essex...70
Churchill Intercontinental Hotel, London W1...115
Cinque Ports Hotel, Hastings...62
Civic Hall, Wallsend...175
Civil Service College, Berkshire...16
Clandon Park, Guildford...168
Clarendon Suites, Edgbaston...179
Claridge's Hotel, London W1...116
Clay House, West Yorkshire...193
Clearwell Castle, Coleford...71
Cleckheaton Town Hall, Cleckheaton...188
Cliff Hotel, Ceredigion...200
Cliveden, Taplow...12
Close Hotel, Tetbury...71
Close House Mansion, Newcastle upon Tyne...173
Clumber Park Hotel, Nottinghamshire...151
Coach House, Essex...70
Cobham Hall, Cobham...93
Coed-y-Mwstwr Hotel, Bridgend...198
Colchester Town Hall, Essex...65
Colwyn Bay Hotel, Conwy...201
Combe Grove Manor Hotel, Bath...9
Combermere Abbey, Whitchurch...154
Combermere Abbey, Whitchurch...VIII
Comedy Store, London...128
Comfort Friendly Inn, Boston...111

INDEX

Comfort Friendly Inn, Newcastle under Lyme...161
Commodore Hotel, South Gloucestershire...158
Compleat Angler Hotel, Marlow...18
Congham Hall, Grimston...137
Coniston Hotel, Kent...99
Conwy Council Offices, Conwy...200
Cooling Castle Barn, Rochester...93
Coombe Abbey Hotel, Binley...180
Coombe Barton Inn, Cornwall...38
Coot on the Tarn, Great Urswick...40
Copper Inn, Pangbourne...13
Coppleridge Inn, Shaftesbury...55
Copthorne Effingham Park Hotel, Surrey...172
Copthorne Hotel, West Sussex...187
Cornist Hall, Flintshire...202
Cornmill Hotel, Hull...99
Cornwallis Arms, Suffolk...168
Cotgrave Place, Stragglethorpe...149
Cottons Hotel, Knutsford...26
Coulsdon Manor Hotel, Surrey...172
Council House, Bristol...17
Country Park Inn, Hessle...60
County Hall, Maidstone...93
County Hotel, Kent...99
County Office, Derbyshire...50
County Thistle Hotel, Newcastle upon Tyne...173
Court Colman Hotel, Penyfai...198
Court Garden House, Marlow...18
Courtyard by Marriott, Ipswich...165
Courtyard by Marriott, Reading...13
Courtyard by Marriott, Ryton on Dunsmore...177
Coventry City FC, Highfield Road...180
Crabwall Manor, Chester...26
Cragside, Morpeth...141
Cragwood Hotel, Windermere...40
Craiglands Hotel, Ilkley...189
Crathorne Hall Hotel, Yarm...144
Craxton Wood Hotel, Puddington...26
Crazy Horse Saloon, Morecambe Bay...100
Cresta Court Hotel, Manchester...134
Crewe Hall, Crewe...26
Crewe Municipal Buildings, Crewe...27
Crewkerne Town Hall, Somerset...158
Cricketer, Poolstock...130
Cricklade Hotel, Cricklade...194
Croft Spa Hotel, Croft on Tees...144
Crondon Park Golf Club, Essex...70
Cross Lanes Hotel, Wrexham...208
Crossmead Centre, Devon...55
Crown Hotel, Boroughbridge...144
Crown Hotel, Carlisle...40
Crown Hotel, Harrogate...144
Crown Hotel, Lyndhurst...76
Crown Hotel, Nantwich...27
Crown Inn at Roecliffe, North Yorkshire...145
Crown Inn, Derbyshire...50
Croydon Clock Tower, Surrey...172
Crudwell Court Hotel, Crudwell..194

Cumberland Banqueting Suite, Essex...65
Cumberwell Park, Bradford-on-Avon...195
Curdon Mill, Williton...156
Cwmwennol Country House, Saundersfoot...204
Cwrt Bleddyn Hotel, Usk...203

D

Dales & Peaks Hotel, Matlock...46
Dalston Hall Hotel, Dalston...40
Darwin Forest Country Park, Matlock...46
Davenport House, Brignorth...154
Davenport House, Brignorth...XVIII
Daw-Yr-Ogof Caves, Swansea...207
De La Warr Pavilion, Bexhill...63
De Montfort Hotel, Kenilworth...177
De Vere Hotel, Wiltshire...197
De Vere Lord Daresbury Hotel, Warrington...27
Deans Place Hotel, East Sussex...65
Deanwater Hotel, Manchester...130
Deer Park Hotel, Honiton...51
Delbury Hall, Craven Arms...155
Devon Hotel, Exeter...51
Devonshire Arms Hotel, Bolton Abbey...145
Devonshire House Hotel, Liverpool...134
Dewsbury Town Hall, Dewsbury...189
Diamond Centre, Northamptonshire...140
Dillington House, Illminster...156
Diplomat Hotel, Llanelli...200
Dissington Hall, Dalton..173
Dolphin & Anchor Hotel, Chichester...184
Dolphin Hotel, St Ives...21
Donington Manor Hotel, Castle Donington...46
Donington Manor Hotel, Castle Donington...XVII
Donington Thistle Hotel, Castle Donington...46
Donington Valley Hotel, Newbury...13
Donnington Manor Hotel, Leicestershire...110
Dorchester Hotel, London W1...116
Dorchester Municipal Buildings, Dorchester...56
Dormy House Hotel, Broadway...82
Dorton House, Aylesbury...18
Dovecliff Hall Hotel, Burton upon Trent...161
Dover Town Hall, Kent...93
Dower House, Bayham...63
Dower House, Padstow......36
Down Hall Hotel, Essex...70
Druidstone Hotel, Newport...204
Duke of Cornwall, Plymouth...52
Duke's Hotel, London SW1...116
Dulwich College, London SE21...16
Duncome Park, Helmsley...145

Dunkenhalgh Hotel, Accrington...100
Dunsley Hall Hotel, Whitby...145
Dunstall Park Centre, Wolverhampton...183
Durant House Hotel, Northam...52

E

Earl of Doncaster Hotel, Bennetthorpe...159
East Court, East Grinstead...184
East Devon Council Offices, Sidmouth...52
East Lancs Masonic Hall, Manchester...134
East Lodge Hotel, Matlock...46
East Lodge, Derbyshire...50
East Riddlesden Hall, Keighley...189
Easthampstead Park, Wokingham...13
Eastnor Castle, Ledbury...83
Eastnor Castle, Ledbury...XVII
Eastwell Manor, Ashford...93
Eathorpe Park Hotel, Leamington Spa...177
Eccle Riggs Manor Hotel, Broughton...40
Edgbaston Conference Centre, Country Ground...180
Edgewarebury Hotel, Elstree...86
Egerton Grey Hotel, Porthkerry...207
Egerton House Hotel, Egerton...130
Eggesford Barton, Chulmleigh...52
Elephant & Castle Hotel, Powys...206
Elfordleigh Hotel, Devon...55
Ellesmere Port Civic Hall, Ellesmere Port...27
Elmbridge Civic Centre, Esher...169
Elmbridge Civic Centre, Esher...VIII
Elmers Court Country Club, Lymington...76
Elms Hotel, Abberley...83
Elsham Hall Barn Theatre, Brigg...111
Elstree Moat House, Borehamwood...87
Elvaston Castle, Elvaston...46
Embleton Hall, Morpeth...141
Ennerdales Hotel, Cleator...40
Epsom Downs Racecourse, Surrey...169
Epsom Downs Racecourse, Surrey...III
Escot House & Gardens, Ottery St Mary...52
Eshott Hall, Morpeth...141
Espley Hall, Morpeth...141
Essebourne Manor Hotel, Andover..76
Essex Country Club, Colchester...65
Everglades Park Hotel, Widnes...27
Ewell Court House, Surrey...172
Ewood Park, Blackburn...100
Excelsior Hotel, London...128

F

Faenol Fawr Hotel, Denbighshire...201
Fairfield Halls, Croydon...116, 172
Fairlawns Hotel, Wallsall...183

211

INDEX

Fairyhill Hotel, Gower...207
Falcon Hotel, Cornwall...38
Falcon Hotel, Farnborough...77
Falcon Hotel, Farnborough...XIV
Falcon Manor Hotel, Settle...145
Falcondale Hotel, Ceredigion...200
Falmouth Beach Resort Hotel, Falmouth...36
Falstaff Hotel, Leamington Spa...177
Fanhams Hall, Ware...87
Fantasy Island, Lincolnshire...113
Farington Lodge, Leyland...101
Farnham House Hotel, Surrey...172
Farthings Hotel, Hatch Beauchamp...157
Feathers Hotel, Shropshire...156
Fence Gate Inn, Burnley...101
Fennes, Braintree...65
Finchcocks, Goudhurst...94
Finney Green Cottage, Wilmslow...27
Fir Grove Hotel, Warrington...28
The Firs, London N21...117
Fischers at Baslow Hall, Derbyshire...50
Fleet Inn, Tewkesbury...71
Flitwick Manor, Flitwick...11
Foley Lodge Hotel, Newbury...13
Ford Green Hall, Stoke on Trent...162
Forest Park Hotel, Brockenhurst...77
Forge Inn, Leek...162
Forte Crest Bristol, Bristol...16
Forte Posthouse Bristol...158
Forte Posthouse Hull Marina, Hull...99
Forte Posthouse Leeds, Bramhope...189
Forte Posthouse, Aylesbury...18
Forte Posthouse, Basildon...66
Forte Posthouse, Derby...47
Forte Posthouse, Gloucester...71
Forte Posthouse, Hull...61
Forte Posthouse, North East Lincolnshire...140
Forte Posthouse, Runcorn...28
Forte Posthouse, Southampton...77
Forte Posthouse, York...198
Fossebridge Inn, Cheltenham...71
Fountain Court Hotel, Hythe...77
Four Seasons Hotel, Hale Barns...28
Four Seasons Hotel, London W1...117
Fourcroft Hotel, Newport...204
Fownes Hotel, Worcester...83
Fox Hotel, Staffordshire...164
Foxfields County Hotel, Billington...101
Frensham Heights, Farnham...169
The Friary, Maldon...66
Friendly Hotel, Walsall...180
Friern Manor Hotel, Brentwood...66
Frimley Hall Hotel, Surrey...172
Frogmill Inn, Cheltenham...71
Fulham Town Hall, London SW6...117
Fydell House, Boston...111

G

Galtres Centre, Easingwold...145
Game Larder, Hampshire...81
Garden Hotel, Faversham...94
Garth Hotel, Staffordshire...164
The Garth, Bicester...151
Garthmyl Hotel, Powys...206
Gateforth Hall Hotel, North Yorkshire...149
Gedling House, Nottingham...149
Gedling House, Nottingham...XII
George Coaching Inn, Cambridgeshire...24
George Hotel, Darlington...59
George Hotel, Huddersfield...189
George Hotel, Isle of Wight...91
George Hotel, Stamford...111
Georgian House Hotel, Bolton...130
Gibbon Bridge Hotel, Preston...101
Gissing Hall, Norfolk...139
Glen Eagles Hotel, Harpenden...87
Glen-Yr-Afon House Hotel, Usk...203
Glenmoor Centre, Ilkley...190
Glenridding Hotel, Ullswater...40
Gliffas Hotel, Powys...206
Glyn Clydach Hotel, Neath...203
Glynde Place, East Sussex...65
Goldney Hall, Bristol...17
Golf Hotel, Woodhall Spa...111
Goodwood House, Chichester...184
Goodwood Racecourse, West Sussex...185
Goring Hotel, London SW1...117
Grafton Manor, Bromsgrove...83
Grafton Manor, Bromsgrove...XI
Granada Studios, Manchester...131
Granary Hotel, Shenstone...83
Grand Hotel, Brighton...63
Grand Hotel, Llandudno...201
Grand Hotel, Tynemouth...175
Grange Hall, Southam...180
Grange Hotel, Alton...77
Grange Hotel, York...197
Grange Park Hotel, Willerby...60
The Grange, Royston...21
Grantley College, North Yorkshire...149
Grapevine Hotel, Stow-in-the-Wold...72
Grasmere House Hotel, Salisbury...195
Great Ballard School, West Sussex...187
Great Fosters, Egham, Surrey...172
Great Tythe Barn, Gloucestershire...74
Green End Park Hotel, Ware...87
Green Lawns Hotel, Falmouth...36
Greenhill Hotel, Wigton...41
Greenway Manor Hotel, Powys...206
The Greenway, Cheltenham...72
Greshams, Cambridge...21
Gretna Chase Hotel, Gretna...41
Greystoke Castle, Penrith...41
Greystoke Castle, Penrith...XI
Grims Dyke Hotel, London...128
Grittleton House, Chippenham...195
Groombridge Place, Groombridge...94
Grosvenor House Hotel, London W1...118
Grosvenor Pulford, Cheshire...35
Grove Court Hotel, Cumbria...45
The Grove, West Yorkshire...193
Grovefield Hotel, Burnham...18
Guide Post Hotel, Bradford...190
Guildford Forte Posthouse, Surrey...169
Guildhall, Bath...9
Guildhall, Lyme Regis...56
Guyers House, Pickwick...195
Gwellian Court Hotel, Carmarthenshire...200
Gwesty Plas Plany-Yr-Athro, Carmarthenshire...200
Gwydir Castle, Llanwryst...200
Gypsy Hill Hotel, Devon...55

H

Habrough Hotel, Habrough...111
Hacienda Club, Manchester...131
Hagley Hall, Stourbridge...181
Haigh Hall, Wigan...131
Haldon Belvedere, Higher Aston...52
Haldon Belvedere, Higher Aston...XII
Haley's Hotel, Headingley...190
Haling Dene Centre, Staffordshire...164
Ham House, London...128
Hambleton Hall, Oakham...108
Hammersmith & Fulham Irish Centre, London W6...118
Hammersmith Town Hall, London W6...118
Hampson House Hotel, Lancashire...107
Hanbury Hall, Droitwich...83
Hanbury Manor Hotel, Ware...87
Hand Hotel, Chirk...208
Hanmer Arms, Hanmer...207
Hannafore Point Hotel, West Looe...36
Hanover International Hotel, Huddersfield...190
Hanover International Hotel, Reading...13
Hanover International Hotel, Skipton...146
Hardwicke Hall Manor Hotel, Co Durham...60
Hare & Hounds Hotel, Tetbury...72
Harris Park Conf Centre, Preston...101
Harrow School, Harrow-on-the-Hill...118
Harte & Garter Hotel, Windsor...14
Hartford Hall, Northwich...28
Hassop Hall, Bakewell...47
Hatfield Hotel, Lowestoft...165
Hatfield Lodge Hotel, Hatfield...88
Hatherly Manor Hotel, Down Hatherly...72
Hatherton Country Hotel, Staffordshire...164
Hatton Court Hotel, Hanslope...19
Hatton Court Hotel, Upton St Leonards...72
Hawker Centre, Kingston upon Thames...169
Hawkwell House Hotel, Iffley...151
Haycock Hotel, Peterborough...21
Haydock Thistle Hotel, Liverpool...136
Haydon House Hotel, Basford...162
Haynes Motor Museum, Sparkford...157

INDEX

Headlam Hall Hotel, Darlington...59
Headland Hotel, Newquay...36
Heanor & Loscoe Town Hall, Heanor...47
Heath Court Hotel, Newmarket...165
Heathrow Hilton Hotel, London...128
Heathrow Park Hotel, London...128
Hellidon Lakes, Northamptonshire...140
Henllys Hall Hotel, Anglesey...203
Hereford Town Hall, Hereford...84
Heritage Park Hotel, Trehafod...206
Herstmonceux Castle, Hailsham...63
Hertford Castle, Hertford...208
Hertford County Hall, Hertford...90
Heybridge Hotel, Ingatestone...66
Heydon Grange, Cambridgeshire...24
Hideout, Wokingham...14
Highbury, Moseley...181
Highclere Castle, Highclere...77
Higher Trapp, Simonstone...101
Highfield Hall Hotel, Northop...202
Highgate School, London N6...118
Highley Manor, West Sussex...187
Highwayman, Winterton on Sea...137
Hill Lodge Hotel, Sudbury...165
Hilton National Hotel, Watford...88
Hilton National, Garforth...190
Hilton National, West Yorkshire...193
Hilton-on-the-Park, London...128
Hinchingbrooke House, Huntingdon...22
Hind Hotel, Northamptonshire...140
Hintlesham Hall, Ipswich...165
HMS Warrior, Portsmouth...78
Holbeck Ghyll Hotel, Windermere...41
Holbrook House Hotel, Holbrook...157
Holdsworth House, Halifax...190
Holiday Inn Crowne Plaza Midland Hotel, Manchester...131
Holiday Inn Maidenhead, Berkshire...16
Holiday Inn Nelson Dock, London SE16...119
Hollington House Hotel, Newbury...14
Hollngs Hall Hotel, West Yorkshire...193
Holly Lodge Hotel, Cheshire...35
Holmbush House, East Sussex...65
Holme Park Hall Hotel, Co Durham...60
Holyland Hotel, Newport...204
Homestead, Derbyshire...50
Hoole Hall, Cheshire...35
Hooton Golf Centre, Cheshire...35
Hopeside Hotel, Colwyn Bay...200
Hopton Court, Kidderminster...84
Horn of Plenty, Devon...55
Horncliffe Mansions, Rawtenstall...102
Hornsbury Mill, Chard...157
Horsham Museum, West Sussex...185
Hotel California, Newquay...37
Hotel Maes-y-Neuadd, Gwynedd...202
Hotel Rembrandt, Weymouth...56
Hotel Rudyard, Leek...162
Hotel St James, Leicester...108
Hotel St Nicholas, Scarborough...146
Howard Hotel, London WC2...119
Hoyle Court, Shipley...191
Huddersfield Town Hall, Huddersfield...191
Hulme Hall, Wirral...134
Hundred House Hotel, Great Witley...84
Hunting Lodge, Adlington...28
Huntsham Court, Tiverton...53
Huyton Suite, Huyton...135
Hyatt Carlton Tower, London SW1...119
Hyatt Regency, Birmingham...183
Hyde Park Hotel, London SW1...119
Hythe Imperial, Hythe...94

I

Ilford Town Hall, Ilford...120
Imperial Hotel, Llandudno...201
Imperial Hotel, Torquay...53
Imperial War Museum, Duxford...22
Indian Community Centre, Derbyshire...50
Indian Community Centre, New Basford...149
Inglenook Hotel, West Sussex...187
Inglewood, Cheshire...35
Inn at Whitewell, Clitheroe...102
Inn on the Green, Berkshire...16
Inn on the Lake, Godalming...170
International Hotel, Derbyshire...50
Ipswich County Hotel, Ipswich...166
Ipswich Guildhall, Ipswich...166
Ireley Grounds, Gloucestershire...74
Irton Hall, Cumbria...45

J

Jarrow Town Hall, Jarrow...173
Jarvis Abbotts Well Hotel, Chester...28
Jarvis Bankfield Hotel, Bingley...191
Jarvis Bowden Hall Hotel, Upton St Leonards...72
Jarvis Comet Hotel, Hatfield...88
Jarvis Crewe, Cheshire...35
Jarvis Elcot Park Hotel, Newbury...14
Jarvis Great Danes Hotel, Maidstone...94
Jarvis Heath Hotel, Bewdley...84
Jarvis International Hotel, Watford...90
Jarvis International, Hemel Hempstead...88
Jarvis International, Solihull...181
Jarvis Newton Park, Derbyshire...50
Jarvis Penns Hall Hotel, West Midlands...183
Jarvis Thatcher's Hotel, East Horsley...170
Judge's Lodgings, Lincoln...112

K

Kedleston Hall, Derby...47
Keele Conference Park, Keele...162
Kelham Hall, Newark...149
Kensington Town Hall, London W8...119
Kenwick Park, Louth...112
Keswick Hotel, Keswick...41
Kettering Park Hotel, Kettering...139
Kilhey Court Hotel, Standish...131
Kimmel Manor Hotel, Conwy...201
King's Lynn Town Hall, Norfolk...137
Kingsbury Country Club, Tamworth...177
Kingsford Park Hotel, Essex...70
Kingston House, Devon...55
Kingswood House Centre, London SE21...120
Kingswood House Centre, London SE21...VII
Kington Manor, Chippenham...195
Kinsale Hall, Holywell...202
Kirkby Suite, Kirkby...135
Kirkley Hall, Ponteland...142
Kitley, Plymouth, Devon...55
Knavesmire Manor Hotel, Wiltshire...197
Knebworth Park, Old Knebworth...88
Knights Out, Berkshire...16
Knowle Restaurant, Higham...95

L

Ladstock Country House, Cumbria...45
Lady Anne's Hotel, Lincolnshire...113
Lains Barn, Wantage...152
Lainston House Hotel, Sparsholt...78
Lake Country House Hotel, Llangammarch Wells...205
Lake Vyrnwy Hotel, Lake Vrynwy...205
Lakeside Hotel, Newby Bridge...41
Lakeside Moat House, Grays...69
Lamport Hall, Northamptonshire...140
Lancashire CCC, Old Trafford...131
Lancashire CCC, Old Trafford...IX
Land's End Hotel, Penzance...37
Landmark London Hotel, London NW1...120
Lanesborough, London SW1...120
Lanesborough, London SW1...XXIII
Langar Hall Hotel, Langar...149
Langdale Chase Hotel, Windermere...42
Langham Hilton, London W1...120
Langland Court Hotel, Swansea...207
Langley Castle Hotel, Hexham...142
Langstone Cliff Hotel, Dawlish...53
Langtry Manor Hotel, Bournemouth...56
Larpool Hall, Whitby...149
Last Drop Village Hotel, Manchester...134
The Lawn, Rochford...66
The Lawn, Rochford...IX
Layer Marney Tower, Colchester...67
Le Gothique, London SW18...118
Le Gothique, London SW18...XIII
Le Meridien London Gatwick, West Sussex...185
Lea Marston Hotel, Lea Marston...178

213

INDEX

Leasowe Castle Hotel, Wirral...135
Leatherhead Golf Club, Surrey....170
Lee Valley Leisure Centre, London N9...120
Leeds Civic Hall, Leeds...191
Leeds Forte Posthouse, West Yorkshire...193
Leeds Marriott Hotel, West Yorkshire...193
Leeds United FC, Elland Road...193
Leeford Place Hotel, East Sussex...65
Leeming House Hotel, Ullswater...42
Leez Priory, Chelmsford...67
Leez Priory, Chelmsford...XXI
Leicester City FC, Filbert Street...108
Leicester Town Hall, Leicester...108
Leicestershire Museum, Leicester...108
Leigh Court, Somerset...10
Leigh Court, Somerset...IX
Leigh Park Hotel, Bradford on Avon...195
Leigh Town Hall, Wigan...102
Leith's at London Zoo, London NW1...121
Lewtrenchard Manor, Okehampton...53
Leyland Masonic Hall, Leyland...102
Limpley Stoke Hotel, Wiltshire...197
Linden Hall Hotel, Northumberland...143
Lingfield Park, Surrey...172
Linthwaite House Hotel, Windermere...42
Linton Springs Hotel, Wetherby...191
Lion & Swan Hotel, Congleton...29
Lion Hotel, Belper...47
Lion Hotel, Shropshire...156
Lisdoonie Hotel, Cumbria...45
Lismoyne Hotel, Fleet...78
Little Silver Hotel, Tenterden...95
Little Thakeham, Storrington...185
Liverpool Marina, Liverpool...136
Liverpool Moat House, Liverpool...136
Liverpool Town Hall, Liverpool...135
Llandidloes Council Chamber, Powys...206
Llangoed Hall, Brecon...205
Locko Park, Sponden...47
Lodge, London...128
Logwood Mill Hotel, Liverpool...136
Long Hall, Chiddingford...170
Longfield Suite, Manchester...134
Longhirst Hall, Morpeth...142
Longleat, Warminster...196
Longleat, Warminster...VI
Longmynd Hotel, Church Stretton...155
Lord Crewe Arms Hotel, Blanchland..59
Lord Hill Hotel, Shropshire...156
Lordleaze Hotel, Chard...157
Lords of the Manor, Upper Slaughter...73
Loseley Park, Guildford...170
Lovelady Shield, Cumbria...45
Low Wood Hotel, Windermere...42

Luckham Park, Colerne...196
Lund Pavilion, Derbyshire CCC...208
Lund Pavilion, Derbyshire...50
Lyceum Library Restaurant, Liverpool...136
Lygon Arms, Broadway...84
Lymm Hotel, Cheshire...35
Lympne Castle, Hythe...95
Lyndhurst Park Hotel, Lyndhurst...78
Lynford Hall, Thetford...137
Lynford Hall, Thetford...XVI
Lythe Hill Hotel, Haslemere...170

M

Mackworth Hotel, Derby...48
Madeley Court Hotel, Shropshire...156
Madonna Hayley Hotel, London...128
Maesmar Hall Hotel, Powys...206
Mains Hall, Poulton-le-Fylde...102
Mains Hall, Poulton-le-Fylde...XVIII
Maison Talbooth, Dedham...67
Makeney Hall, Milford...48
Manchester Airport Moat House, Cheshire...35
Manchester Town Hall, Manchester...132
Manchester United FC, Old Trafford...134
Manoir Aux Quat' Saisons, Great Milton...152
Manor Barn, Bexhill...63
Manor Hotel, Dorchester...56
Manor Hotel, Hendford...157
Manor House Hotel, Devon...55
Manor House Hotel, Leamington Spa...178
Manor House Hotel, Moreton-in-the-Marsh...73
Manor House, Aldermaston...14
Manor House, Castle Combe...196
Manor House, Cheshire...35
Manor of Groves Hotel, Hertford...91
Manor Parc Hotel, Cardiff...199
Manor School of Fine Cuisine, Widmerepool..150
Manor, Guildford...171
Manor, St Albans...88
Mansfield Civic Centre, Nottinghamshire...150
Mansion House Hotel, Poole...57
Mansion House, Bristol...17
Mansion House, Littlehampton...185
Margam Orangery, Port Talbot...203
Marine Hall, Fleetwood...107
Marine Hotel, Hartlepool...81
Market Hall, Holdsworthy, Devon...55
Market House, Kingston upon Thames...171
Marlborough Golf Club, Wiltshire...197
Marlborough Hotel, Ipswich...166
Marle Place, Burgess Hill...185
Marriott Goodwood Park Hotel, Chichester...186
Marriott Goodwood Park Hotel, Chichester...XXII

Marriott Hotel, Metro Centre...175
Marsden Mechanics Hall, Marsden...191
Marshalls Meadow Hotel, Berwick upon Tweed...142
Marston Farm Hotel, Warwickshire...179
Marygreen Manor Hotel, Essex...70
Mash & Air, Manchester...132
Mawdsleys Eating House, Ormskirk...102
May Fair Intercontinental Hotel, London W1...121
May Fair Intercontinental Hotel, London W1...IV
Maynard Arms Hotel, Grindleford...48
Medland Manor, Devon...55
Melton Mowbray Council Offices, Leicestershire...108
Merchant Adventurers' Hall, York...198
Merchant Taylor's Hall, York...198
Mere Golf & Country Club, Mere...29
Merewood Hotel, Windermere...42
Michael's Nook, Grasmere...43
Mickleover Court Hotel, Mickleover...48
Middx & Herts Country Club, Harrow...121
Midland Hotel, Derby...48
Milford Hall Hotel, Salisbury...196
Mill House Hotel, Reading...15
Mill House Hotel, Reading...XXIV
Millers Hotel, Nuneaton...178
Millstream Hotel, Bosham...186
Mirage at Milton Hall, Brampton...43
Miskin Manor, Pontyclun...206
Missenden Abbey, Great Missenden...19
Moat House Hotel, Staffordshire...162
Moat House Restaurant, Acton Trussell...162
Moller Centre, Cambridgeshire...24
Mollington Banastre Hotel, Chester...29
Monkey Island Hotel, Bray...15
Montague Arms Hotel, Hampshire...81
Moor Hall Hotel, West Midlands...183
Moore Place Hotel, Milton Keynes...11
Moorland Lodge, West Yorkshire...193
Moorlands Link Hotel, Yelverton...53
Moormead Country Hotel, Wiltshire...197
Morley Hayes, Derby...48
Morritt Arms Hotel, Rokeby...59
Mosborough Hall Hotel, Mosborough...159
Mosimann's, London SW1
Mottisfont Abbey, Romsey...78
Mottram Hall Hotel, Cheshire...29
Mount Ephraim Gardens, Faversham...95
Mount Pleasant Hotel, Rossington...159
Moxhull Hall Hotel, Warwickshire...179
Mullion Cove Hotel, Cornwall...38
Muncaster Castle, Ravensglass...43

Museum of Costume, Bath...9
Mytton Fold Farm Hotel,
　　Blackburn...103

N
Nailcote Hall Hotel, Coventry...181
Nanteos Mansion, Aberystwyth...205
Nantyffin Motel, Newport...204
National Railway Museum,
　　York...146, 198
Naworth Castle, Brampton...43
Neston Civic Hall, Neston...29
Netherfield Place, Battle...63
Netherwood Hotel, Cumbria...45
New Bath Hotel, Matlock Bath...49
New Connaught Rooms,
　　London WC2...121
New House Hotel, Cardiff...199
New Mill Restaurant, Eversley...15
New Mill Restaurant, Eversley...X
New Oysterfleet, Canvey Island...67
New Place Management Centre,
　　Southampton...79
New Priory Hotel,
　　Stretton Sugwas...84
Newburgh Priory,
　　North Yorkshire...149
Newcastle United FC,
　　St James' Park...173
Newick Park, Newick...64
Newick Park, Newick...V
Newland Hall, Chelmsford...67
Newnham College, Cambridge...22
Newport Guildhall, Newport...155
Newsholme Manor Hotel,
　　Keighley...191
Newstead Abbey, Basford...150
Newtown House Hotel,
　　Hayling Island...79
Nizel's Golf Club, Hildenborough...95
Nonsuch Mansion, Surrey...172
Normanton Park Hotel, Oakham...109
North Euston Hotel, Fleetwood...103
North Lakes Hotel, Penrith...43
North Shore Hotel, Skegness...112
Northcote Manor, Burrington...53
Northcote Manor, Langho...103
Northorpe Hall, Lincolnshire...113
Northumberland County Hall,
　　Northumberland...143
Northwood House, Cowes...91
Norton Grange Hotel, Rochdale...132
Norwich City FC, Carrow Road...138
Norwood Park, Southwell...150
Noseley Hall, Billesdon...109
Nunsmere Hall Hotel, Northwich...29
Nutfield Priory Hotel, Surrey...172
Nuthurst Grange Hotel,
　　Hockley Heath...178

O
Oak Lodge Hotel, Enfield...122
Oakham Castle, Leicestershire...109
Oakland Hotel, Northwich...30
Oaklands Hotel,
　　North East Lincolnshire...140
Oaklands Manor, Buxton...49
Oaklands, Grimsby...112
Oaks Hotel, Burnley...103
The Oaks, Manchester...134
Oakwell Hall, Birstall...192
Oakwood Hall Hotel,
　　West Yorkshire...193
Oakwood House, Maidstone...95
Oatlands Park Hotel, Weybridge...171
Ockendon Manor, Cuckfield...186
Offley Place, Great Offley...89
Old Bell, Wiltshire...197
Old Bridge Hotel, Huntingdon...22
Old England Hotel, Bowness...43
Old Forde House, Newton Abbott...54
Old Hall Hotel, Sandbach...30
Old Lodge Hotel, Malton...146
Old Mill, Aldermaston...15
Old Municipal Buildings, Taunton...158
Old Orleans, Cheshire...35
Old Palace, Hatfield...89
Old Park Hotel, Isle of Wight...91
Old Rectory Hotel,
　　Gloucestershire...74
Old Rectory, Somerset...158
Old Ship Hotel, Brighton...64
Old Swan Hotel, North Yorkshire...149
Old Thorns Hotel, Liphook...78
Old Vicarage Restaurant,
　　Derbyshire...50
Olde England Kiosk, Darwen...103
Olde Stocks Restaurant,
　　Grimston...109
Oliver's Lodge Hotel, St Ives...22
One Whitehall Place,
　　London SW1...122
Orangery, Malton...146
Ormesby Hall, Ormesby...174
Orsett Hall Hotel, Grays...67
Orwell Park, Ipswich...166
Osborne House, Isle of Wight...91
Osterley Park House, Isleworth...122
**Osterley Park House,
　　Isleworth...XIII**
Otterburn Hall, Northumberland...143
Overmead Hotel, Devon...55

P
Pack Horse Hotel, Manchester...134
Packfords Hotel, London...128
Packfords Hotel, Woodford Green...68
Paddington House Hotel,
　　Paddington...30
Painswick Hotel, Stroud...73
Painswick House, Painswick...73
Palace Pier, Brighton...64
Paradise Room, Lancashire...107
Park Hall Hotel,, Chorley...103
Park Hotel, Barnstaple...54
Park Hotel, Cardiff...199
Park Hotel, Redcar...175
Park Hotel, South Gloucestershire...159
Park Hotel, Tynemouth...175
Park Lane Hotel, London W1...122
Park Royal International Hotel,
　　Warrington...30
Parkgate Hotel, Cheshire...30
Parkhill Hotel, Hampshire...81
Parkhouse Hotel, Shifnal...155
Parkside Hotel, Bristol...17
Parkway Hotel, Cwnbran...207
Parsonage Farm, Theydon Bois...68
Patten Arms, Cheshire...35
Pavilions of Harrogate,
　　North Yorkshire...149
Pear Tree at Purton, Wiltshire...196
Pearse House, Bishops Stortford...89
Peckforton Castle, Peckforton...30
Penally Abbey, Newport...204
Pendley Manor Hotel, Hertford...91
Pendrell Hall College,
　　Wolverhampton...163
Pengethley Manor Hotel,
　　Ross on Wye...85
Penmaenchaf Hotel, Gwynedd...202
Penmere Manor Hotel, Falmouth...37
Penrhos Court, Kington...85
Penshurst Place, Penshurst...96
Petwood House Hotel,
　　Woodhall Spa...112
Philpots Manor, Hildenborough...96
Phyllis Court Club,
　　Henley on Thames...152
**Phyllis Court Club,
　　Henley on Thames...XX**
Pickering Park Country House,
　　Garstang...104
Pine Hotel, Chorley...104
Pine Lodge Hotel, Bromsgrove...181
Pinewood Studios, Iver...19
Pinewood Thistle Hotel,
　　Handforth...31
Pink Geranium, Melbourn...22
Pittville Pump Room, Cheltenham...73
**Pittville Pump Room,
　　Cheltenham...VIII**
Plas Dolguog Hotel, Machynlleth...206
Plas Hafod Hotel, Mold　202
Plas Maenan, Conwy Valley...200
Plough at Eaton, Cheshire...35
Pockerley Manor, Co Durham...59
Polhawn Fort, Torpoint...37
Polhawn Fort, Torpoint...XIX
Ponsbourne Park Hotel, Hertford...69
Pontlands Park Hotel, Chelmsford...68
Port Vale FC, Vale Park...163
Portal Golf & Country Club,
　　Tarporley...31
Portal Premier, Tarporley...31
Porthminster Hotel, Cornwall...38
Portsmouth F C, Fratton Park...79
Portsmouth Marriott, Hampshire...79
Potters Heron Hotel, Ampfield...79
Powderham Castle, Exeter...54
Powderham Castle, Exeter...II
Powdermills Hotel, Battle...64
Powis Castle, Welshpool...206
Prestbury House Hotel, Prestbury...73
Preston Cross Hotel, Surrey...172
Preston Marriott, Lancashire...104
Prestwold Hall, Loughborough...109
Pride Park Stadium, Derbyshire...50

INDEX

Prince Regent Hotel, London...128
Prince Regent Hotel,
 Woodford Bridge...68
Priory Barn, Sudbury...166
Priory Hotel, Conwy...201
Priory Wood Beefeater, Orrel...104
The Priory, Ware...89
Priston Mill, Somerset...10
Puckrup Hall, Tewkesbury...74
Pulman Lodge Hotel, Seaburn..175
Pump House, London SW18...122
Pump House, London SW18...V
Pump Room & Roman Baths,
 Bath...10
Purbeck House Hotel, Swanage...57
Putteridge Bury, Hertford...91

Q

QEII Conference Centre,
 London SW1...123
Quaffers Theatre Restaurant...132
Quality Clock Hotel, Welwyn...89
Quality Cobden Hotel,
 Edgbaston...182
Quality Friendly Hotel, Boldon...174
Quality Friendly Hotel, Cardiff...199
Quality Friendly Hotel,
 Loughborough...109
Quality Friendly Hotel, Norfolk...139
Quality Friendly, Cheshire...35
Quality Kimberly Hotel,
 Harrogate...147
Quality Norfolk Hotel,
 Edgbaston...182
Quality Royal Hotel, Hull...99
Quayside Restaurant, London...128
Queen Elizabeth Hall,
 Manchester...134
Queen Elizabeth Hall, Oldham...104
Queen Hotel, Chester...31
Queen's Hotel, Brighton...64
Queen's Hotel, Cheltenham...74
Queen's Hotel, Penzance...37
Queen's House, London SE10...123
Queen's Hotel,
 Burton upon Trent...163
Queen's Hotel, Staffordshire...164
Queens, Leeds...192
Quex House, Birchington-on-Sea...96
Quorn Country Hotel,
 Loughborough...110
Quy Mill Hotel, Cambridgeshire...24

R

Raby House Hotel, Willaston...135
Radbrook Hall Hotel, Shropshire...156
Radcliffe Civic Hall, Manchester...134
Radisson Edwardian Hotel, Hayes...123
Radisson SAS Portman Hotel,
 London W1...123
Radlett Centre, Hertford...91
Rake Hall Hotel, Little Stanney...31
Ramada Hotel, London...128
Ramblers Restaurant, Corbridge...142
Ramsbottom Civic Hall,
 Manchester...134

Rangeworthy Court Hotel,
 Rangeworthy...158
Raven Country Hotel,
 Co Durham...60
Raven Hall, North Yorkshire...149
Ravens Ait, Surbiton..123, 172
Ravenswood, Sharpthorne...186
Ravenwood Hall,
 Bury St Edmunds...166
Read's Restaurant, Faversham...96
Reading Town Hall, Berkshire...16
Reasenheath Hall, Cheshire...35
Red Lion Inn, Staffordshire...164
Redcoats Farmhouse Hotel,
 Hertford...91
Redditch Town Hall, Redditch...85
Regent Banqueting Suite,
 London N3...124
Regents Park Marriott, London...128
Reigate Manor Hotel, Surrey...173
Rembrandt Hotel, London SW7...124
Rhinefield House Hotel,
 Brockenhurst...79
Riber Hall, Matlock...49
Richmond Gate Hotel,
 Richmond...124
**Richmond Gate Hotel,
 Richmond...XXII**
Richmond Hill Hotel, Richmond...124
Richmond Theatre, Richmond...124
Ringwood Hall Hotel, Chesterfield...49
Ripley Castle, Harrogate...147
Ripley Castle, Harrogate...XV
Ripon Spa Hotel,
 North Yorkshire...149
Risley Hall Hotel, Risley...49
Ritz Hotel, London W1...124
Rivers & Boaters, Benson...152
Riverside Hotel, Branston...16
Riverside Hotel, Warwickshire...179
Robinson College, Cambridge...23
Rochdale Town Hall, Rochdale...132
Rock Inn Hotel, Halifax...192
Roebuck, Buckhurst Hill...68
Roffen Club, Rochester...96
Roffen Club, Rochester...XXII
Rogerthorpe Manor Hotel,
 Pontefract...192
Romans Hotel, Hampshire...81
Roof Gardens, London W8...125
Rookery Hall Hotel, Nantwich...32
Rose & Crown Hotel, Colchester...68
Rose-in-Vale Hotel, St Agnes...38
Rosehill House Hotel, Burnley...104
Rossett Hall Hotel, Wrexham...208
Rowhill Grange, Wilmington...96
Rowley Manor Hotel,
 Little Weighton...61
Rowton Castle Hotel, Shropshire...156
Rowton Hall Hotel, Rowton...32
Royal Armouries, Fareham...80
Royal Berkshire Hotel, Ascot...16
Royal British Legion, Ely...24
Royal Cambridge Hotel,
 Cambridge...23
Royal Chase Hotel, Shaftesbury...57

Royal Crescent Hotel, Bath...10
Royal Duchy Hotel, Falmouth...38
Royal Garden Hotel, London W8...125
Royal Geographical Society,
 London...128
Royal Hotel, Bideford...54
Royal Hotel, Scarborough...147
Royal Northern College of Music,
 Manchester...133
Royal Oak, Marlborough...197
Royal Pavilion, Brighton...64
Royal Regency Banqueting Suite,
 Ilkeston...49
Royal Society of Arts,
 London WC2...125
Royal Victoria Hotel, Gwynedd...202
Royal Wells Inn, Tunbridge Wells...97
Royals Hotel, Wythenshaw...133
Rudding Park Hotel, Harrogate...147
Rudloe Hall Hotel, Corsham...197
Rudstone Walk, South Cave...61
Rumwell Manor Hotel, Somerset...158
Runnymeade Hotel, Egham...171
Rushden Hall, Rushden...140
Rushpool Lodge Hotel, Seaburn...175
Russ Hill Hotel, Surrey...173
Ruthin Castle, Ruthin...201

S

Sacha Court, Elland...192
Saddleworth Hotel, Saddleworth...133
St Andrews & Blackfriars Hotel,
 Norwich...138
St Augustines', Westgate-on-Sea...97
**St Augustines',
 Westgate-on-Sea...XVII**
St Brides Hotel, Saundersfoot...204
St David's Park Hotel, Flintshire...202
St David's School, Ashford...125
St David's School, Surrey...173
St Elphins School, Matlock...50
St George's Hotel, Llandudno...201
St Leonards Hotel, St Leonards...80
St Mary's Guildhall, Coventry...182
St Mellion Hotel & Golf Club,
 Saltash...38
St Mellons Hotel,
 Neath Port Talbot...204
St Michael's Hotel, Cornwall...38
Salford Hall Hotel, Evesham...85, 178
Salisbury Guildhall, Wiltshire...197
Salomons Centre, Tunbridge Wells...97
Salterns Hotel, Poole...57
Samling at Dovenest, Windermere...44
Sandhole Farm, Congleton...32
Sandown Park, Esher...171
Sandringham Hotel, Isle of Wight...91
Saunton Sands Hotel, Devon...55
Saville Court Hotel, Surrey...173
Savoy Hotel, Blackpool...105
Savoy Hotel, London WC2...125
Saxon Cross, Cheshire...35
Scafell Hotel, Cumbria...45
Scaitcliffe Hall Hotel, Todmorden...105
Scandic Crown Hotel, London...128
Scarisbrick Hotel, Southport...136

Sconner House Inn, Cornwall...38
Scotch Corner Hotel, North Yorkshire...147
Sculthorpe Mill, Norfolk...139
Seabank Hotel, Lancashire...107
Searcy's, London SW1...126
Seedy Mill Golf Club, Lichfield...163
Seiont Manor Hotel, Gwynedd...202
Sevenoaks Town Council Offices, Kent...97
Shanklin Manor, Isle of Wight...91
Sharsted Court, Newnham...97
Shaw Hill Hotel, Chorley...105
Sheene Mill Hotel, Melbourn...23
Sheffield Wednesday FC, Hillsborough...160
Shendish Manor, Apsley...90
Sheraton Skyline Hotel, Hayes...126
Sherborne Hotel, Sherborne...57
Shireburn Arms Hotel, Whalley...105
Shotton Hall, Peterlee...60
Shrewsbury Castle...155
Shropshire Hotel, Shropshire...156
Shrubbery Hotel, Ilminster...158
Shugborough Estate, Milford...163
Shurland, Eastchurch...97
Shuttleworth Centre, Bedfordshire...11
Sibson Inn, Cambridgeshire...24
Silverstone Circuit, Northamptonshire...140
Sir Christopher Wren's House, Berkshire...16
68 Fareham, Hampshire...81
Sketchley Grange Hotel, Burbage...110
Skiddaw Hotel, Keswick...44
Slaley Hall, Northumberland...143
Sleepers Hotel, Cheshire...35
Slepe Hall Hotel, St Ives...23
Smithills Coaching House, Bolton...105
Smoke House, Mildenhall...167
Soho House, London W1...128
Solberge Hall, Newby Wiske...147
Solent Hotel, Fareham...80
Solihull Conference Centre, Solihull...182
Solna Hotel, Liverpool...136
Somerhill, Tonbridge...98
Somerleyton Hall, Suffolk...167
Sonning Golf Club, Berkshire...16
Sopwell House Hotel, St Albans...90
Soughton Hall Hotel, Northop...202
South Lodge Hotel, Chelmsford...69
South Lodge Hotel, West Sussex...187
South Shields Town Hall, South Shields...174
South Walsham Hall, Norfolk...139
Southam Community Hall, Warwickshire...179
Southdowns Hotel, Petersfield...80, 186
Spa Hotel, Tunbridge Wells...98
Sparth House Hotel, Accrington...105
Spread Eagle Hotel, Midhurst...186
Springfield Hotel, Flintshire...202
Springfield House Hotel, Pilling...106
Springfield Park Hotel, Kirkburton...193

Sprowston Manor Hotel, Norwich...138
SS Golden Hinde, London SE1...117
SS Great Britain, Bristol...17
Stafford Hotel, London SW1...126
Stafford House, Dorchester...57
Stage Hotel, Wigston Fields...110
Stakis Bedford Hotel, West Yorkshire...193
Stakis Birmingham Metropole, NEC...182
Stakis Corby Hotel, Northamptonshire...140
Stakis Keswick Lodore, Keswick...44
Stakis Norwich, Norfolk...138
Stakis Sheffield Hotel, Sheffield...160
Stakis St Ermins Hotel, London SW1...126
Stallingborough Grange Hotel, North East Lincolnshire...140
Stanhill Court Hotel, Charlwood...172
Stanneylands Hotel, Wilmslow...32
Stanwell House Hotel, Hampshire...81
Stapleford Park Hotel, Melton Mowbray...110
Statham Lodge Hotel, Lymm...32
Stephen Joseph Theatre, Scarborough...148
Stirk House Hotel, Gisburn...106
Stockport Town Hall, Stockport...133
Stoke by Nayland Golf Club, Suffolk...167
Stoke Park, Stoke Poges...19
Stoke Park, Stoke Poges...XI
Stoke Rochford Hall, Grantham...113
Stone House Hotel, Staffordshire...164
Stonehouse Court Hotel, Stonehouse...74
Stonor Arms Hotel, Stonor...152
Stourport Manor Hotel, Stourport on Severn...85
Stowe Gardens, Buckingham...19
Stowe School, Buckingham...19
Stragglethorpe Hall, Lincoln...113
Strathmore Hotel, Morecambe...106
Stratton House Hotel, Cirencester...74
Studley Priory Hotel, Horton cum Studley...153
Sudbury House Hotel, Faringdon...153
Summer Lodge Hotel, Evershot...58
Sun Hotel, Hertford...91
Sunley Management Centre, Northampton...140
Sutton Coldfield Town Hall, Sutton Coldfield...182
Sutton Court Hotel, Sutton Coldfield...183
Sutton Hall, Macclesfield...32
Sutton House, London E9...126
Swainston Manor Hotel, Newport...91
Swallow Gosforth Park, Gosforth...175
Swallow Highcliff Hotel, Bournemouth...58
Swallow Hotel, York...198
Swallow Hotel, Peterborough...23
Swallow Hotel, Sheffield...160

Swallow Hotel, South Normanston...50
Swallow Hotel, Stockton...175
Swallow Hotel, West Yorkshire...193
Swallow Royal Hotel, Bristol...17
Swallows Leisure Centre, Sittingbourne...98
Swan at Hay Hotel, Hay on Wye...206
Swan Hotel, Bibury...74
Swan Hotel, Newby Bridge...44
Swan Hotel, Suffolk...168
Swansea Mariott Hotel, Swansea...207
Swarling Manor, Canterbury...98
Swinfen Hall Hotel, Staffordshire...164
Swiss Gardens, Bedfordshire...11
Sywnford Paddocks, Cambridgeshire...24

T

Tabley House, Knutsford...33
Talbot Hotel, Northamptonshire...140
Tall Trees Hotel, Yarm...175
Tan Hill Inn, Keld...148
Taplow House Hotel, Taplow...16
Tarantella Hotel, Sudbury...167
Tattershall Castle...113
Tatton Park, Knutsford...33
Taverham Hall School, Norfolk...139
Tavistock Town Hall, Tavistock...54
Taylor's Restaurant, Conwy...201
Telford Moat House, Shropshire...155
Temple Park Centre, South Shields...174
Templeton, London SW15...127
Tenterden Town Hall, Kent...98
Tern Hill Hall Hotel, Shropshire...156
Tewin Bury Farm, Welwyn...90
Tewkesbury Park Hotel, Gloucestershire...74
The Corn Exchange, Faringdon...151
The Mill at Croston, Lancashire...103
The Visitors' Centre, Aberdare...207
Theatre Royal, Bath...10
Theatre Royal, Newcastle upon Tyne...175
Thornbury Castle, Thornbury...159
Thornton Hall Hotel, Thornton Hough...136
Thorpeness Country Club, Suffolk...167
Three Rivers Country Club, Cold Norton...69
Three Swans Hotel, Market Harborough...110
Thurning Hall, East Dereham...138
Thurning Hall, East Dereham...V
Thurrock Masonic Hall, Essex...70
Tickled Trout, Salmesbury...106
Tickton Grange, East Yorkshire...61
Tillmouth Park Hotel, Cornhill on Tweed...143
Tiverton Castle, Tiverton...55
Tiverton Hotel, Tiverton...55
Todmorden Town Hall, West Yorkshire...193
Tom Cobleigh's Weetwood House, Sheffield...160

INDEX

Tonbridge Castle, Kent...98
Tottington Manor, Henfield...187
Towcester Racecourse,
　　Northamptonshire...140
Tower Hotel, Harwich...69
Tower Thistle Hotel, London E1...127
Town Hall, Great Yarmouth...138
Trafalgar Tavern, London SE10...127
Tre-ysgawen Hall, Anglesey...202
Trearddur Bay Hotel, Anglesey...203
Tredegar House,
　　Neath Port Talbot...204
Tree Tops Hotel, Formby...136
Trent College, Nottingham...150
Trent College, Nottingham..XV
Trent Lock Golf Centre,
　　Nottinghamshire...151
Trentham Gardens,
　　Stoke on Trent...164
Trevigue, Bude...38
TS Queen Mary, London WC2...127
Tu Tu L'Auberge, South Godstone...172
**Tu Tu L'Auberge,
　　South Godstone...II**
Tuddenham Mill, Newmarket...167
Tufton Arms, Appleby...44
Tullie House Museum, Carlisle...45
Tuxedo Royale, Gateshead...174
Ty Penlan, Llandelio...200
Tyddyn Llan Hotel, Denbighshire...201
Tyglyn Aeron. Lampeter...200
Tylney Hall, Hampshire...81
Tyne Theatre & Opera House,
　　Newcastle upon Tyne...175
Tynedale Farmer Function Suite,
　　Northumberland...143
Tyrells Ford Hotel, Hampshire...80
Tythrop Park, Aylesbury...20

U

Uckfield Civic Centre, Uckfield...65
Ufford Park Hotel, Woodbridge...168
Ullswater Hotel, Penrith...45
Under the Clock Tower,
　　Wakefield...193
Undercliff, Ferryside...200
Upper House, Staffordshire...164
Uttoxeter Racecourse,
　　Staffordshire...164
Uttoxeter Town Hall, Staffordshire...164

V

Vale Mascal, Bexley...8
Vale Mascal, Bexley...XVI
Valley Club, Cornwall...38
Victoria Hotel, Menai Bridge...202
Victoria Park Hotel, Barrow...45
Village Hotel, Whiston...136
Village Leisure Hotel,
　　Bromborough...136
Village Leisure Hotel,
　　Nottingham...151
Village Leisure Hotel, Prestwich...133
Villiers Hall, Buckingham...20
Vintage Court Hotel, Puckeridge...90

W

Waddesdon Manor (The Dairy)...20
Wadenhoe House, Peterborough...23
Waldorf Hotel, London WC2...127
Wallington Hall, Northumberland...143
Walls Eating House, Oswestry...156
Walnut Tree Hotel, Somerset...158
Waltham Court Hotel,
　　Canterbury...208
Walton Hall, Warrington...33
Walworth Castle Hotel, Walworth...60
Wandsworth Town Hall, London...128
Warmington Grange, Sandbach...33
Warpool Court Hotel, St Davids...204
Warren Golf Club, Malden, Essex...70
Washington Central Hotel,
　　Cumbria...45
Washington Old Hall,
　　Washington Village...175
Waterford House, Middleham...148
Waterside Inn, Bray...16
Waterton Park Hotel, Wakefield...193
Waverley Borough Council Offices,
　　Godalming...172
Weetwood Hall, Leeds...193
Welcombe Hotel,
　　Stratford upon Avon...178
Wensum Lodge Hotel, Fakenham...139
Wentbridge House Hotel,
　　West Yorkshire...193
Wentworth Club, Surrey...173
Wessex Centre, Winchester...81
West Bromwich Moat House...183
West Lodge Park Hotel,
　　Hadley Wood...128
West Retford Hotel, East Retford..151
West Thames College, Isleworth...128
West Tower Hotel, Ormskirk...106
Westcliff Hotel, Essex...69
Westerfield House Hotel, Ipswich...168
Westley Hotel, West Midlands...183
Westmead Hotel, Hopwood...183
Weston Park Golf Club,
　　Weston Longville...139
Westover Hall, Milford on Sea...81
Whately Hall Hotel, Banbury...153
Whatley Manor, Malmesbury...197
White Friars Hotel, East Sussex...65
White House Hotel,
　　Denbighshire...201
White Lion Inn, Crewe...33
White Lodge, Linton...99
White Swan Hotel, Alnwick...143
White Swan, London W9...128
Whitechapel Manor, Devon...55
Whitehall Hotel, Broxted...69
Whitewalls Restaurant, Lancashire...107
Whitley Hall Hotel, Sheffield...160
Whoop Hall Inn, Carnforth...106
Wildboar Hotel, Tarporley...33
Willington Hall Hotel, Tarporley...34
Wilmslow Moat House Hotel,
　　Wilmslow...34
Wiltshire Country Hall, Wiltshire...197
Wimborne Minster Town Hall,
　　Dorset...58

Wimpole Hotel, West Sussex...187
Wincham Hall Hotel, Wincham...34
Winchester Guildhall, Hampshire...81
Windyridge, Kent...99
Winnington Hall, Northwich...34
Winston Manor Hotel, East Sussex...65
Winter Garden, Surrey...173
Winter Gardens Hotel,
　　Bournemouth...58
Winter Gardens, Bath...10
Wiston House, Steyning...187
Wivenhoe House Hotel,
　　Colchester...70
Woburn Abbey, Woburn...11
Wokingham Town Hall, Berkshire...16
Wood Hall Hotel, Linton...148
Wood Norton Hall, Evesham...85
Woodbridge Town Council,
　　Suffolk...168
Woodhey Hotel, Cheshire...35
Woodhorn Colliery Museum,
　　Ashington...143
Woodhouse Hotel, Warwickshire...179
Woodland Comfort Inn,
　　Northwold...139
Woodlands Manor Hotel,
　　Bedfordshire...11
Woodlands Park Hotel,
　　Stoke D'Abernon...172
Woodstock Town Hall,
　　Oxfordshire..153
Wooley Hall, Wakefield...193
Wordsworth Hotel, Grasmere...45
Worsley Court Hotel, Manchester...134
Wortley House Hotel,
　　Scunthorpe...140
Wrea Head Country House,
　　Scalby...148
Wroxton House, Banbury...153
Wyck Hill House Hotel,
　　Gloucestershire...74
Wycombe Swan, High Wycombe...20
Wythenshaw Hall, Wythenshaw...134

Y

Yarner, Bovey Tracey, Devon...55
Yenton Hotel, Bournemouth...58
Yew Lodge Hotel, Kegworth...50
Ynys Hewel Centre, Crosskeys...204
Ynyshir Hall Hotel, Ceredigion...200
York House, Twickenham...128
Yotes Court, Kent...99

Entries in **bold** *denote that the venue appears in the colour section.*

NOTES

NOTES